9.81 m/sec²

The Science behind Sikhara's Journey

Shanmugam Selvakumar

notionpress
.com

INDIA · SINGAPORE · MALAYSIA

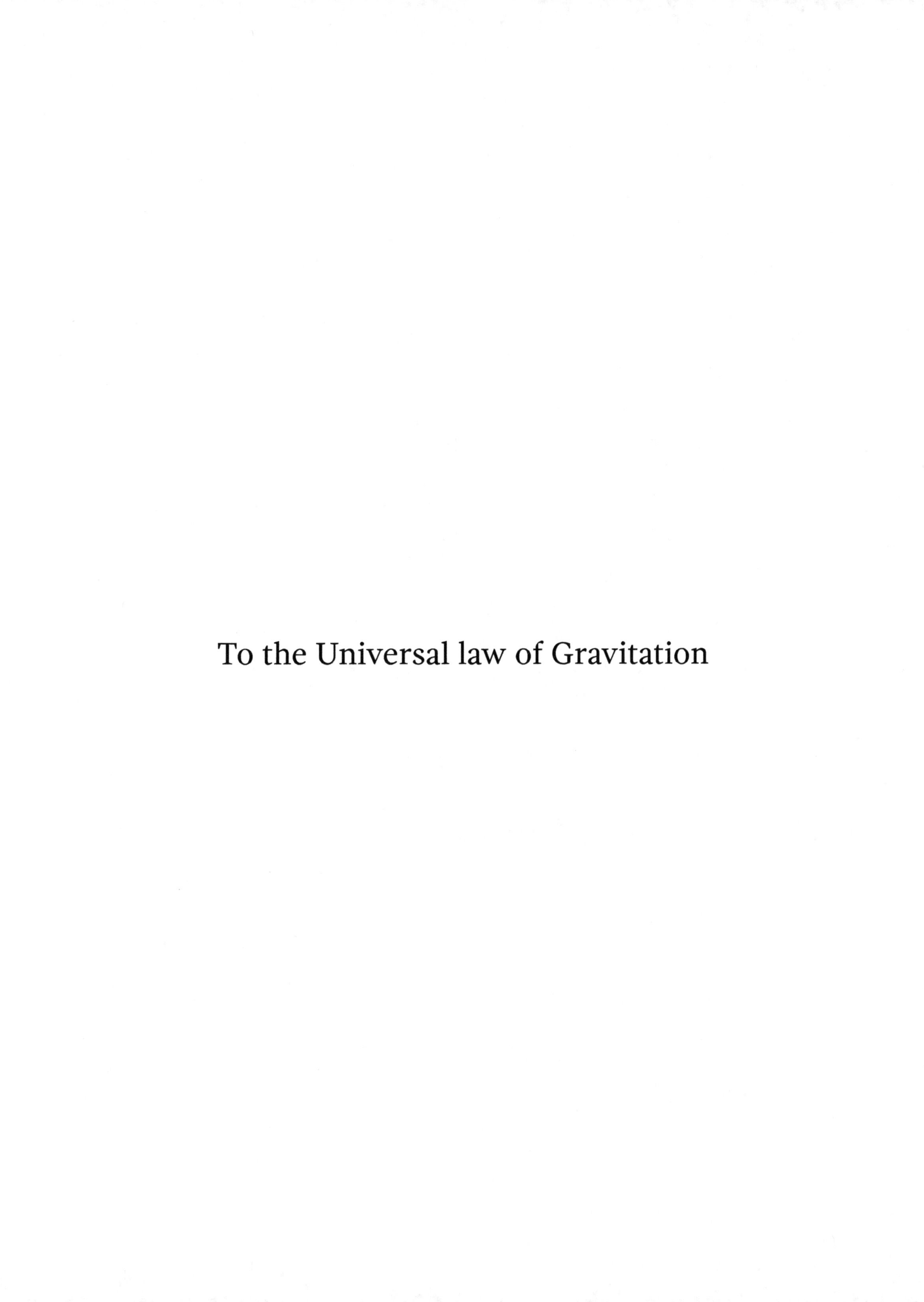

To the Universal law of Gravitation

Contents

Preface

Ancient India was a culture that valued knowledge.

Tamil Nadu has historically been a region noted for its scientific and mathematical prowess and knowledge power, and the ancient Tamil culture was an advanced knowledge society.

As a result of invasions and colonial dominance, most of its institutions were destroyed, and its fundamental competencies were removed and buried.

Tamils have long been known as master temple builders, with their Kings serving as generous patrons of the arts.

Large temples built by ancient Tamil Engineers in the Chola dynasty exhibited masterful Architectural and Engineering talents that are unmatched even today. Their architectural prowess allowed them to build monuments to their legacy.

Architects and Engineers who worked on Tanjore Big temple were experts in advanced science and math, and they knew how to seamlessly handle a difficult undertaking by combining science and maths into a well-thought-out strategy.

As far as we can gather, inscriptions commemorate the King's achievements in the military, naval, and excellent administrative capacities, but they do not sufficiently portray the Cholas' amazing mastery of Engineering and the unique tactics engaged in the temple construction.

The question is whether the Kingdom purposely left it out to safeguard its intellectual property rights, or whether the inscription and proof were buried and removed on purpose during any invasion, colonial dominance, or altering work.

Many Engineering-related questions about this temple remain unresolved and unanswered.

How did the 81 tonnes Sikara or the Capstone climb all the way to the top without modern equipment a thousand years ago? The main mystery.

It held the secret and amazing kernel of an engineering solution that had been hidden and unknown for centuries.

How did the massive Lord Shiva statue fit through the narrow entrance in to the sanctum?

The grand Vimana hides incredible science and engineering secrets for eager and curious minds to discover .

It had not been thoroughly researched, displayed, or projected.

In search of a credible Engineering explanation, I made an unwavering effort to research the magnificent Science and Engineering that were involved and covertly hidden in the construction of the Tanjore Big Temple a thousand years ago during the Emperor Raja Raja Cholan's dynasty.

One finding leads to another.

Astonishing discoveries about the temple began to emerge one after another as I worked through my meticulous research analysis and calculations. The research findings enhanced the image of Tamil culture by demonstrating the advanced scientific concepts and ideas used by the ancient Tamil Engineers.

These facts inspired me to create a book, which I hope will promote awareness and elevate the image of this incredible Temple and Tamil worldwide.

Without the support and encouragement of the Director, Dr. Arunraj, and the ASI Trichy Circle officials, I would not have been able to complete the above journey.

My heartfelt gratitude goes to the ASI team for granting me access to the detailed documented measurements, photographs, and levels, as well as allowing me to personally verify the information at the temple.

I am extremely grateful to Mr. J. Kumaragurubaran, IAS, the commissioner of HRCEB, for granting permission and allowing me to view and verify the details at the temple complex.

The HRCEB and ASI officials at the temple complex were extremely helpful and encouraging throughout my research visits.

Finally, working with a professional publisher has been an amazing experience. My sincere respect and appreciation to Notion Press for their insights, and I consider myself fortunate to have had the pleasure of working with a team of competent and talented editorial and production staff to illustrate this research journey, for which I am also deeply grateful.

Shanmugam Selvakumar
(shanmugamselvakumar9.81@gmail.com)

Science Ignores the Size

Whether something is large or small, simple or complex, it obeys and delivers on time and every time as long as the laws of Physics are truly, faithfully, and unwaveringly mastered!!

1

Journey to the Summit

Gravity is the reason! and a result of the Universal Law of Gravitation!

History has demonstrated that those who dare to imagine the impossible are the ones who break all human limitations.

Dr. APJ Abdul Kalam

Science ignores the size.

Whether something is large or small or simple or complex to make, as long as the law of physics is truly, faithfully, and unwaveringly masterminded, it is unaffected by size and obeys and delivers on time and every time.

Unique to Tamil history, the feat was especially impressive given the lack of high-tech lifting equipment a thousand years ago.

The Tanjore Big Temple!

It was built in the Dravidian architectural style and is also known as the Peruvudayar Temple or the Brihadiswara Temple. Its Vimana, which holds the magnificent Sikhara at its summit, is a massive block of granite that was lifted and installed on the summit at the perfect line, level, and equilibrium, and is said to weigh 81 metric tonnes (MT).

It may appear impossible to lift such a massive weight to 50 m above ground level and install it in perfect equilibrium against the gravitational pull and field a thousand years ago, but the ancient Tamil engineers under the Chola regime did it with great courage and skill!

In his inscription, Emperor Raja Raja Cholan openly credited the engineers and architects led by Kunjara Mallan Raja Raja Perunthachan for this magnificent achievement.

The team's confidence, courage, grit, and determination enabled them to start a great game and reach the perfect climax.

An inspired climax of the Chola's architectural engineering marvel, which is still standing with a zero-degree inclination in the perfect line of equilibrium sustaining major earthquakes, was sparked by the emperor's spur-of-the-moment idea of selecting and involving the right kind of players on the field to handle the universal gravitational aspects in every part of engineering.

Architecture and structural engineering are both stunning in their own right. Approximately 130,000 MT of large blocks of granite mass was handled and heaped in the project to create this spectacular mountain scenery with its perfect interlocked alignment against the gravitational pull at higher elevations.

With their exceptional ability in architecture and structural engineering, the ancient Tamil architects, engineers, and artisans captivate and inspire every visitor to this temple.

Engineers must have had the psychology of optimal experience with a perfect deep-rooted understanding and knowledge of precision engineering by integrating the principles of science and mathematics, in addition to their inherent confidence, courage, and resolve!

Many engineering-related questions remain unanswered to this day.

The massive granite stone block, the 81 MT Sikhara, has long been a central mystery!

The Sikhara's journey to the summit is still a mystery.

Everyone who visits this monument is fascinated by the central mystery that has remained unsolved for centuries, and there is no clear and reliable engineering answer to this day.

Many incorrect views, interpretations, and made-up stories have accumulated over the centuries, possibly as a result of ignorance and misunderstanding. The popular belief on the traditional method of laying a long, inclined plane from 6.6 km, dragging and installing it on the summit by deploying a large number of elephants, manpower, and so on fails to produce any citing evidence to support this idea of the traditional theory.

While the king has spelt out the names of engineers, architects, and artisans who have contributed to the construction, the details of the construction methodology have been left out.

To date, this is untraceable and invisible!

The debate is whether the kingdom left it out on purpose to protect its intellectual property rights, or whether the inscriptions and pieces of evidence were intentionally buried and destroyed during any invasion, alteration, or maintenance work.

The Herculean efforts of the ancient Tamil engineers and architects captivated, astounded, and inspired me, as they do every visitor to this temple.

It was a thousand years ago, and they had achieved the perfect climax despite the lack of advanced technology and high-end lifting equipment.

The central mystery is how the massive granite stone block, the 81 MT Sikhara, made its way to the summit!

How did the massive Lord Shiva statue, weighing 25 MT, fit through the narrow entrance and into the sanctum?

How did these Herculean tasks get done a thousand years ago? It has stumped scientists and engineers for centuries.

It must contain the scientific kernel of truth!

There must also be outstanding engineering intelligence and a solution that has been hidden and unexplored for centuries. It will stimulate everyone's interest in the central mystery that remains unsolved.

As an engineer, I've been driven by a sense of curiosity to systematically explore and find a reliable engineering answer to this unresolved mystery.

As a result, I'm making a concerted effort to invite everyone to join me on a journey back to the time when the temple was built a thousand years ago by following the Sikhara's footpath with close attention and understanding, to reach the summit of Vimana together.

The Vimana holds incredible science and engineering secrets waiting for eager and curious minds to explore it, and this book takes us on a journey to discover the science behind it!

A close focus and clear understanding are required to explore and establish all the facts with a systematic investigation.

Let us begin with the research rather than the results.

To get the most out of this volume's logical investigation, readers are strongly encouraged to study the accompanying physical illustrations, physics principles, mathematical equations, graphical information, structure arrangements, analyses, and computations at the end of each chapter side by side.

Nothing complicated, very simple, and easy to understand.

A science-and-math-based engineering solution to the mystery will emerge.

Vimana front view

The Sikhara front view

The Sikhara corner view

Vimana – Pyramidal view

2

Site Investigation Report

It is a process of learning all the details in the proposed layout area before deciding on a project location and beginning any major project. A large project necessitates a detailed 'Site Investigation Report' (SIR) and careful engineering consideration for proper location and site selection.

When the emperor had an impulsive thought of building an impressive temple with a tall Vimana over the sanctum for Lord Shiva out of the hardest granite construction material, his engineers identified and selected the appropriate project site.

Topography and surroundings had a major influence in completing the project on time and preserving the temple layout from natural disasters.

The overall temple layout measures 120 m × 240 m, and the main Vimana tower is facing towards the east.

It was designed to be surrounded by water on all sides, as evidenced by the surroundings shown in the attached images. Deep moats surround the east and west sides. On the northern side, a larger and deeper Siva Ganga Tank has been constructed. The Kallani Canal encircles the south. According to legend, the original moat on the south side was converted as part of the Kallani Canal stretch adjacent to the temple layout during the British regime.

Moats are typically filled with water and used to defend against invasion and attack. Apart from protecting and safeguarding the layout against any intrusion, it was also linked to several engineering reasons.

It demonstrated engineering intelligence by providing a deep moat around the temple's perimeter and a much deeper adjacent tank far below the level of the main Vimana's foundation.

The vertical deeper excavation cuts all around the layout had given the ancient design engineers a clear perspective and fair idea of the in-situ ground conditions, geo-technical information, and other ideas about the series and type of various soil layers lying beneath the layout.

In the absence of mechanised drilling and advanced soil exploration methods during ancient times, this must have greatly aided the Cholas' engineering team in judging and arriving at all the uncertainty factors hidden within the soil stratum before freezing their final design.

The second engineering reason is that keeping the moat bed level and water table level far below the level of the courtyard and Vimana foundation allows a large amount of rainwater collected from the entire layout to be quickly drained off all sides.

The final and most important engineering reason could be to completely cut off and minimise the effect of high-intensity earthquake waves hitting and damaging the temple foundation structures by isolating the entire temple layout and high Vimana structure from its complete connectivity with the adjoining lands.

The water body filled up deep inside the moats, and the large water body in the Siva Ganga Tank added cushioning effect as a shock absorber against the high-intensity earthquake waves.

There are five wells around the Vimana that are roughly 1.2 m × 1.2 m at the top and follow a circular profile to a depth of 15 to 18 m.

The higher level of the courtyard and the deeper drainage system via moats and drainage canals had been formed to quickly collect and drain off the large quantity of rainwater into the Siva Ganga Tank, and the water table was aimed to be kept far below the foundation structure. This arrangement greatly reduces the impact of any severe damage caused by a sudden increase in pore water pressure during an earthquake.

The original dimensions of the moat had to be much wider and deeper than the currently visible dimensions. Silt and sediment deposits may have narrowed and shortened their size over centuries.

The topsoil for a depth of 1.5 m is hard laterite soil, and the limestone rock begins after 1.5 m and must extend far deeper from the ground level according to visual perception inside the well near Saint Karuvurar Shrine. It appears that the massive homogeneous limestone layer that begins as a hillock from the ground level at a depth of 1 to 1.5 m directly bears the enormous load of the temple tower.

The limestone rock appears to slope down from a hilltop and can be seen at the bottom of the moat wall on the east, west, and around the Siva Ganga Tank.

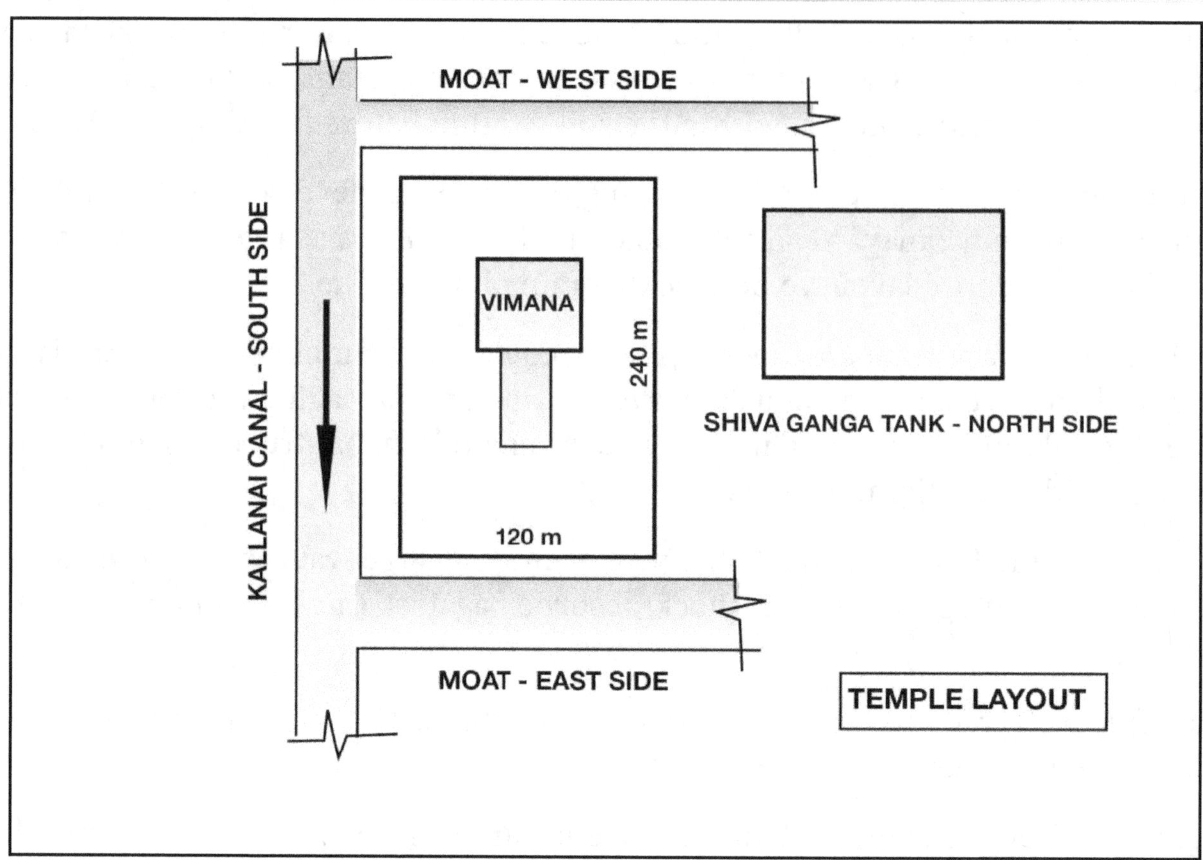
MOAT - WEST SIDE
KALLANAI CANAL - SOUTH SIDE
VIMANA
240 m
120 m
SHIVA GANGA TANK - NORTH SIDE
MOAT - EAST SIDE
TEMPLE LAYOUT

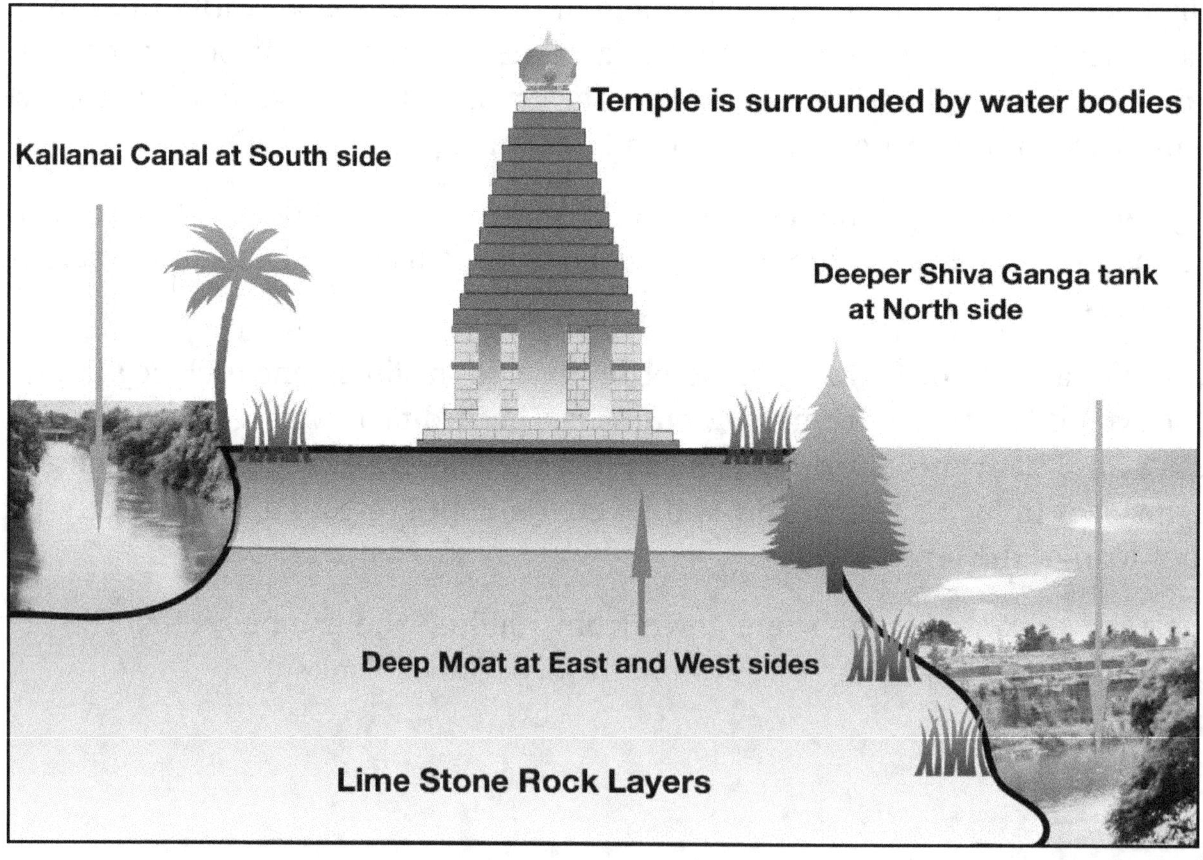
Temple is surrounded by water bodies
Kallanai Canal at South side
Deeper Shiva Ganga tank at North side
Deep Moat at East and West sides
Lime Stone Rock Layers

Bird's eye View

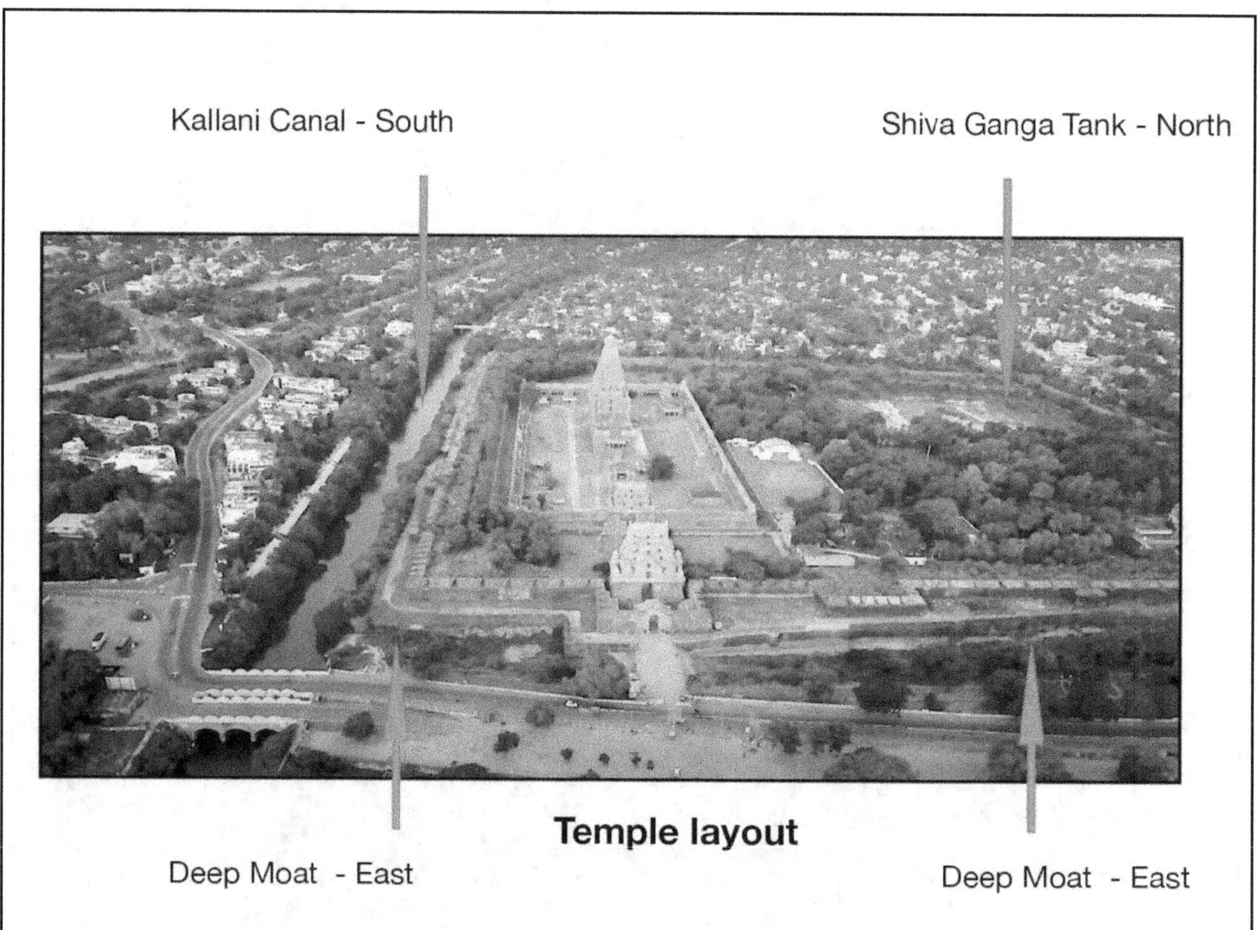

Temple layout

View from Western side

Siva Ganga Tank located at North side

Kallani Canal running at South side

Deep Shiva Ganga Tank - North side

Deep moat - East side

Over centuries, the huge moat was reduced in size by the accumulation of silt and sediment.

Underground well near saint Karuvurar shrine (15 to 18 m Deep)

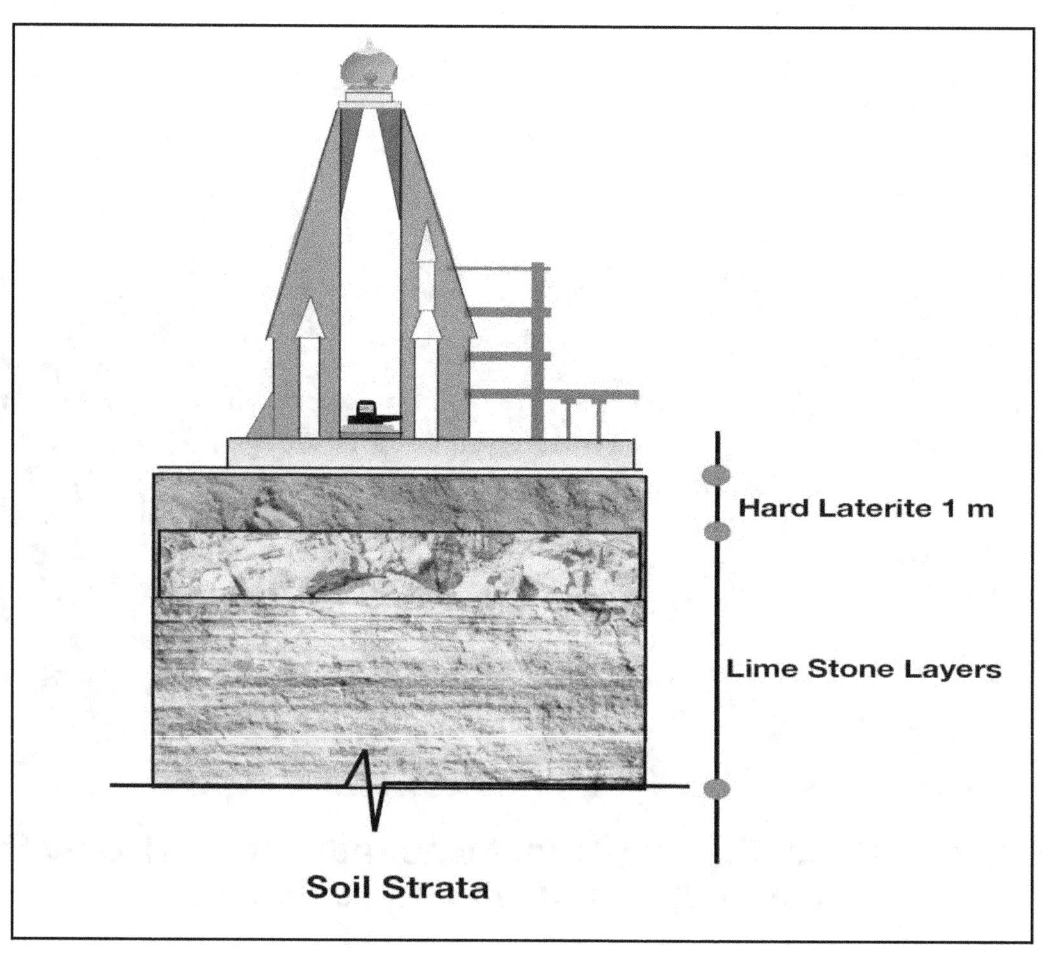

3

Configuration

A systematic investigation for detailed research and analysis necessitates a thorough understanding of the external profile, as well as a deeper micro-level scanning of the inner profile, levels, and dimensions of the various components involved in the main Vimana structure.

The drawings at the end of this topic cover the plan of the sanctum sanctorum and the overall structure's cross-sectional details that show the heights, levels, sizes, and dimensions in greater detail.

Let us now delve into the specifics.

Vimana

The main Vimana tower's measurements, levels, and tiers are sourced and referenced from Archaeological Survey of India (ASI) documents and publications.

Height

The Vimana rises like a pyramid from the courtyard square base to +49.50 m, and the Sikhara is majestically seated around this level as its base.

The Sikhara consists of three decorative granite features: the bottom square slab, the drum-shaped Griva, and the spherical dome. Four pairs of holy bulls face eight directions from the corners.

The combined height of the above three components is roughly 8.25 m, and the height of the gold finial installed over the Sikhara's centre is 3.81 m.

Let us refer to all three components together including the holy bulls either as "Cap Stone" or "Sikhara unit" or "Sikhara."

There are no records to verify and observe the nature, type, and depth of the foundation beneath the courtyard level. The Vimana rises to a total height of 57.75 m from the courtyard, and the Sikhara's base is seated close to 50 m from the courtyard, with the level having to be precisely at +49.50 m.

The total height from the courtyard to the tip of the gold finial is 49.50 m (structure height) + 8.25 m (Sikhara block's height) + 3.81 m (gold finial) = 61.56 m.

Plinth

The Vimana, with its impressive scale, is linked to the massive square plinth. According to the ASI publication, the central shrine's plinth measures 45.72 m in total, and the shrine proper measures 30.48 m in total. The solid and massive plinth rises 4.47 m from the courtyard to the sanctum floor level.

Sanctum Sanctorum

The sanctum (Garbagriha) has a magnificent Shivalingam said to weigh approximately 25 MT and stand 3.66 m tall in the centre, and the profile of the sanctum chamber is a perfect square measuring 7.93 m × 7.93 m.

Enclosures with Massive Walls

Massive internal and external granite walls surround the sanctum chamber. The thickness of the internal wall is 3.36 m, and the thickness of the external wall is 3.97 m. A circumambulatory cavity with a width of 1.87 m surrounds the sanctum in both the ground and first stories between both walls.

Both walls rise vertically above the massive square plinth for the ground and the first storey, totalling 11.85 m from the ground floor, and the floor of the sanctum is referred to as the ground floor.

The external wall follows the slope from the top of the second storey, which is at + 16.50 m from the courtyard floor, to align with the main Vimana slope and rise to reach the base of the Sikhara. More clearly, the outside slope begins above the level of the second massive drip cornice course and ends at Sikhara's base level, which is near +49.50 m.

While the external Vimana sloped surface has been entirely ornamented and covered with massive architectural characteristics, the interior wall has unique and more interesting structural features visible from the sanctum chamber.

The inner wall rises upright from the sanctum floor as a quadrangular perfect square shaft, maintaining its square size up to 28.53 m height from the plinth level. When the massive plinth height of 4.47 m is added, the total height of this upright vertical inner wall is constructed to straight plumb from the level of the courtyard base +33.00 m.

Vimana's Interior

Up to +33.00 m level, the walls are straight vertical to the plumb, with corbel projections gradually jutting out from the four corners above + 33.00 m level.

The square-sized sanctum vertical walls are gradually converged into an octagonal shape, and the extended masonry from + 33.00 m level at the four corners is gradually jutted out from the main body of the inner walls to take the profile of four massive spread-out spherically curved triangular pendentives vaulting for a height of 6.85 m connecting at the walls' centre.

When viewed from the bottom, the upper square base of the sanctum can be seen gradually converging to an octagonal shape from +33.00 m to +39.85 m level (33.00 + 6.85 = 39.85 m). Beyond +39.85 m, the octagonal profiles and the corner pendentives gradually fade away, converging to regular concentric circular bases to support the subsequent corbelling with smaller diameters. The circular corbelling takes up the majority of the height all around, with clear visibility beginning at +41.25 m and gradually reaching +49.50 m, where it touches the bottom surface of Sikhara.

The triangular pendentives are structural features in the engineering design that allow the weight of the circular dome to transition to a square supporting structure below without any massive pillars or columns interfering with the internal space.

Pendentives are simple in appearance but more complex in geometry. In masonry, the pendentives receive the outward force from the dome and transfer the weight downwards into the corners where it can be received by the piers beneath. Essentially, a pendentive is a spherical triangle that serves as an arch.

Circumambulatory

Circumambulatory way refers to the 1.87 m wide space provided between the massive internal and external walls. It surrounds the inner wall of the sanctum and extends vertically straight up to 11.85 m high, covering the ground and first stories.

From level 11.85 m, the width of 1.87 m gradually narrows due to the jutted-out corbelling from both the inner and outer walls, and the two massive walls merge gradually and roughly at a height of 4.61 m, forming a triangular cavity with a vertex of 4.61 m and a base of 1.87 m.

The merged level from the sanctum floor is approximately 11.85 m + 4.61 m = 16.46 m, and from the courtyard, it is 16.46 m + 4.47 m = 20.93 m. The cavity disappears after merging as a single massive wall, and this is only applicable to the south, west, and north sides. On the east side, there is a 1.90 m × 3.8 m rectangular shaft opening between two walls and extending beyond 20.93 m up to the level of 31.60 m, similar to a lift pit shaft. Its centre exactly coincides with the centre of the eastern side of the terrace third-floor hall, which must also coincide with the centre of the Vimana's Eastern face.

All of the dimensions listed above are taken as references from ASI records for further study and analysis.

Three Equal Parts of Vimana

It is evident from an overall examination of the structural cross-section, elevation, configuration, and heights of various levels that the Chola engineers divided the height of Vimana (49.50 m) into three equal parts for engineering purposes.

Part one is up to +16.50 m from the courtyard floor and from where the corbels are just jutted out by gradually narrowing the circumambulatory surrounding width from 1.87 m to merge as a single massive wall at+20.93 m.

Part two is next 16.50 m in height up to 33 m, and is the bottom point of the pendentives where the vertical alignment of the straight sanctum chamber wall ends. The triangular stretched-out pendentive extends from the main body of the inner wall at each corner from this +33 m level, gradually converting the square chamber into an octagon.

Part three is the final part of 16.50 m, from +33 m and up to +49.50 m, and is most likely the final seating position for the massive Sikhara unit.

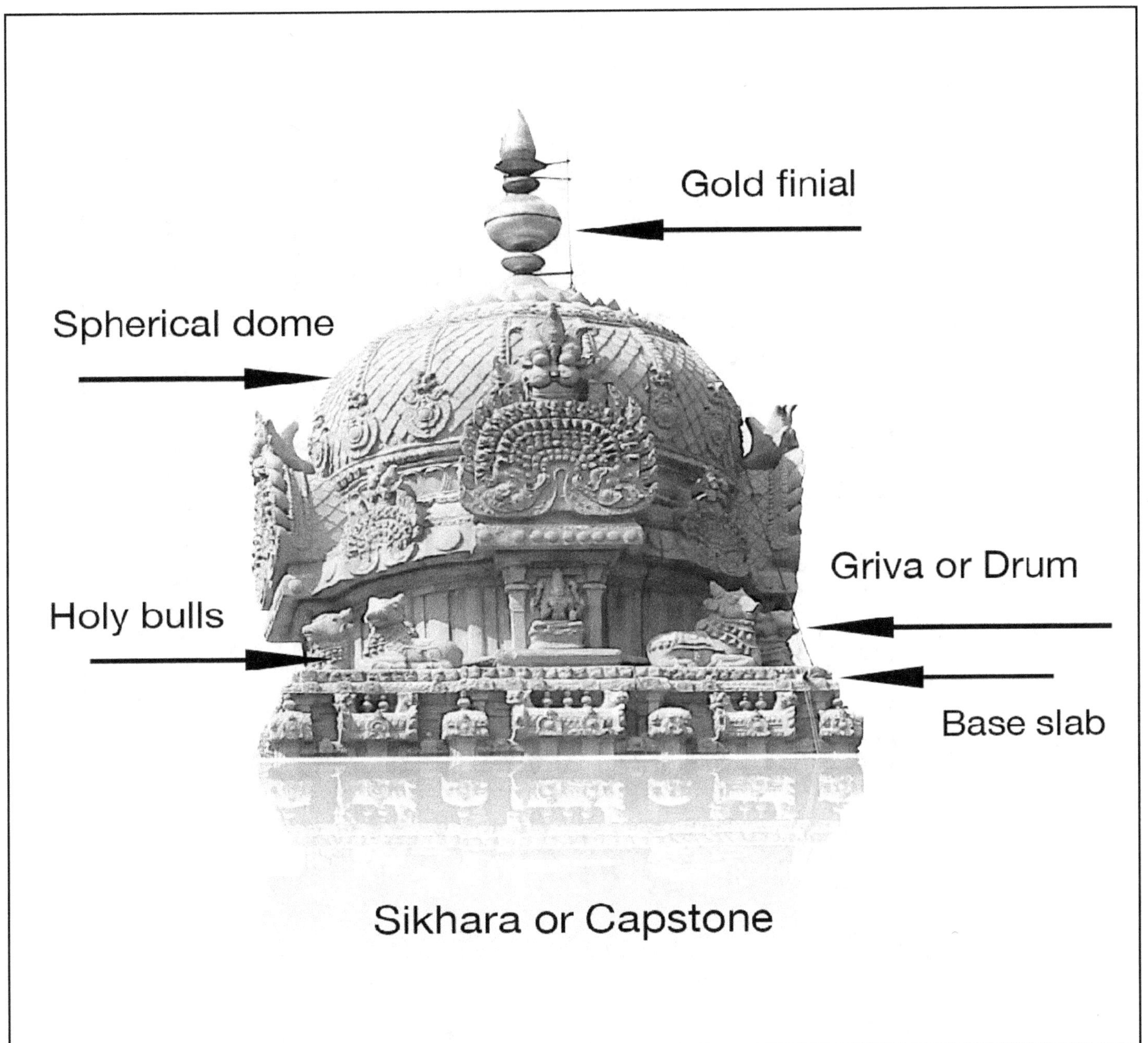

Gold finial
Spherical dome
Griva or Drum
Holy bulls
Base slab
Sikhara or Capstone

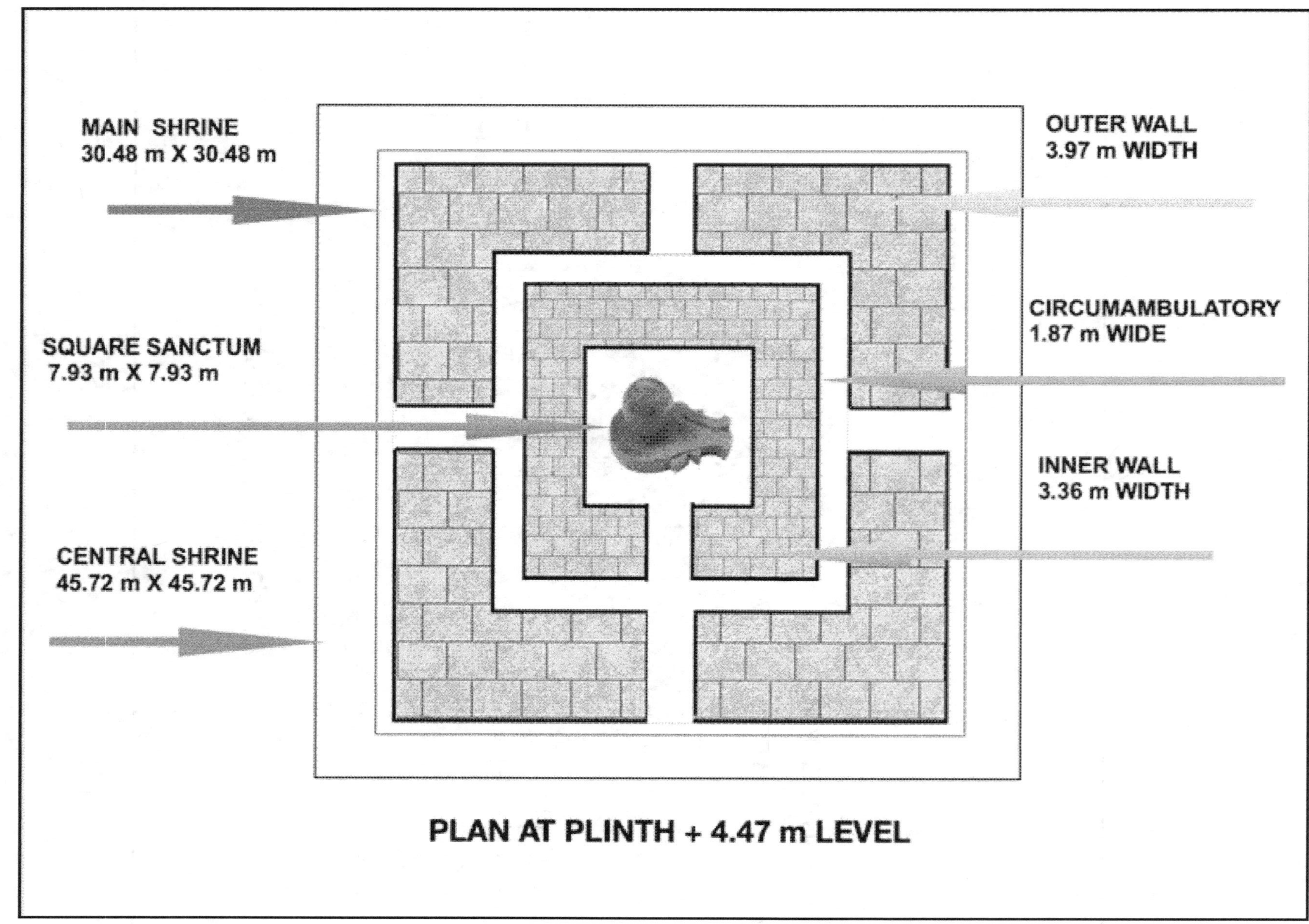

PLAN AT PLINTH + 4.47 m LEVEL

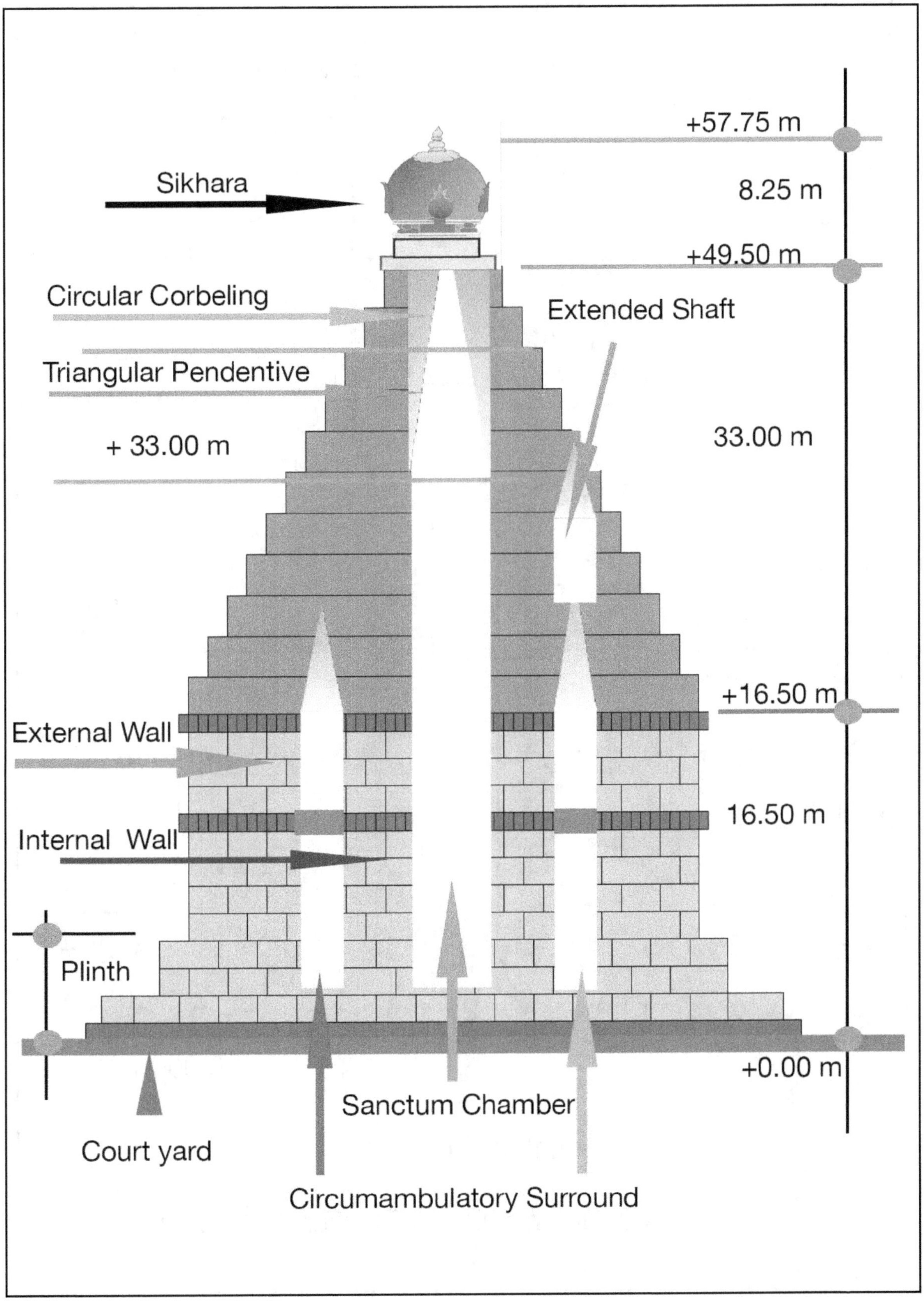

Structure – Cross section

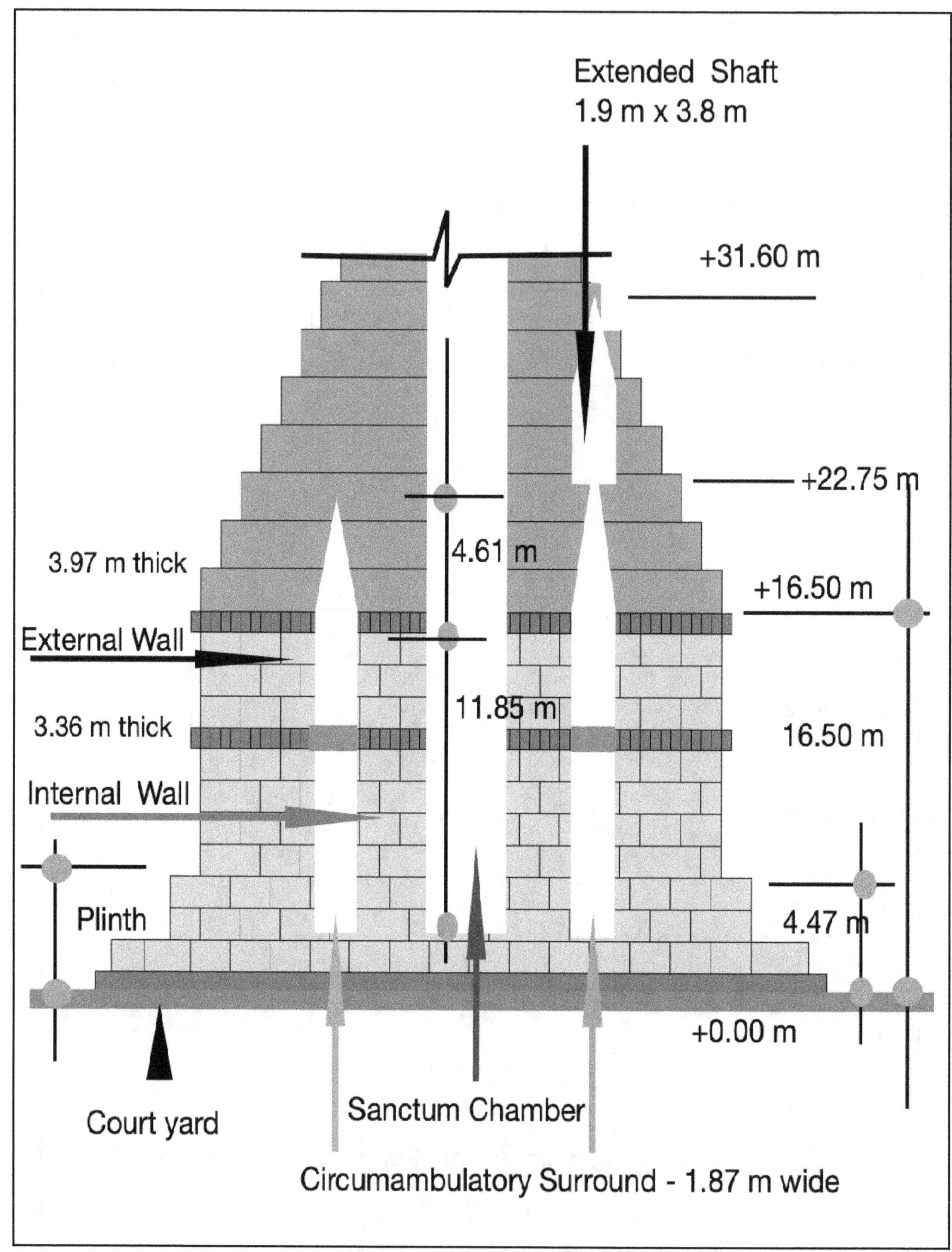

Circumambulatory arrangement

Four spread out corner triangular shaped spherically curved pendentives start from +33 m level

**Typical triangular shaped spherically curved
Pendentive construction at each corner**

Inside top view showing triangular shaped spherically curved Pendentives at corners

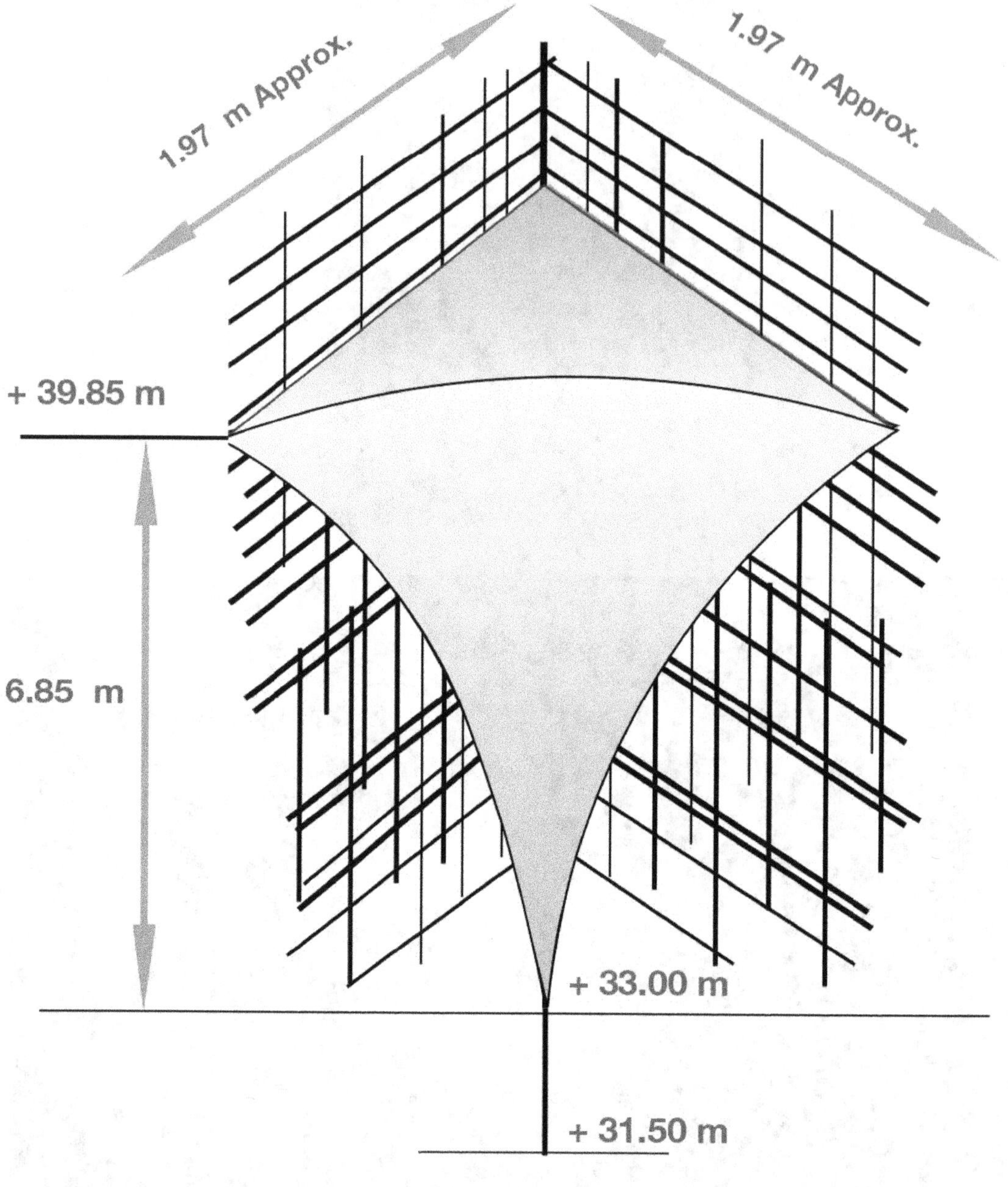

Vimana's interior - Corner Pendentive starts at + 33.00 m level

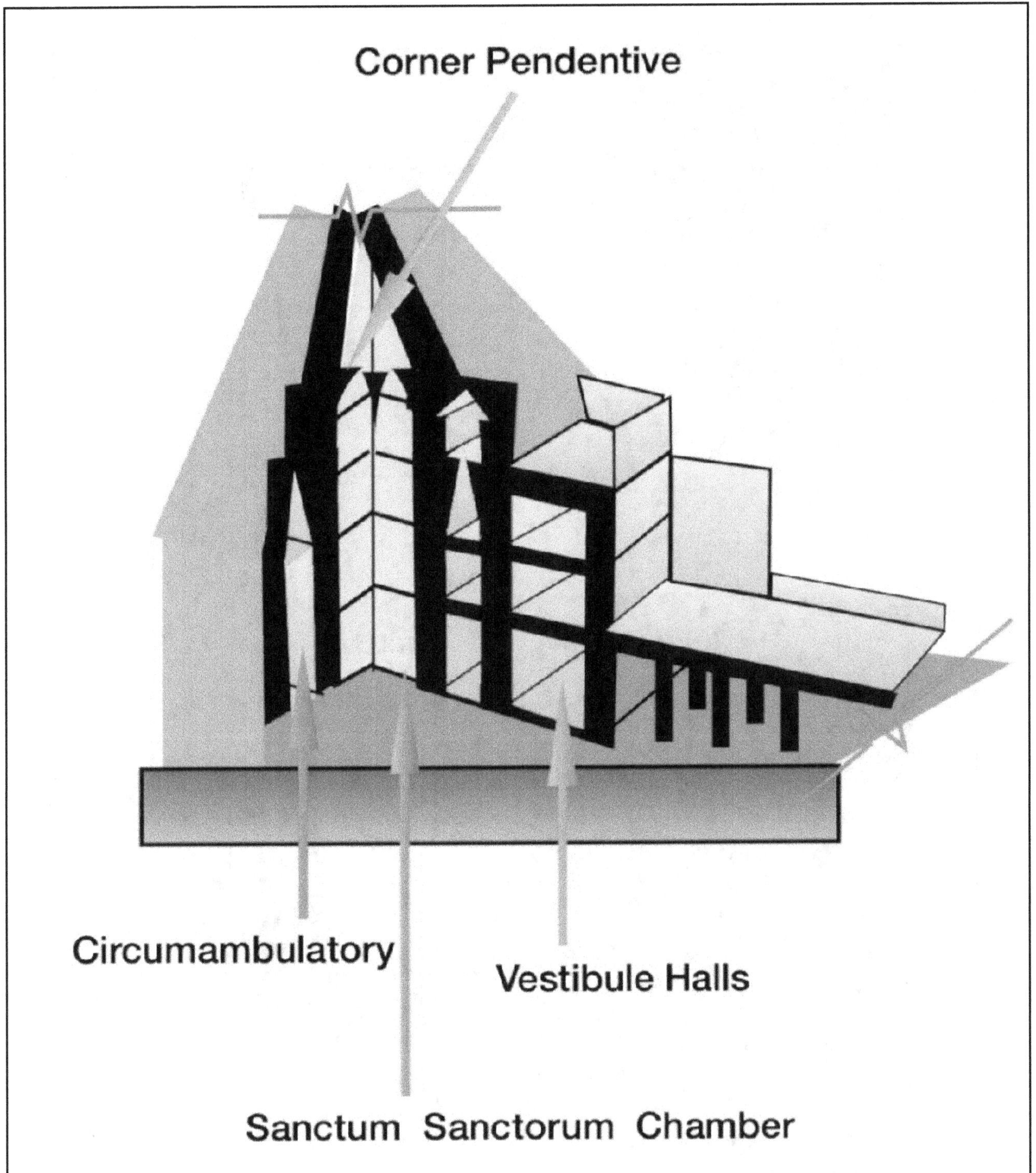

Corner Pendentive
Circumambulatory
Vestibule Halls
Sanctum Sanctorum Chamber

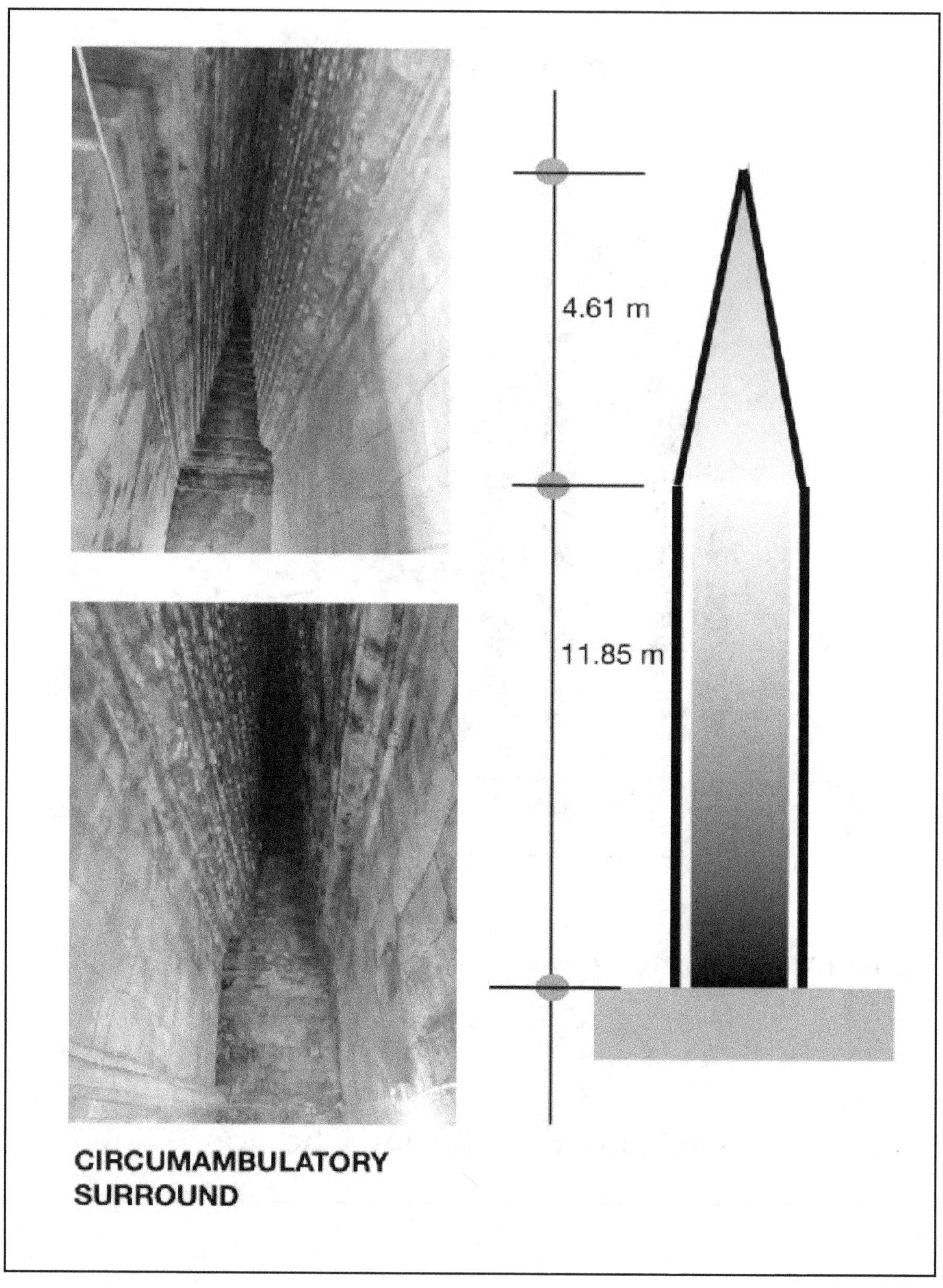

4.61 m
11.85 m
CIRCUMAMBULATORY
SURROUND

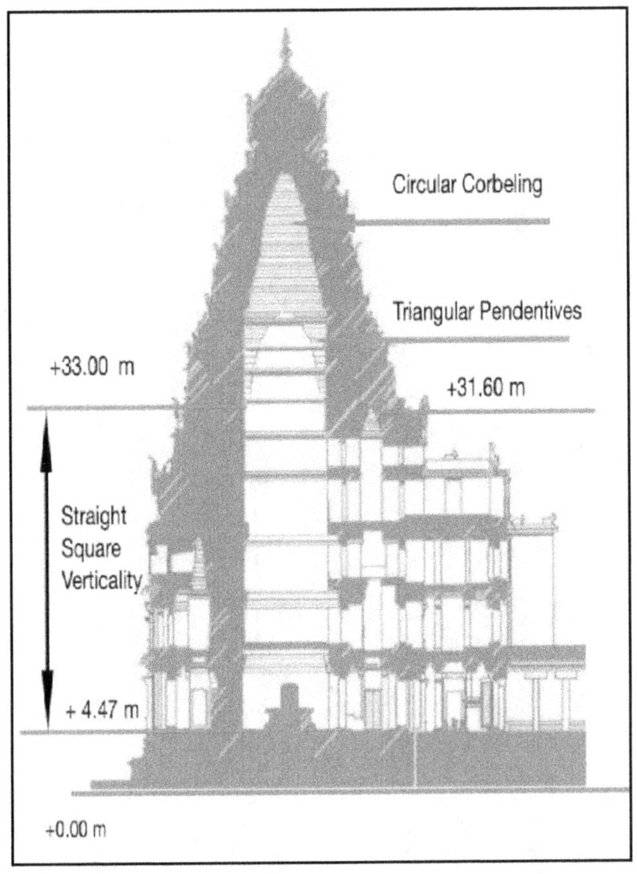

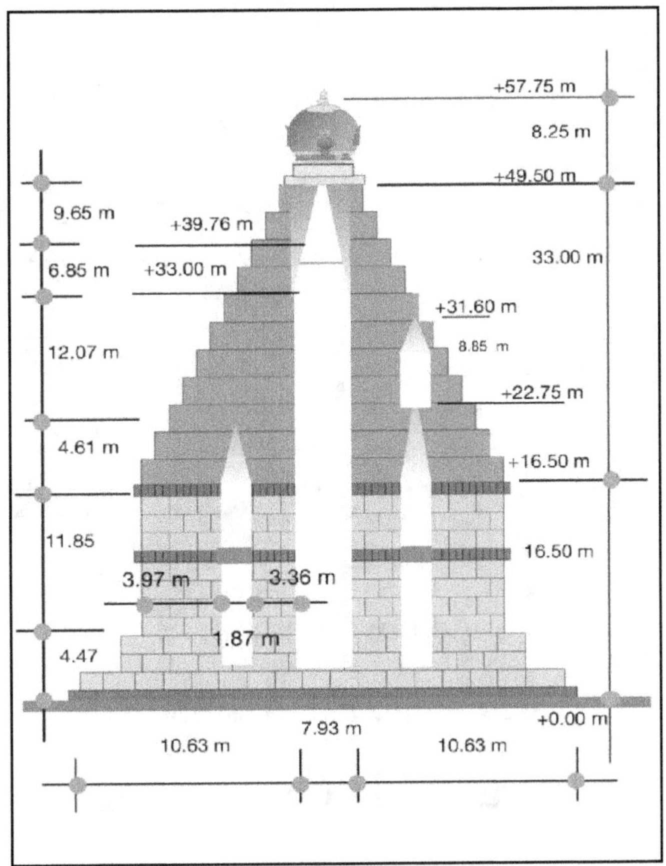

Cross sectional view showing dimensions

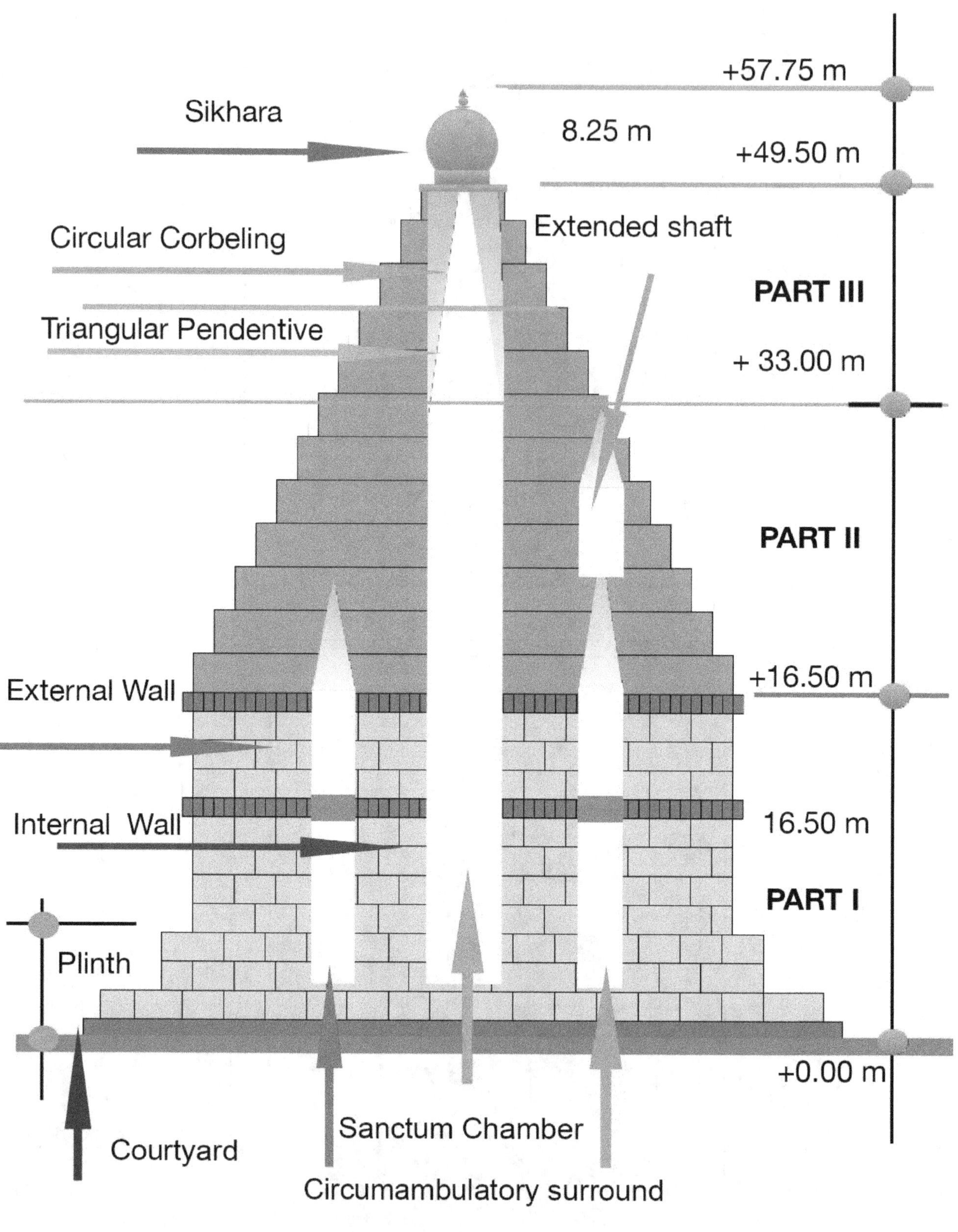

Structure in three parts

Vimana in three parts

4

Annexe

The annexe is the adjoining rectangular structure attached to the eastern face of Vimana. From the ground floor, it projects vertically in the form of rectangular vestibule halls stacked one on top of the other, as shown in the drawings and images.

It rises vertically over the massive plinth for three closed stories and an open terrace hall. The third story, which is open to the sky as an open terrace hall, is surrounded by massive granite parapet walls that are 1.68 m thick and 4.51 m high on three sides east, north, and south. The north and south walls are tightly interlocked and secured at the ends by the slanted Vimana facade. The inclined Vimana face serves as a west side wall for all of the halls beginning on the ground floor, resulting in a perfect configuration of a rectangular shape with nearly identical sizes on the ground, first, and second floors, with only a slight variation on the third-floor open terrace.

The inner dimensions of the hall are 13.80 m in length and 7.30 m in width roughly for both the first and second stories. The dimensions are nearly identical to the inner clear dimensions of the ground floor, which is 13.80 m × 7.30 m, connecting the two side massive stairways from the courtyard. The third-level terrace hall is also approximately 13.80 m × 7.30 m in size and is open to the sky, surrounded by higher, thicker parapet walls.

Inner, Outer, and Terrace Wall Openings

All of the above halls have entrance door openings of approximately 1.5 m × 2.1 m at the centre, which can be seen from the courtyard and more visibly and closely from the ground floor terrace. The third-floor-level open terrace has a 1 m × 1.5 m accessible opening and a 0.6 m × 0.9 m inaccessible opening on the eastern face of the Vimana wall, as displayed and explained in the sketches and images.

The openings from the halls are constructed by connecting the inside sanctum chamber directly.

The massive upper-storied rectangular halls, stacked one on top of the other, appear to be unused halls; their purpose is unknown at this stage of research.

The openings are visible from the halls and extend through the Vimana walls by directly connecting to the sanctum chamber. The inaccessible opening of 0.6 m × 0.9 m roughly corresponds to the mid-height of Vimana, which is + 24.75 m from the courtyard floor. This arrangement of all such openings could be for providing adequate ventilation and lighting to dark interior spaces during routine maintenance and renovation work. However, there are no more door entrances and openings beyond the level of the terrace for any such adequate ventilation and lighting requirement!

The above openings on Vimana's Eastern side are visibly seen.

The halls are stacked and arranged one on top of the other from the plinth and up to +27.26 m as rectangular boxes, nearly matching all of their inner dimensions from the ground to the open terrace parapet level.

It appears that the hallways, which must be stacked one on top of the other, played an important part and assignment during construction. The design, its necessity, and its purpose must also have played a significant role in bolstering the "Cholas' masterminded engineering approach."

We will look into and investigate all of this further.

Annexe - Rectangular shaped vestibule halls

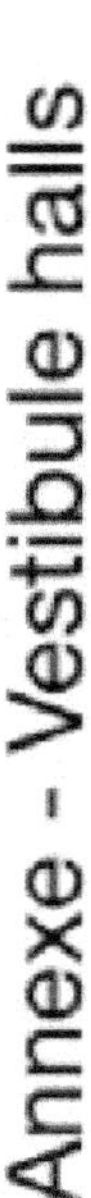

Annexe - Vestibule halls

Annexe

Annexe - Rectangular shaped vestibule halls - Birds eye view

Openings inside the Sanctum chamber's eastern wall connecting to Annexe

Annexe vestibule hall inside

Annexe - 3rd level open terrace encircled by
massive walls around

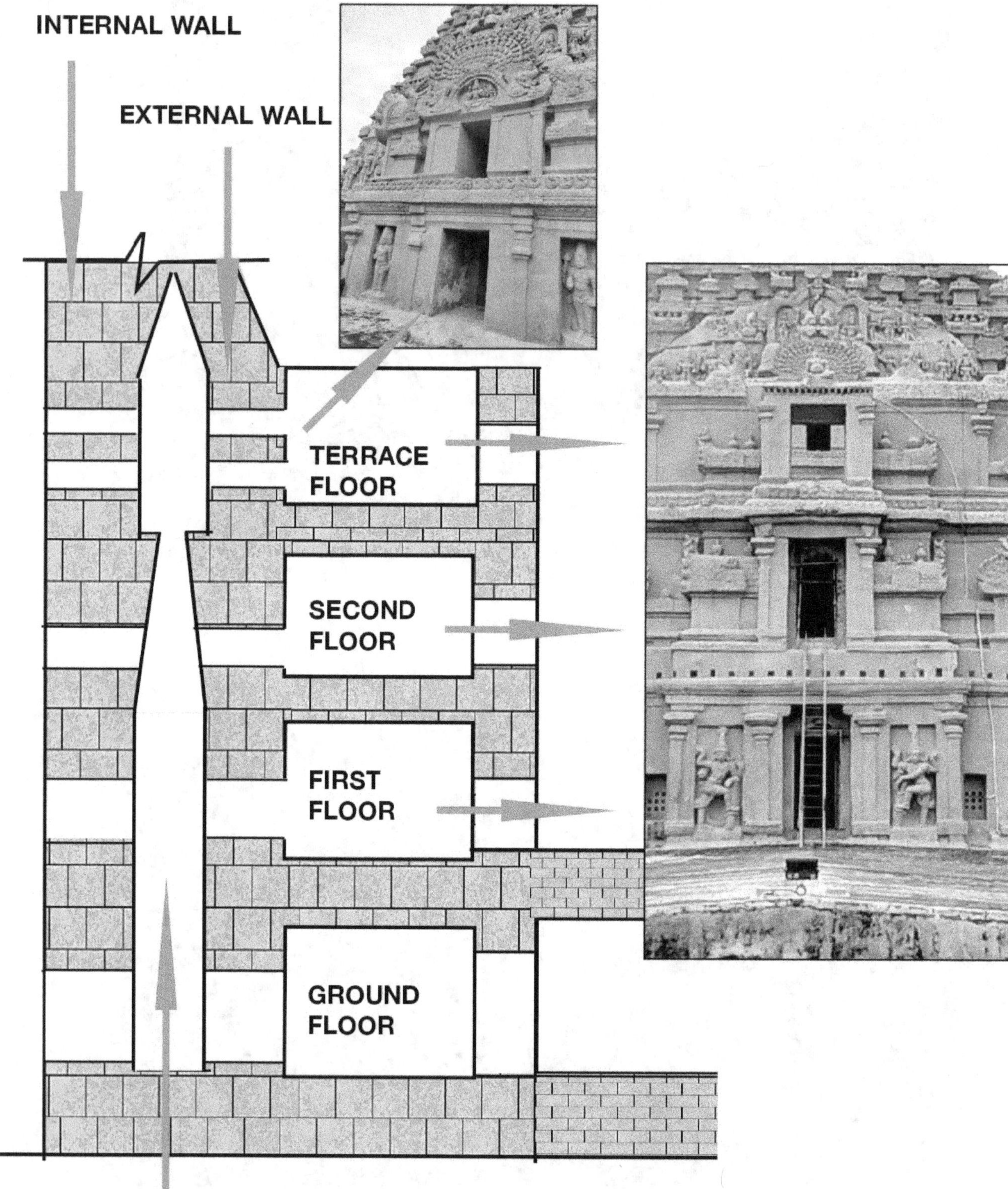

Annexe building & Circumambulatory – Cross section

5

Mass

Over the years, it has been widely accepted that the Sikhara is approximately 81 MT in weight.

A total of three main granite components make up the Sikhara as a single unit.

The first component is a top spherical dome placed over the second component, an octagonal drum known as Griva in the middle. They rest on a square bottom horizontal slab, which is the third component.

A long-held belief of 81 MT raises questions and doubts.

Which part refers to the weight of 81 MT?

Does it only refer to the spherical dome or the drum, or the combined weight of both the spherical dome and the drum? What about the weight of the horizontal square granite part that serves as a slab for both the drum and the spherical dome? Furthermore, there are four pairs of holy bulls sitting majestically on the slab's corners, each weighing a significant amount of weight.

A small round aperture, which appears to represent the container's mouth, can be seen at the centre of the bottom slab when viewed from inside the Vimana, with the rest of the bottom slab being completely covered by ornate circular corbelling.

In the following, doubt arises and questions erupt.

Is the entire capstone unit a solid monolithic carved out of a single massive block of rock consisting of a solid horizontal slab, a vertical solid drum, and a curved solid spheroid?

Or

Is there a hollowness and open vacuum space inside the drum and spherical dome unit?

Because the temple has a few huge monolithic sculptures, such as the entrance guardian deities (gatekeepers), huge holy bull, entrance pillar, water cistern, and so on, the carving skills of the Cholas cannot be understated or ruled out from a massive block of rock.

Calculation of Mass

The dimensions and sketches obtained from the ASI were used to make the calculations for the two assumptions.

The first assumption is that the entire unit is a single solid monolithic block made up of the base resting slab, the drum-shaped Griva, and the spherical dome with a pair of holy bulls seated at each of the four corners.

The second assumption is that hollowness with free space both inside the drum and in the spherical dome is considered. The probable wall thickness for the stem and shell had been arrived at based on dimensions and sketches obtained from the ASI.

Inferences were also drawn from other similar structural features within the temple complex to determine the shell and drum's closest and most likely wall thickness.

Completely Solid

When considered as a complete single monolithic solid block, the mass involved in the slab, drum, spherical dome, and four pairs of holy bulls seated at the corners would be approximately 675 MT (675,000 kg), as calculated and detailed in the table.

Hollow Spherical

The wall thickness of the spherical cell has been approximated and logically determined to be between 90 and 100 mm, while the thickness of the supporting Griva drum wall is between 100 and 150 mm.

This is based on the ASI drawings' external projection of 450 mm spherical Sikhara from the face of the Griva wall (drum wall) and also inferences derived from other structural features available within the temple complex.

Logical Inference from Water Cistern

A massive parabolic curve-shaped water cistern is lying in the long southern corridor adjacent to the ASI Museum Office. The cistern measures 2.7 m x 0.90 m x 0.9 m and must weigh between 1500 and 1750 kg (1.5 to 1.75 MT).

It has been brilliantly sculpted out of a single massive block of rock with no joints to a beautiful parabolic curved profile all over. To allow water to drain, the cistern must be water-tight and have a drainage hole at the bottom. Inside and out, the granite surfaces are finely chiselled and dressed to a high standard, with curved profiles reaching the ends.

It exemplifies the sculptor's high quality with his meticulous attention to its spherical curving and carving skills on all sides.

An inference is drawn and used as a reference from this huge parabolic cistern.

Based on the evidence and reasoning presented above, the weighted average thickness of this water-tight curved cistern is estimated to be between 90 and 100 mm, as shown in the calculations.

The sculptor who designed this water cistern may also have been involved in the modelling of the spherical dome, which must have used his spherical carving skill to the thickness of 90–100 mm for the dome shell and 100–150 mm for the drum wall.

Based on the references and logical inferences provided above, the total mass contained in the hollow Sikhara, including the base slab and the holy bulls seated at the corners, is estimated to be 139.10 MT (139,100 kg), as shown in the table.

With a weighted average thickness of only 100 mm for the spherical shell and 150 mm for the drum wall, the total mass contained in the entire unit is nearly 140 MT.

With various combinations of calculations taking into account the nearby shell and wall thicknesses, the overall mass is likely to range between 140 and 160 MT.

Lifting and installing a block with a limited technological advantage against the gravitational field a thousand years ago would appear impossible and extremely difficult, regardless of whether it is a solid 650 MT or a hollow 140 MT of mass.

With logical reference and inference, and taking into account the hollowness inside, the entire dome unit could have a mass of around 140 MT, and even hoisting and installing such a massive block of granite rock in the gravitational field is a Herculean and extremely difficult operation.

In this context, the unit of measurement for large masses is MT, which refers to the solid matter contained in the Sikhara in the form of granite carved rock material rather than weight.

Mass (M) = volume × density in physics and the unit in the SI system is kilograms (kg)

$M = m^3 \times kg / m^3 = kg$

1000 kg = 1 Metric Tonne, abbreviated as 1 MT.

The gravitational force acting on a mass in a gravitational field is known as weight, and its SI unit is 'Newton'.

Weight (W) is defined as the mass of the body multiplied by the acceleration due to the gravity of the earth ($W = M \times g$), with 'Newton' as the SI unit.

$W = kg \times m / sec^2$ and 1 kg m per sec^2 equals 1 Newton and 1000 N = 1 kilo Newton (kN).

People in common parlance refer to weight in kg or MT.

While the Sikhara's mass is 140 MT, its weight is computed as follows.

W = M × g

= 140 MT × 1000 kg × 9.81 m/sec²

= 1373,400 kg m/sec² and 1 kg m/sec² equals 1 N

= 1373400 N

= 1373.40 kN

Similarly, the exact weight of 160 MT mass is calculated as 1569.60 kN.

We can also refer to the mass of 140 MT as the "140 MT force," meaning that the force of gravity is acting on the 140 MT of mass in the gravitational field.

In summary, depending on the exact weighted average thickness of the shell and drum, the Sikhara's total weight can range between 140 and 160 MT force. However, unless it is supported by calculations and physical evidence, the long-held assumption and belief that the entire capstone weighs only 81 MT are likely to be challenged.

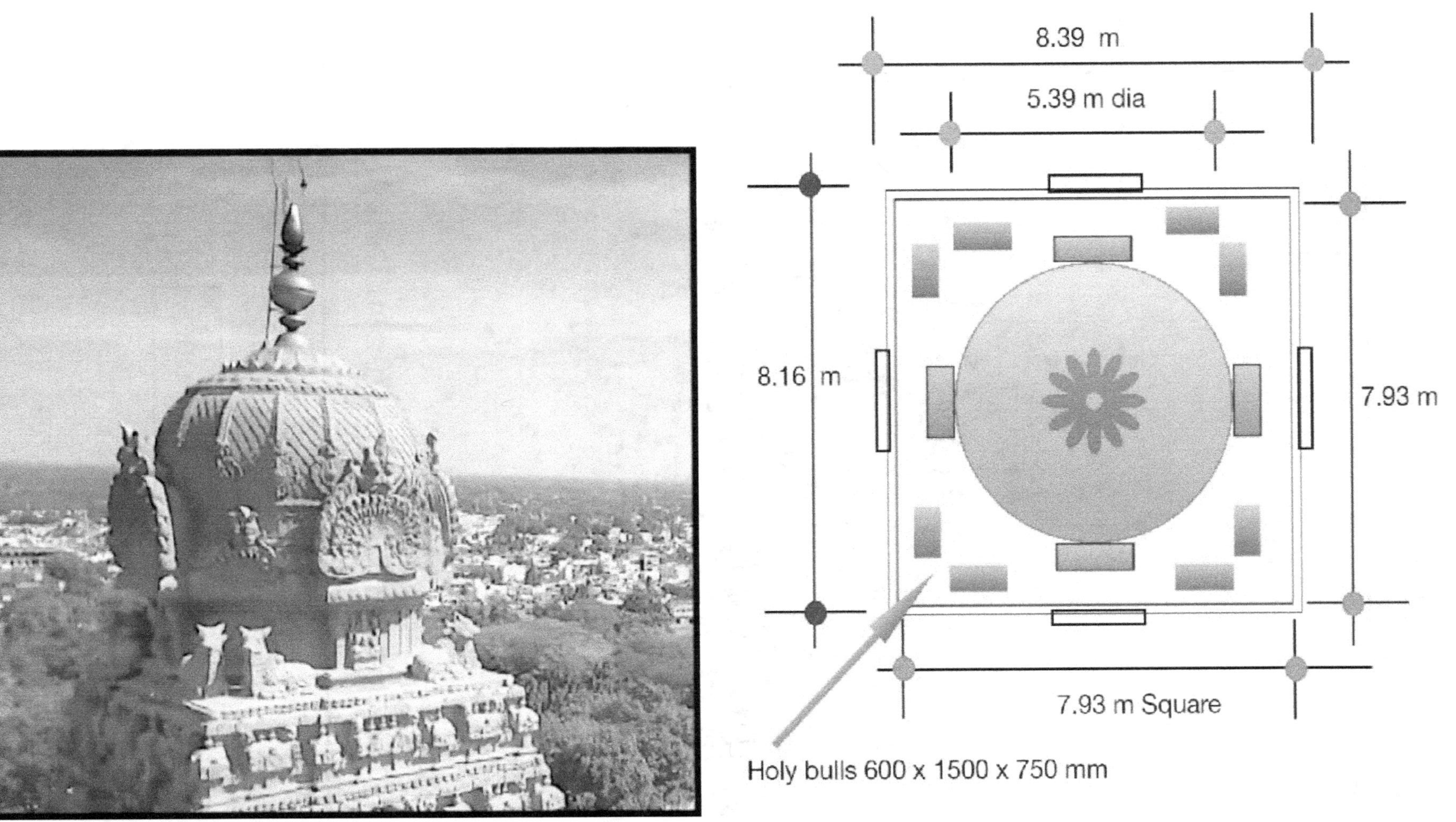

8.39 m
5.39 m dia
8.16 m
7.93 m
7.93 m Square
Holy bulls 600 x 1500 x 750 mm
Sikhara - Top View

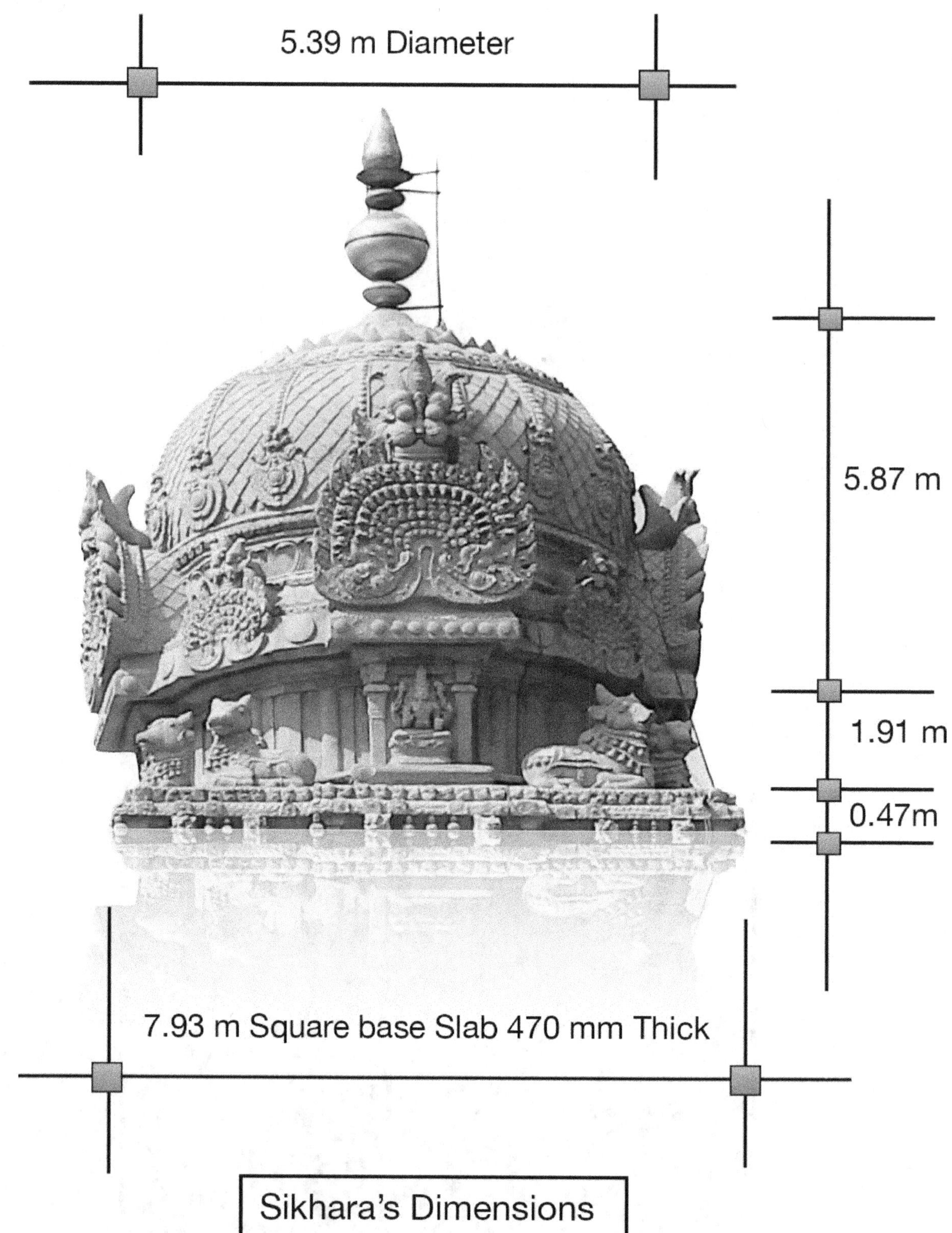

Sikhara's Dimensions

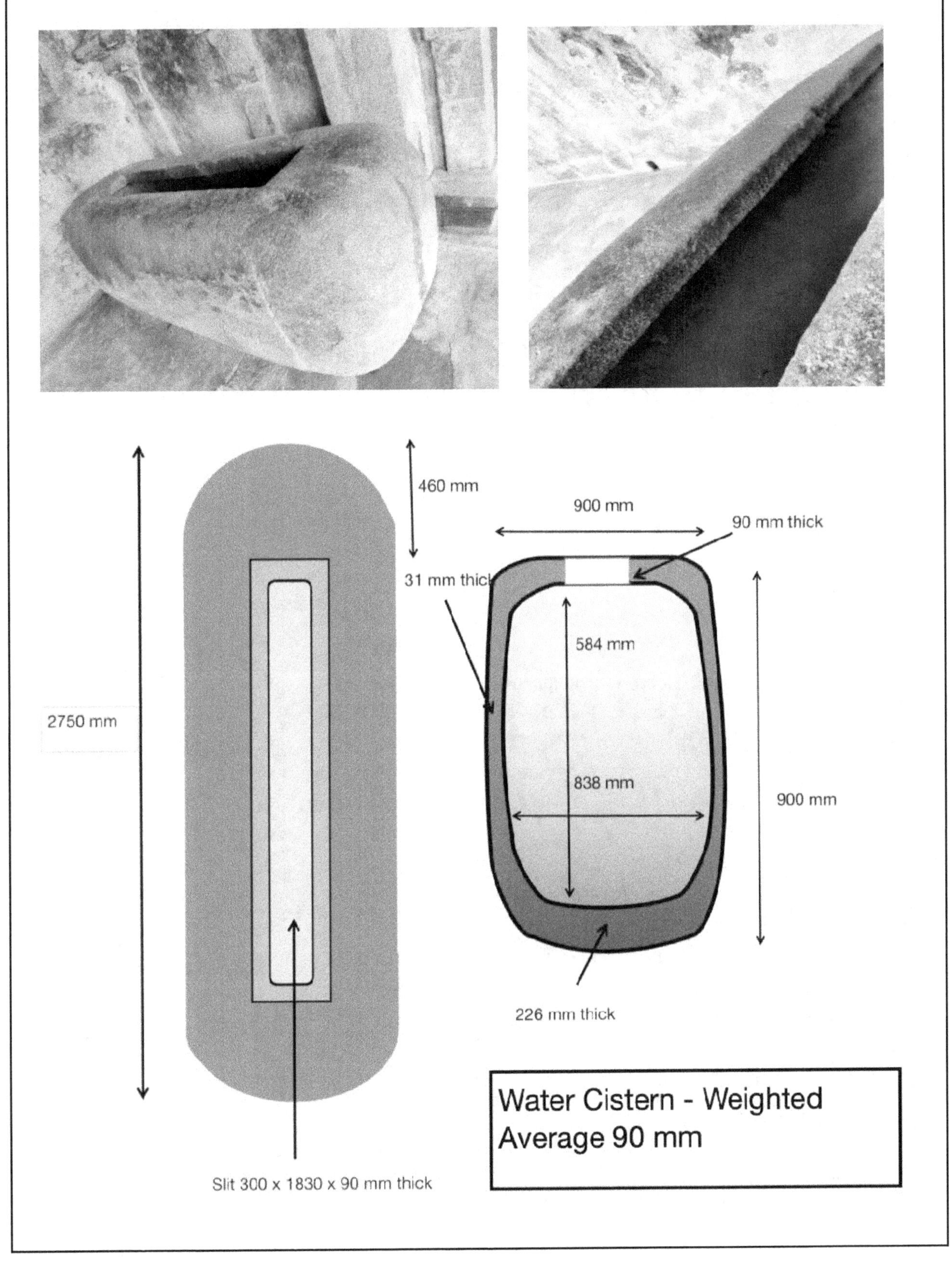
460 mm
900 mm
90 mm thick
31 mm thick
584 mm
2750 mm
838 mm
900 mm
226 mm thick
Slit 300 x 1830 x 90 mm thick
Water Cistern - Weighted
Average 90 mm

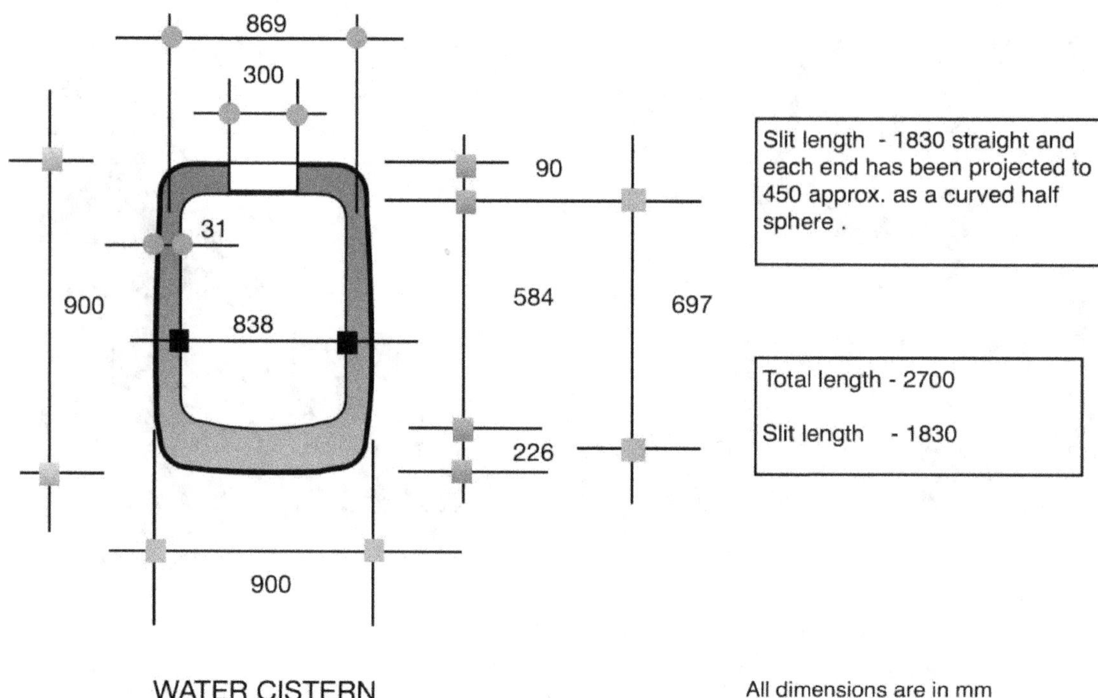

Water cistern - weighted average wall thickness calculation		
The cross sectional shape is similar to a parabola		
Area of parabola outer = 2/3 (a x b)	a = 584+226 = 810 mm	b = 900 mm
A1 = 2/3 x 0. 810 x 0.9 = 0.486 m²		
Area of parabola inner = 2/3 (a x b)	a = 584 mm	b = 838 mm
A2 = 2/3 x 0. 584 x 0.838 = 0.326 m²	Arc length = 1.715 m	
Variance A1 and A2 = 0.486 -0.326 = 0.160 m²		
Volume of granite = 0.160 x 1.83 = 0.2928 m ³		
Average side wall thickness = 0.2928/(1.715 x1.83) = 0.0933 m	0.932 m = 93 mm	
Top = 1.83 x 0.9 x 0.09 - 1.83 x 0.3 x 0.09 = 0.09882 m³		
Sphere wall volume considering 900 mm outer dia and wall thick 90 mm		
0.3817- 0.19543 = 0.18627 m³		
Total volume of granite = 0.2928+.09882+0.18627 = 0.58 m³	@ 2.7 MT/m³ = 1.57 T	
Total weighted average		
Arc area 1.83 x 1.715 + top 0.90 x 1.83 - 0.3 x 1.83 + sphere 2.061 m² =	6.297 m² = Total surface area	
Weighted average = volume/surface area = 0.58 / 6.297 = 0.092 m	say 90 mm	

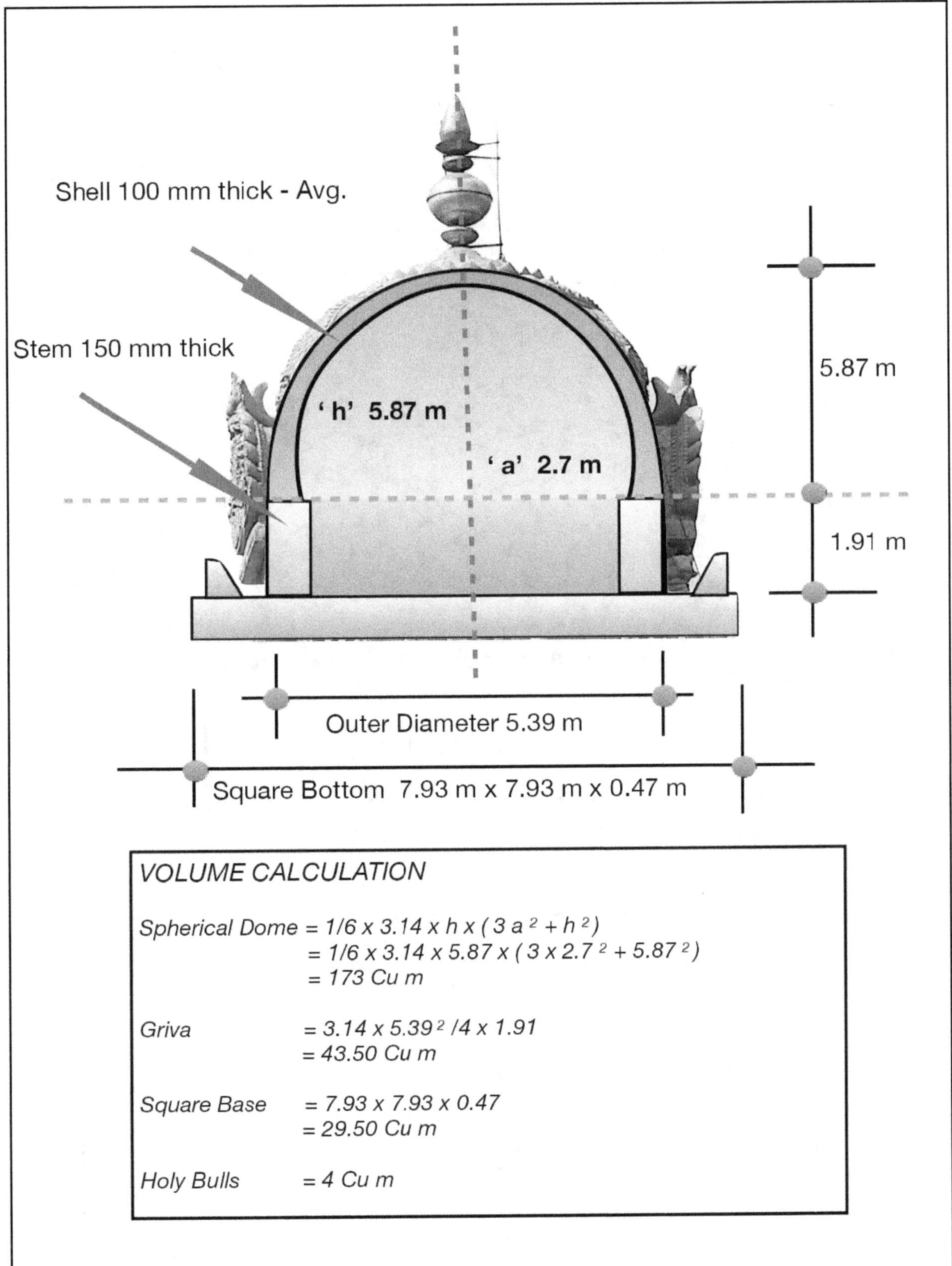

VOLUME CALCULATION

Spherical Dome $= 1/6 \times 3.14 \times h \times (3 a^2 + h^2)$
$= 1/6 \times 3.14 \times 5.87 \times (3 \times 2.7^2 + 5.87^2)$
$= 173$ Cu m

Griva $= 3.14 \times 5.39^2 / 4 \times 1.91$
$= 43.50$ Cu m

Square Base $= 7.93 \times 7.93 \times 0.47$
$= 29.50$ Cu m

Holy Bulls $= 4$ Cu m

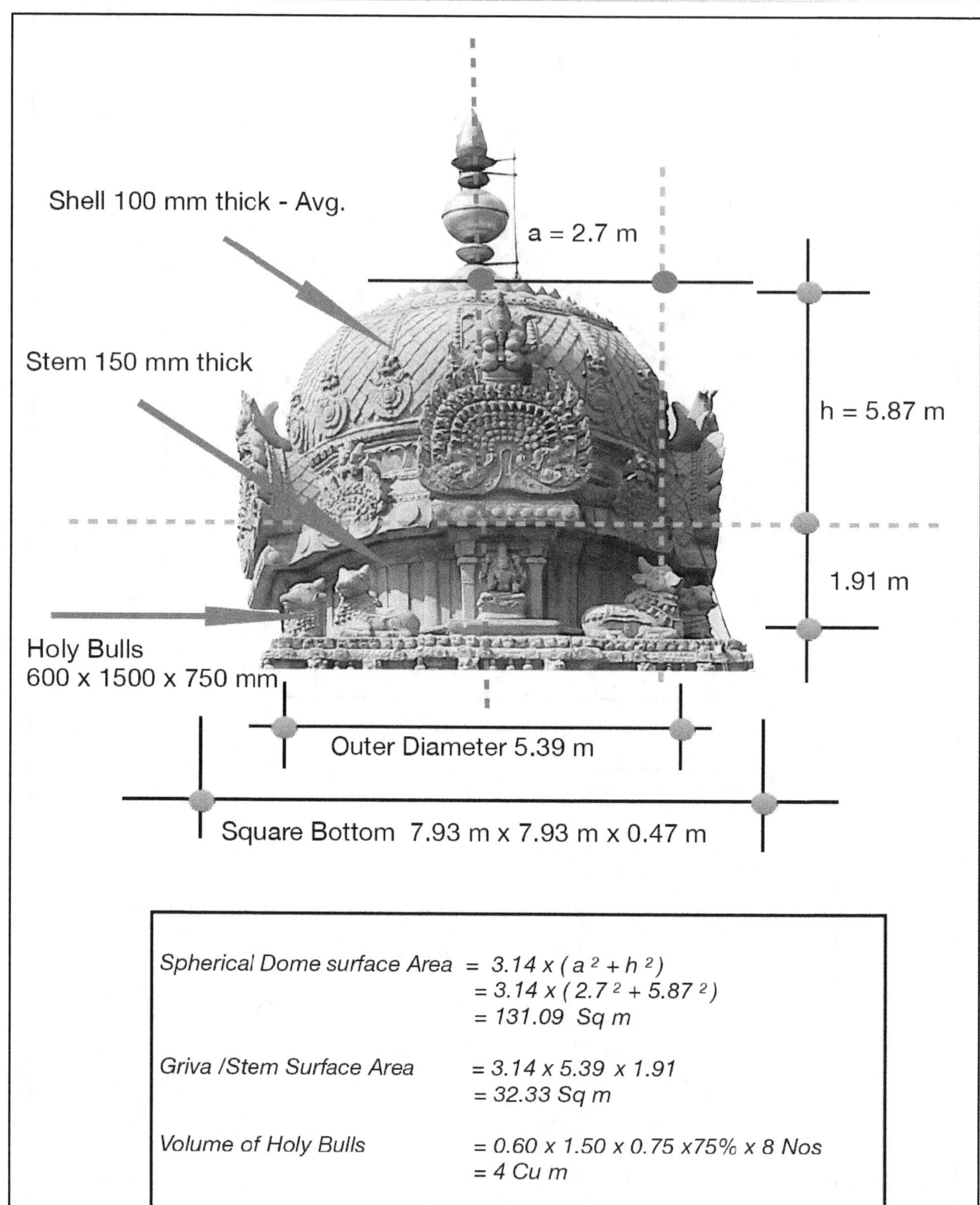

Spherical Dome surface Area $= 3.14 \times (a^2 + h^2)$
$= 3.14 \times (2.7^2 + 5.87^2)$
$= 131.09$ Sq m

Griva /Stem Surface Area $= 3.14 \times 5.39 \times 1.91$
$= 32.33$ Sq m

Volume of Holy Bulls $= 0.60 \times 1.50 \times 0.75 \times 75\% \times 8$ Nos
$= 4$ Cu m

Projected length from the Drum wall surface - 450 mm

Mass and weight of solid Sikhara unit

Monolithic spherical diameter 5.39 m , height 5.87 m , Griva 1.91 m high & slab 0.47 m thick

Description	Unit	Spherical dome	Griva or Drum	Slab	Holy bulls	Total
Total outer volume	m³	173	43.50	29.50	4	250.00
Granite density	MT/m³	2.7	2.7	2.7	2.7	
Total	MT	467.10	117.45	79.65	10.8	675.00
Total mass						675 MT
Total weight						675 MT force
Weight in kN		675 x 1000 x 9.81 = 6621.75 kN			say	6622 kN

Mass and weight of hollow Sikhara unit

Monolithic spherical diameter 5.39 m , height 5.87 m , Griva 1.91 m high & slab 0.47 m thick.

Description	Unit	Spherical dome	Griva or Drum	Slab	Holy bulls	Total
Total outer volume	m³	173	43.50	29.50	4	250.00
Surface area	m²	131.09	32.33	62.88		
Average wall thick.	mm	100	150	470		
Granite volume	m³	13.11	4.85	29.55	4	51.51
Granite density	MT/m³	2.7	2.7	2.7	2.7	
Total	MT	35.39	13.09	79.79	10.80	139.08
Total mass					say	140 MT
Total weight						140 MT force
Weight in kN		140 x 1000 x 9.81 = 1373.40 kN			say	1373 kN

Complete Solid - 675 MT of Mass (approx.)

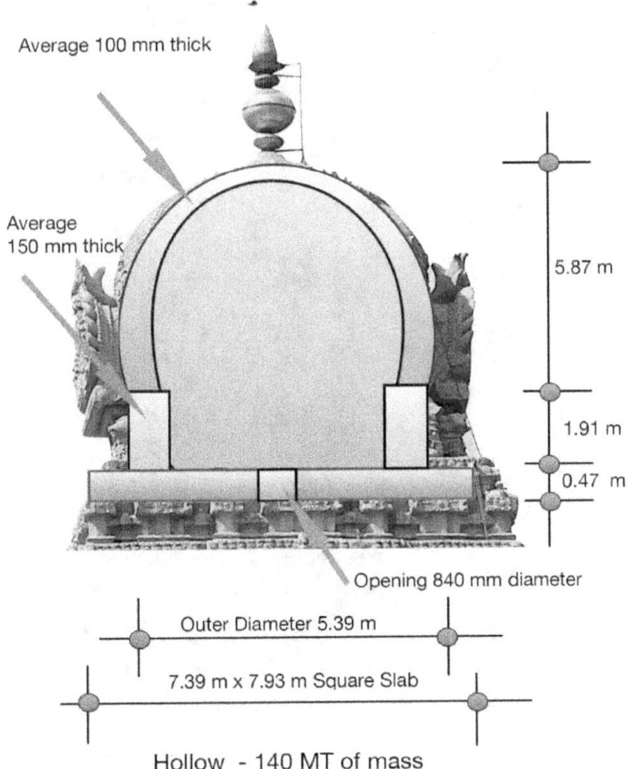

Hollow - 140 MT of mass

Single monolithic Granite Units - 6 m high Approx.

Holy Bull carved out from Single Monolithic Granite Block 2.1 m length and 2.1 m High

Hollow Water Cistern 2.75 m x 0.90 m x 0.90 m made from Single Monolithic Granite Block of 5 m length approx.

Door deity Made from a Single Monolithic Rock Mass of 5 to 5.5 m High

Pillar Made from a Single Monolithic Rock Mass of 12 to 14 m High

6

Ramp & Elephants

It is a long-held belief that a huge ramp measuring 6.6 km had been built from a place called Sarapallam to move the heavier stones and the Sikhara block to higher elevations by deploying a large number of elephants, bulls, and highly skilled workers, and the remains of the ramp can still be seen around the temple complex.

The temple was built more than a thousand years ago. No evidence or documentation exists to support the claim that the above-mentioned conventional methodology and process occurred.

Practicality and technicality must coexist harmoniously in the methodology.

A thorough investigation into conventional ramp methodology and its practicality are therefore required.

Physical Ramp Configuration

Consider the traditional method of constructing an inclined plane from Sarapallam, 6.6 km from the temple, to the summit of Vimana. The base in Sarapallam is zero, and the temple tower is more than 50 m high, requiring a lot of compacted earth and sand fill to last for 5 to 6 years of construction duration.

To keep the earth pressure from the filled ramp at bay, two massive retaining walls of sufficient width are required as shown in the drawing. The retaining walls around the temple plinth should be 17 to 20 m wide, approximately, and made of solid granite masonry to withstand 50 m height of lateral earth pressure.

In such an arrangement, the maximum weight of the masonry retaining wall is also transferred to the base in this configuration around the tower in addition to the weight of the main structure. Furthermore, a large amount of compacted sand and earth filling is necessary between the vertical side of the retaining wall and the Vimana, with a sufficient compaction factor to survive at least 6 1/2 years including monsoons and until the completion time.

In addition, the architectural embellishments on the Vimana facade require additional sand packing, which adds further weight to the tower. Finally, the vertical empty space inside the sanctum shaft up to + 50 m elevation, as well as the voids of the circumambulatory and annexe halls, must be filled with sand and soil, adding immense weight to the foundation.

The total combined weight of the two retaining walls, compacted sand inside the chamber, and the filling over the tower and around the plinth may exceed that of the main Vimana.

The total weight of the structure combined with all of the above temporary fillings and retaining wall arrangements will exert heavy pressure on the soil layers, which are most likely limestone rock strata, as determined and validated in the site-assessment procedure previously. The soil strata must bear all the above high-intensity loading within the permissible safe bearing capacity (SBC) and by meeting the minimum factor of safety criterion as engineering norms.

The maximum SBC of limestone with a very good rock mass classification is 162 T/m² or nearly 1620 kN/m². If there are localised fissures, clay weathering, shear zones, and alternate hard and soft layers present in the rock mass, they add to the uncertainty of the aforementioned figure.

Assuming that the rock mass classification is very good under the temple tower, the stress distribution and expected settlement are within acceptable limits.

The overall final safe permissible design loading must be determined from the ultimate bearing capacity by considering the factor of safety, and margin to arrive at the maximum SBC value. In general, a factor of safety of 2 to 3 is used to calculate a rock mass's maximum SBC from its ultimate bearing capacity.

According to the calculation in Table 1, the total mass of the Vimana exerts 72 MT of force per square metre on the soil or 700 Kilo Newton per square metre (kN/m²) in terms of weight.

This is based on the assumption of a 1.5 m thick foundation raft, which is widely believed to be the case. If the rock quality and rock mass classification are both good, the total weight of the structure, 700 kN/m², is less than the SBC of the soil, 1620 kN/m², and the structure is safe when only its total weight is considered.

The Chola engineers appear to have compared the soil loading pattern to the entire weight of the structure's safety limit to ensure that the maximum intensity of the loading should be within the soil's maximum SBC.

This is only considering the weight of the entire granite structure over a 30 m × 30 m courtyard base.

What about the weight of the 50-meter-plus high solid retaining wall enclosure and the compacted sand fill inside, which, together with the weight of the main structure, will exert enormous pressure on the soil? In such a case, what is the total combined load transfer on the soil, in addition to the weight of the Vimana structure?

According to Tables 1 and 2, the maximum load value reaches 1836 kN/m², which is above the permitted upper limit of SBC.

The total load transferred on the soil exceeds the maximum allowable SBC value without taking into account the other uncertainty factors present beneath the soil strata, which is not safe for the stability of the structure and is not permitted.

It is widely assumed and stated that the structure is standing on filled-up and compacted sand.

Technically, the compacted sand cannot withstand the pressure of 1836 kN/m² because its maximum SBC value is only 450 kN/m², which is four times less than the intensity of the actual load from the Vimana, and the soil tends to settle during the construction stage itself.

Even though the base soil is of massive limestone rock of good classification, the intensity of loading from the conventional ramp and elephants method is 1836 kN/m², which exceeds the maximum safe permissible SBC of 1620 kN/m², and it is technically not advisable or permissible to transfer load beyond the safe permissible value.

As a result, the traditional ramp and elephant system of covering the structure with compacted sand and dragging the granite blocks are technically, practically, and logically impossible, and is only a made-up and imagined solution that may be due to ignorance and misunderstanding.

Furthermore, the weight of the two temporary massive retaining walls required to sustain the lateral soil and sand pressure is not included in the above figure because the data on the raft's extension from the main Vimana foundation beneath the courtyard was not visible and could not be retrieved.

Now that the courtyard has been covered with flooring, the raft foundation may or may not extend beyond the visible base width of the Vimana. Due to a lack of information, it is unknown whether the temporary retaining wall built to support the massive sand filling also transferred its weight to the main Vimana foundation.

Assuming a 50-m-high granite masonry retaining wall, the intensity of loading from that wall alone is 1530 kN/m², which is directly transferred just adjacent to the main foundation.

The mass is 57.75 m³ × 2.7 T/m³ = 156 MT/m², and the weight is 1530 kN/m².

In this case, the main Vimana foundation and the retaining wall base are just adjacent, and the closely spaced footings interfere. When two foundations are placed next to each other in similar soil conditions, the ultimate bearing capacity of each foundation may change due to the interference effect of the failure surface in the soil.

This will have a significant effect on bearing capacity as well as other failure mechanisms like footing settlement and tilting.

Deployment and Involvement of Elephants

Over the centuries, it has been widely accepted that a large number of elephants were used for shifting and pulling operations from Sarapallam, a 6.6 km distance from the temple complex.

Elephants may have been used to pull and move huge stones and blocks on the ground level operations in a horizontal plane. Even though the slope of the ramp is gentle by connecting the Vimana's top, the feasibility, practicality, and technicalities must be investigated.

To begin with, how many elephants were used to tow the massive 140 MT force or even the traditionally stated and accepted weight of 81 MT? Long-held beliefs and erroneous views persist that a large number of elephants were also employed for the installation operation at the summit level of 50 m above ground level.

An African elephant's shoulder height is typically between 3 and 4 m, while an Asian elephant is closer to 3 m in height. The trunk length of an elephant can vary from 1.8 m to 2 m. Elephants can effectively carry a weight of 1 to 1.5 m above their shoulders, which can reach a maximum height of 4.5 m.

We'll assume that the Sikhara is made up of eight separate pieces that have been put together and connected so that it functions as a single, enormous monolithic unit. Even if one takes into account the 81 MT total traditional weight, a single piece weighs about 10 MT.

As a result of the physical characteristics of an elephant described above, how can an elephant efficiently do any lifting operation over 9 to 10 m to install a granite element perfectly in the equilibrium for the total Sikhara's height of 8.25 m?

It's up for debate and discussion.

Furthermore, elephants can only efficiently lift between 250 and 350 kg above their shoulder level. In such a case, the number of elephants needed to lift and install a single piece weighing 10 tonnes around the square Sikhara's block requires 33 elephants.

In 32 m of peripheral length, a maximum of 8 to 12 elephants can be accommodated in the 8 m × 8 m Sikhara base, allowing some working area clearance. How can 33 elephants be stationed and lined up even to lift a single piece of 10 MT weight?

Lifting 81 MT vertically as a single monolithic unit requires 270 elephants to be stationed around the Sikhara base at the summit for perfect equilibrium, which is logistically impossible, raising serious issues and questions.

It's even more controversial and disputed!

As a result, the complex conventional method of laying a huge length ramp of 6.6 km and employing a large number of elephants' technical and practical feasibility is called into question.

Considering all of the constraints and obstacles, it is evident that the Chola engineers played a strategic game of a different kind by applying their engineering expertise and intelligence.

There must be a simple lifting and installation mechanism from the engineering team, who must have meticulously masterminded the technicalities and managed to hoist the block vertically through inside the sanctum shaft with a unique setup and arrangement.

To establish the facts, the inner and outer structural features and constructional details, as well as other engineering aspects that may have supported the lifting and installation operation, must be extensively scanned and analysed.

Table - 1 Total load (weight) transfer on the soil from the main structure

	Area at top - A1 in m²	1No x 7.93 m x 7.93 m	62.88
	Area at 16.50 m lvl in m ²	1No x 25.93 mx 25.93 m	672.36
	Height of above 16.32 m lvl in m	49.50-16.50 =33.18	33.00
	A 1 x A 2 in m²	62.88 x 672.36	42,278.00
	√ A1 x A2 in m²	√62.88 x 672.36	205.62
	Super structure volume - m³		
1	Volume above 16.50 m lvl	H/3 (A1+A2 + √ A1 x A2))	10,349.46
2	Volume below 16.50 m lvl	25.93 x 25.93 x 16.50	11094.02
3	Less sanctum shaft	7.93 x 7.93 x (49.50 -4.47)	-2831.49
4	Less circumambualtory	16,52 x 4 x (16.50 -1.05-4.47) x 1.87	-1356.79
5	Less triangualr top cavity	0.5 x 1.87 x 4.61 x16.52x4	-284.83
6	Less extended rectangular Shaft from +22.75 m	1.90 x 3.8 x (31.60 -22.75)	-63.897
7	Circular corbelling above +39.75 m	1/2 x 3.545 x 9.75 x (7.93- 2 x 1/3x3.545)x3.14	302.08
8	50% of Annexe structure slab and beam	7.30 x 13.80 x 3.35 X 50%	168.74
9	Annexe columns	6 x 0.65 x 0.65 x (22.75-4.47-3.35) x 50%	18.92
10	Annexe walls	(7.3x2+13.80)x 1x 22.79 x 50%	322.34
	Total - m³		17718.56
	Add 20 % for wastage and dressing work left out for final finish in the arch. carvings	20%	3543.71
	Grand total for super structure - m³		**21262.27**
	Raft foundation - assumed 1.5 m thick	29.20 x 29.20 x1.50 m	1278.96
	Total granite volume over all - m³		**22541.23**
	Total load exerted on the soil from the structure per m²	22541.23 x2.7 /(29.20 x29.20) = 71.35 MT /m² x 9.81 = 700 kN / m²	**Or 72 MT force per m²**

Table - 2 Total load on the soil - conventional sand covering method

Sand /earth covering over the ctructure	29.20 x 29.20 x 57.75 m	49239.96
Compaction factor & additional (25%+10%)	35%	17233.99
Less granite structure (super structure) volume		-21262.27
Net volume of sand and earth from super structure		45211.68
Considering monsoon period and density of wet sand and earth @ 2.08 MT / m^3		94040.29
Summary		
Mass of the granite structure including raft	22541.23 x 2.70 MT/m^3	60861.32
Mass of sand and earth cover	45211.68 x 2.08 MT/m^3	94040.29
Total in MT		**154901.61**
Add miscellaneous load , other live loads & contingencies	3%	4647.05
Total mass involved in the conventional sand covering method - MT		159548.66
Over all mass involved - MT / m^2	159548.66 / (29.20 x 29.20) =	187.12
Total intensity of loading on the soil	187.12*1000*9.81/1000 =1836 kN/ m^2	1836 kN per m^2
Maximum safe bearing capacity of well compacted sandy soil	450 kN/m^2	
Maximum safe bearing capacity of good rock mass classification of lime stone rock	1620 kN/ m^2	
Total Intensity of loading exceeds the limit of maximum SBC value in both the cases of sand and lime stone rock bed layers !	*450 kN / m^2 & 1620 kN/m^2 are less than 1836 kN/m^2*	*Not safe & technically not feasible*

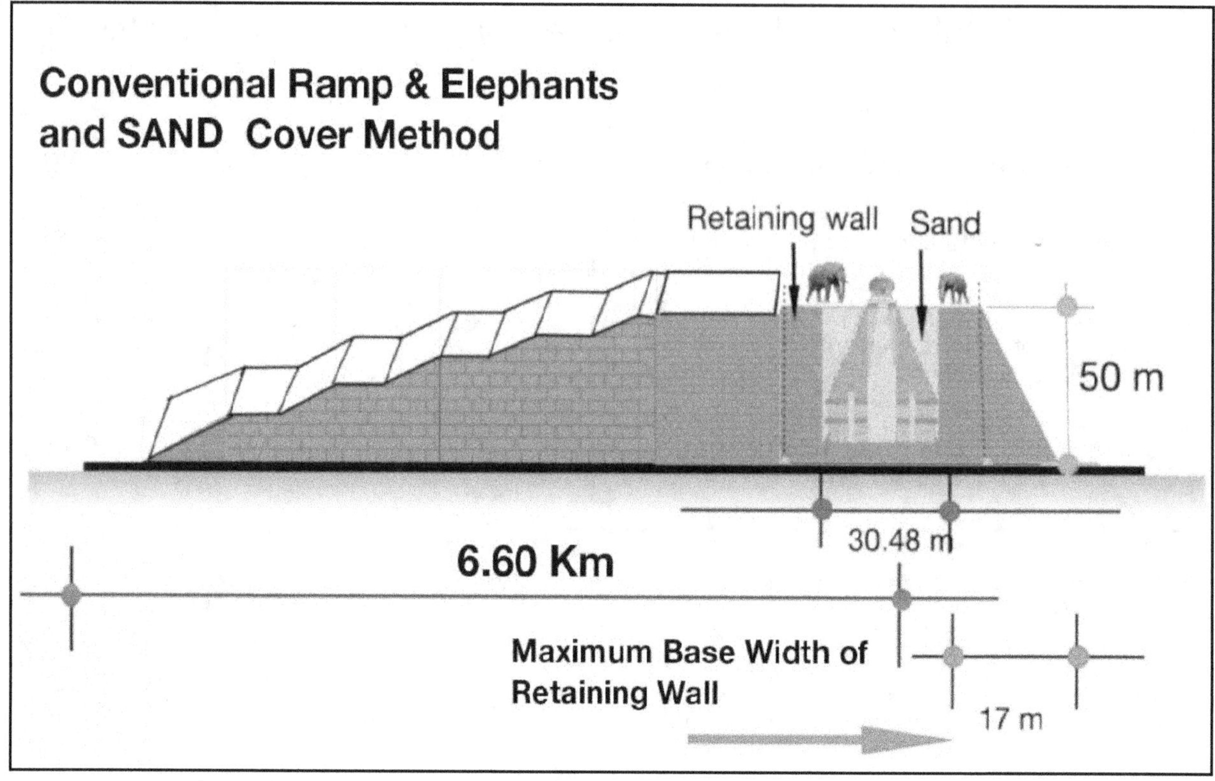

Conventional Ramp & Elephants
and SAND Cover Method
Retaining wall
Sand
50 m
30.48 m
6.60 Km
Maximum Base Width of
Retaining Wall
17 m

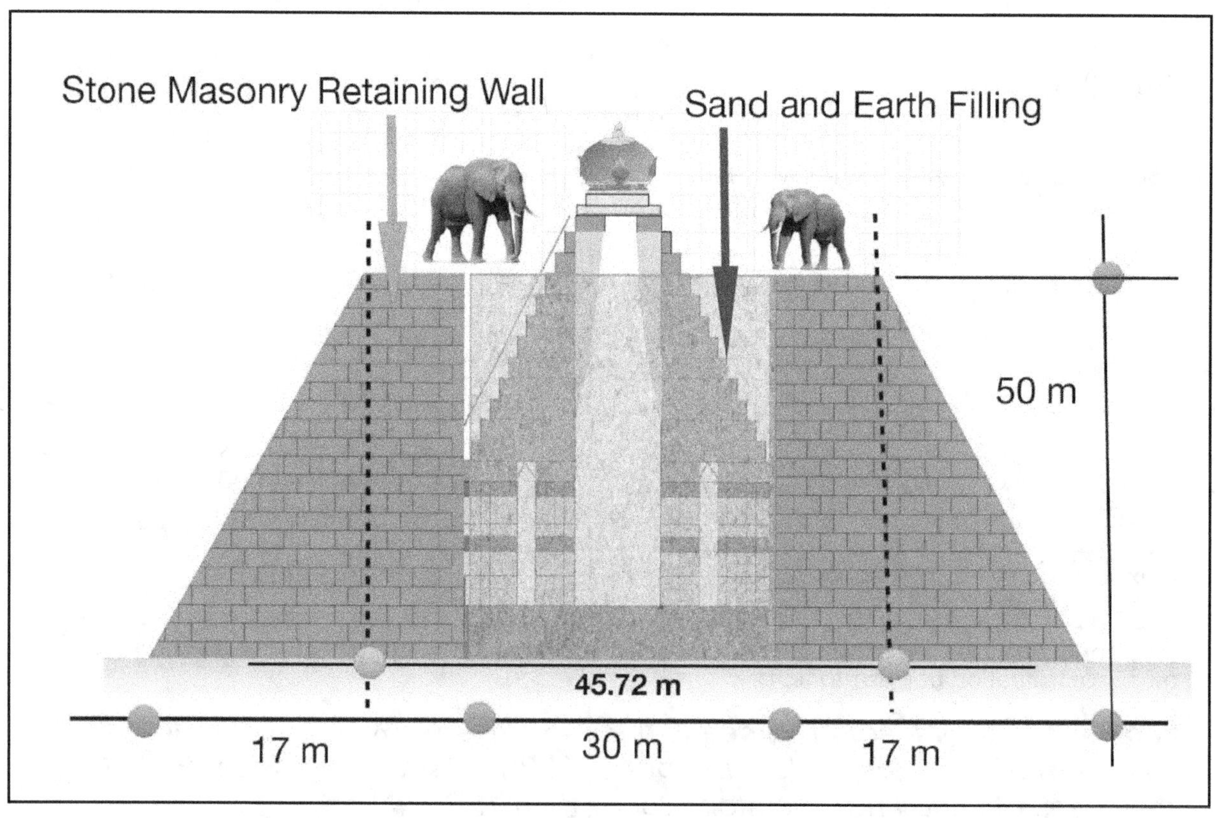

Stone Masonry Retaining Wall
Sand and Earth Filling
50 m
45.72 m
17 m
30 m
17 m

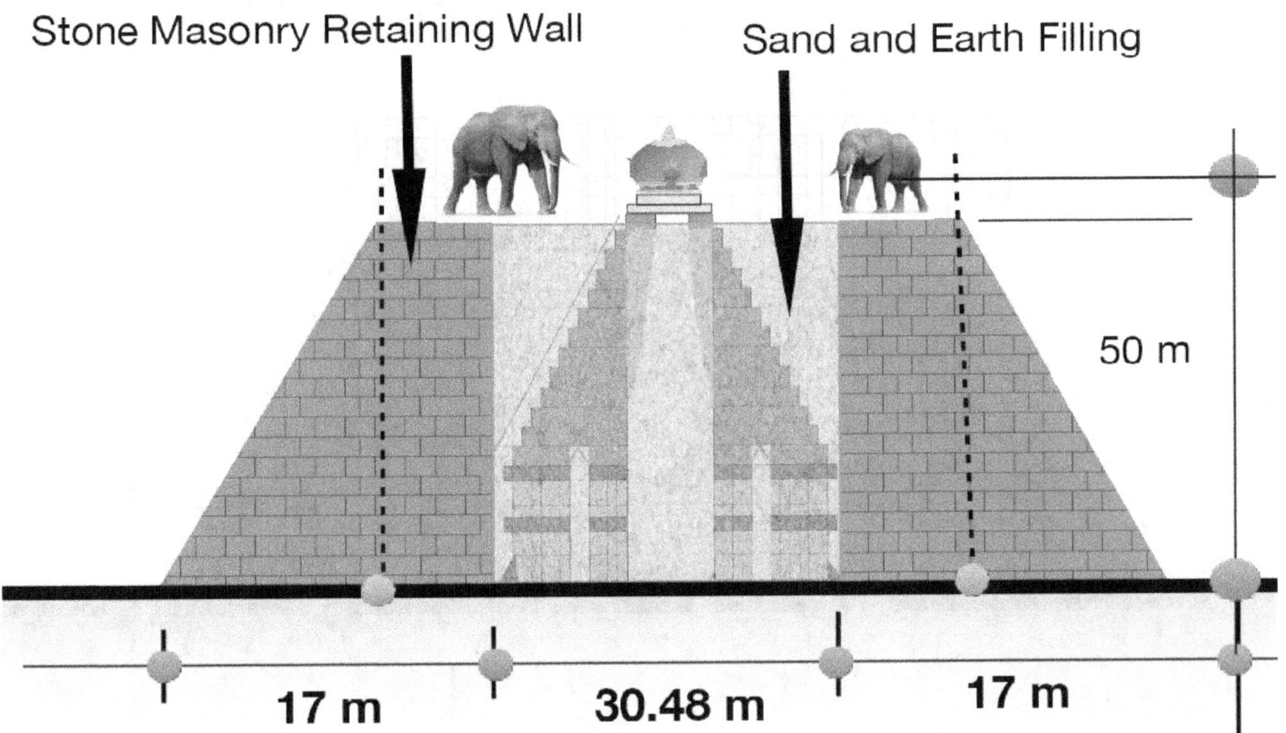

Total Intensity of Loading
187 MT / Sq m or
1836 KN / Sq m

*Total Intensity
exceeds SBC value*

Safe bearing capacity of
Soil 162 MT / Sq m or
1620 KN/ Sq m (approx.)

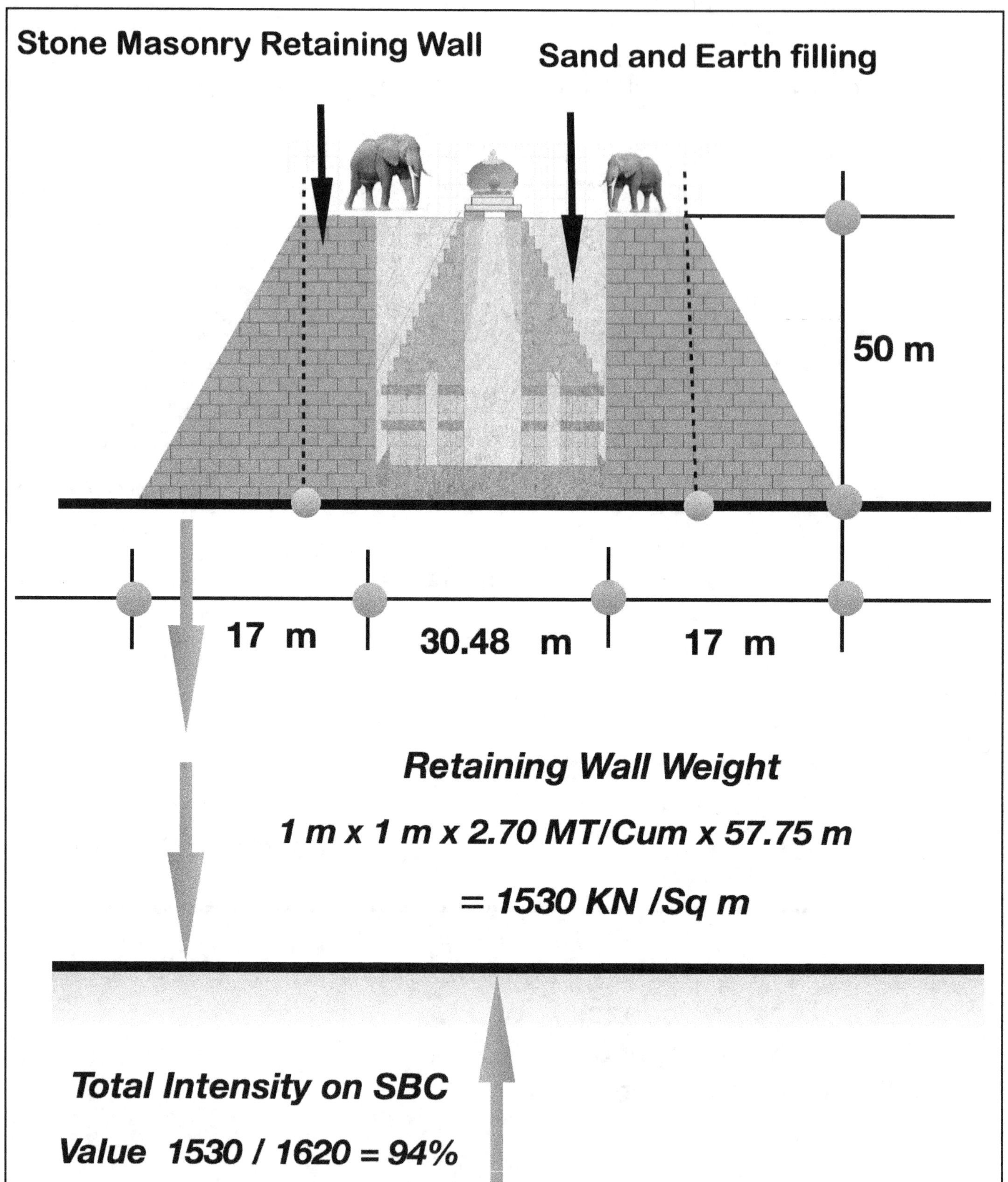

Stone Masonry Retaining Wall
Sand and Earth filling
50 m
17 m
30.48 m
17 m
Retaining Wall Weight
1 m x 1 m x 2.70 MT/Cum x 57.75 m
= 1530 KN /Sq m
Total Intensity on SBC
Value 1530 / 1620 = 94%

AN ARTISTIC IMPRESSION ON THE CONVENTIONAL METHOD OF USING RAMP AND ELEPHANTS

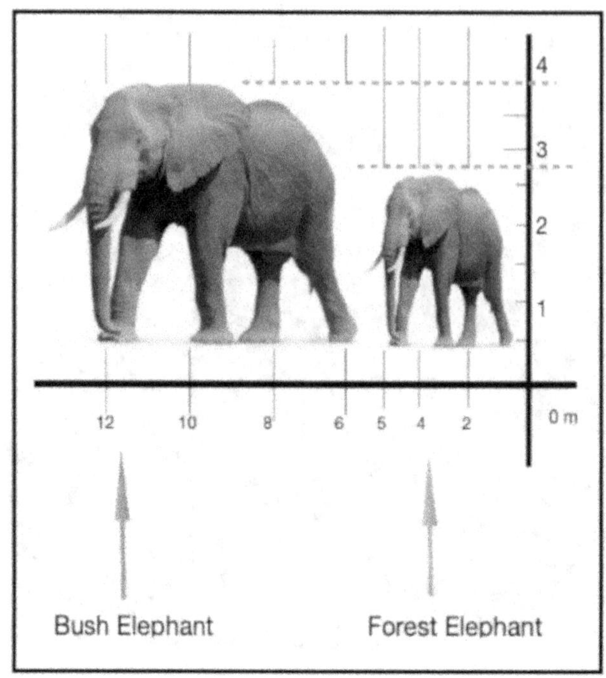

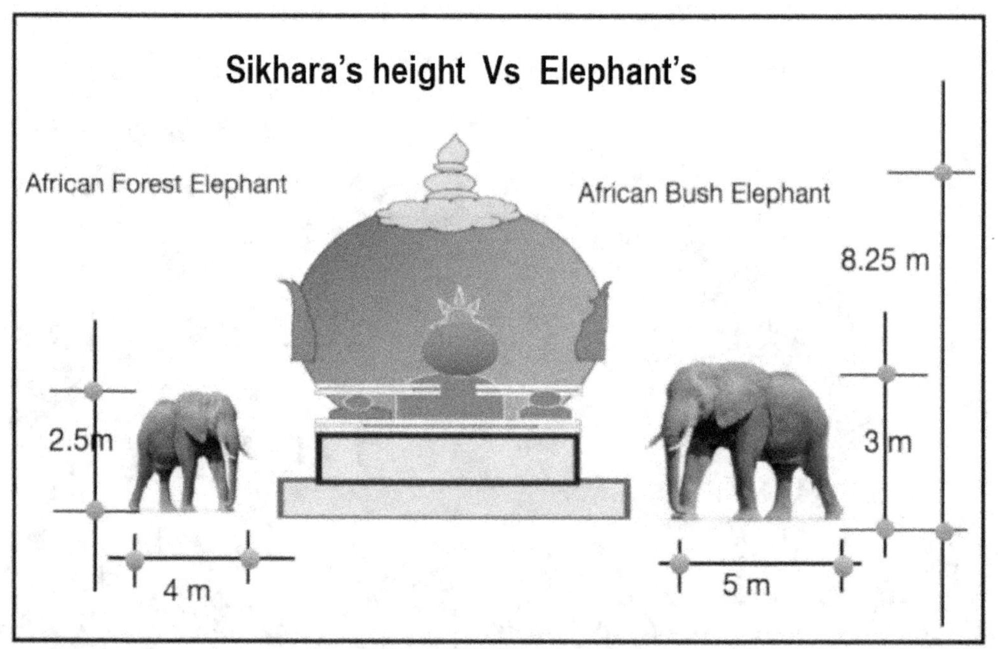

PHYSICAL CHARACTERISTICS OF ELEPHANTS

7

Cavities

The sanctum sanctorum chamber, which is 7.93 m × 7.93 m in size, has a total floor area of 62.88 m². Between the interior and external walls of the circumambulatory corridor is a space of 123.56 m² and is arrived by 16.52 m × 4 sides × 1.87 m = 123.57 m².

The floor area of the circumambulatory is nearly double that of the sanctum chamber, resulting in a 1:2 ratio.

The floor spaces of the four side passages are not included in this comparison and will be examined in detail later.

The volume of Circumambulatory Cavities

The circumambulatory has a volume of 1357 m³ along the 1.87 m corridor up to the level of +16.50 m, as shown in the table illustrating the calculation and workings.

The volume of the three-side open spaces is roughly 126 m³ and the total combined volume of free spaces in the vertical length of circumambulatory is 1483 m³ up to +16.50 m elevation. In addition to the above-mentioned free space, the circumambulatory construction features 285 m³ as triangular cavities above +16.50 m level for a height of 4.61 m and 26 m³ inside the extended rectangular spaces up to the terrace mid-level +24.75 m.

Accordingly, the whole circumambulatory has an overall total volume of 1794 m³ inside the structure as arrived in detail and illustrated in the tabulation "Volume of circumambulatory and summary."

Vestibule Halls in the Annexe

Annexe vestibule halls are rectangular and have a total free volume of 1741 m³. The detailed calculations are shown in the table "Annexe building volume."

The Vimana structure inside has a total of 3535 m³ of free space that was planned and built. This doesn't include the main sanctum square shaft and the empty spaces inside it. The free spaces in the circumambulatory and the annexe building have almost the same volume, with less than a 5% difference. It looks like they were made to hold the same amount of open space up to the middle height of the Vimana, which is +24.75 m.

Why was the structure built with such a large amount of empty spaces inside?

What is the purpose of Vimana's annexe building, which is attached to it?

Why do the vestibule halls have so much dead space, almost as much as the free volume of circumambulatory surround?

What purpose and contribution did the whole free volume serve?

This open space and volume need to be looked at and studied from a technical point of view.

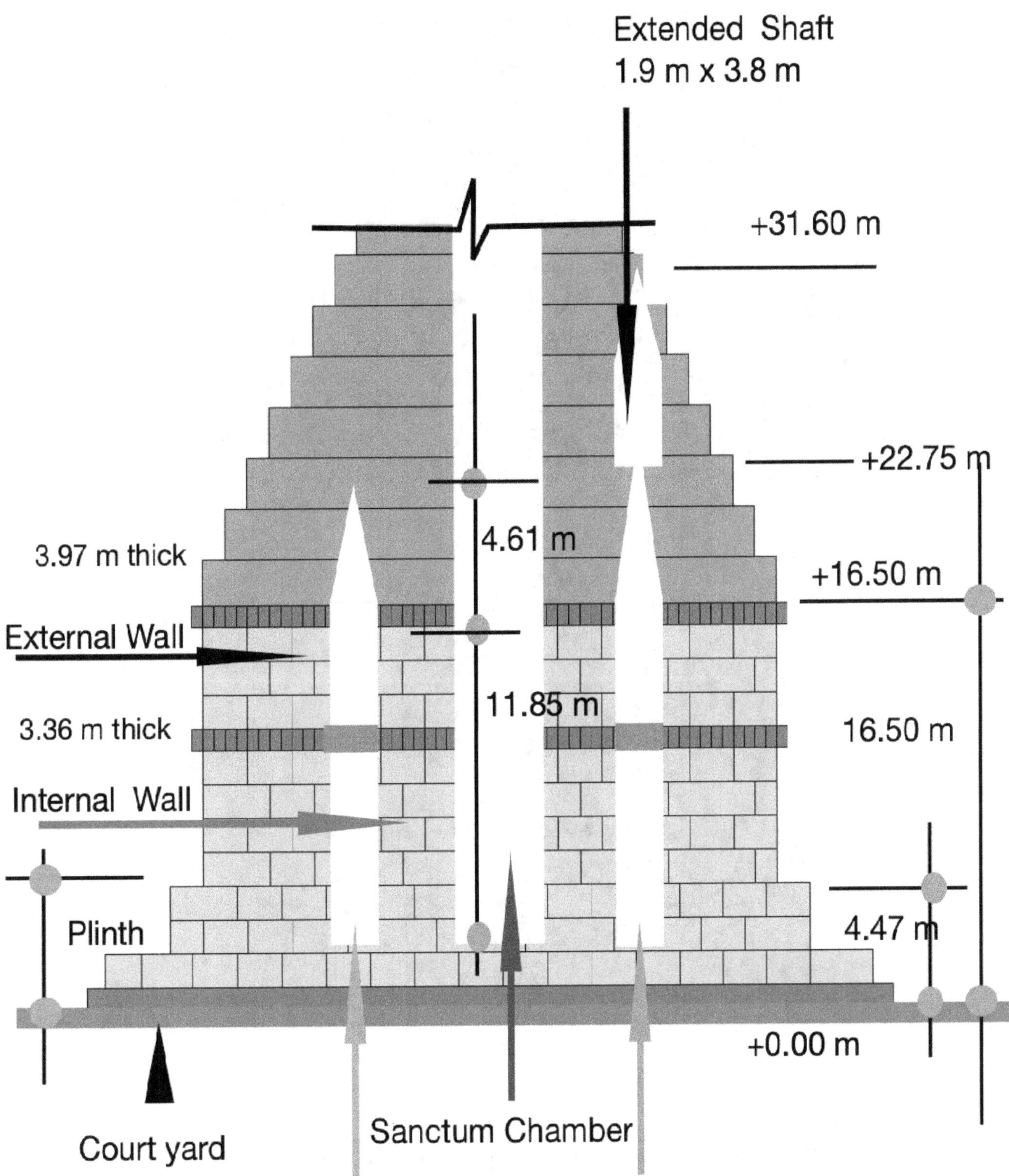

Cavities inside the Structure

Annexe - Rectangular shaped vestibule halls

First and second level - Covered by granite roof
Third level - Open terrace encircled by massive walls

Annexe - Vestibule halls - Birds eye view

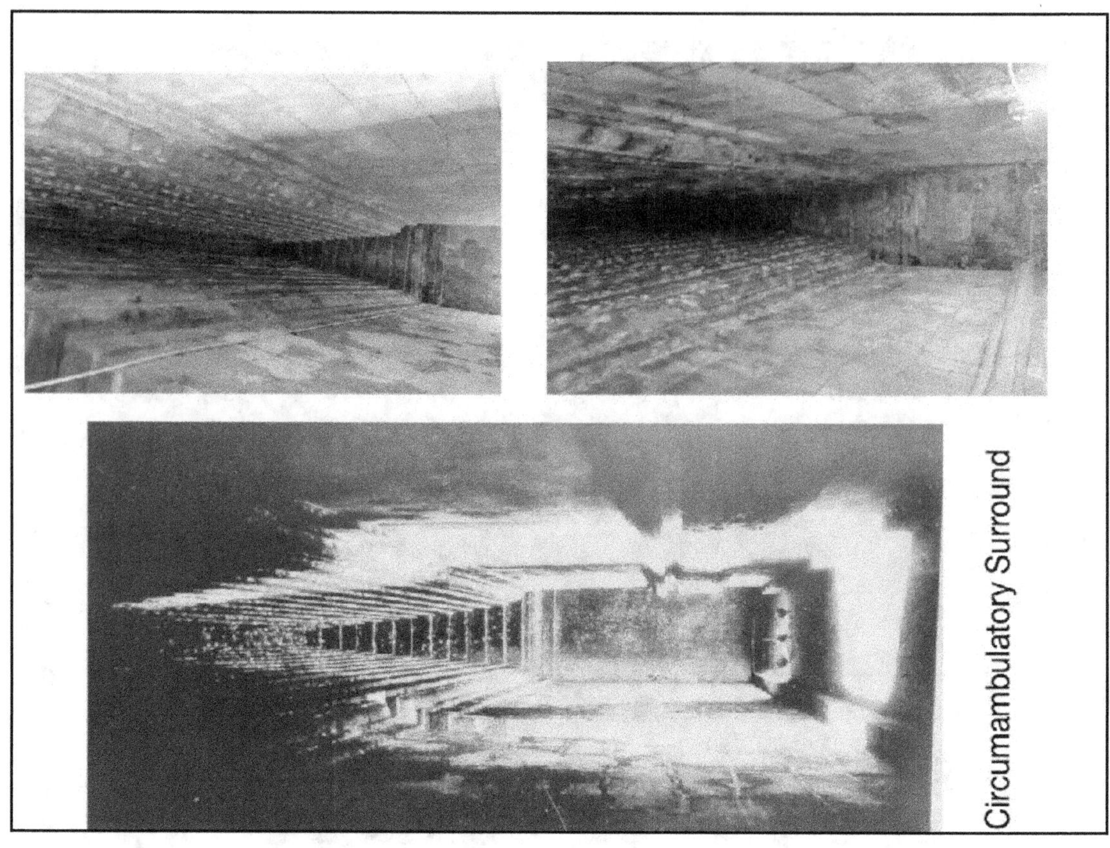

Circumambulatory Surround

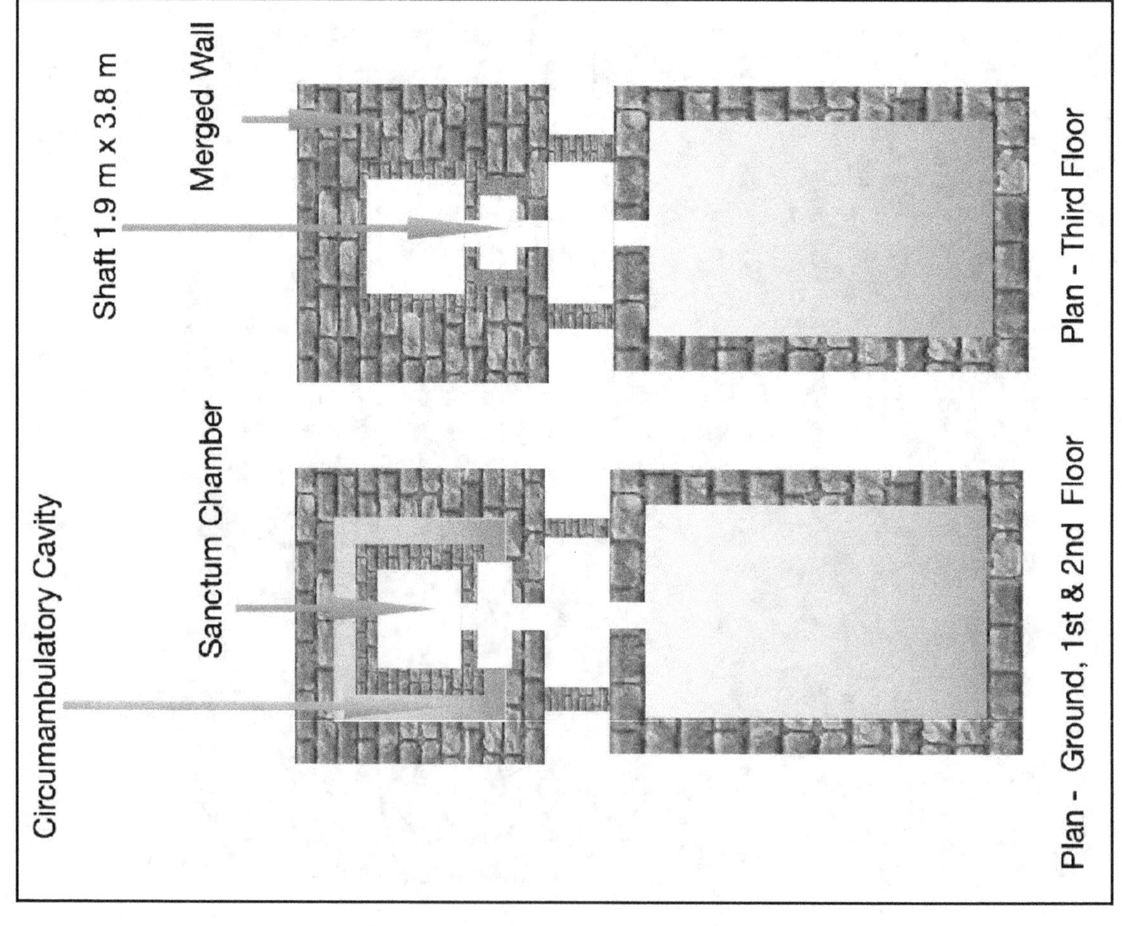

Shaft 1.9 m x 3.8 m
Merged Wall
Circumambulatory Cavity
Sanctum Chamber
Plan - Third Floor
Plan - Ground, 1st & 2nd Floor

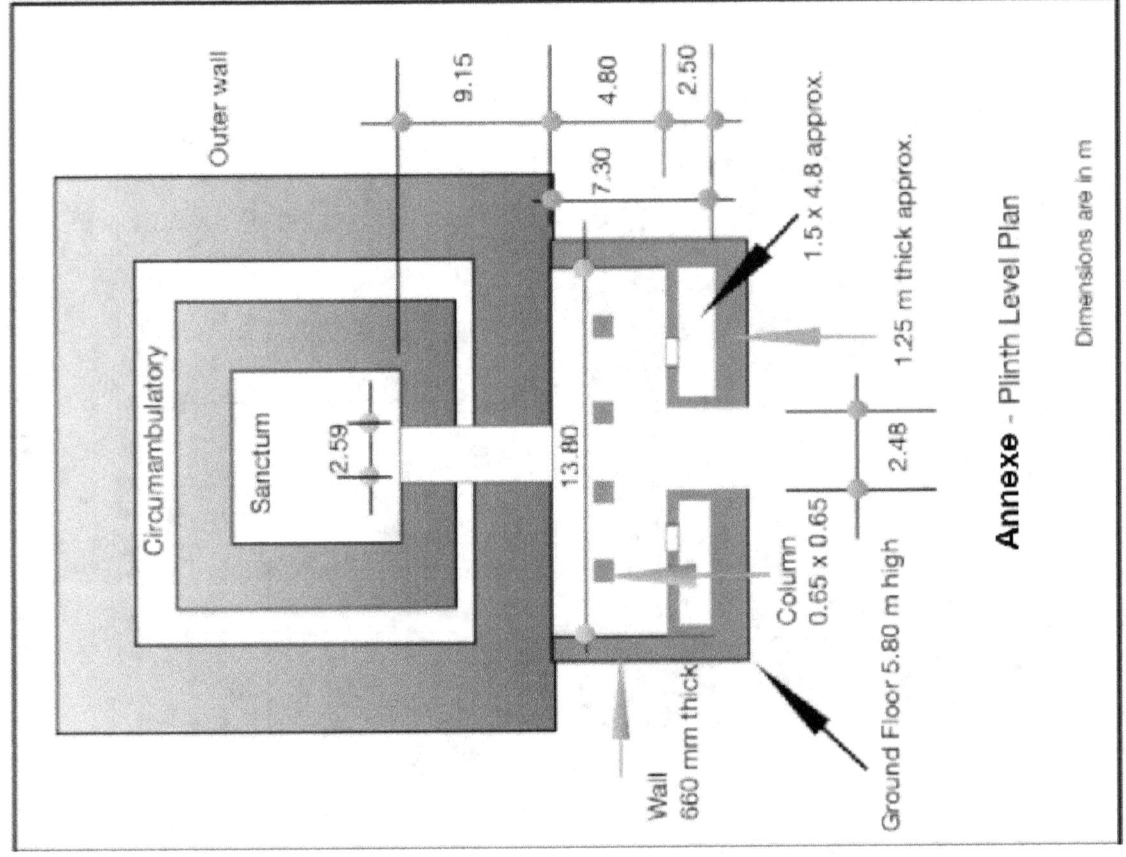

Annexe – First Level Plan

Annexe – Plinth Level Plan

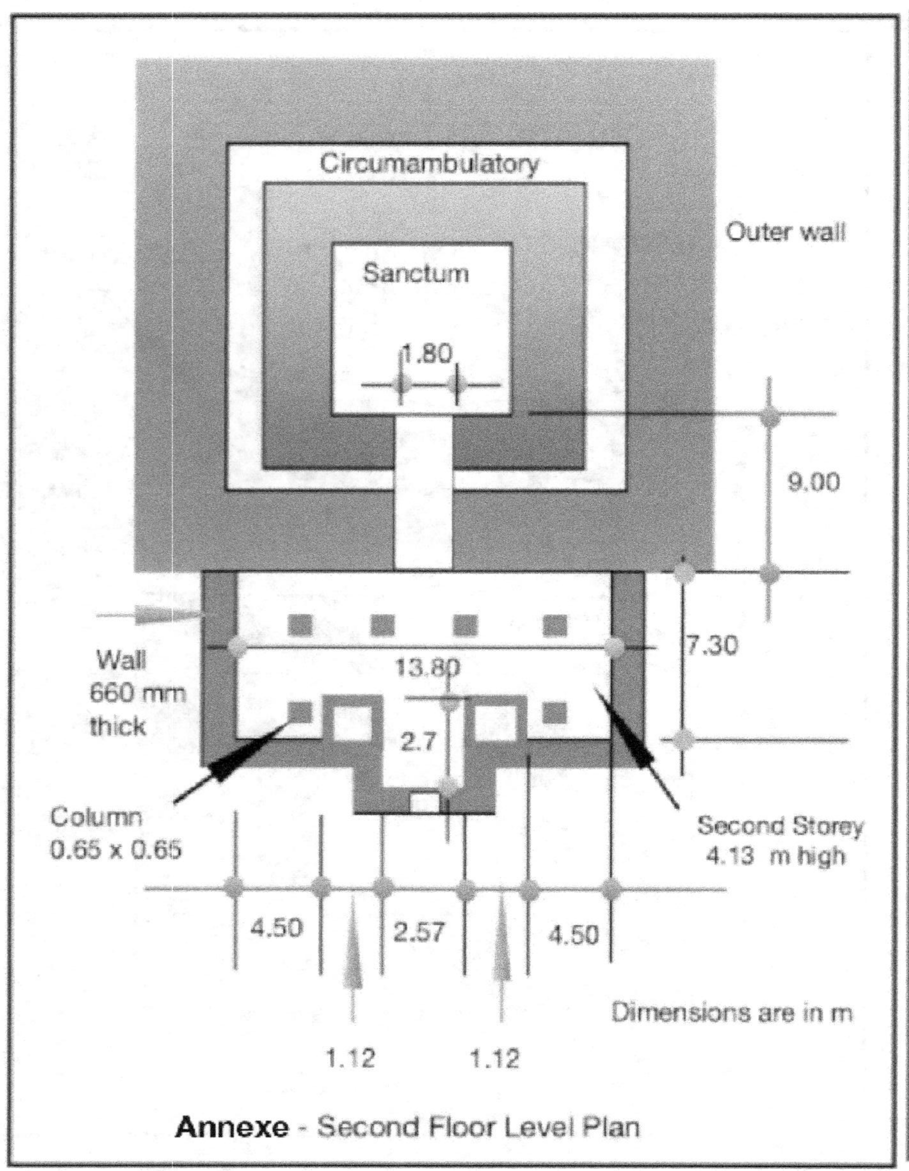

Annexe - Second Floor Level Plan

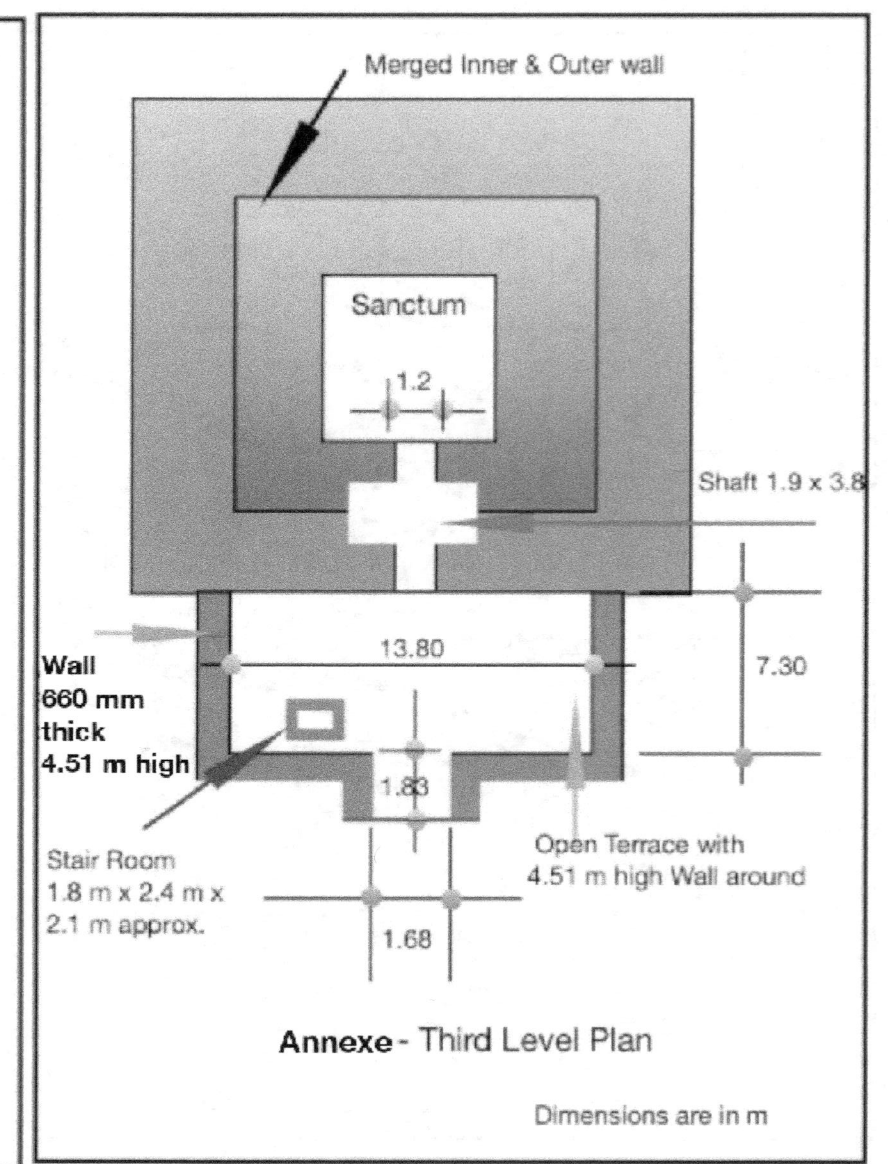

Annexe - Third Level Plan

Annexe building volume

Sl no	Location	Calculation	Volume	Unit
A	Annexe			
1	Ground floor			
	Vestibule hall	13.80 x 7.30 x 5.80 m high	584.29	m³
	Less room walls	2 Nos x 5.6 x 1 x 5.8	-64.96	
	Less room walls	2 Nos x 1.5 x1 x 5.8	-17.40	
	Less columns	4 x 0.65 x 0.65 x 5.8	-9.80	
	Less brackets	4 x 2 x 1 x 0.65 x 0.65	-3.38	
	Total ground floor		488.75	m³
2	First floor			
	Hall	13.80 x 7.30 x 5 m high	503.70	
	Less columns	6 x 0.65 x 0.65 x 5	-12.68	
	Less brackets	6 x 2 x 1 x 0.65 x 0.65	-5.07	
	Total first floor		485.96	m³
3	Second foor			
	Main hall	13.80 x 7.30 x 4.13 m high	421.09	
	Less columns	6x 0.65 x 0.65 x 4.13	-10.47	
	Less brackets	6 x 2 x 1 x 0.65 x 0. 65	-5.07	
	Total second floor		405.55	m³
4	Terrace floor			
	Main open terrace hall	13.8 x7.30 x 3.66 m high	368.71	
	Less stair way	1.2x1.2x 5.75	-8.28	
	Total terrace floor		360.43	m³
	Grand total		1740.69	m³
		Say	1741	m³

Volume of circumambulatory and summary

Sl no	Location	Calculation	Volume	Unit
B	Circumambulatory			
	Vertical from +4.47 to +16.50	(7.93 + 2 x 3.36 +1.87) x 1.87 x (16.50 -4.47-1.05) 4 sides	1,356.79	
	Triangular 4.61 m high	0.5 x (7.93 + 2 x 3.36 +1.87) x 1.87 x (16.50 -4.47) x 4.61 m	284.83	
	Three side openings	1.98 x 3.92 x (5.8+5.0)x3 nos x 50%	125.74	
	Extension	(1.9 x 3.8) x (1.62 +2) m high	26.14	
	Total		1,793.50	m³
		Say	1,794	m³
	Summary			
A	Annexe		1,741.00	
B	Circumambulatory		1,794.00	
	Grand total		3,535.00	m³

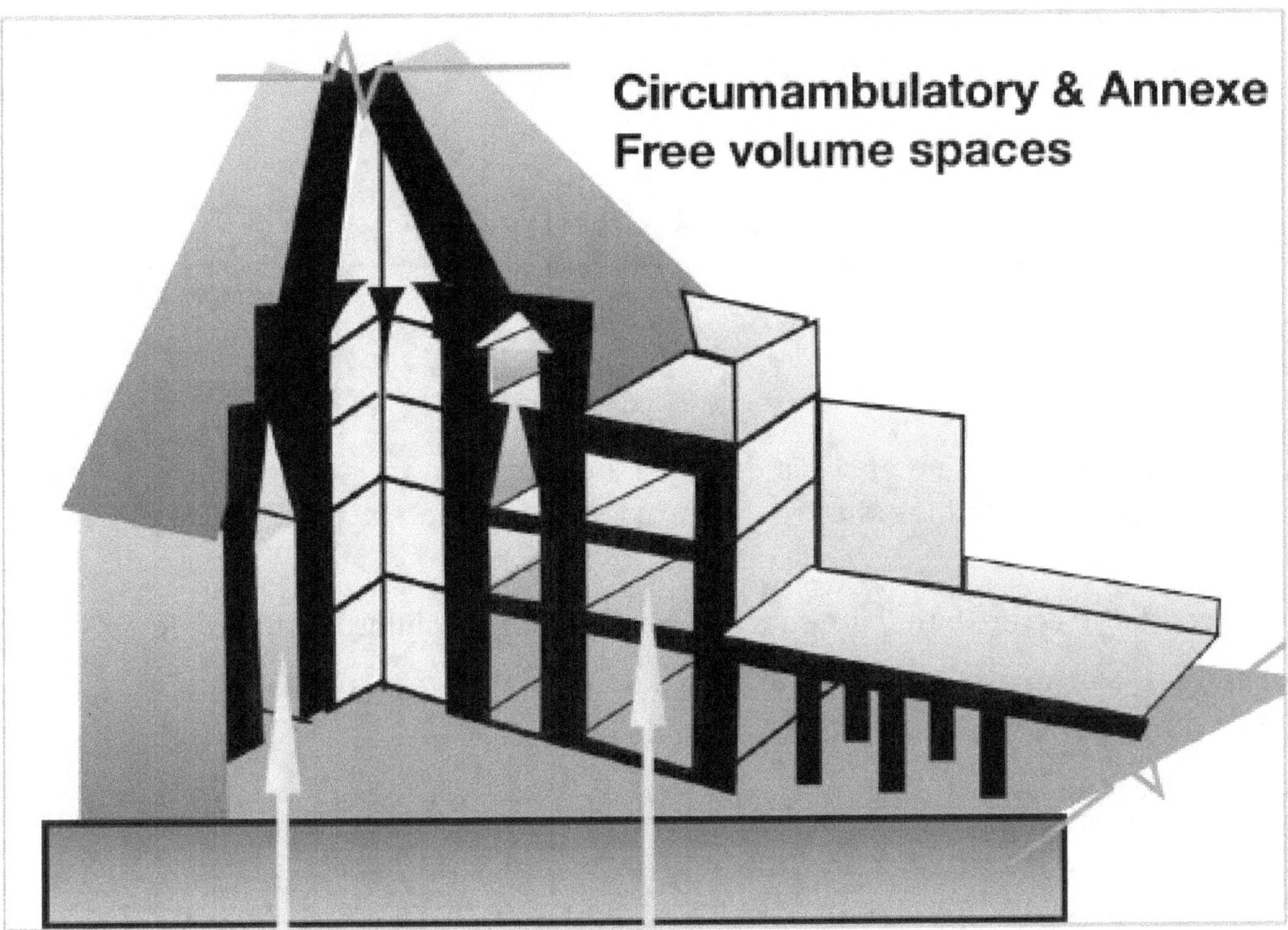

Annexe Building Volume - 1741 m^3

Circumambulatory Volume - 1794 m^3

Total Volume - 3535 m^3

8

Voids Volume

The overall empty volume of space designed and provided inside the Vimana building is roughly 3535 m³, excluding the free vertical voids volume extended inside the sanctum shaft.

Why was the structure built with so much free space and volume on the inside?

What was the main function of the Vimana's annexe, which got attached to it? Why is there so much space and free volume in its vestibule halls?

The circumambulatory cavity's free volume contributed to what?

The significant open spaces inside the building appear to have been designed and created to hold vast amounts of water, making the operation of lifting the heavy-weighted granite stones and blocks scientific and simple!

According to legend, the Cholas were water-management professionals who travelled extensively on the sea, managed the Cauvery River, and were knowledgeable about the behaviour and properties of water. The manner the Cauvery River was diverted, conserved, and harvested for agricultural purposes during their regime is recorded in the annals of the past.

Tanjore, which was surrounded by waterways, was essentially a water-based community, and they must have had an in-depth understanding and knowledge of fluid statics and dynamics mechanics.

If the cavities inside the main structure were to hold a large volume of water, the Chola's construction team may have employed water buoyancy and fluid pressure from a larger depth of water column to plan and lift heavier granite stone blocks and the massive Sikhara effortlessly to higher heights to counteract gravity!

Annexe halls and circumambulatory voids might have been specifically designed and created to contain a significant volume of water that extends up to half the height of the Vimana tower to generate the buoyancy and adequate pressure at the base from the deeper water column matching the weight of the load.

Wood floats in water due to buoyancy, and wood was the most prevalent buoyancy material used in ancient times. Good floatable wood has a specific gravity range between 0.4 and 0.8.

Archimedes described that the water displaces the equal weight of an object when immersed.

For example, a ship that is launched sinks into the ocean until the weight of the water it displaces is equal to its own weight. When the object is placed on a wooden flotation device, the weight of the total displaced volume of water equals the combined weight of the wood and the object.

Water has a density of 1000 kg/m^3 of volume. A density of less than 1000 kg/m^3 of a wooden flotation device is required to exert positive buoyancy for carrying and elevating any weight. To counterbalance the negative buoyancy effect of heavier materials placed on it, the flotation system must anticipate the required operating lift and level.

The goal is to be near neutrally buoyant or gain more positive buoyancy in order to lift an object at the operational height.

In our case, when water from the vestibule halls and circumambulatory voids is allowed to flow down into the sanctum shaft from a larger height, a solid and straight cylindrical wooden flotation system with granite stone blocks stacked on top will rise vertically due to pressure and the buoyant force of water.

The flotation device can be a long square or cylinder, or a combination of both, with the flexibility for modification to change the shape as and when required according to specific usage.

However, the Vimana structure required a significant quantity of heavy granite stone pieces of varying sizes for its superstructure construction, and the lifting operation must have occurred periodically in line with the vertical physical construction progress right from ground level.

Before raising a load of granite stones, the vestibule annexe halls and circumambulatory cavities must be periodically filled with vast quantities of water to operate each cycle.

How was the enormous volume of water raised and periodically filled up in the higher-level storage halls above the surface?

A deeper calculation and technical analysis reveal the Chola engineers' remarkable mastering strategy and their operation is scientific and simple!

From the overall cross-section, heights, and levels of the structural components inside the main Vimana and annexe structure, as shown in the drawing, the maximum permissible water level inside the sanctum appears to have been planned and designed not to exceed 50% of the Vimana height or 24.75 m.

The Chola engineering team appears to have chosen and used a specific type of wood with a density of around 500 kg/m³ for the wooden floating unit based on the maximum safe water level rise planned and designed which is up to the mid-height of Vimana. If a block of wood has a density in this range, it will float with a net positive buoyancy of 50% above the free water surface when immersed in water.

One cubic metre of such wood generates approximately 5 kN (0.5 MT) of positive buoyant force when immersed in water, enough to support the weight of equal measures of heavier stone and lighter water.

The neutrally close buoyant condition is what keeps the thing floating, as previously stated. The height of the float can be increased to maximise the positive buoyant force for carrying any additional weight.

Using the same wooden float designed to lift and hoist large granite stones, large amounts of water can also be carried from ground level and elevated to be refilled in the annexe building's vestibule halls and circumambulatory storage spaces on a regular basis. In such a case, the sanctum chamber must have been dug deeper and extended into the ground to a depth greater than the height of the Vimana and most likely greater than 49.50 m.

For using the natural buoyancy and for an effortless operation, a float with a smaller diameter or a square shape may have been designed and employed to lift stones and elevate water up to +33 m, and the condition is that the magnitude of the buoyant force matches the weight of the load.

To raise the load above +33 m, before each lift, water must be filled periodically in the empty spaces of the annexe and circumambulatory and made to flow down into the well for operating each cycle so that the wooden flotation device with its density of 500 kg/m³ raises the load after gaining buoyancy from the ground level that will move up to reach higher elevations.

The same float may have been finally modified to raise and install the massive Sikhara block, which is the final step in completing the Vimana superstructure.

Let's examine the technique.

For operating a cycle to elevate a granite load to +33 m height, water is allowed to flow down from a ground-level source by connecting an inlet to the sanctum so the water level rises in the well and the wooden float carrying the stone weight can slowly rise from the well after gaining the required buoyancy.

After the stone blocks are unloaded at the required higher elevations, the water inside the well is drained through a deeper outlet point, allowing the empty float to naturally lower to receive the next cycle's material.

To lift the granite stones above 33 m heights, each cycle requires a large amount of water that must be lifted and stored in each compartment of the annexe building and the circumambulatory to allow the water to flow down and raise the level inside the sanctum shaft. The float which carries the load can naturally move due to its lesser density and buoyant force along with the level of water.

The flotation device must lift heavy stone blocks and large amounts of water cyclically for this purpose.

The structural cross-section shows that water can be stored up to the maximum height of the terrace parapet top level, which is just above the mid-height of Vimana, and the parapet top level is approximately +27.26 m. When the same flotation unit that must raise stones and water is required, it must be built to obtain positive buoyancy to raise the load beyond +24.75 m to hold and transfer water from the ground level.

Adding 8.25 m to +24.75 m, a float with half the density of water must be 66 m long for loads of granite to be lifted effortlessly to a height of 33 m. For operations above + 33 m, the stored water is allowed to flow down to raise the float along with the load for the entire height of the Vimana.

As a result, before starting the foundation raft, the ancient engineers planned and built a 66 m deep underground well to fit the dimension of a square sanctum. The raft foundation was interlocked and attached to the solid limestone rock mass underneath to form the main Vimana foundation.

The Sikhara has a square base that is the same size as the sanctum's dimensions. To allow for any free vertical movement, a square base of the same dimensions cannot be placed inside the same-sized sanctum without appropriate clearance around all the sides. The inner sanctum's square dimension, which corresponds to the Sikhara square base, has already been fixed, and the superstructure walls have been built; therefore, changes inside the walls are not possible.

So, what is the option?

Tilting a square base horizontally by 45 degrees allows the four diagonal ends that extend beyond the square dimension to be secured inside the wall by forming four triangular cavities, specifically at the middle of the sides of the inner wall, as shown in the drawings.

These four cavities have been extended vertically with clearances around for the entire height up to + 49.50 m so that the four corners of the Sikhara base can fit and be secure inside; these grooves can be used as guides to move vertically when the float ascends due to buoyancy.

Overall, it strongly resembles an open square sanctum shaft with four triangular cavities formed to accommodate the four projected corners of the square base at the inner wall's centre. The sanctum shaft penetrates the massive plinth and extends from the plinth up to +49.50 m level in the superstructure and deep down as a square open underground well for 66 m below the level of the courtyard floor.

The purpose of the well and the four triangular cavities was to catch the displaced water as well as allow the water to flow down inside the well and shaft from higher-level storage to develop the required buoyancy force and lift the weights through the long cylindrical wooden flotation system while also serving the four projected corners of the Sikhara's base to get accommodated inside the slots for a synchronised gradual rising.

The heavy granite blocks kept on the deck of the flotation system might have been hoisted up to the desired levels of Vimana by creating positive buoyancy from the ground level by just allowing water to get filled up inside the well from a ground-level water source by gravity as well as from higher-level storage with an appropriate drainage system inside the well at its mid-depth to drain off the water.

While a smaller-diameter wooden system can adequately serve the superstructure construction and periodically lift the enormous quantity of water, a large-diameter cylindrical flotation system is required to be designed specifically for lifting the heavy Sikhara by this method, as stated earlier.

A square floating structure with sanctum dimensions of 7.93 m × 7.93 m is difficult to handle and rotate horizontally to move the square base away from the triangular cavities through the circumferential cut formation made in the well's side wall. A vertical cylindrical shape of a diameter lesser than the dimension of 7.93 m and 66 m in height may easily fit within the square sanctum dimension of 7.93 m × 7.93 m by providing appropriate clearance all around for obstruction-free vertical movement.

The float diameter and the sizes of the triangular cavity formation in the inner wall were required to be designed for the magnitude of the buoyant force that matches the weight of the load and the operating height. By taking into account the extended corners of the square Sikhara base inside the triangular cavities and the wooden float with a density of 500 kg/m³, a minimum free space of roughly 50% of the area of the sanctum chamber was required to be created around the float to receive the displaced water. Accordingly, the free spaces around the float must be 50% of 7.93 m × 7.93 and roughly equal to 32 m².

The above-mentioned 32 m² was required to be equally apportioned to both the inside and outside of the chamber of the triangular cavity formations, as explained and shown in the drawings.

That means roughly 50% of the area occupied around the float inside the chamber (50% of 32 m²) and the remaining 50% (50% of 32 m²) was equally shared by the four triangular cut cavities formed in the wall; the detailed accurate calculation can be arrived at latter.

Assume the entire Sikhara block is mounted on a cylindrical wooden float suspended in water without touching any hard surface at the bottom, so the ground frictional resistance opposing any motion is zero. The system is in equilibrium because the upward buoyant force from the water and the downward force due to the weight of the wooden float and Sikhara in the gravitational field balance each other.

Since there is no frictional force, the long vertical cylindrical float along with the weight can be rotated horizontally for a circular motion at a very slow movement of 45 degrees with minimal force. To make the process easier, the vertical downward force caused by the weight of the wooden float and Sikhara has already been balanced out by the upward buoyant force of water, and the long flotation device inside the water has already experienced apparent weight loss.

Only the weight of the Sikhara unit, which is mounted above the water's surface on the wooden deck, the weight of the projected part of the float above the water's surface, and the submerged part below the water's surface must be managed. When there is no ground frictional force, and the entire system is rotated clockwise in a circular horizontal motion for 45 degrees at a very low velocity, the prevailing force is only the skin friction from water along the submerged surface of the float which will resist the motion to some extent. Managing this minimal force is not difficult because the horizontal rotation moves at a very slow pace for only a 3.11 m distance. To reduce such drag force, a cylindrical curved smoothened float surface would be naturally more user-friendly.

A drag force is a resistive force caused by the motion of a body through a fluid like water. The drag force of water acts in the opposite direction of motion. To reduce drag, the float's surfaces are smoothed, polished, and coated with an oily substance similar to that used on the hull surfaces of ships and boats.

The square smaller-sized floating device might have cyclically lifted the smaller granite stone pieces and the required volume of water during the progress of superstructure construction work by creating the required buoyant force by filling the well from the ground-level water source.

A float with a large diameter of less than and near to the size of the sanctum chamber size 7.93 m and a long cylindrical shape could have been designed specifically for hoisting the massive weight of Sikhara, which can be easily handled due to the curved wall surface all around, and for making a 45-degree horizontal turn before the final installation, which will be discussed at length in the lifting process later.

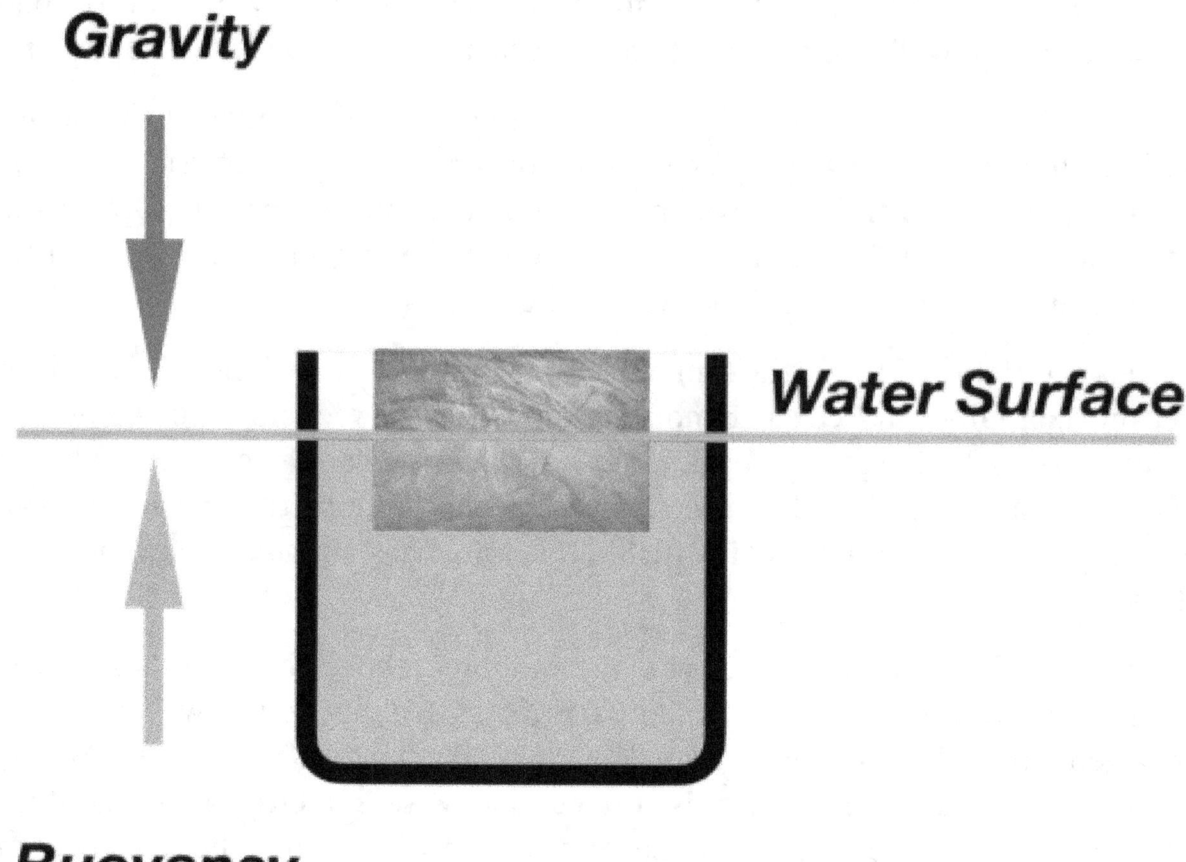

Forces of Buoyancy and Gravity balancing each

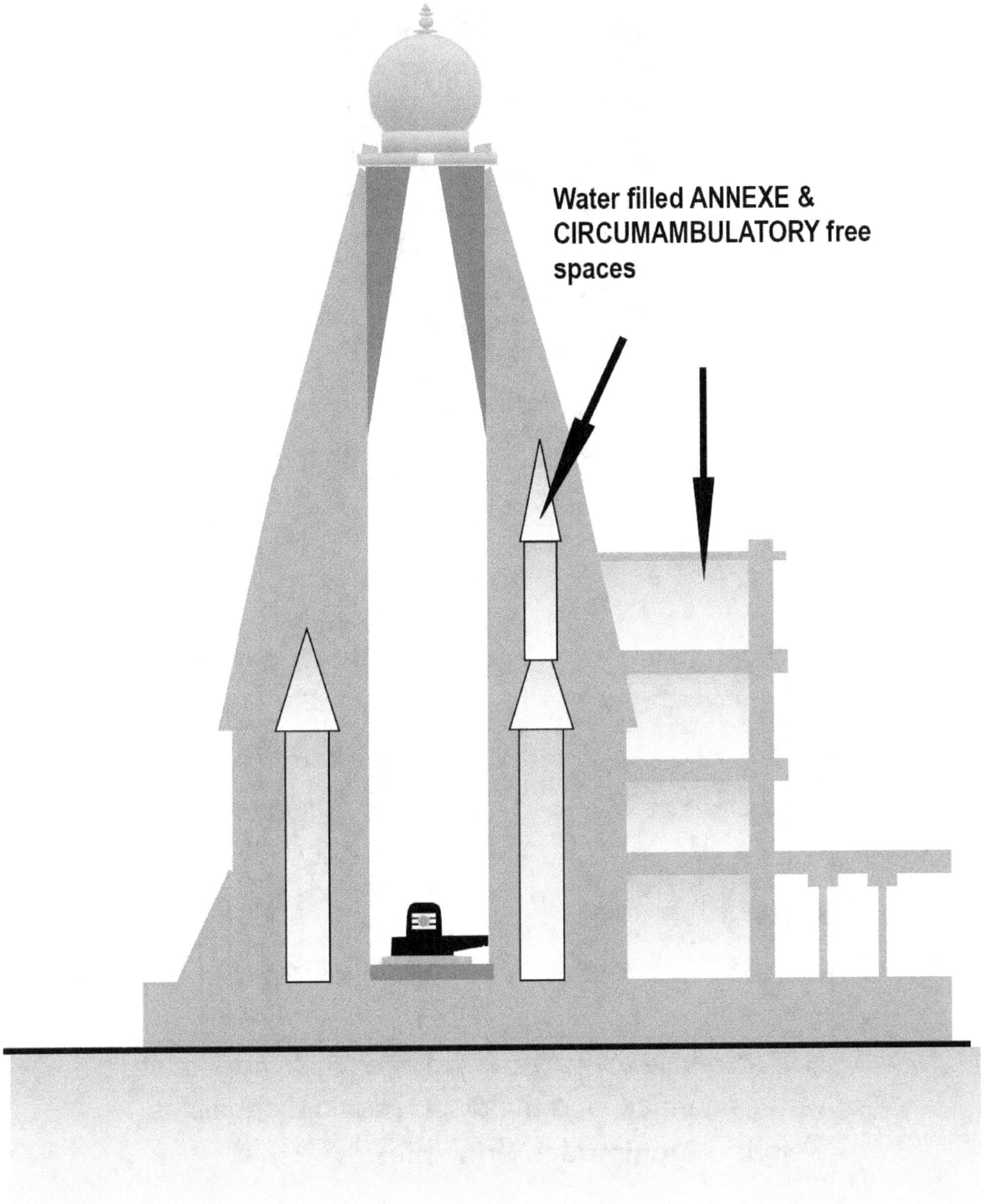

Water filled ANNEXE &
CIRCUMAMBULATORY free
spaces

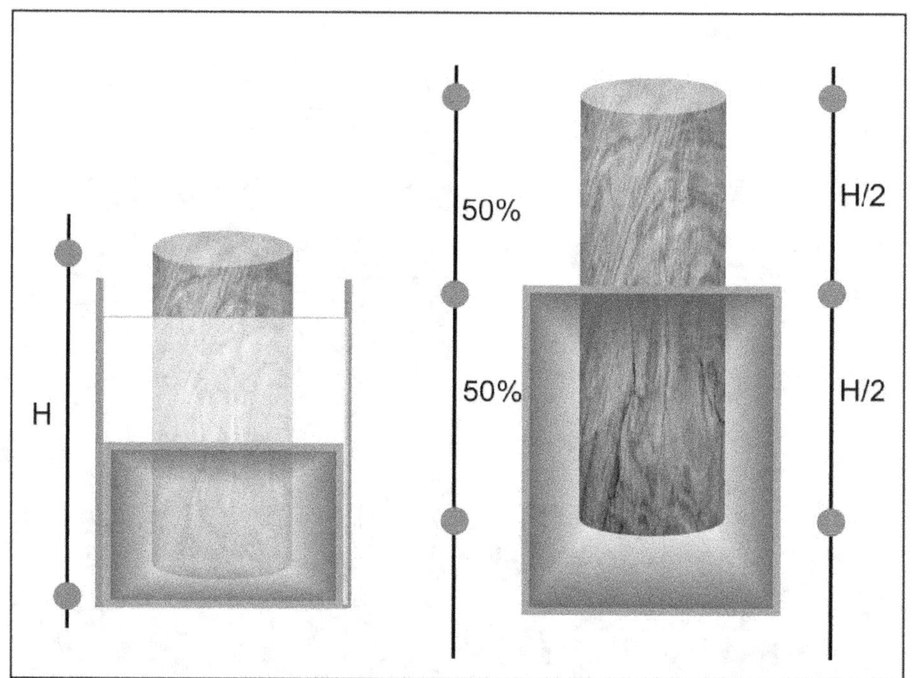

Half as dense as water, wood rises 50% above the water's surface, and the displaced fluid equals its weight - **Archimedes Principle**

Archimedes
(C.287 - C.212 BC)

Buoyancy

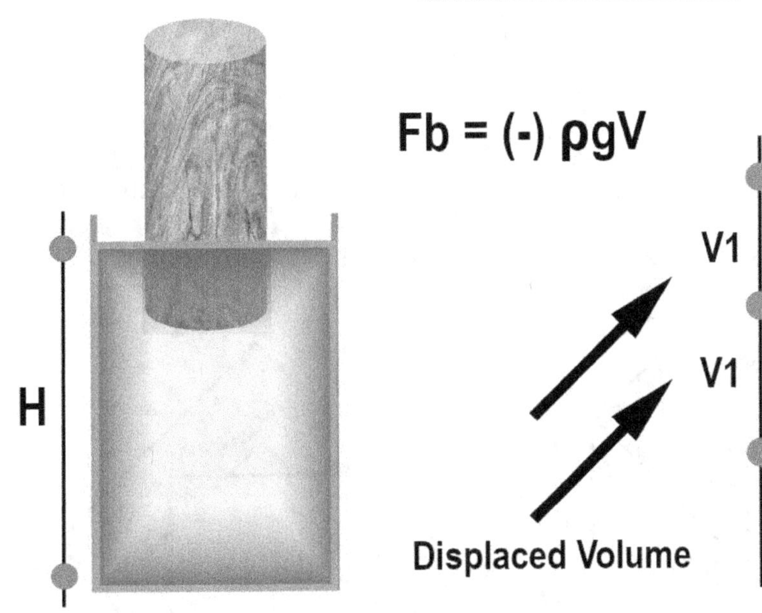
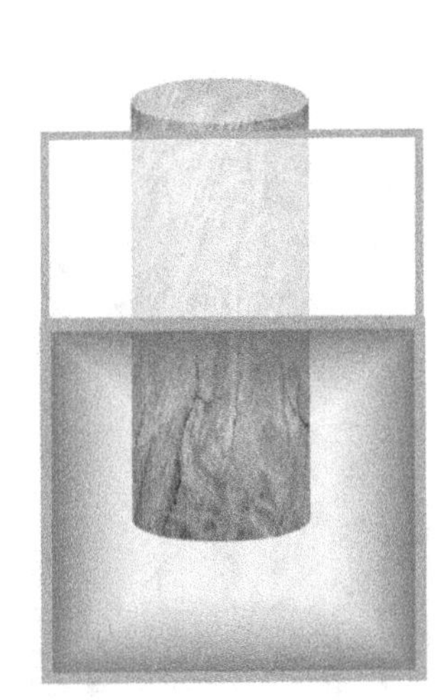

Fb = Buoyant Force
ρ = Fluid Density
g = Acceleration due to Gravity 9.81 m /Sec^2
V = Displaced Volume

OUTER WALL
TRIANAGULAR SHAPED CAVITY
INNER WALL
CIRCUMAMBULATORY

PLAN

Square of same size can be horizontally rotated for 45 degrees and the projected corners can get secured inside the triangular shaped cavities for free vertical movement .

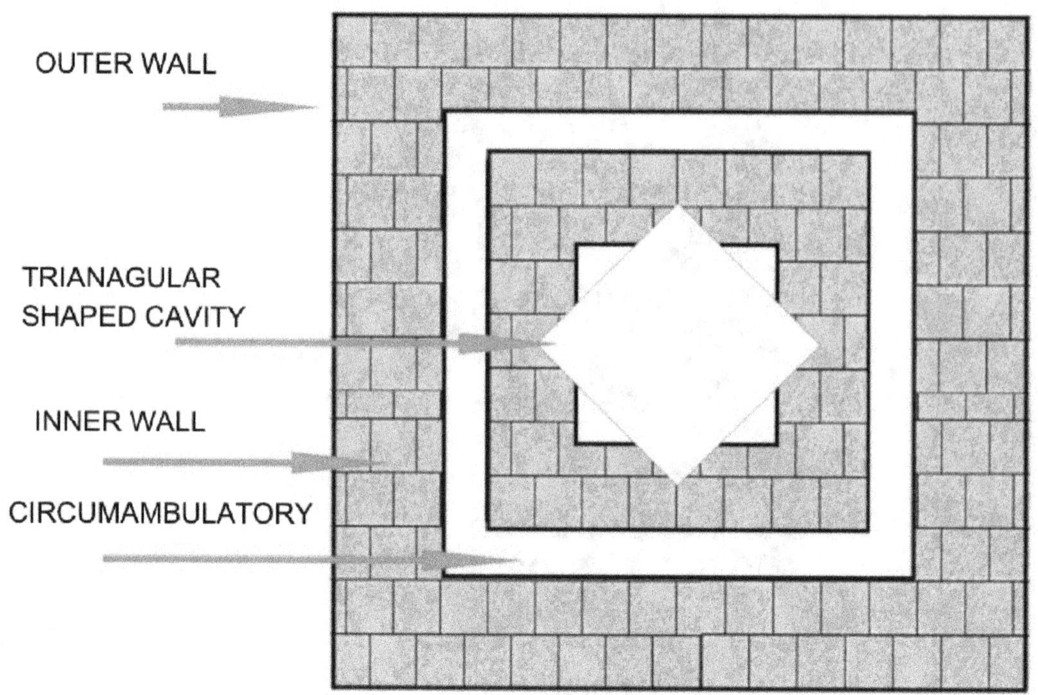

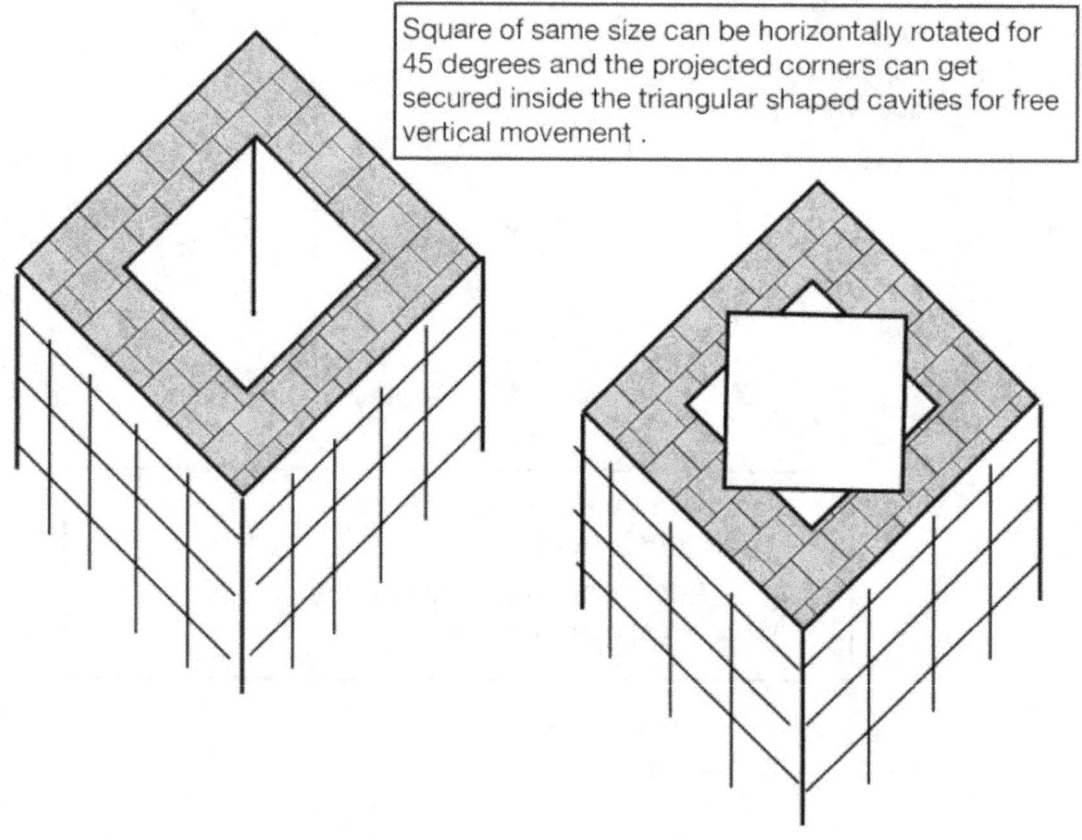

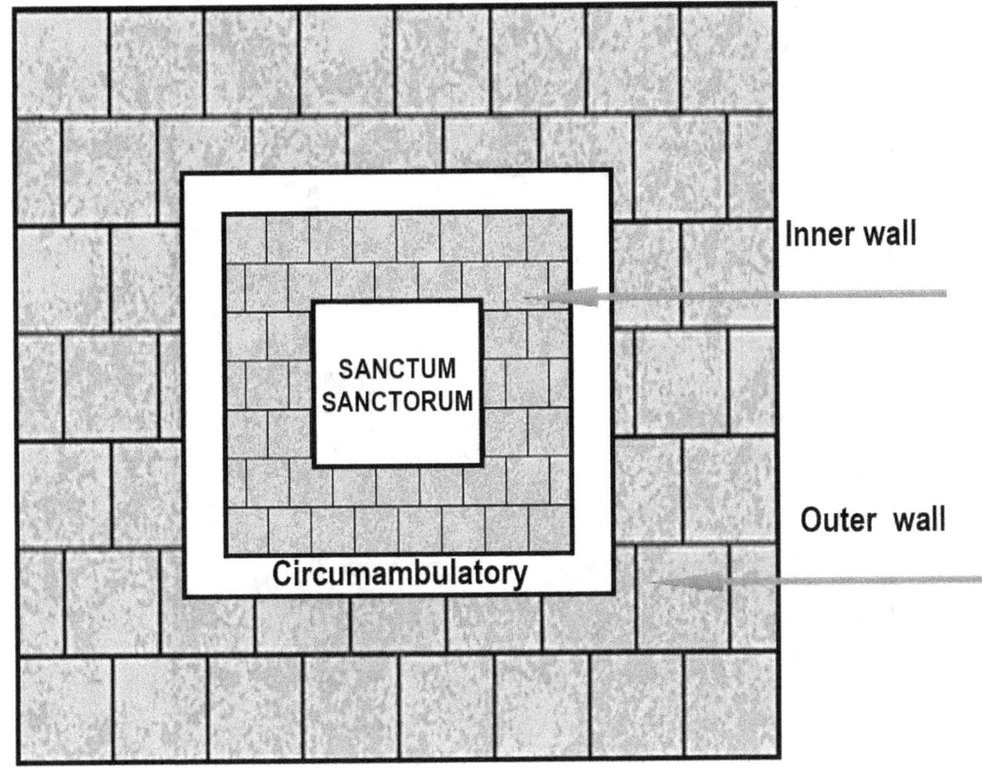

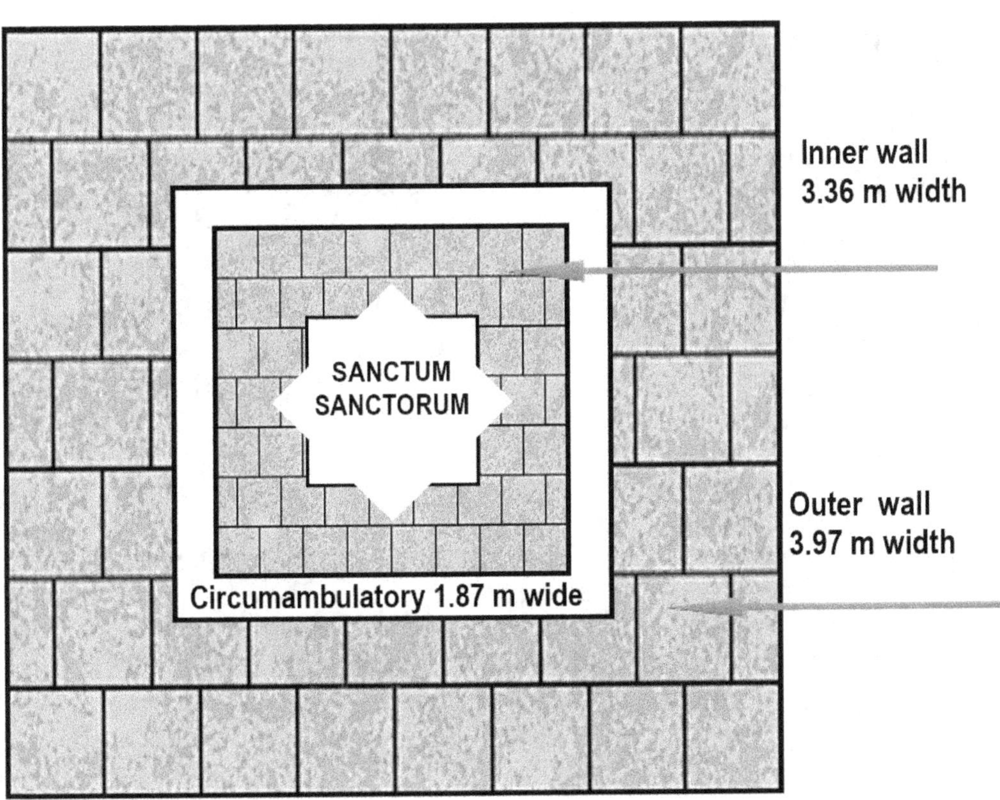

PLAN - After triangular shaped cavity construction

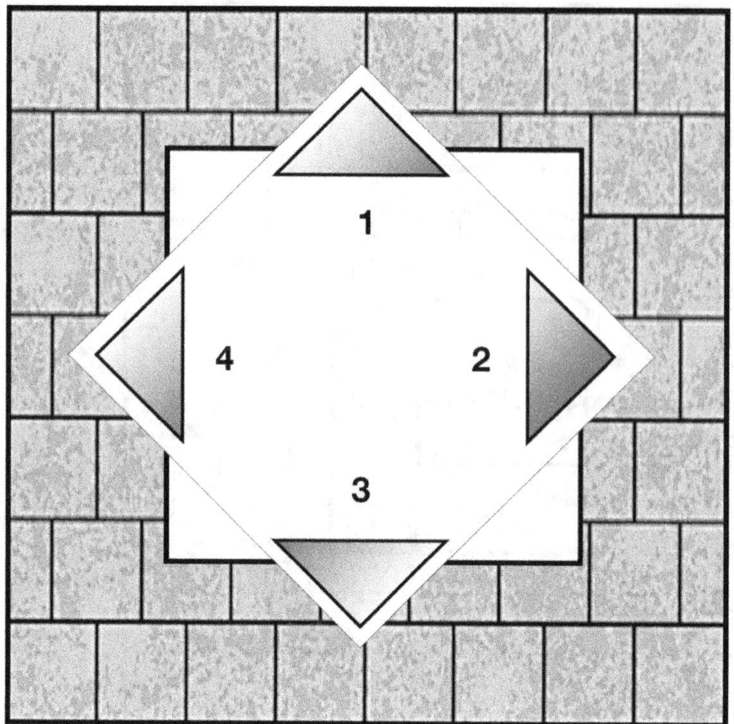

Four triangular shaped cut cavities made in the inner wall - PLAN

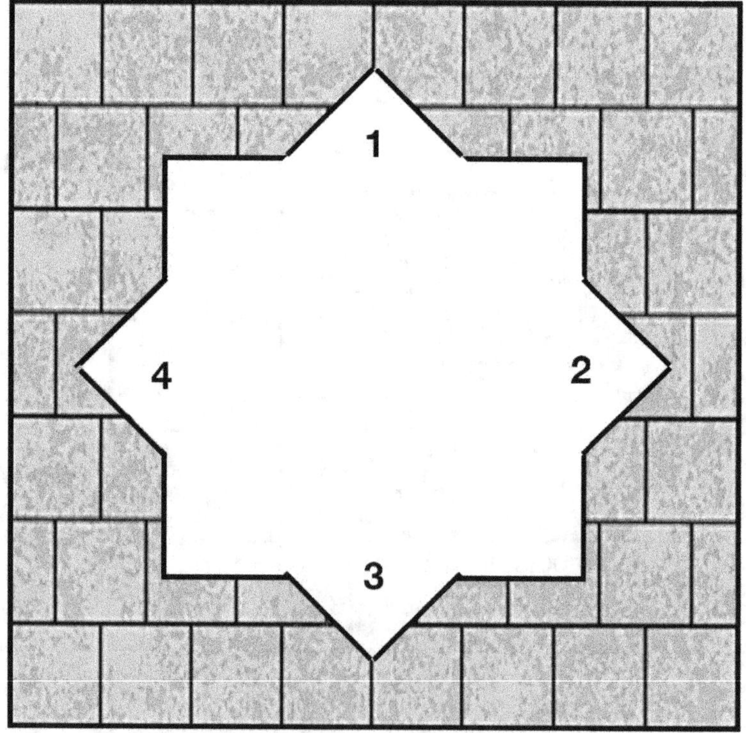

Four Triangular shaped cavities constructed in the inner Wall - PLAN

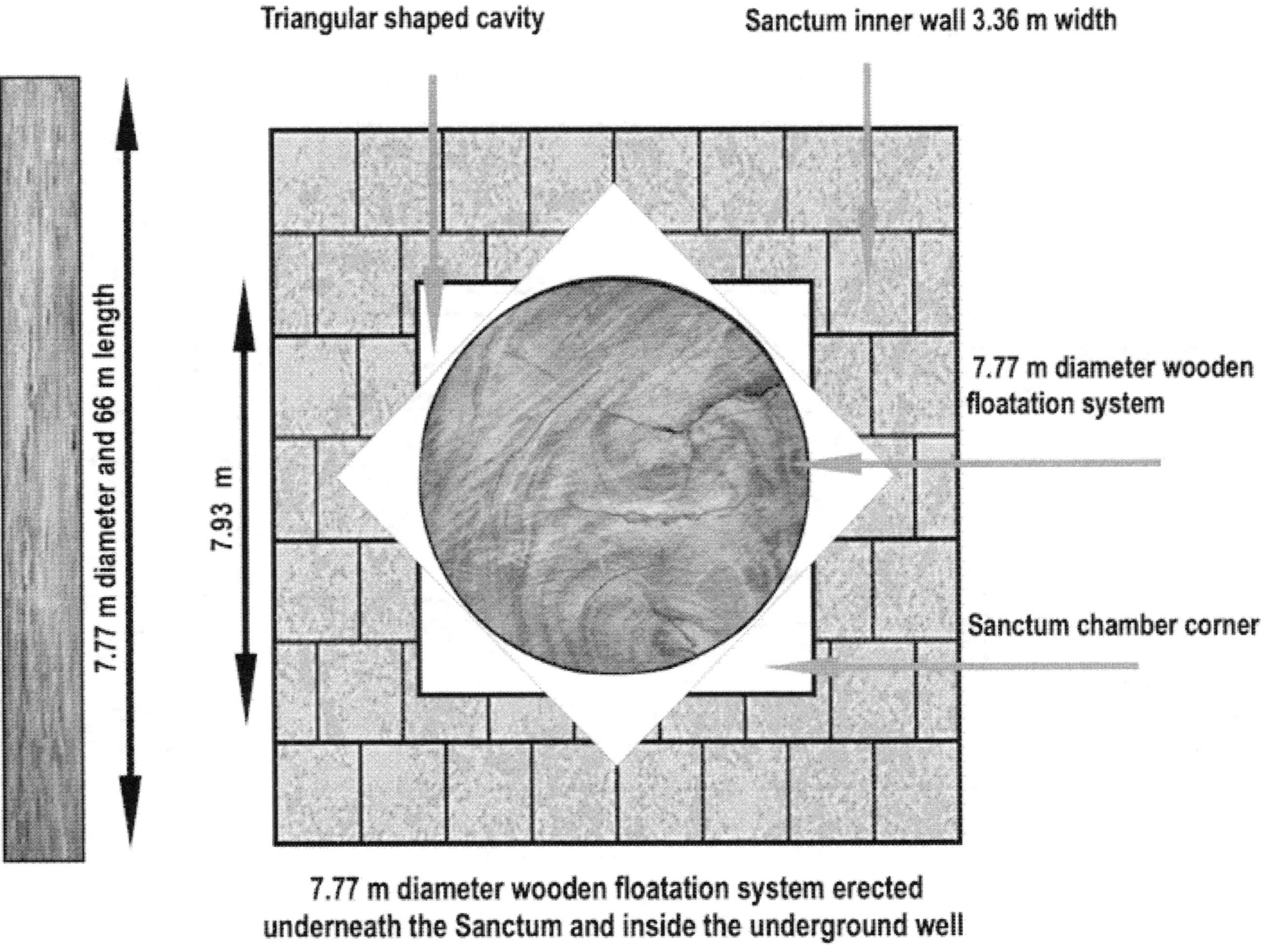

Triangular shaped cavity
Sanctum inner wall 3.36 m width
7.77 m diameter and 66 m length
7.93 m
7.77 m diameter wooden floatation system
Sanctum chamber corner
7.77 m diameter wooden floatation system erected underneath the Sanctum and inside the underground well

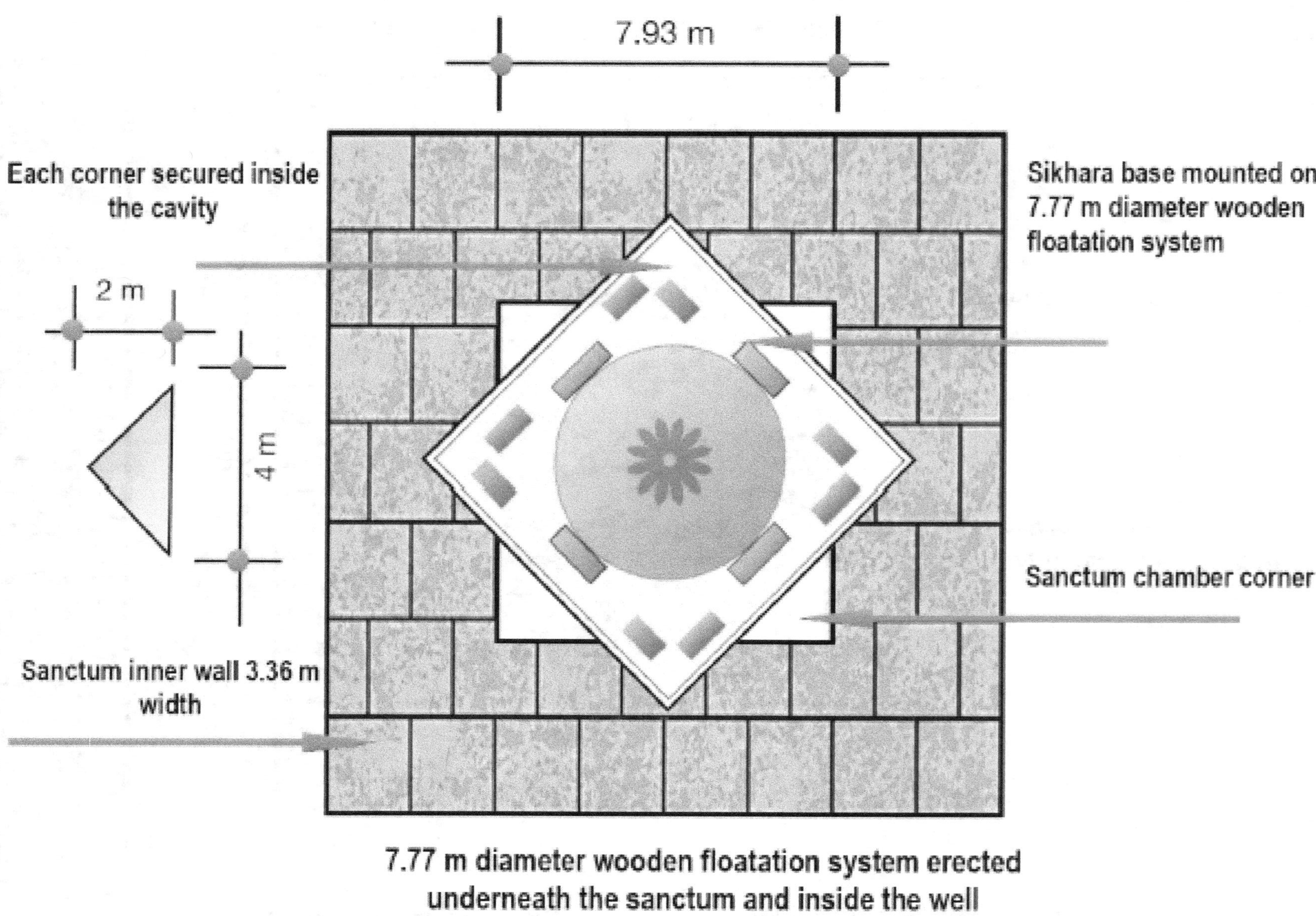

7.93 m
Each corner secured inside the cavity
Sikhara base mounted on 7.77 m diameter wooden floatation system
2 m
4 m
Sanctum chamber corner
Sanctum inner wall 3.36 m width
7.77 m diameter wooden floatation system erected underneath the sanctum and inside the well

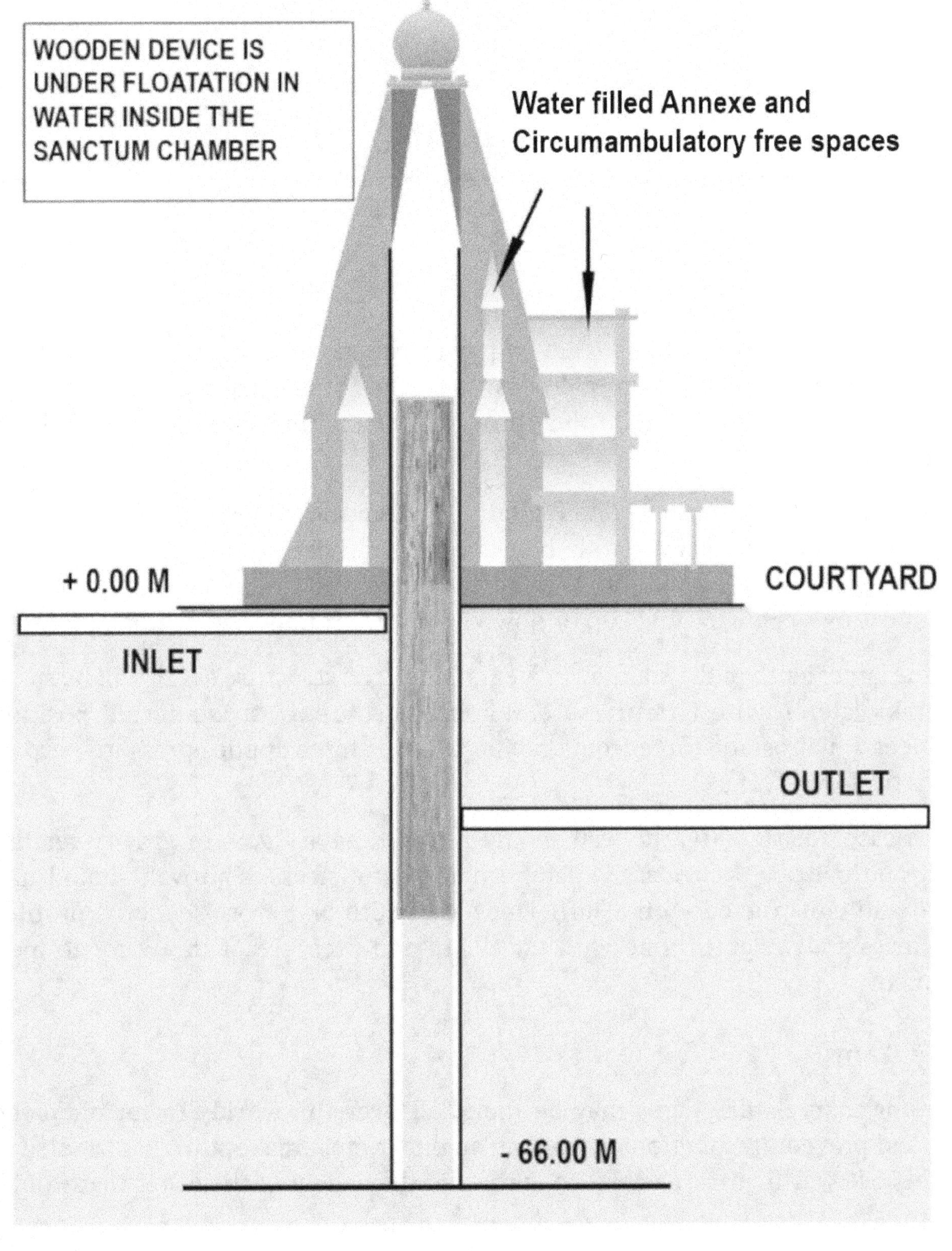

WOODEN DEVICE IS UNDER FLOATATION IN WATER INSIDE THE SANCTUM CHAMBER
Water filled Annexe and Circumambulatory free spaces
+ 0.00 M
INLET
COURTYARD
OUTLET
- 66.00 M

9

Structural Study

Suppose that the Chola's building team employed the method of providing the appropriate buoyant force against gravitation pull to hoist the heavy-density granite stones to varying heights. It was only possible to do this through the sanctum shaft located inside the main Vimana structure.

To begin, a sturdy, large-scale wooden flotation system should be used to accommodate and raise the heavy-density granite stone blocks of various sizes. Additionally, a large amount of water must also be pumped into the sanctum shaft and drained out periodically for the wooden floating system to travel up or down from the ground-level loading point.

Due to the large depth of the standing water column, the structure's wall will be subjected to considerable lateral hydrostatic pressure. When it is in the perfect equilibrium position, water experiences a hydrostatic force from gravity, and this force applies pressure perpendicular to the vertical wall surface.

In such a case, for stability, the wall should act as a gravity dam or gravity-retaining wall to resist and balance such massive lateral hydrostatic stress. The wall should have been designed and constructed with a sufficient base width and cross-sectional profile for the needed mass and weight in line with the depth and pressure of the water to meet these requirements.

Gravity Dam

Engineering marvels like dams may be found all over the world. To maintain the dam's balance and prevent it from tipping over, an engineer must make sure that the structure has sufficient base width, mass, and size to withstand the weight of the water that would collect behind it.

A gravity wall system resists lateral water pressure and is designed to be stable solely by its weight.

Gravity dams are made of concrete or stone masonry and are designed to resist horizontal water pressure while holding back water by their weight. To prevent slipping in a gravity dam, the wall's components must have a cross-sectional profile that corresponds linearly to the water depth and horizontal pressure and its elementary profile would be a right-angle triangle if it is subjected to horizontal pressure from water and its weight.

In the dam engineering design, forces must be balanced for the structure to be stable and maintain its equilibrium.

Newton's Laws of Motion

For a system to be stable, Newton's third law of motion follows that every action must have an equal and opposite reaction. In other words, an equivalent stabilising force is needed to counteract a destabilising one.

Water's hydrostatic force acts as a destabilising force in a dam structure; hence, the wall's entire weight must operate as an equivalent resisting or stabilising force.

Newton's second law of motion governs the behaviour of objects whose forces are not evenly distributed among them. According to this law, the net force is precisely proportional to the acceleration and is equated to the product of mass time's acceleration.

Mathematics defines the corresponding physics formula as follows:

Force (F) = Mass (M) × Acceleration (a)

Newton's second law further states that the downward force on an object on the earth's surface is equal to its mass times the acceleration.

Since gravitational acceleration contributes to the total weight of an object, in the modified form of the above formula,

Force (F) = Mass (M) × Gravity (g)

where M is the object's mass in kilogram, and 'g' is the gravitational acceleration in m/s^2.

The weight of the granite stone wall should act as a stabilising factor in the Tanjore Temple scenario, protecting the structure from the lateral water pressure exerted on it by the filled-up water column.

How does the water exert the lateral hydrostatic destabilising force on the wall?

It is caused by a fluid's properties and behaviour, and it corresponds to the fluid's theory and principle.

According to scientist Stevin's Hydrostatics law, the pressure at any point within a fluid at rest (of a certain density) depends only on the depth of that point.

This hydrostatic law also states that the rate of pressure increase in a vertically downward direction must be equal to the specific weight of the fluid at that point.

The formula for calculating the water pressure at depth 'h' is

$P = \rho \times g \times h$

The formula for calculating the hydrostatic force at a depth 'h' is

$F = 1/2 \times (\rho \times g \times h) \times h$

where 'F' denotes the hydrostatic force, $(\rho \times g)$ is the specific weight of water calculated by multiplying its density by the acceleration due to gravity (9.81 m/sec²), and 'h' denotes the total height of the water.

The pressure in a liquid column is zero at the top of the water surface and maximum at the bottom. The total pressure acting normal to the wall is shown in the pressure diagram, which is triangular in shape. The area of the triangle is the total water pressure acting on the wall, which is mathematically defined in the above formula.

Because the pressure diagram is triangular in shape, the combined total lateral hydrostatic pressure is acting at 1/3ʳᵈ height from its base, which is the centre of water pressure and is acting perpendicular to the wall surface.

If the Tanjore Temple tower granite wall was designed in the concept of a dam structure, the Chola engineers must have taken into account all of the failure mechanisms that must be verified, such as sliding, overturning and crushing of the dam foundation and the development of tension in the dam.

Sliding

In this mode of failure, the dam fails in sliding, as shown in the sketch, and the forces acting on the dam must be balanced and equated for stability as follows.

The stabilising force = The destabilising force

For stability, the weight of the Vimana wall should act as a stabilising force against the lateral hydrostatic force from water which is the destabilising force.

Weight of the Vimana tower = Lateral hydrostatic pressure

The final mathematical equation is $M \times g = 1/2 \times \rho \times g \times h \times h$

Newton's second law states 'M×g' is the weight which is the force upon a mass in the gravitational field and is equated to the hydrostatic force from the depth of the water column in the above equation.

Frictional Coefficient

The total weight of the wall structure touching and transferring the load to the soil beneath the foundation is denoted by 'W,' which is equal to 'M × g' as seen above.

When the structure is subjected to sliding, the base, which is in contact with the soil surface, experiences friction to oppose any sliding motion. Hence, the total weight shall be factored into the frictional coefficient, and the greatest available frictional force opposing and resisting the motion of the structure against sliding due to lateral hydrostatic pressure equals

Frictional Force = μ × W

where 'μ' is the coefficient of friction, which is the ratio of frictional force to normal force between the structure base and the surface of the soil on which the structure rests. The coefficient of friction (μ) for granite material is 0.65.

Dam wall design must take into account the first and foremost criteria of preventing a dam's sliding failure, as seen above. As a result, if the Vimana wall of the Tanjore Big Temple was designed like a gravity dam, it must be secure against the sliding collapse caused by hydrostatic lateral pressure.

By this rule, the resistive force 'μ × W' must be larger than or equal to the lateral hydrostatic pressure exerted from water, which is the first criterion the Chola engineers must have taken into account in their design.

Prerequisite for Overturning

An overturning moment can also cause a gravity-retaining wall or dam structure to fail apart from a sliding failure, as shown in the sketch.

All the forces acting on the dam cause moments. Some of the forces help maintain the stability of the dam, while others try to disturb the stability. The moments of the forces, helping the dam to maintain its stability are known as resisting moments, and the moments of the forces that try to disturb the stability of the dam are known as overturning moments.

Due to the moment of the force, the structure will rotate around or overturn a given point or axis, resulting in this failure; structure components must be stable and robust enough to resist overturning moments to prevent overturning failures, according to this rule.

The dam or retaining wall resistance causes the system to tumble or twist (overturn) in the event of an overturning failure due to excessive lateral water pressure. Because of this, the only criterion is that the stabilising or the resisting moment generated by the structural weight must be larger than the destabilising or overturning moment generated by the hydrostatic force.

Resisting Moments from Structure Weight > Destabilising Moment from Hydrostatic Force

In conclusion, the external forces and moments acting on the dam structure must be balanced such that their net effect is equal to zero, and wall thickness must be kept for the maximum dimension to meet both requirements to maintain the structure's safety and stability.

Safety is a consideration here. To fully protect the structure from both sliding and overturning failures, a good and safe engineering design will include an additional safety margin and widen it beyond the aforementioned maximum requirement.

The Indian Standard design code of practice directs the consideration of the following safety elements for a safer design against sliding and overturning.

IS Code 456-2000 – Clause 20 – Page 33 STABILITY OF THE STRUCTURE

Clause 20.2 – Sliding or Shear

The above clause states that the structure shall have a factor against sliding of not less than 1.4 under the most adverse combinations of the applied characteristic forces. In this case, only 0.9 times the characteristic dead load shall be taken into account.

When the wall is at the point of sliding:

For the limiting equilibrium, $0.9 \times (\mu) \times (W) = 1.4\ Ph$

Where 'μ' is the coefficient of friction, 'W' is the total weight of the retaining wall and 'Ph' is the horizontal component of water pressure acting at a height of h/3 from above the bottom of the base slab.

The effective factor of safety against sliding is

$(\mu \times W)/(Ph) = 1.4/0.9 = 1.56$

Clause 20.1 – Overturning

The above clause states that the stability of the structure as a whole against overturning shall be ensured so that the restoring moment shall not be less than the sum of 1.2 times the maximum overturning moment due to the characteristic dead load and 1.4 times the maximum overturning moment due to the characteristic imposed loads. In cases where dead load provides the restoring moment, only 0.9 times the characteristic dead load shall be considered. Restoring moments due to imposed load shall be ignored.

W is the total weight of the retaining wall which acts at a distance of 'X' from the toe end;

'Ph' is the horizontal component of water pressure acting at a height of 'h/3' from above the bottom of the base slab.

For the limiting equilibrium, $1.4 \times Ph \times h/3 = 0.9\,(W) \times (X)$

The effective factor of safety against overturning is

$(W) \times (X) / (Ph \times h/3) = 1.4 / 0.9 = 1.56$.

To ensure the structure is adequately protected against hydrostatic pressure, IS 1904–1986 specifies in Clause 17 that the minimum allowable safety factor against sliding and overturning is 1.5 when dead load, live load, material pressure, and seismic or wind forces are all taken into account.

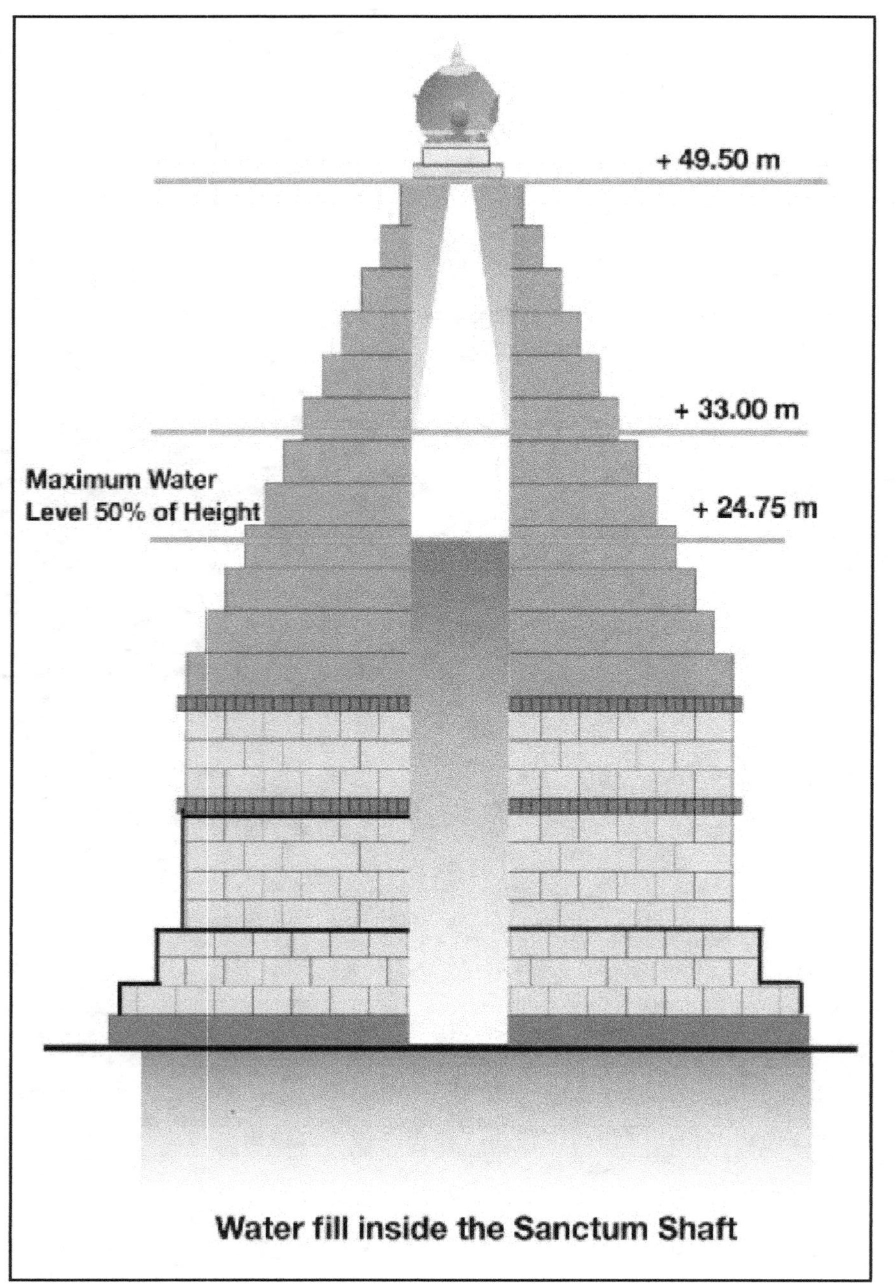
+ 49.50 m
+ 33.00 m
Maximum Water Level 50% of Height
+ 24.75 m
Water fill inside the Sanctum Shaft

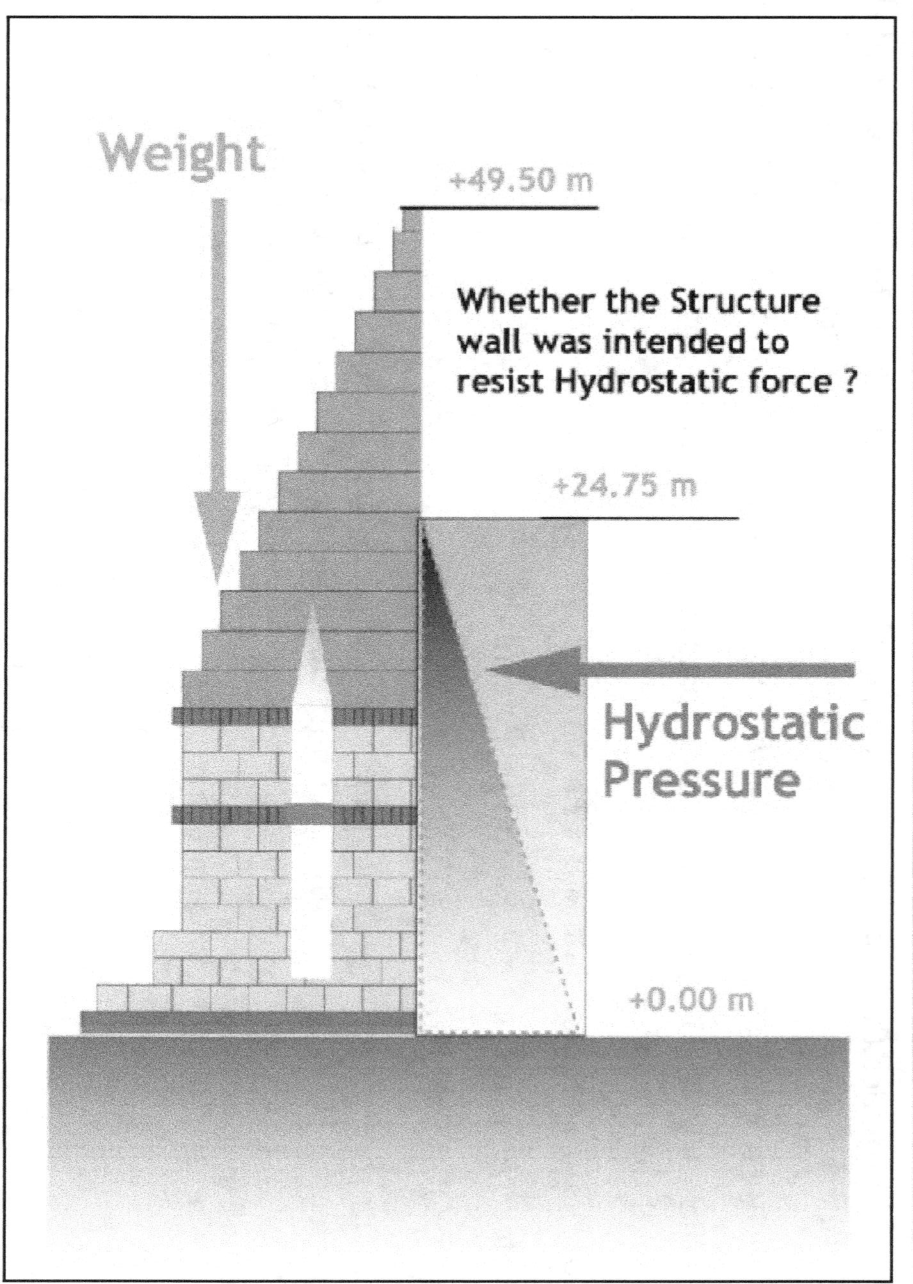
Weight
+49.50 m
Whether the Structure wall was intended to resist Hydrostatic force ?
+24.75 m
Hydrostatic Pressure
+0.00 m

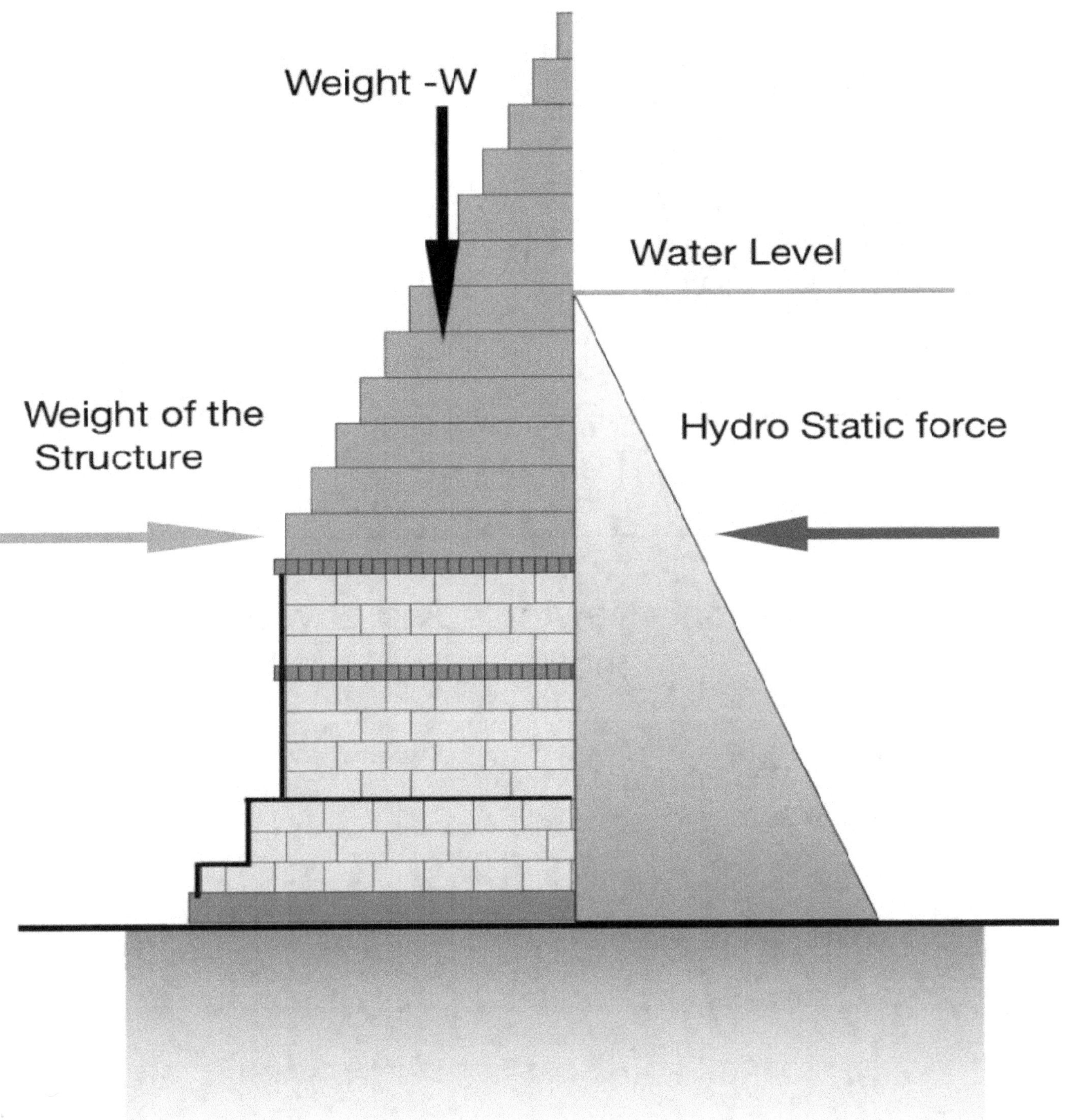

Forces acting on the Wall

$$F = ma$$

$$F = G \frac{m_1 m_2}{r^2}$$

Gravitation - Newton's 2nd Law of motion

$$F = ma$$

m -mass

Weight

Weight = Mass x Gravity

$$W = m \times g$$

The Weight of an object is the gravitational force that the planet exerts on the object. The weight always acts downward towards the centre of the planet.

m is the mass the body

g is the gravitational acceleration $9.81 m/Sec2$

when the mass increases, its weight increases proportionately

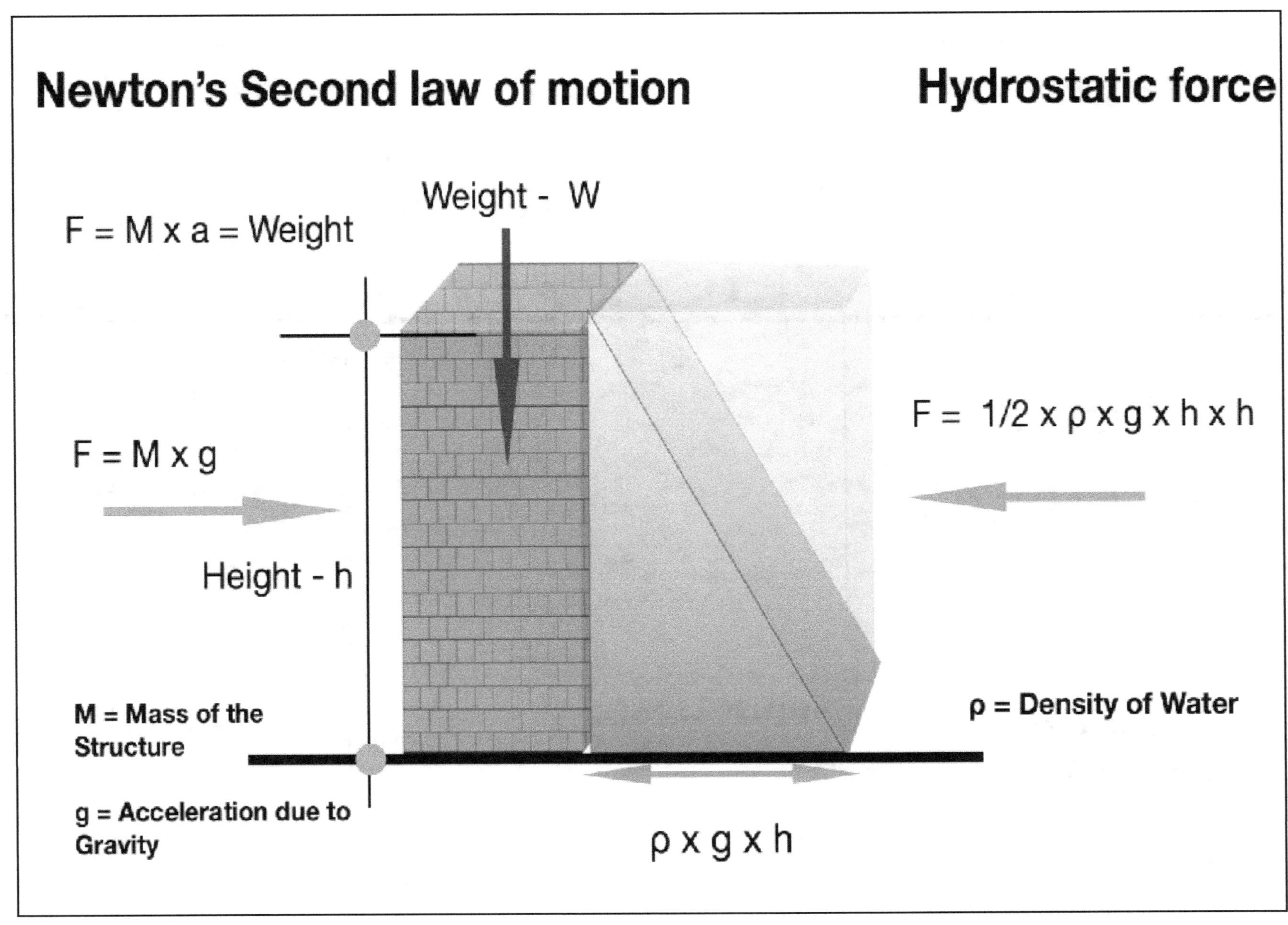

Newton's Second law of motion
Hydrostatic force
F = M x a = Weight
Weight - W
F = M x g
F = 1/2 x ρ x g x h x h
Height - h
M = Mass of the Structure
g = Acceleration due to Gravity
ρ = Density of Water
ρ x g x h

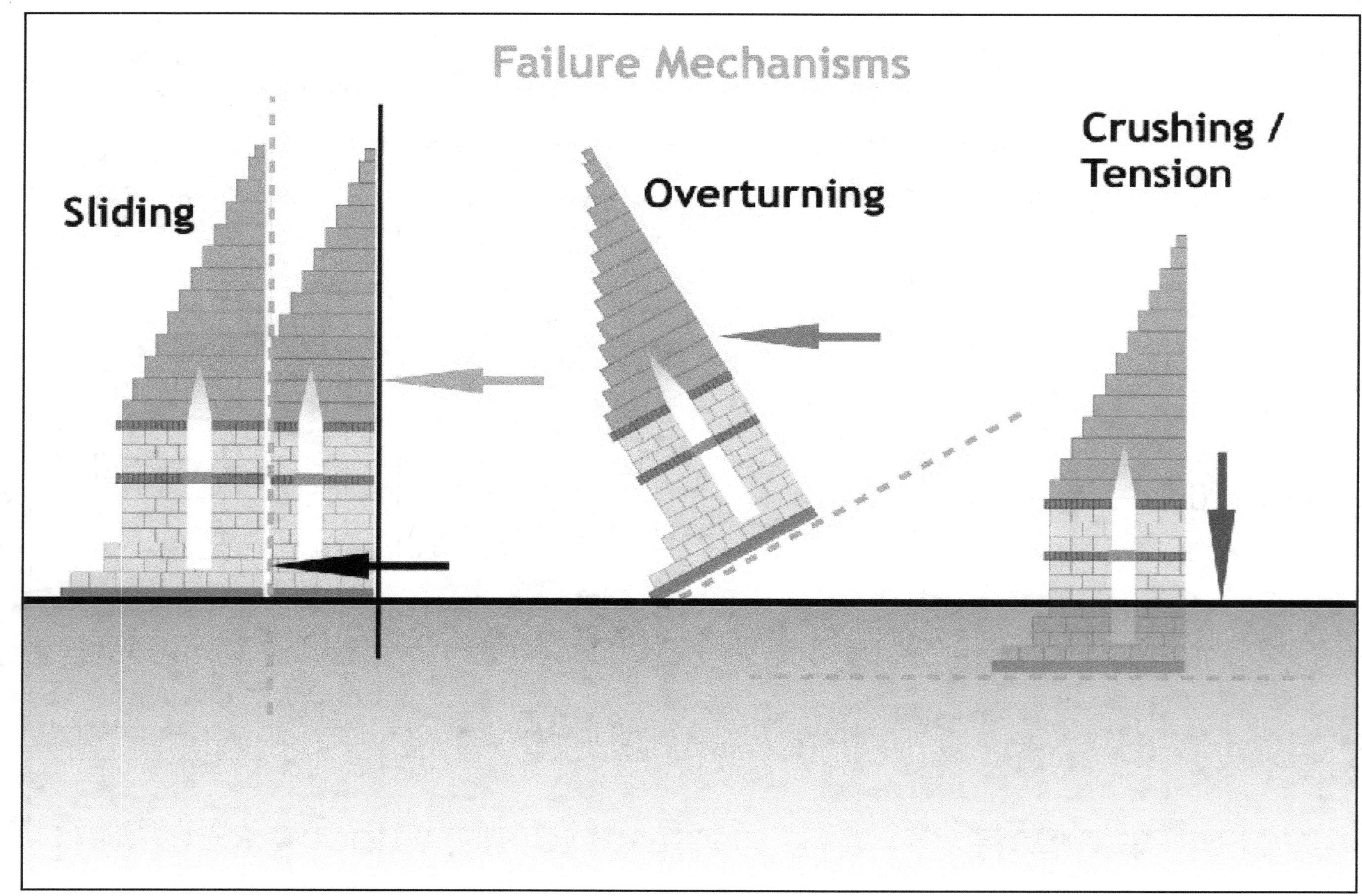

Failure Mechanisms
Sliding
Overturning
Crushing /
Tension

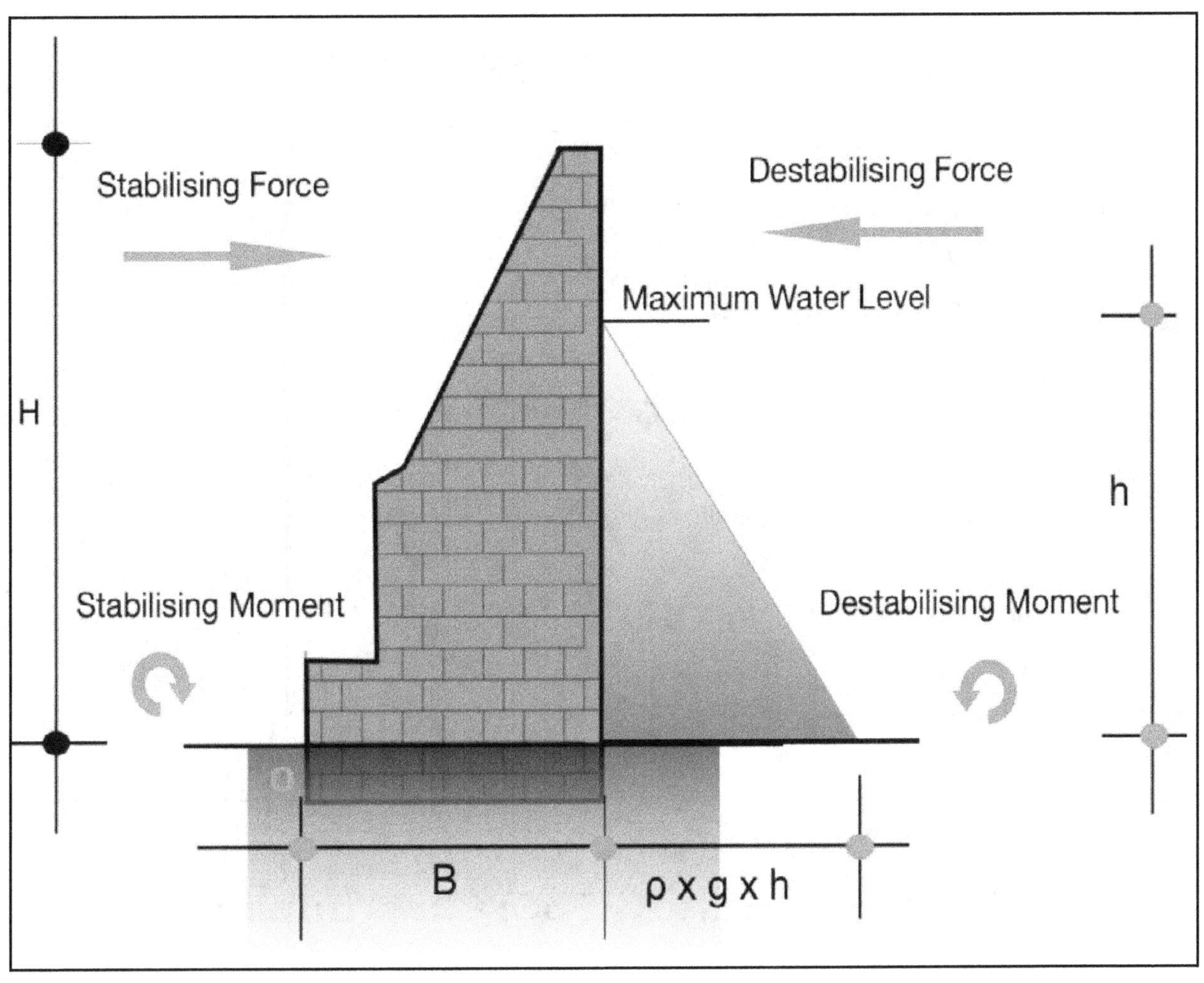

A - Sliding criteria		
Stabilising force		Destabilising force
$F = M \times g$	=	$F = 1/2 \times \rho \times g \times h \times h$
Stability factor $\times \mu \times (L \times B \times H) \times \gamma gr$	=	Stability factor $\times 1/2 \times \rho \times g \times h \times h$
B = ?		
B - Overturning criteria		
Stabilising moment		Destabilising moment
$Mst = M \times g \times B/2$	=	$Mot = 1/2 \times \rho \times g \times h \times h \times h/3$
Stability factor $\times (L \times B \times H) \times \gamma gr) \times B/2$	=	Stability factor $\times 1/2 \times \rho \times g \times h \times h \times h/3$
B = ?		
Maximum value of B shall be considered		

Factor of Safety (FoS) - Sliding

- When the wall is at the point of sliding

- For the Limiting Equilibrium

- $0.9 \times \mu \times W = 1.4\,Ph$ (μ is Coeff of Friction)

- Effective FOS against Sliding

- $(\mu \times W)/(Ph) = 1.4/0.9 = 1.56$

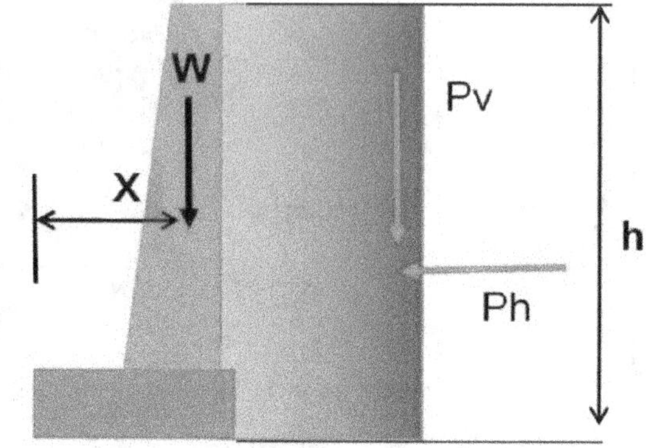

Factor of Safety (FoS) -Overturning

- W - Total vertical load due to weight of the wall which acts at 'X' distance from the toe end

- 'Ph' is the horizontal component of water pressure acting at a height of 1/3 of h from above the bottom of the base slab

- For the Limiting Equilibrium
- $1.4 \times Ph \times h/3 = 0.9\,W \times X$

- Effective FOS against Over turning

- $(W \times X)/(Ph \times h/3) = 1.4/0.9 = 1.56$

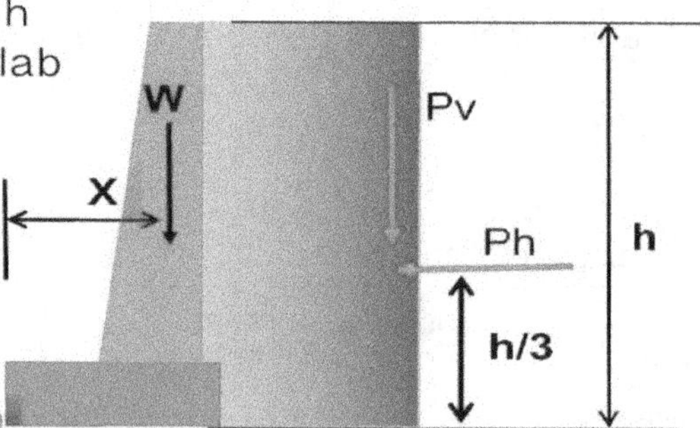

IS : 1904 - 1986

16.3.4 The permissible value of settlement for different types of structures are given in Table 1.

16.3.5 Differential settlement and/or tilt (angular distortion) of the structures shall not be more than the permissible values. The differential settlement shall be obtained by taking the difference maximum and minimum settlement. Tilt shall be calculated by dividing the differential settlement by the distance between points of related maximum and minimum settlement.

16.4 Settlement Analysis for Deep Foundation

16.4.1 The permissible value of total settlement, differential settlement, and tilt (angular distortion) have been specified in the relevant Indian Standard (*see* 3). The settlement shall be calculated according to IS : 8009 (Part 2)-1980*.

17 STABILITY AGAINST OVERTURNING AND SLIDING

17.1 The stability of the foundation against sliding and overturning shall be checked, and the factors of safety shall conform to the following requirements.

17.1.1 *Sliding* — The factor of safety against sliding of structures which resist lateral forces (such as retaining walls) shall be not less than 1·5 when dead load, live load and earth pressures are considered together with wind load or seismic forces. When dead load, live load and earth pressure only are considered, the factor of safety shall be not less than 1·75.

NOTE — For structures founded on soils with low frictional coefficient (that is, slippery material), safety against sliding may be improved by providing anchor type cut-off walls or piles to take the excess load over that resisted by friction or an inclined underside of the base.

17.2 Overturning — The factor of safety for shallow foundation against overturning shall be not less than 1·5 when dead load, live load and earth pressures are considered together with wind load or seismic forces. When dead load, live load and earth pressures only are considered, the factor of safety shall be not less than 2. The factor of safety of other types of foundation is covered in relevant Indian Standard (*see* 3).

18. BEARING CAPACITY

18.1 The safe bearing capacity for shallow foundation shall be calculated in accordance with IS : 6403-1981†. The method of computation of safe bearing capacity for other types of foundations has been specified in the

---

*Code of practice for calculation of foundations: Part 2 Deep foundations subjected to symmetrical static vertical loading.

†Code of practice for determination of bearing capacity of shallow foundations (*first revision*).

IS code guidelines for stability against overturning and sliding

IS 456 : 2000

effects due to temperature fluctuations and shrinkage and creep can be ignored in design calculations.

19.6 Other Forces and Effects

In addition, account shall be taken of the following forces and effects if they are liable to affect materially the safety and serviceability of the structure:

- a) Foundation movement (*see* IS 1904),
- b) Elastic axial shortening,
- c) Soil and fluid pressures [*see* IS 875 (Part 5)],
- d) Vibration,
- e) Fatigue,
- f) Impact [*see* IS 875 (Part 5)],
- g) Erection loads [*see* IS 875 (Part 2)], and
- h) Stress concentration effect due to point load and the like.

19.7 Combination of Loads

The combination of loads shall be as given in IS 875 (Part 5).

19.8 Dead Load Counteracting Other Loads and Forces

When dead load counteracts the effects due to other loads and forces in structural member or joint, special care shall be exercised by the designer to ensure adequate safety for possible stress reversal.

19.9 Design Load

Design load is the load to be taken for use in the appropriate method of design; it is the characteristic load in case of working stress method and characteristic load with appropriate partial safety factors for limit state design.

20 STABILITY OF THE STRUCTURE

20.1 Overturning

The stability of a structure as a whole against overturning shall be ensured so that the restoring moment shall be not less than the sum of 1.2 times the maximum overturning moment due to the characteristic dead load and 1.4 times the maximum overturning moment due to the characteristic imposed loads. In cases where dead load provides the restoring moment, only 0.9 times the characteristic dead load shall be considered. Restoring moment due to imposed loads shall be ignored.

20.1.1 The anchorages or counterweights provided for overhanging members (during construction and service) should be such that static equilibrium should remain, even when overturning moment is doubled.

20.2 Sliding

The structure shall have a factor against sliding of not less than 1.4 under the most adverse combination of the applied characteristic forces. In this case only 0.9 times the characteristic dead load shall be taken into account.

20.3 Probable Variation in Dead Load

To ensure stability at all times, account shall be taken of probable variations in dead load during construction, repair or other temporary measures. Wind and seismic loading shall be treated as imposed loading.

20.4 Moment Connection

In designing the framework of a building provisions shall be made by adequate moment connections or by a system of bracings to effectively transmit all the horizontal forces to the foundations.

20.5 Lateral Sway

Under transient wind load the lateral sway at the top should not exceed $H/500$, where H is the total height of the building. For seismic loading, reference should be made to IS 1893.

21 FIRE RESISTANCE

21.1 A structure or structural element required to have fire resistance should be designed to possess an appropriate degree of resistance to flame penetration; heat transmission and failure. The fire resistance of a structural element is expressed in terms of time in hours in accordance with IS 1641. Fire resistance of concrete elements depends upon details of member size, cover to steel reinforcement detailing and type of aggregate (normal weight or light weight) used in concrete. General requirements for fire protection are given in IS 1642.

21.2 Minimum requirements of concrete cover and member dimensions for normal-weight aggregate concrete members so as to have the required fire resistance shall be in accordance with 26.4.3 and Fig. 1 respectively.

21.3 The reinforcement detailing should reflect the changing pattern of the structural section and ensure that both individual elements and the structure as a whole contain adequate support, ties, bonds and anchorages for the required fire resistance.

21.3.1 Additional measures such as application of fire resistant finishes, provision of fire resistant false ceilings and sacrificial steel in tensile zone, should be adopted in case the nominal cover required exceeds 40 mm for beams and 35 mm for slabs, to give protection against spalling.

21.4 Specialist literature may be referred to for determining fire resistance of the structures which have not been covered in Fig. 1 or Table 16A.

IS code direction on Sliding and Overturning

10

Intensive Research

An in-depth explanation of gravity dam forces and collapse mechanisms was provided in the preceding chapter and the Vimana wall's engineering design can be analysed for these considerations and precautions.

Maximum water levels and total volume have been determined in the circumambulatory and annexe building vestibules. An examination of the structure's empty spaces suggests that it could have held the water up to +24.75 m deep, which is half the height of Vimana.

To evaluate the structural wall's viability as a gravity dam, the prescribed cross-sectional area must meet the hydrostatic pressure from the large depth of water. To function and act as a gravity dam, the wall must have a sufficient base width considering sliding and overturning failures. The overall cross-sectional area is designed to accommodate the required mass and weight to withstand the hydrostatic pressure linearly with the height by closely following a right triangular profile.

Data like the Vimana's overall height and maximum water height can be inferred from the Vimana's actual cross-sectional and physical profile, which were most likely maintained and operated by the Chola engineers during the construction period. A comprehensive calculation necessitates the inclusion of additional variables such as water density, granite stone density, and friction coefficient, in addition to the information and guidelines provided by the Indian Standard code norms and regulations, all of which are listed and included in the table "Data for Analysis."

The objectives of this exercise are

- To determine the minimum thickness of the wall required to arrive at the total cross-sectional area that would safely withstand and balance the hydrostatic force exerted by the 24.75 m height of the water column; and
- To verify whether the structure was designed in accordance with the design requirements of a gravity dam by the Chola engineers.

123

Two calculations are required for this exercise:

- To determine the minimum wall thickness for sliding failure criteria, the self-weight of the structure wall must be equated to the hydrostatic force of water while taking frictional coefficient and safety factors into account in the first calculation.
- In the second step, the moments of stabilising and destabilising forces must be equated to obtain the minimum wall thickness required for the overturning failure criterion.

The maximum of the above variables determines the average width and wall cross-sectional area of the structure, which must have been fixed during physical construction.

The tables show the results of the sliding and overturning criteria exercises and calculations based on a one-metre length of the sanctum wall.

Exercise No. 1 – The structure progressed to the height of 33 m and the water level was maintained at 24.75 m from the floor level of the courtyard.

The detailed calculations for Exercise No. 1 are shown in the table "Structure height 33 m and water level +24.75 m," and the results are further illustrated in the respective drawing.

With a 1.5 safety factor, 9 m was found to be the minimum average wall width required to meet both the sliding and overturning criteria.

For a water column with a height of 24.75 m, a minimum cross-sectional area of 9 m × 33 m = 297 m² should have been allowed in the actual construction.

Exercise No 2 – The structure progressed to the height of 49.50 m and the maximum permitted water level up to +24.75 m

The detailed calculations for Exercise No. 1 are shown in the table "Structure height 49.50 m and water level +24.75 m," and the results are further illustrated in the respective drawing.

With a 1.5 safety factor, 7.37 m was found to be the minimum average wall width required to meet both the sliding and overturning criteria and hence for a water column with a height of 24.75 m, a minimum corresponding cross-sectional area of 7.37 m × 49.50 m = 364.82 m² should have been considered and provided in the overall actual construction up to the height of +49.50 m.

Exercise No. 3 – The structure reached 49.50 m, and the water level hit +31.60 m from +24.75 m upon sudden system failure during the lifting operation

The detailed calculations for Exercise No. 3 are shown in the table "Structure height 49.50 m and water level +31.60 m," and the results are further explained in the respective drawing.

With a 1.5 safety factor, the base must be 10.63 m to meet the sliding and overturning conditions when the water column unexpectedly rises to +31.60 m from +24.75 m.

The gravity dam's basic and practical profile is generally created in the shape of a right-angled triangle. The width is maximum at the structure's base and reduces linearly with the water column's hydrostatic pressure reduction and depth.

The maximum width derived from each exercise shall be used to calculate the overall cross-sectional area, and the result should be identical and comparable to determine whether the structure was designed and constructed in the concept and profile of a gravity dam from the base. There may have been practical difficulties in carrying and precisely arranging the heavy granite materials during construction, but the physical construction profile and area should be comparable to the design, even if the values aren't quite matching. Only then can it be demonstrated that the massive wall was designed to withstand the hydrostatic pressure and that the entire wall construction was used as a gravity dam.

Analysis of Exercise No. 1

The table "'Structure height 33 m and water level +24.75 m" Exercise No. 1 shows the sliding and overturning exercises and calculations.

With a safety factor of 1.5, the minimum average wall width required to meet both the sliding and overturning criteria was determined to be 9 m. As a result, Exercise No. 1 requires a cross-sectional area of 297 m² (9 m × 33 m = 297 m²) in one-half of the standing structure.

The actual area physically constructed and provided in the various zones is illustrated in the drawing "Actual Area Calculation – Exercise No. 1," and the values were calculated using ASI-documented measurements up to the height of +33 m.

The drawing shows that one-half of the total actual constructed area from the face of the wall is 300 m², which more precisely meets the design criteria requirement of 297 m².

Even though the structure is only halfway up, this is exactly in line with the intended result of 297 m², and it appears that the Chola engineers have carefully and precisely designed the profile and allocated various zones to meet the design requirement and in line with the hydrostatic pressure.

Analysis of Exercise No. 2

The study established 7.37 m as the minimum average wall thickness to satisfy both the sliding and overturning criteria with a 1.5 safety factor.

The actual temple cross-sectional area will be compared to that based on the 7.37 m wall thickness.

When the outcome of Exercise no. 2 requires a minimum width of 7.37 m and an overall area of 7.37 m × 49.50 m = 364.82 m², this is the most optimal area required to meet the overall performance of the structure when the structure has reached its completion, taking into account the maximum water pressure from a height of 24.75 m.

The area physically provided in one-half of the structure from the face of the inner wall is approximately 360 m², as featured in the drawing "Actual Area Calculation – Exercise No. 2."

The 360 m² area physically available in the standing structure is astonishingly very close to meeting the design figure of 364.82 m². The difference of less than 5 m² is insignificant and could be the result of measurement error.

Because it is widely assumed and traditionally stated that the construction has just 5 to 6 feet of foundation depth, an assumption of only a 1.83 m thick raft is considered, incorporated, and verified in the overall total.

Surprisingly, the actual constructed area closely matches the design requirement in both Exercises 1 and 2, confirming that hydrostatic pressure played a significant role in designing the wall width and profiling the wall structure like a gravity dam.

The cross-sectional geometry is similar to that of a gravity dam, which is typically a right-angled triangle, as shown in the drawing. The above two exercises firmly establish that the structure and zones have been organised and fashioned like a dam, and they validate the Chola engineers' purpose of using the structural wall as a gravity dam to withstand the hydrostatic force applied by the considerable height of water.

In conclusion, the actual cross-section area of the structure in Exercise 2 matches the designed area based on an average wall thickness of 7.37 m, which is required to maintain stability against the hydrostatic force acting from a depth of 24.75 m in the water column to keep the structure in overall equilibrium.

Analysis of Exercise No. 3

The safety of the structure also has to be duly addressed in the design, and the structure should function properly in case of any system failure with the above dimensional measurements.

If the wooden floating mechanism carrying the heavy Sikhara breaks or crushes between +24.75 m and the highest +49.50 m level before final installation, the entire system may collapse, and the Sikhara will slide and forcefully drop into the sanctum well and submerge.

When the Sikhara slides down and is immersed, the water level surges up from + 24.75 to hit + 33 m for the height of the Sikhara by displacing and raising the equivalent volume of water suddenly for certain moments.

In such a severe and high-risk circumstance, how can the main structure be protected from the abrupt increase in hydrostatic pressure on the wall?

To safely meet the above circumstance, the Chola engineers have made a careful safety precautionary measure and provision in the physical construction that displays openings and an extension of the circumambulatory cavity provided up to +31.60 m level to quickly catch and drain the surged-up water from the inner chamber.

Though the sudden rise in water level is only for a few moments, other temporary strengthening measures, such as thicker temporary walls around the base or additional temporary supporting arrangements, such as sand-filled gunny bags or stone boulders stacking as counterweight around the base for a certain height, must be taken as a safety precautionary measure before carrying out the final lifting and installation.

These additional temporary supporting arrangements will also compensate to a major extent for the shortfall in mass and weight due to any temporary cavities or cut-outs made in the circumambulatory inside.

The corresponding calculations were also verified to find out how thick the walls would have to be if the water unexpectedly and suddenly rose from +24.75 m to +31.60 m.

The result of this was that the walls would have to be at least 10.63 m in width at the courtyard base, as arrived through the calculation.

The sanctum's inner width is 7.93 m, and when the above wall thickness of 10.63 m is added for both sides of the sanctum, the overall total dimension of the base at the level of the courtyard must be maintained for 7.93 m + 10.63 × 2 sides = 29.19 m.

The above number should be verified and must be very close to the actual dimension provided in the standing structure at the base of the courtyard.

If the measurement is close to 29.19 m, it increases the confidence that the research is on the right track and that the ancient Tamil engineers have designed the structural wall system in the style of a gravity dam.

Taking into account the sudden surge of water up to +31.60 m where the cavities merge and the height of Sikhara is 8.25 m, Chola engineers most likely fixed the maximum water level as +23.35 m from the courtyard by considering a free board of 1.4 m from +24.75. This may reduce the width of the base and the cross-sectional area of the construction to some extent.

ASI Base Width Measurement of 30.48 m

The ASI publication measure of 30.48 m base width most likely is at the bottom-most level of the foundation raft, the depth of which must be roughly 1.6 m or approximately 5 feet as traditionally believed, and stated below the current level of the courtyard. In that case, the wall will be subjected to additional water pressure from a depth of 1.6 m, and the maximum safe base dimension must be calculated and fixed while taking the additional water pressure into account.

As a result, the total wall height is 49.5+1.6 = 51.10 m, and the water level is 31.60+1.6 = 33.20 m.

With a safety factor of 1.5, the calculated and arrived base width is 11.276 m.

When the above wall thickness of 11.276 m for both sides of the sanctum is added, the overall total dimension of the base 1.6 m below the level of the courtyard must be maintained for 7.93 m + 11.276 × 2 sides = 30.48 m, as shown in the sketch "ASI Measure."

Stability Verification

Though the designed area corresponds nearly to the overall physically constructed area, it should be noted that the structure inside has significantly large voids in the circumambulatory and in the triangular cavity formation, resulting in a significant reduction in the structure's cross-sectional area and the corresponding mass and weight.

The vertical wall and the Vimana's sloped outer surface have large-sized extensive architectural features that may significantly contribute to compensating for the reduction in mass and weight caused by the large voids present inside the structure.

It necessitates a careful exercise in calculating and arriving at the actual weighted average thickness of these architectural features and projections from the outer and inner wall faces.

The design requires an average width of 7.37 m when the maximum water level is +24.75 m, but one-half of the structure's base width is 10.63 m, as per Exercise No. 3, and the wall structure appears to have been enlarged and profiled from a larger base width.

During operation, the inside of the circumambulatory will have voids, while the sanctum chamber and triangular cavity inside will be filled with water to a depth of +24.75 m. With the empty spaces inside the circumambulatory, one-half of the Vimana structure from the inner face of the wall should be stable enough to withstand the hydrostatic pressure of the large water column, and a "Dam stability Check Analysis" based on the designed dimensions will provide more accurate information on the actual cross-sectional area required while taking stability and safety factors into account.

Given their in-depth design awareness, for overall stability, the Chola engineers must also have taken into account the following two additional important factors to ensure that the structure wall was designed perfectly in the style of a gravity dam.

A dam structure can collapse due to issues such as crushing or compression, development of tension, in addition to sliding, and overturning. The induced normal stresses in the dam or the foundation should not exceed the permissible value.

To maintain optimal stability and avoid tension development, the "Middle Third Rule" must be followed, which stipulates that the resultant force must pass through inside the middle third of the structure's foundation.

The maximum normal stresses should be limited within the safe carrying capacity of the soil.

For sliding criteria, a minimum factor of safety of 1.5 is typically fixed, whereas a safety factor of 2 is considered against overturning effect.

It is also possible that the Chola engineers knew what the Middle Third Rule meant when they came up with the idea and built the structure more like a gravity dam.

It necessitates a thorough examination further.

Data for analysis

Sl no	Description		Data	Remarks
1	Acceleration due to gravity	g	9.81m / Sec²	
2	Density of water	ρ_w	1000 kg / m³	
3	Density of granite	ρ_{Gr}	2700 kg / m³	
4	Specific weight of water. $\gamma_w = \rho_w \times g$	γ_w	1000 × 9.81 m / sec² =9810 kgm / sec² = 9.81 kN / m³	1 kg m /sec² = 1 N and 1000 N = 1kN
6	Specific weight of granite. $\gamma_{Gr} = \rho_{Gr} \times g$	γ_{gr}	2.7 × 9.81 kN / m³ = 26.49 kN / m³	
7	Total height of Wall	H	49.50 m	
8	Depth of water	h	Exercise No 1 & 2- 24.75 m Exercise No 3 - 31.60 m	
9	Length of wall	L	Per running meter considered for analysis	
10	Width of wall	B	To be determined	
11	Coefficient of friction - granite	μ	0.65	
12	Stability safety factor - dead load	FoS	0.9 time - as per IS 456-2000	sliding
13	Stability safety factor - applied forces	FoS	1.4 times - as per IS 456-2000	sliding
14	Stability safety factor - restoring moment	FoS	0.9 time - as per IS 456-2000	overturning
15	Stability safety factor - overturning moment	FoS	1.4 times - as per IS 456-2000	overturning

Exercise no 1 - Structure height 33 m & water level +24.75 m

A Sliding

Stabilising force	=	Destabilising force
$F = Ma$ and $Ma = Mg$		$F = 1/2 \times \rho g \times h \times h$
Mg	=	$1/2 \times \rho g \times h \times h$
$FoS \times \mu \times (LxBxHx\gamma gr)$		$FoS \times 1/2 \times \rho g \times h \times h$
$0.9 \times 0.65 \times (1xBx33x2.7x9.81)$	=	$1.4x\ (1/2 \times 1x\ 9.81 \times 24.75 \times 24.75)$
$511.332\ B$	=	4206.4667
B	=	4206.4667/511.332
B for 1.56 FoS	=	8.23 m
B for 1.5 FoS	=	$8.23 \times (1.50) / (1.56)$
B w.r.t sliding criteria		7.91 m

B Overturning

Stabilising moment	=	Destabilising moment
$Mg \times B/2$		$1/2 \times \rho g \times h \times h \times h/3$
$FoS \times (LxBxHx\gamma gr) \times B/2$	=	$FoS \times 1/2 \times \rho g \times h \times h \times h/3$
$0.9x(1xBx33\ x2.7x9.81\ ) \times B/2$	=	$1.4x\ (1/2 \times 1 \times 9.81x\ 24.75 \times 24.75 \times 24.75/3)$
$393.332 \times B^2$	=	34703.350
B^2	=	34703.350/ 393.332
B	=	$\sqrt{(34703.35/ 393.332)}$
B	=	$\sqrt{(88.23)}$
B for 1.56 FoS	=	9.39 m
B for 1.5 FoS	=	$9.39 \times (1.50)/(1.56)$
B w.r.t overturning criteria	=	9.00 m

Exercise no 2 - Structure height 49.50 m & water level +24.75 m

A	Sliding		
	Stabilising force	=	Destabilising force
	$F = Ma$ and $Ma = Mg$		$F = 1/2 \times \rho \times g \times h \times h$
	Mg	=	$1/2 \times \rho \times g \times h \times h$
	$FoS \times \mu \times (LxBxHx\gamma gr)$		$FoS \times 1/2 \times \rho g \times h \times h$
	$0.9 \times 0.65 \times (1 \times B \times 49.50 \times 2.7 \times 9.81)$	=	$1.4 \times (1/2 \times 1 \times 9.81 \times 24.75 \times 24.75)$
	$767\ B$	=	4206.4667
	B	=	$4206.4667\ /767$
	B for 1.56 FoS	=	$5.48\ m$
	B for 1.5 FoS	=	$5.48 \times (1.50) / (1.56)$
	B w.r.t sliding criteria		$5.27\ m$
B	Overturning		
	Stabilising moment	=	Destabilising moment
	$Mg \times B/2$		$1/2 \times \rho \times g \times h \times h \times h/3$
	$FoS \times (LxBxHx\gamma gr) \times B/2$	=	$FoS \times 1/2 \times \rho \times g \times h \times h \times h/3$
	$0.9 \times (1 \times B \times 49.50 \times 2.7 \times 9.81) \times B/2$	=	$1.4 \times (1/2 \times 1 \times 9.81 \times 24.75 \times 24.75 \times 24.75/3)$
	$590 \times B^2$	=	34703.35
	B^2	=	$34703.35 / 590$
	B	=	$\sqrt{(34703.35 / 590)}$
	B	=	$\sqrt{(58.82)}$
	B for 1.56 FoS	=	$7.669\ m$
	B for 1.5 FoS	=	$7.669 \times (1.50) /(1.56)$
	B w.r.t overturning criteria	=	$7.37\ m$

Exercise no 3 - Structure height 49.50 m & water level +31.60 m

A	Sliding		
	Stabilising force	=	Destabilising force
	$F = Ma$ and $Ma = Mg$		$F = 1/2 \times \rho \times g \times h \times h$
	Mg	=	$1/2 \times \rho g \times h \times h$
	$FoS \times \mu \times (LxBxHx\gamma gr)$		$FoS \times 1/2 \times \rho g \times h \times h$
	$0.9 \times 0.65 \times (1 \times B \times 49.50 \times 2.7 \times 9.81)$	=	$1.4 \times (1/2 \times 1 \times 9.81 \times 31.60 \times 31.60)$
	$767\ B$	=	6857.112
	B	=	$6857.112\ /767$
	B for 1.56 FoS	=	$8.94\ m$
	B for 1.5 FoS	=	$8.94 \times (1.50) / (1.56)$
	B w.r.t sliding criteria		$8.60\ m$
B	Overturning		
	Stabilising moment	=	Destabilising moment
	$Mg \times B/2$		$1/2 \times \rho \times g \times h \times h \times h/3$
	$FoS \times (LxBxHx\gamma gr) \times B/2$	=	$FoS \times 1/2 \times \rho g \times h \times h \times h/3$
	$0.9 \times (1 \times B \times 49.50 \times 2.7 \times 9.81) \times B/2$	=	$1.4 \times (1/2 \times 1 \times 9.81 \times 31.60 \times 31.60 \times 31.60/3)$
	$590 \times B^2$	=	7228.2413
	B^2	=	$72228.2413 / 590$
	B	=	$\sqrt{(72228.2413/ 590)}$
	B	=	$\sqrt{(122.421)}$
	B for 1.56 FOS	=	$11.06\ m$
	B for 1.5 FOS	=	$11.06 \times (1.50) /(1.56)$
	B w.r.t overturning criteria	=	$10.63\ m$

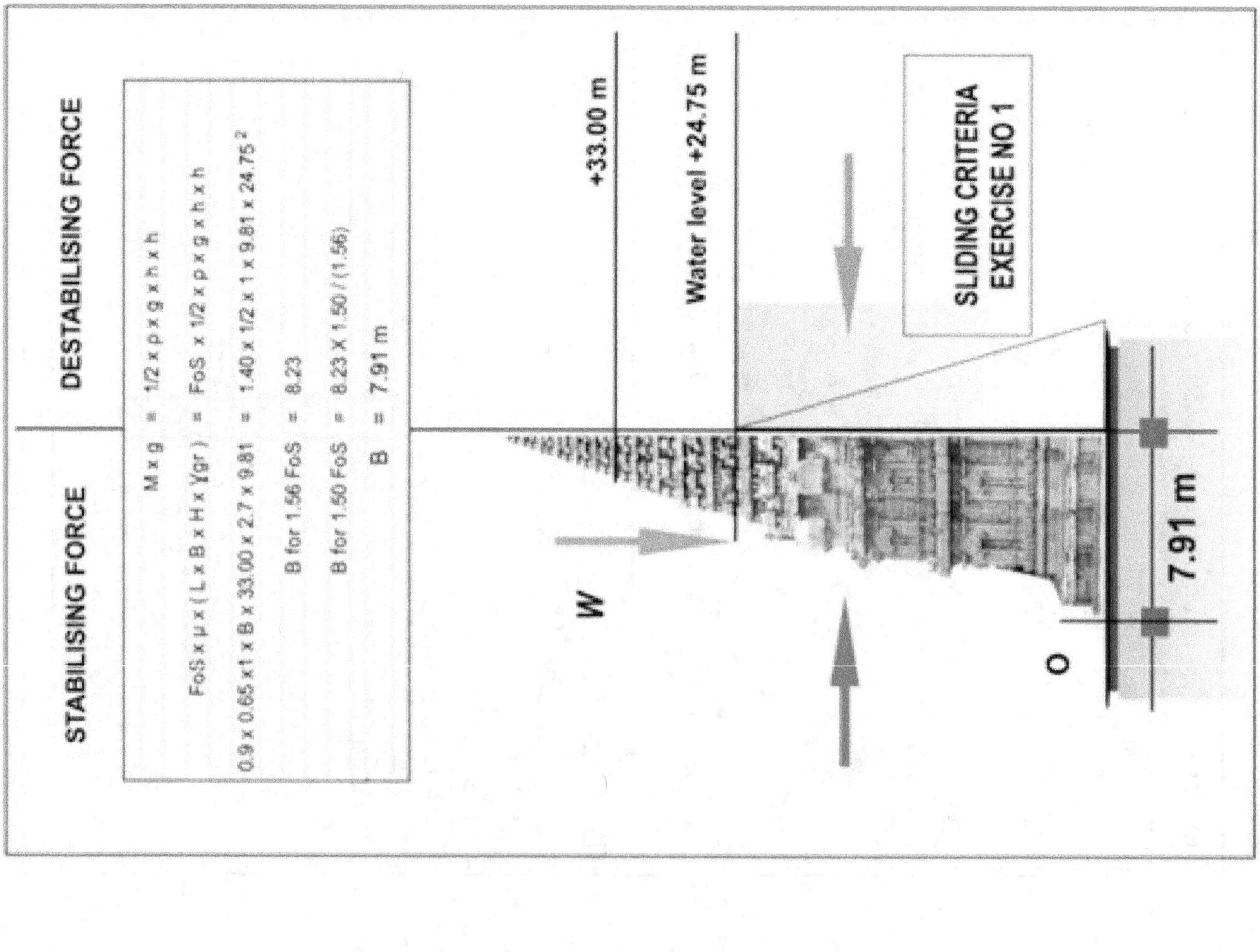

STABILISING FORCE	DESTABILISING FORCE
$M \times g$ =	$1/2 \times \rho \times g \times h \times h$
$FoS \times \mu \times (L \times B \times H \times \gamma_{gr})$ =	$FoS \times 1/2 \times \rho \times g \times h \times h$
$0.9 \times 0.65 \times 1 \times B \times 33.00 \times 2.7 \times 9.81$ =	$1.40 \times 1/2 \times 1 \times 9.81 \times 24.75^2$
B for 1.56 FoS =	8.23
B for 1.50 FoS =	$8.23 \times 1.50 / (1.56)$
B =	7.91 m

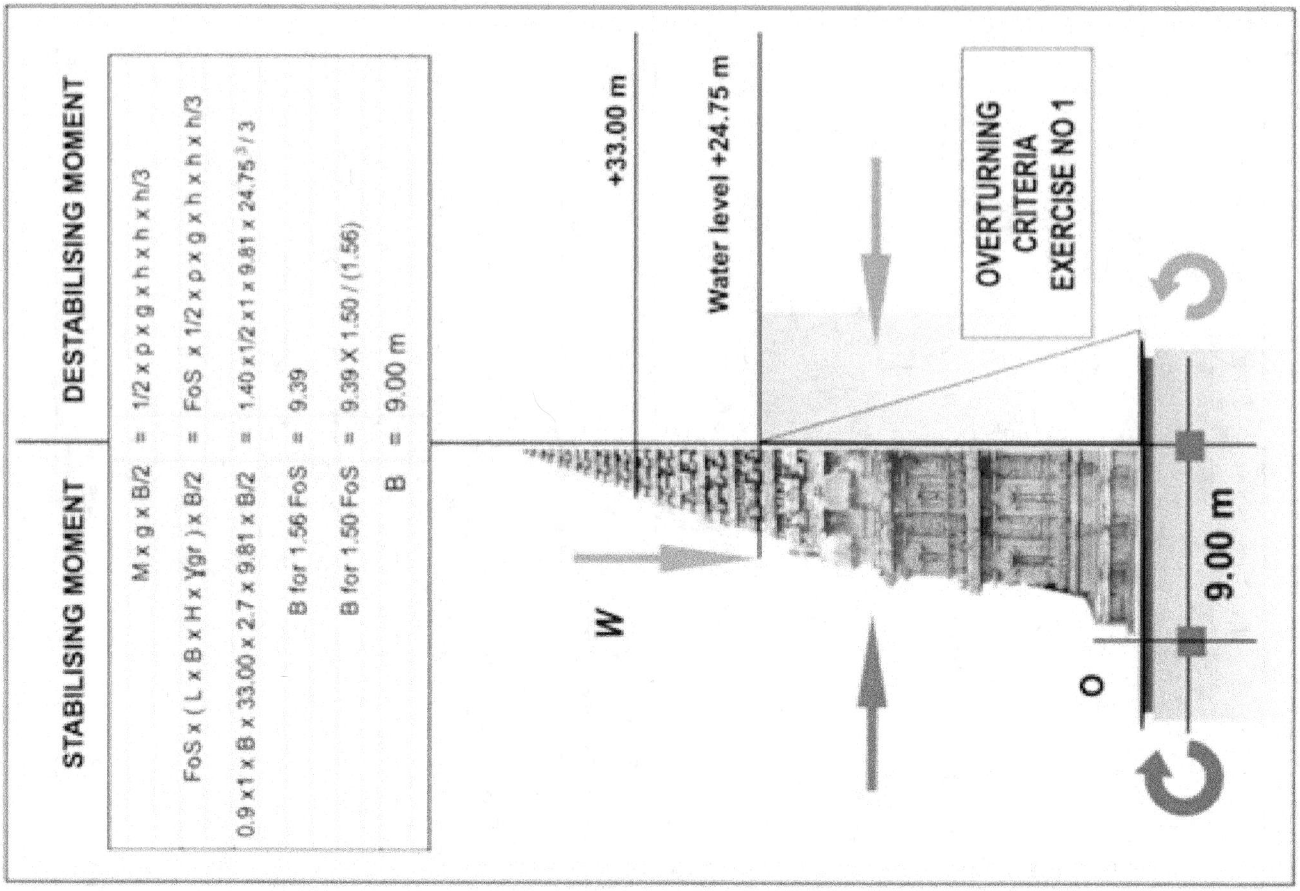

STABILISING MOMENT	DESTABILISING MOMENT
$M \times g \times B/2$ =	$1/2 \times \rho \times g \times h \times h \times h/3$
$FoS \times (L \times B \times H \times \gamma_{gr}) \times B/2$ =	$FoS \times 1/2 \times \rho \times g \times h \times h \times h/3$
$0.9 \times 1 \times B \times 33.00 \times 2.7 \times 9.81 \times B/2$ =	$1.40 \times 1/2 \times 1 \times 9.81 \times 24.75^3/3$
B for 1.56 FoS =	9.39
B for 1.50 FoS =	$9.39 \times 1.50 / (1.56)$
B =	9.00 m

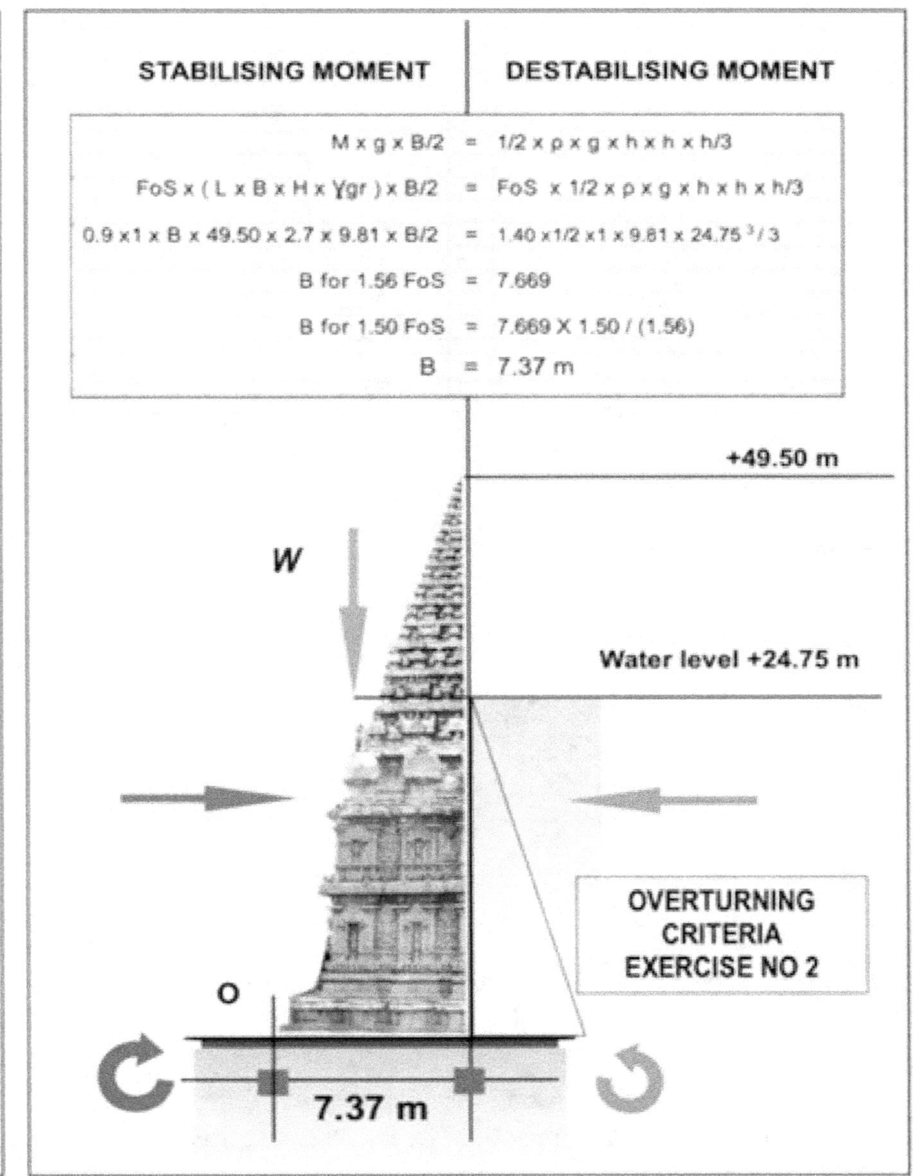

STABILISING FORCE
DESTABILISING FORCE
M x g = 1/2 x ρ x g x h x h
FoS x μ x (L x B x H x Ɣgr) = FoS x 1/2 x ρ x g x h x h
0.9 x 0.65 x1 x B x 49.50 x 2.7 x 9.81 = 1.40 x 1/2 x 1 x 9.81 x 24.75 2
B for 1.56 FoS = 5.48
B for 1.50 FoS = 5.48 X 1.50 / (1.56)
B = 5.27 m
+49.50 m
W
Water level +24.75 m
SLIDING CRITERIA
EXERCISE NO 2
O
5.27 m

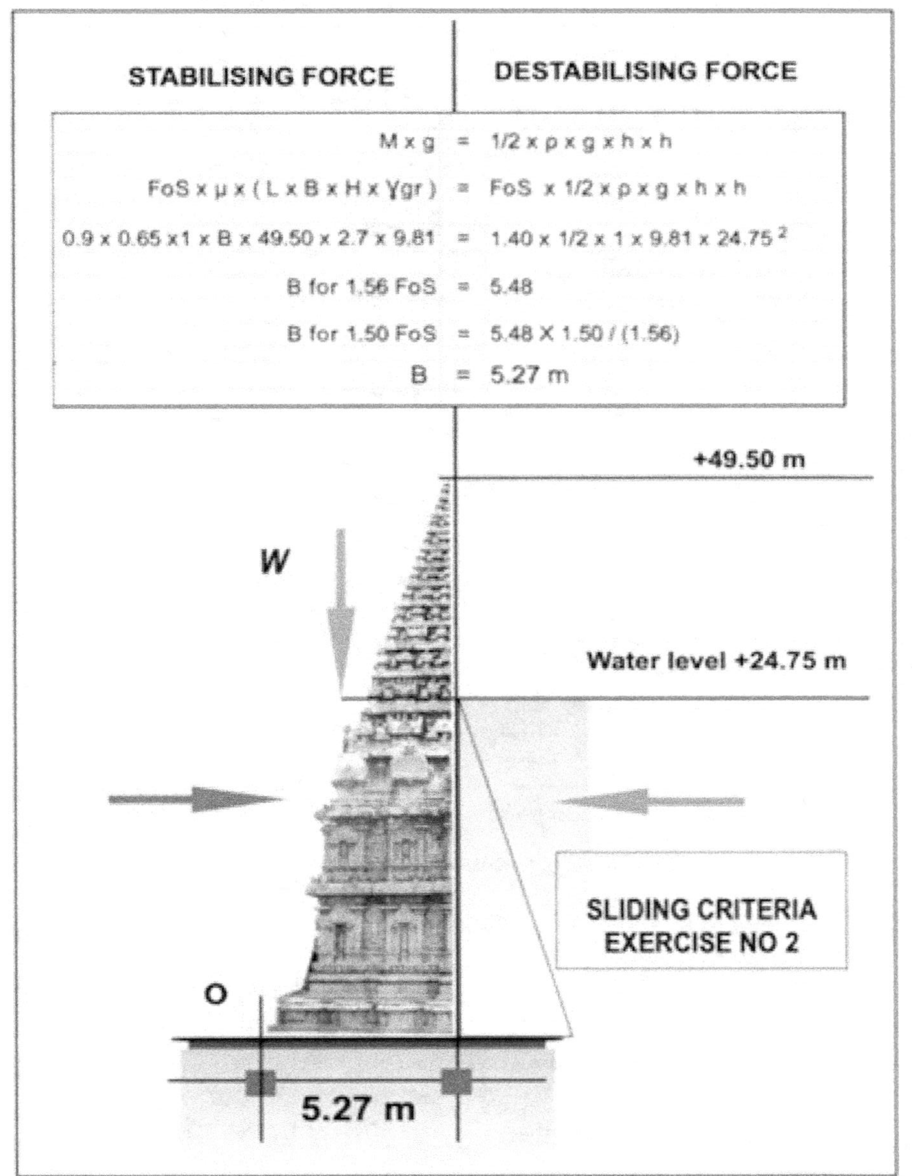

STABILISING MOMENT
DESTABILISING MOMENT
M x g x B/2 = 1/2 x ρ x g x h x h x h/3
FoS x (L x B x H x Ɣgr) x B/2 = FoS x 1/2 x ρ x g x h x h x h/3
0.9 x1 x B x 49.50 x 2.7 x 9.81 x B/2 = 1.40 x1/2 x1 x 9.81 x 24.75 3/3
B for 1.56 FoS = 7.669
B for 1.50 FoS = 7.669 X 1.50 / (1.56)
B = 7.37 m
+49.50 m
W
Water level +24.75 m
OVERTURNING
CRITERIA
EXERCISE NO 2
O
7.37 m

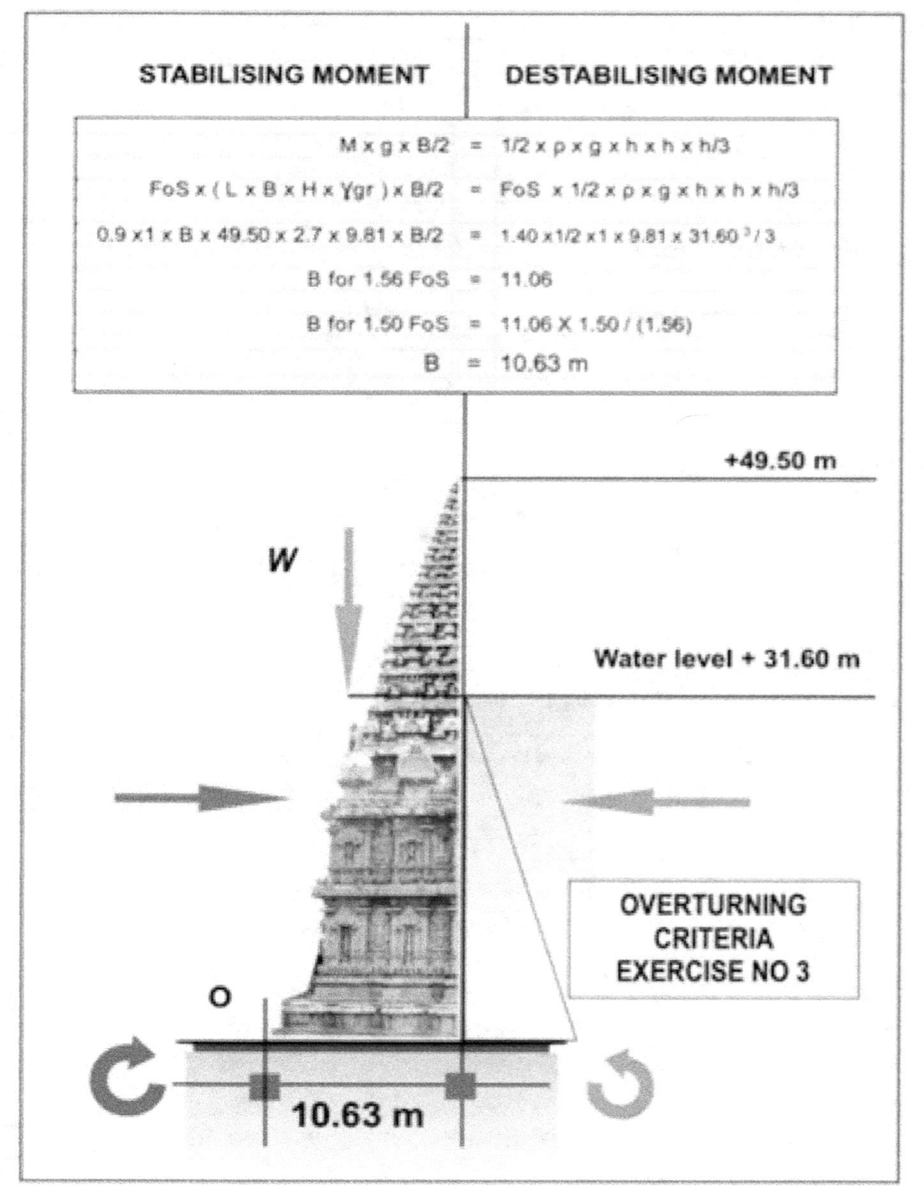

STABILISING FORCE
DESTABILISING FORCE
M x g = 1/2 x p x g x h x h
FoS x μ x (L x B x H x Ygr) = FoS x 1/2 x p x g x h x h
0.9 x 0.65 x1 x B x 49.50 x 2.7 x 9.81 = 1.40 x 1/2 x 1 x 9.81 x 31.60²
B for 1.56 FoS = 8.94
B for 1.50 FoS = 8.94 X 1.50 / (1.56)
B = 8.60 m
+49.50 m
W
Water level +31.60 m
SLIDING CRITERIA EXERCISE NO 3
O
8.60 m

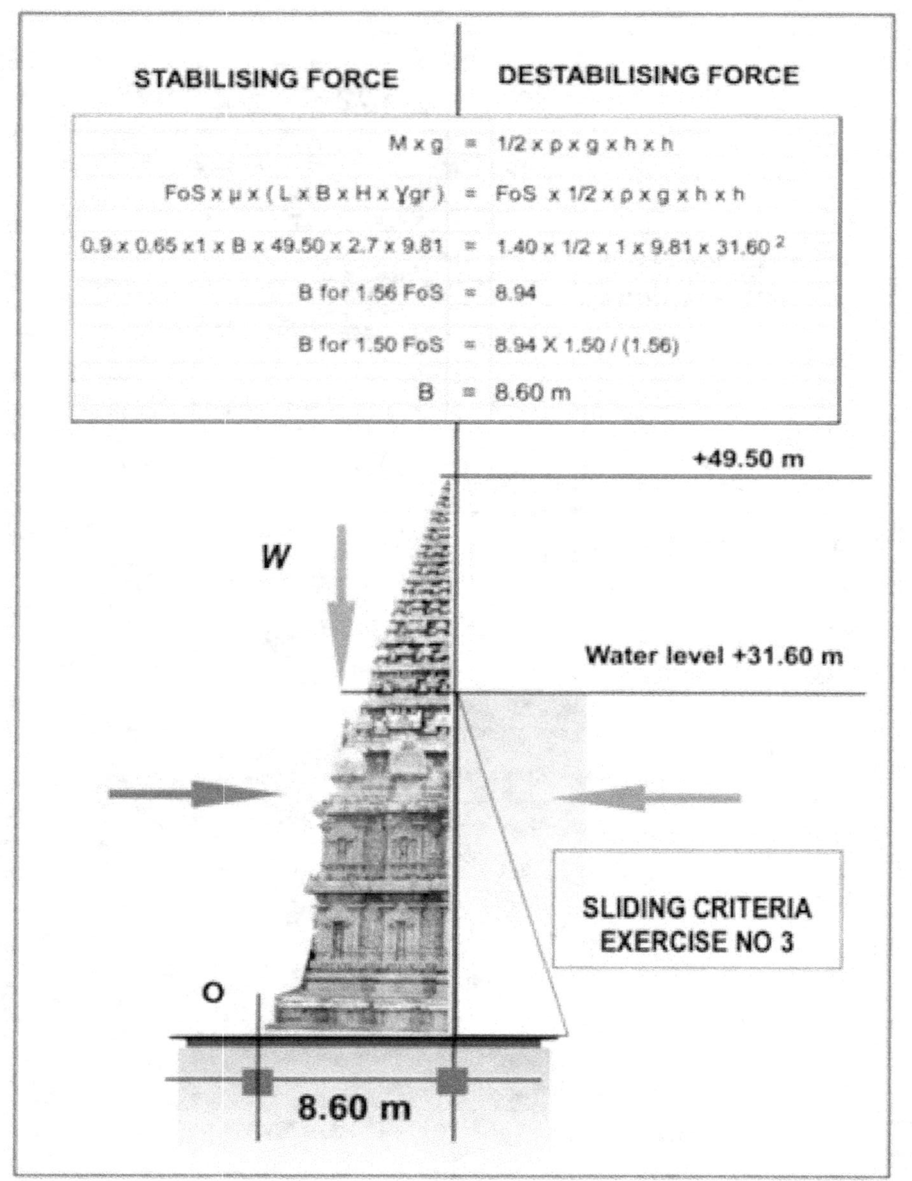

STABILISING MOMENT
DESTABILISING MOMENT
M x g x B/2 = 1/2 x p x g x h x h x h/3
FoS x (L x B x H x Ygr) x B/2 = FoS x 1/2 x p x g x h x h x h/3
0.9 x1 x B x 49.50 x 2.7 x 9.81 x B/2 = 1.40 x1/2 x1 x 9.81 x 31.60³ /3
B for 1.56 FoS = 11.06
B for 1.50 FoS = 11.06 X 1.50 / (1.56)
B = 10.63 m
+49.50 m
W
Water level + 31.60 m
OVERTURNING CRITERIA EXERCISE NO 3
O
10.63 m

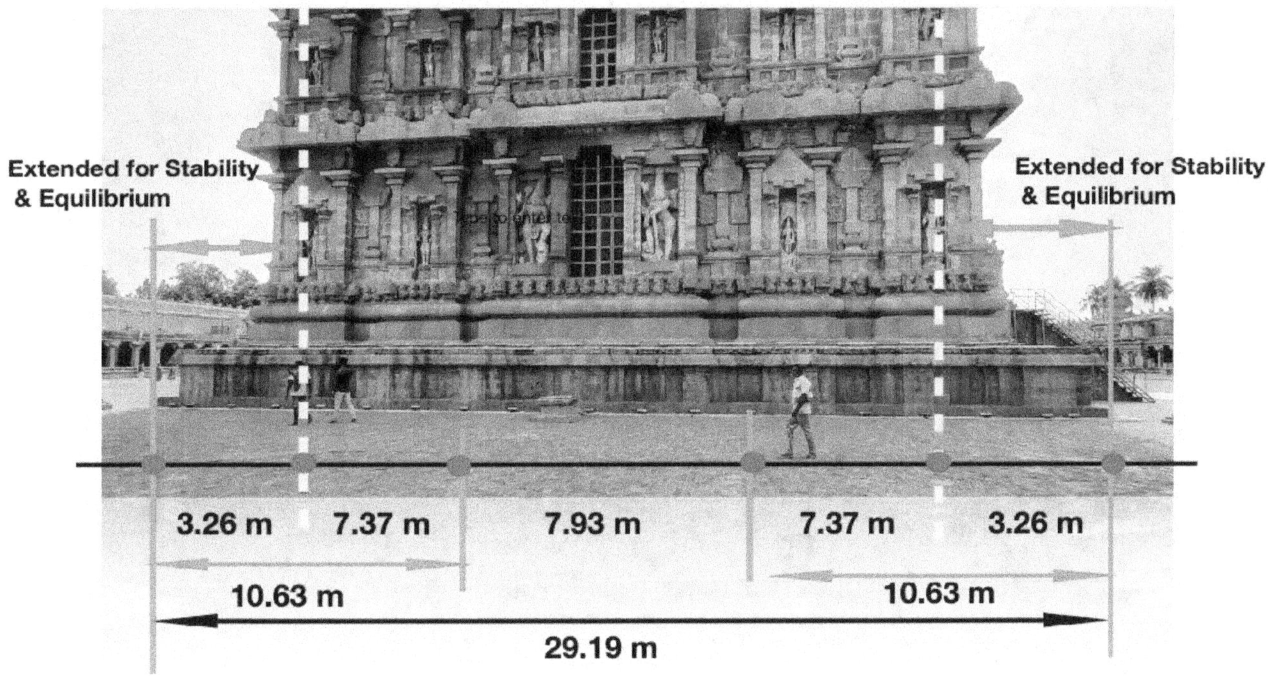

Exercise No 2 & 3

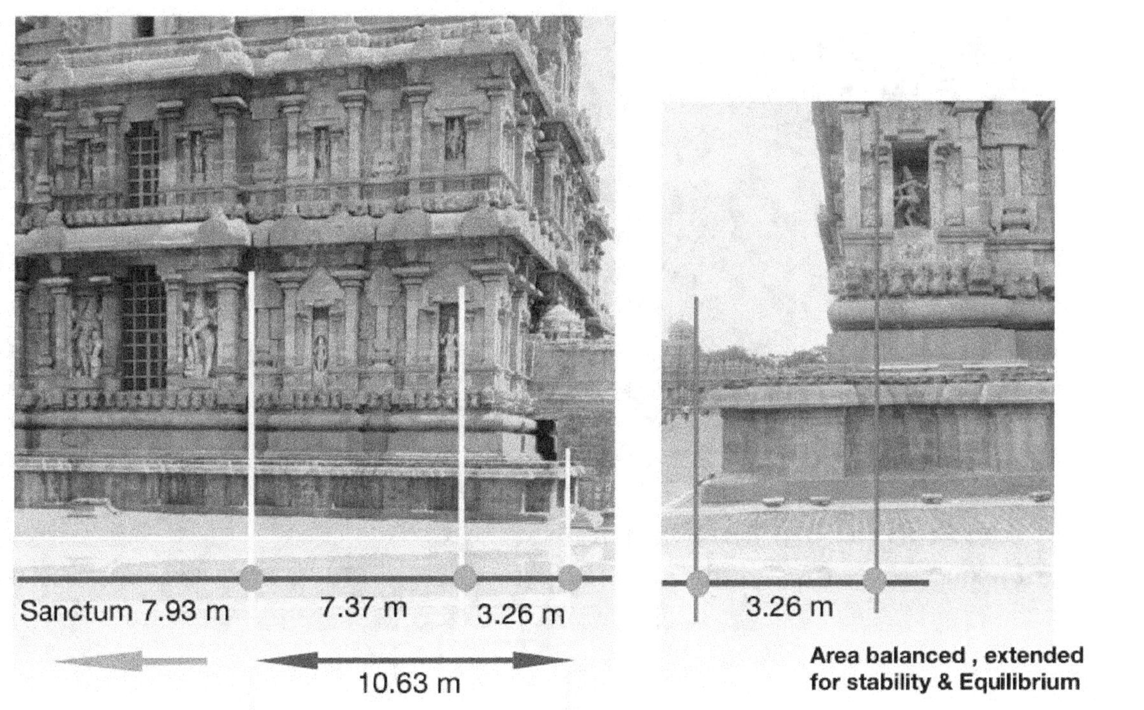

Exercise No 2 & 3

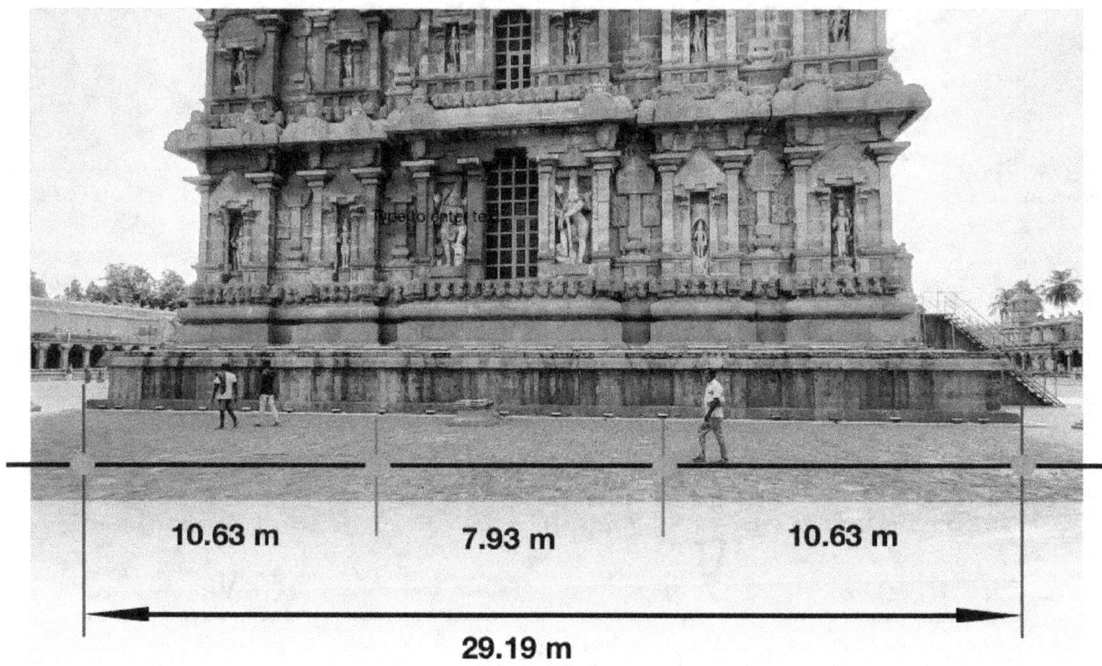

Exercise No 3

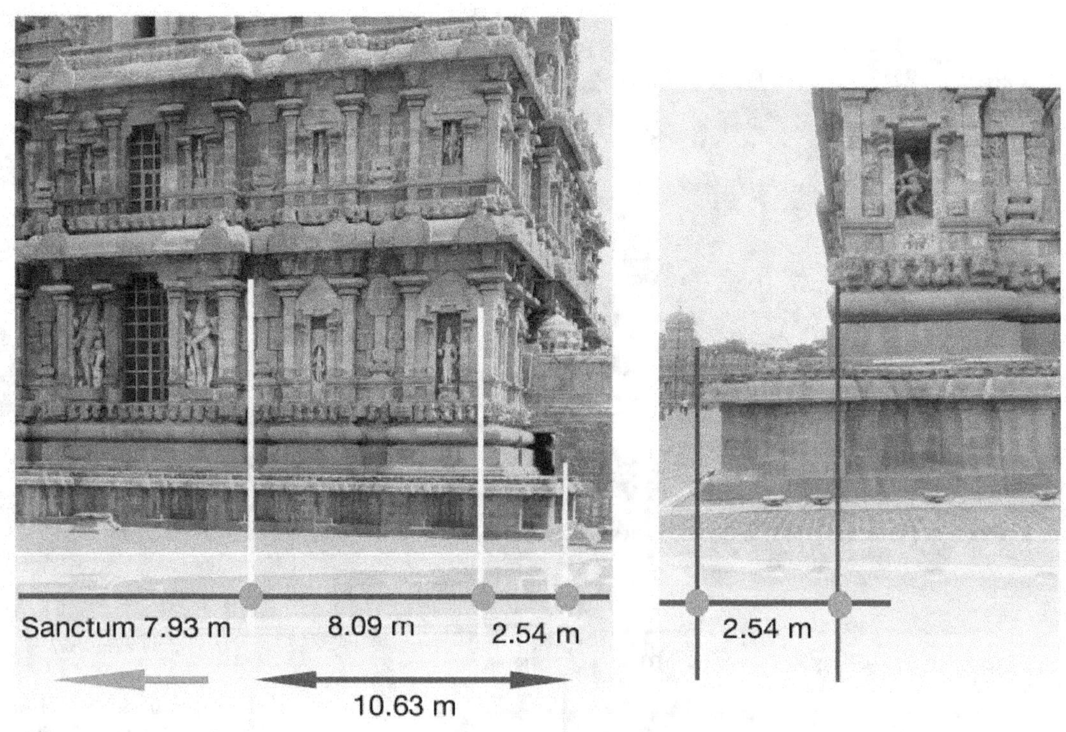

Exercise No 3

7.37 m
2.54 m
10.63 m

2.54 m

3rd Exercise outcome   10.63 m +7.93 m +10.63 m = 29.19 m

RIGHT TRIANGLE - DAM LIKE PROFILE

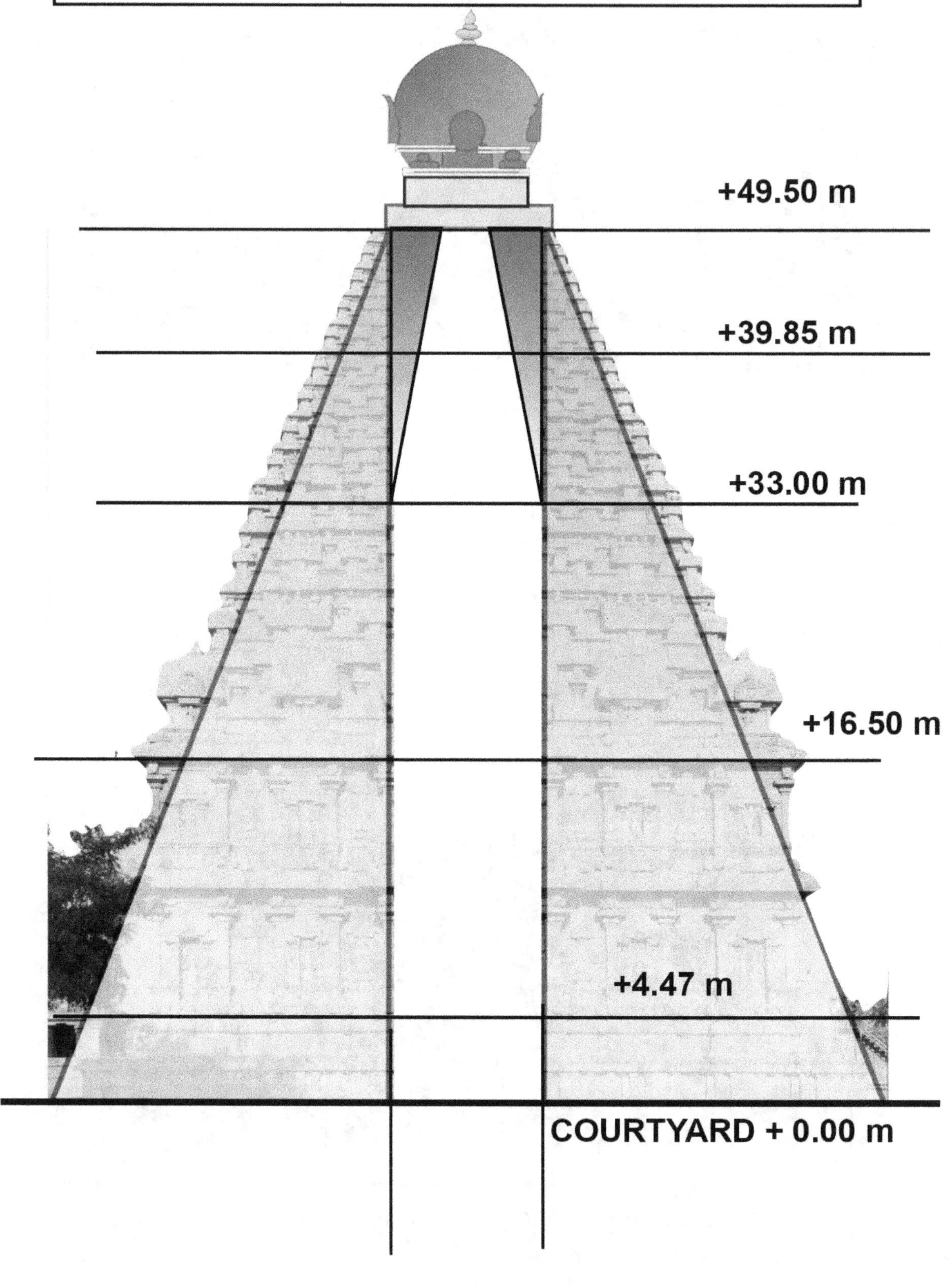

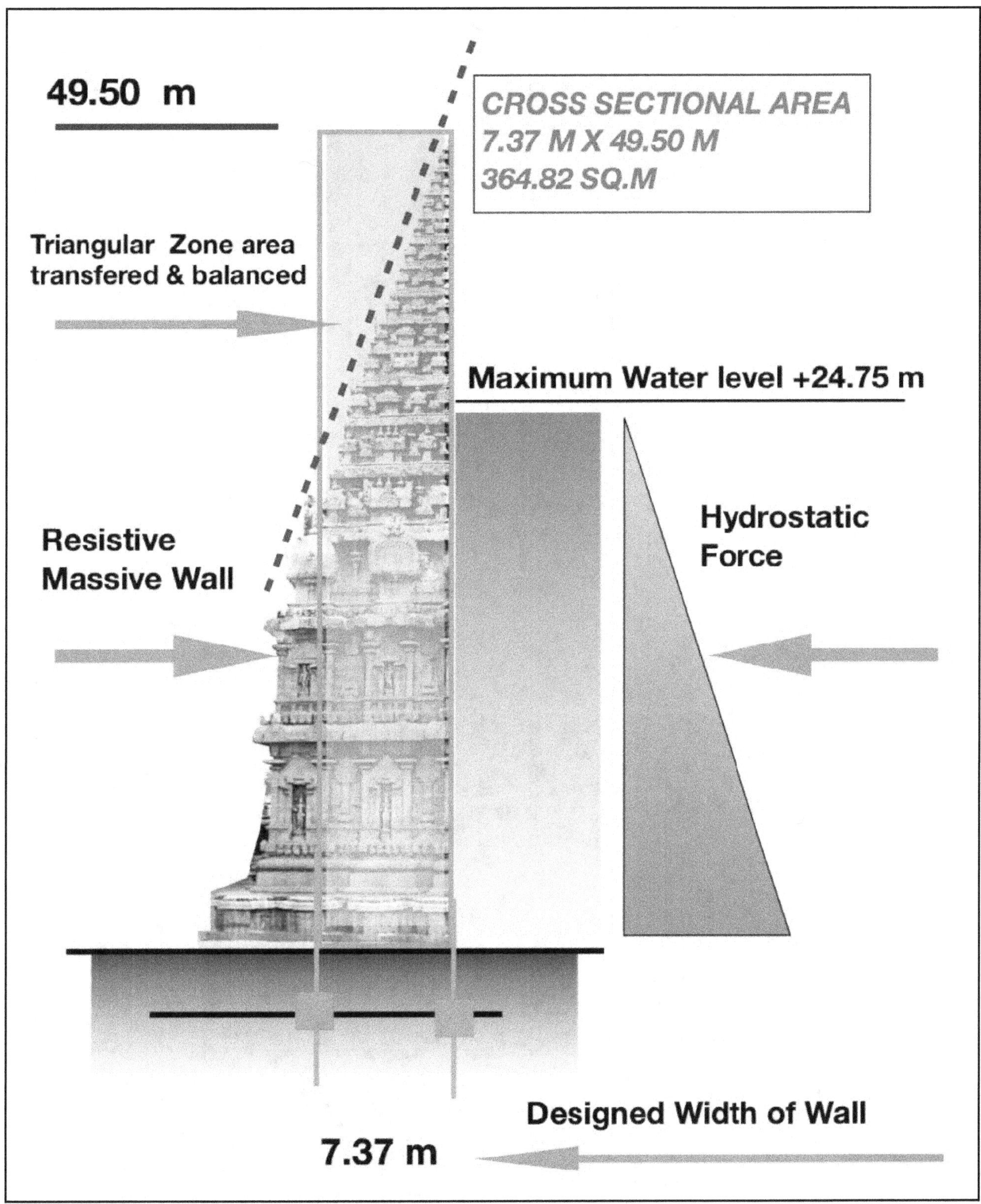

Area w.r.t Designed Wall width

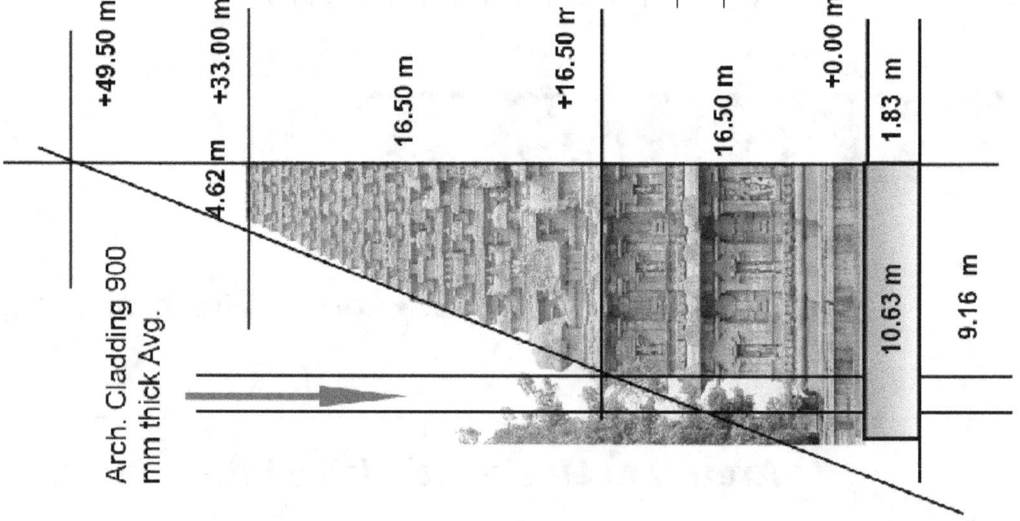

Actual Area Calculation - Exercise No 1							
Foundation Raft	10.63	x	1.83			=	19.45
up to +16.50 m	9.16	x	16.5			=	151.14
above +16.50 m	0.5	x	16.5	x	(4.62+9.16)	=	113.69
Outer Wall Cladding	0.9	x	16.5			=	14.85
TOTAL in Sqm						=	299.13

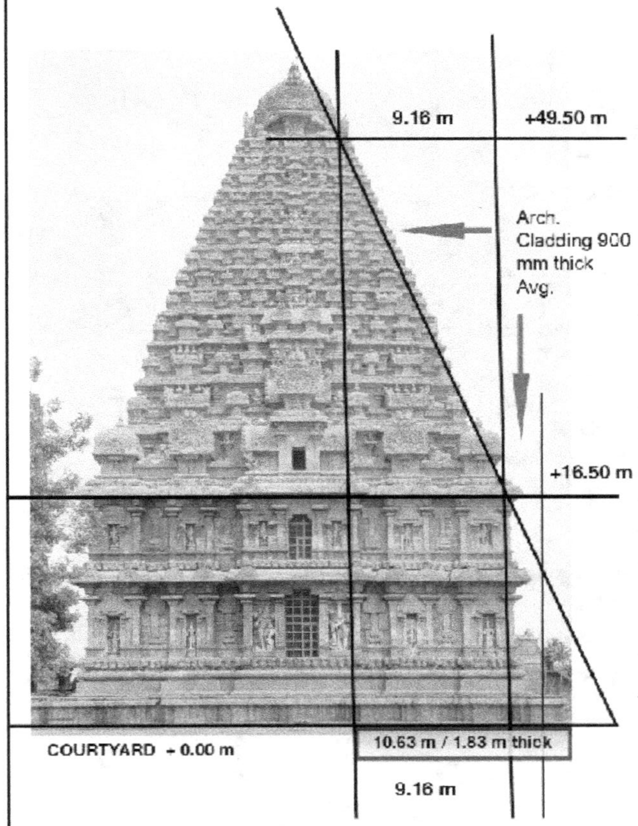

Actual Area Calculation - Exercise No 2

Foundation Raft	10.63	x	1.83		=	19.45
up to +16.50 m	9.16	x	16.5		=	151.14
above +16.50 m	0.5	x	9.16	x 33	=	151.14
Cladding over slope	0.9	x	34.25		=	30.83
Side wall Cladding	0.9	x	16.5		=	14.85
TOTAL in Sqm					=	367.41

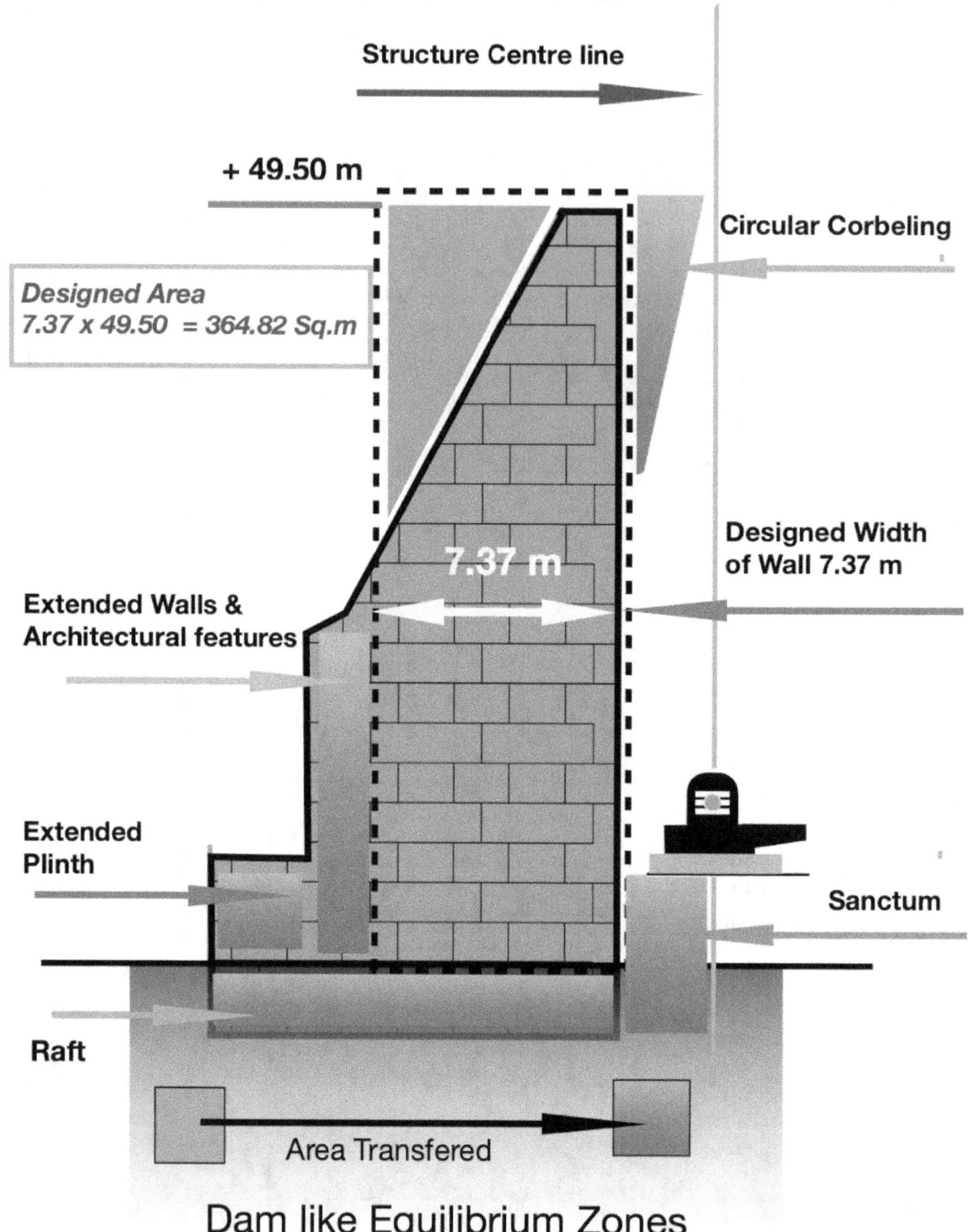

Dam like Equilibrium Zones

ASI Measure

$$M \times g \times B/2 = 1/2 \times \rho \times g \times h \times h \times h/3$$

$$FoS \times (L \times B \times H \times \gamma_{gr}) \times B/2 = FoS \times 1/2 \times \rho \times g \times h \times h \times h/3$$

$$0.9 \times 1 \times B \times (49.50+1.60) \times 2.7 \times 9.81 \times B/2 = 1.40 \times 1/2 \times 1 \times 9.81 \times (31.60+1.60)^3/3$$

$$B \text{ for } 1.56 \, FoS = 11.727$$

$$B \text{ for } 1.50 \, FoS = 11.276$$

$$B = 11.276$$

+ 0.00 m

Raft 1.6 m depth below Courtyard

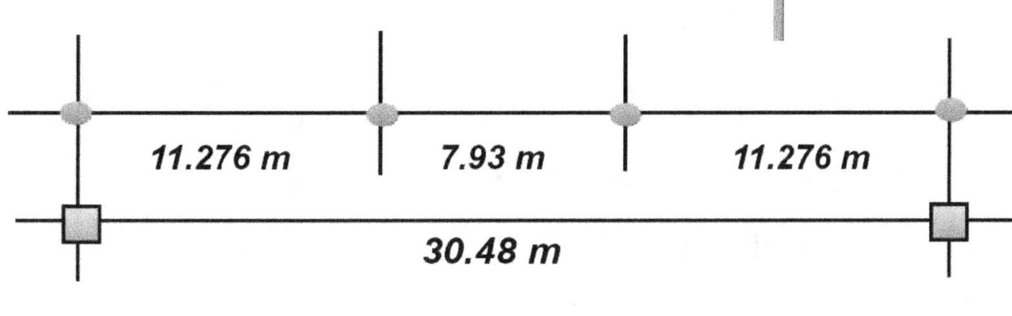

11

Stability

When the structure was designed in the concept and style of a gravity dam, the first and foremost criterion was that there should not be any tension to develop.

The resultant of the forces should pass through within the middle third of the base, with eccentricity less than one-sixth of the width of the base and normal stresses not exceeding the soil's maximum allowable SBC.

The temple construction has been stable for millennia.

If the structure followed the design of a gravity dam, the Chola civil engineers may have applied the Middle Third Rule and other stability assessments to achieve the engineering requirements and assured stability in the construction accordingly.

Analysis

Analysis of a gravity dam's structural stability by an experienced structural design engineer using the analytical technique is described here.

When a cross-section is taken, a right triangle will emerge in about one-half of the cross-section, as shown in the drawings.

Now let us consider a unit length of the wall from one-half of the structure's cross-section.

Step 1: Algebraic Sum of Vertical and Horizontal Forces (ΣV and ΣH)

The first step is to calculate the algebraic sum of all vertical and horizontal forces operating on the structure.

In this scenario, the vertical downward force is the weight of the granite construction for a running metre length, and the horizontal force is the hydrostatic pressure acting laterally on the wall for a running metre length from the maximum water height inside the sanctuary shaft.

There is no uplift pressure to operate against the vertical weight of the structure; hence, it is ignored.

There is also no passive soil pressure to act horizontally against the hydrostatic force that is not considered because the foundation and depth data are not accessible and the structure is analysed only above the courtyard level.

The algebraic sum of the vertical and horizontal forces is calculated and denoted as ΣV and ΣH respectively.

Step 2: Algebraic Sum of Moments of the Forces (ΣMr and ΣMo)

The next step is to find out the algebraic sum of the moments of the forces from the edge of the toe to determine the overturning moment. From the algebraic sum of the moments, the net moment as ΣM and as follows.

$\Sigma M = \Sigma Mr - \Sigma Mo$ where ΣMr and ΣMo are the total resisting and overturning moments respectively.

Step 3: Position of the Resultant Forces from the Toe end (x)

The next requirement is to determine the position of the resultant force R, from the toe end.

$$X = \frac{\Sigma Mr - \Sigma Mo}{\Sigma V}$$

Step 4: Eccentricity (e)

Determine the eccentricity (e) of resultant R from the centre of the base 'b' where b is the base width of the structure.

Eccentricity 'e' = (b/2) - X

Step 5: Normal Stresses (Maximum and Minimum Stress at the Foundation)

The normal stresses at the toe and heel are determined by the following equation:

$$\sigma = \left(\frac{\Sigma V}{b} \right) \times \left(1 \pm \frac{6 \times e}{b} \right)$$

Step 6 Factor of Safety (FoS)

Find out the factor of safety against sliding by the following expression:

$$\text{FoS Sliding} = \frac{\mu \times \Sigma V}{\Sigma H} \quad \text{where } \mu \text{ is the coefficient of friction}$$

Find out the factor of safety against overturning by the following expression:

$$\text{FoS Overtunring} = \frac{\Sigma Mr}{\Sigma Mo}$$

Stability Criteria and Middle third Rule

The eccentricity 'e' shall be less than one-sixth of the base width.

Eccentricity e < (b/6) and the resultant shall pass through within the middle third of the base width.

Reservoir in Full and Empty Conditions

If the structure inside is filled with water to its maximum water level, there will be maximum pressure at the toe, and the resultant will pass towards the toe and close to the outer border of the middle third, ensuring a maximum stabilising moment.

If the structure is empty and there is no water within, the pressure will be highest on the heel side, and the resultant will pass towards the heel to the inner edge of the middle third for stability.

Permissible Stress value

In a dam or retaining-wall design, negative stresses must not be permitted to develop, and the maximum normal stress must be kept within the soil's maximum safe carrying capability or safe bearing capacity (SBC).

The maximum permitted SBC for the limestone rock is 1620 kN/m² and hence the allowable stress must be less than 1620 kN/m².

$\sigma < 1620 \text{ kN/m}^2$

The Final Factor of Safety

For sliding criteria a minimum factor of safety of 1.5 is typically fixed whereas a safety factor of 2 is considered against overturning effect.

FoS sliding ≥ 1.50

FoS overturning ≥ 2

If all of the preceding engineering principles are addressed in the design, it will be firmly established that the structure was designed in the style of a gravity dam by the engineers of the Chola kingdom in order to validate the study findings.

Findings

As shown in the tabulations, the calculations and analyses were performed for both scenarios when the structure inside is filled with water and when the structure is empty.

Exercise A – Reservoir Full Condition (Water inside the Chamber)

When the chamber inside is filled to the maximum water level of +24.75 m, the eccentricity value is 1.77 m, which is exactly equal to b/6 of 1.77 m. The path of the resultant forces is towards the toe and precisely intersects the outer boundary of the inner middle third; this is the maximum permissible eccentricity for no tension at the structure's base, and it does not cross the middle third, making it safe.

The highest developed normal stress at the toe end is 1405 kN/m^2, whereas the minimum stress at the heel is 1.26 kN/m^2. Both readings do not exceed the soil's maximum SBC of 1620 kN/m^2 and are safe.

Finally, the structural design reveals that the factor of safety for sliding failure is 1.62 and for overturning is 2.07, which are greater than the minimum requirements of 1.5 and 2, respectively, and thus the structure will be safe for overall stability.

Exercise B – Reservoir Empty Condition (No Water inside the Chamber)

The eccentricity value in the empty condition, as indicated in the table, is (–) 1.46 m, which is less than the value of b/6, which is 1.77 m. The resultant path is towards the heel to the inner boundary of the middle third, and it is safe because it is well within the middle third.

The heel has the highest developed normal stress of 1250 kN/m^2, whereas the toe has the lowest stress of 121 kN/m^2. Both readings are safe because there is no negative stress development and the maximum does not exceed the soil's maximum SBC of 1620 kN/m^2; hence, the design is safe.

The exact intersection of the eccentricity at the outer edge of the inner middle third is the maximum possible outermost position of the resultant for no tension to develop, which strongly suggests that the Chola engineers attempted to design the structure for the maximum possible stabilising moment by fixing the water level at +24.75 m. However, by keeping the lower water level to the actual operating weight and lift requirement, the eccentricity value can be adjusted and reduced to well within the middle-third limits, making the structure extremely safe.

The results above clearly show that the design and construction were planned in the style of a gravity dam and that all of the empty spaces inside the circumambulatory and the annexe structure were designed for holding such a huge volume of water.

The dam's elementary profile would be a right-angle triangle if it is subjected to horizontal pressure from water and its own weight.

Half of the structure's cross-section is visible here and exactly resembles a right triangle as drawn and displayed in the drawing.

It is clear that the buoyancy has worked in tandem with gravity.

A gravity–buoyancy seesaw lifted the large stones of granite material and the massive weight of Sikhara to the summit, conclusively.

What is the maximum weight that the Chola engineers have lifted, and how did the lifting operation and process go?

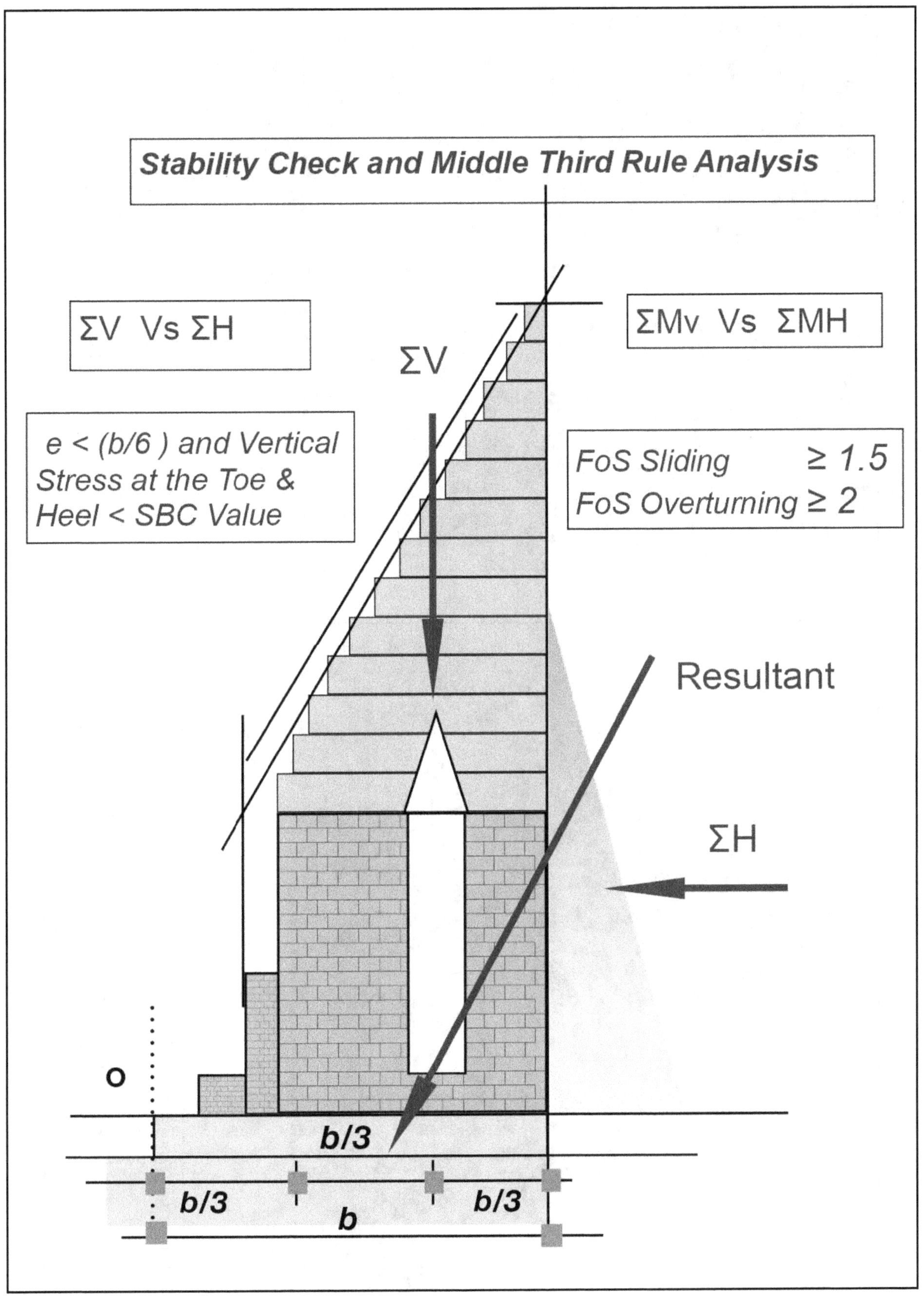

Stability Check and Middle Third Rule Analysis
ΣV Vs ΣH
ΣMv Vs ΣMH
ΣV
e < (b/6) and Vertical Stress at the Toe & Heel < SBC Value
FoS Sliding ≥ 1.5
FoS Overturning ≥ 2
Resultant
ΣH
o
b/3
b/3
b/3
b

Arch. features and Cornice projections from the face of the Wall
Weighted Average - 900 mm thick

Architectural features (Weighted)

Arch. features and Cornice projections from the face of the Wall
Weighted Average - 900 mm thick

Arch. features and Cornice projections from the face of the Wall
Weighted Average - 900 mm thick

Weighted Average thickness of Architectural features from the Main External Wall

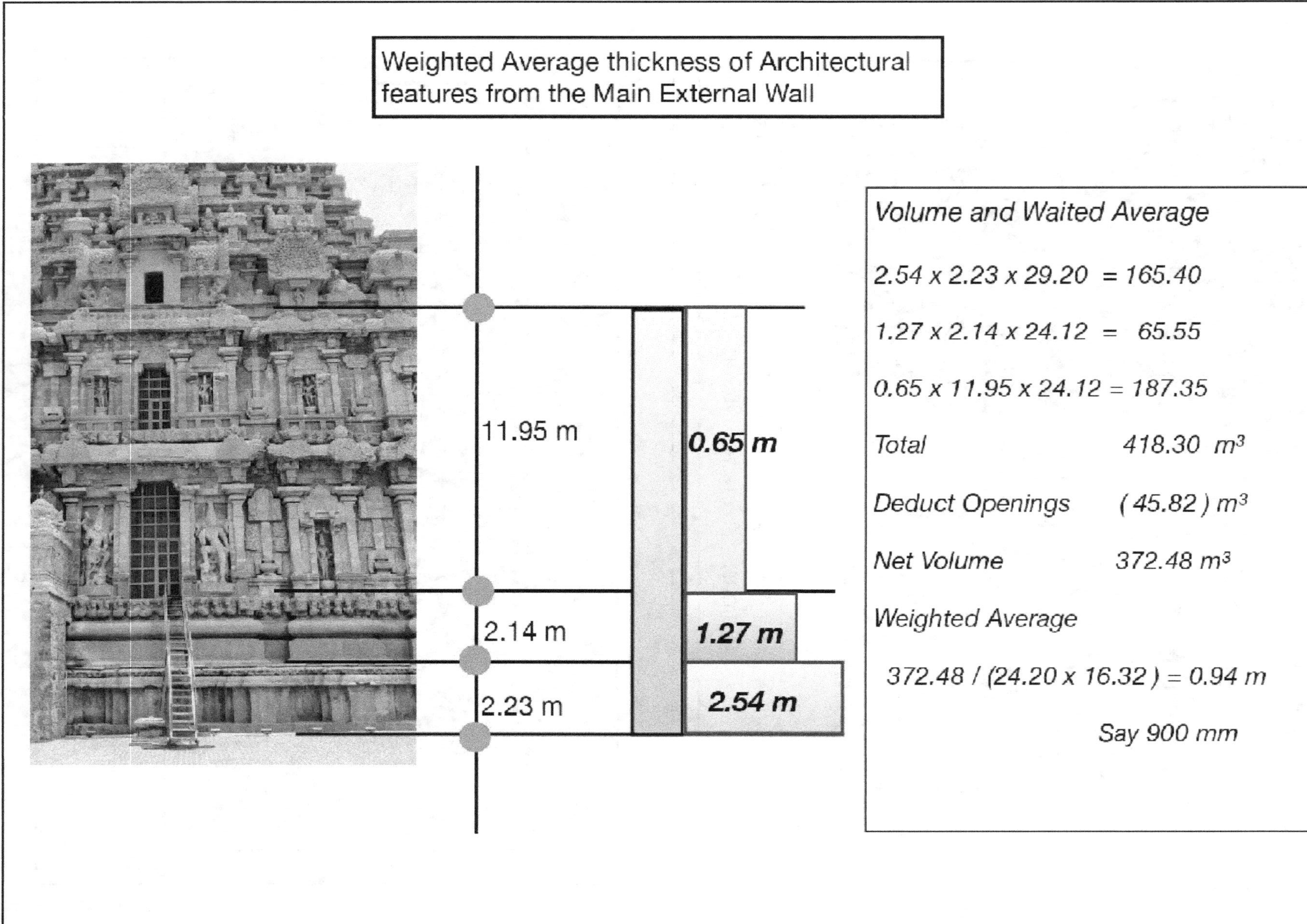

Architectural Features /Projections average thickness

For 2.23 m from Court yard					
Lower block	1	29.20	2.54	2.23	165.39
Deduct lower block voids					
Openings Type 1 - 0.784 x .253	-8	0.78	0.25	1.90	-3.01
Openings Type 2 - (0.784+0.253+0.253) x 0.253	-8	1.29	0.25	1.90	-4.95
Openings Type 3	-8	2.31	0.25	1.90	-8.85
Deduct corner Cutouts	-2	0.81	0.81	1.90	-2.49
Deduct	-1	24.20	0.30	1.27	-9.22
slope Architrave at 1.91 m level	1	27.45	0.13	0.36	1.22
Top Horizontal Edge Flower Architrave - 230 mm wide	1	41.39	0.12	0.30	1.43
Top Edge 1 " x 6 " band	1	41.39	0.025	0.15	0.16
From +2.23 m to +4.37					
Upper block	1	24.20	1.27	2.14	65.77
Deduct 18" non projected panels	1	15.24	0.45	2.14	-14.68
Deduct Voids between panels	4	0.45	0.60	2.43	-2.62
From +4.37 m to 16.32 m					
Central panel	1	6.56	11.95	0.90	70.55
Other panels	1	11.08	11.95	0.45	59.58
Intermediate panels architectural design	4	1.50	11.80	0.05	3.54
Add Cornice	2	25.10	0.84	0.84	35.42
Add corince top Horizontal	2	25.10	0.84	0.30	12.65
Total Volumen m³					369.89
Average projection for 24.11 x 16.32					
369.89 / (24.11 x 16.32). = 0.940 m					
Weighted average thickness of Architectural features up to +16.32 m		Say	900 mm		

Average projection of corner pendentive and extended column from the face of the sanctum wall

Sanctum size	7.93 m x 7.93 m		
Diagonal of the sanctum	$\sqrt{(7.93^2 + 7.93^2)}$	11.21	m
Deduct slab outer to outer		-8.51	
Projected length		2.70	
Projected length per corner	2.70 / 2 = 1.35 m		
Triangular platform	1/2 x 2.70 x 1.35		
Area of triangle	1/2 x 2.70 x 1.35	1.82	
Average volume for 6.85 m height	1.82 x 50% x 6.85	6.23	
Extended platform (16.50 m-6.85 m) high	(16.50 - 6.85) x 1.82	17.56	
Total volume for the chamber length of 7.93 m		23.80	
Volume per rm	23.80 / 7.93	3.00	
Average width of projections from the face of the wall	3.17 /(16.50 m)	0.182	m
	say	**180**	**mm**

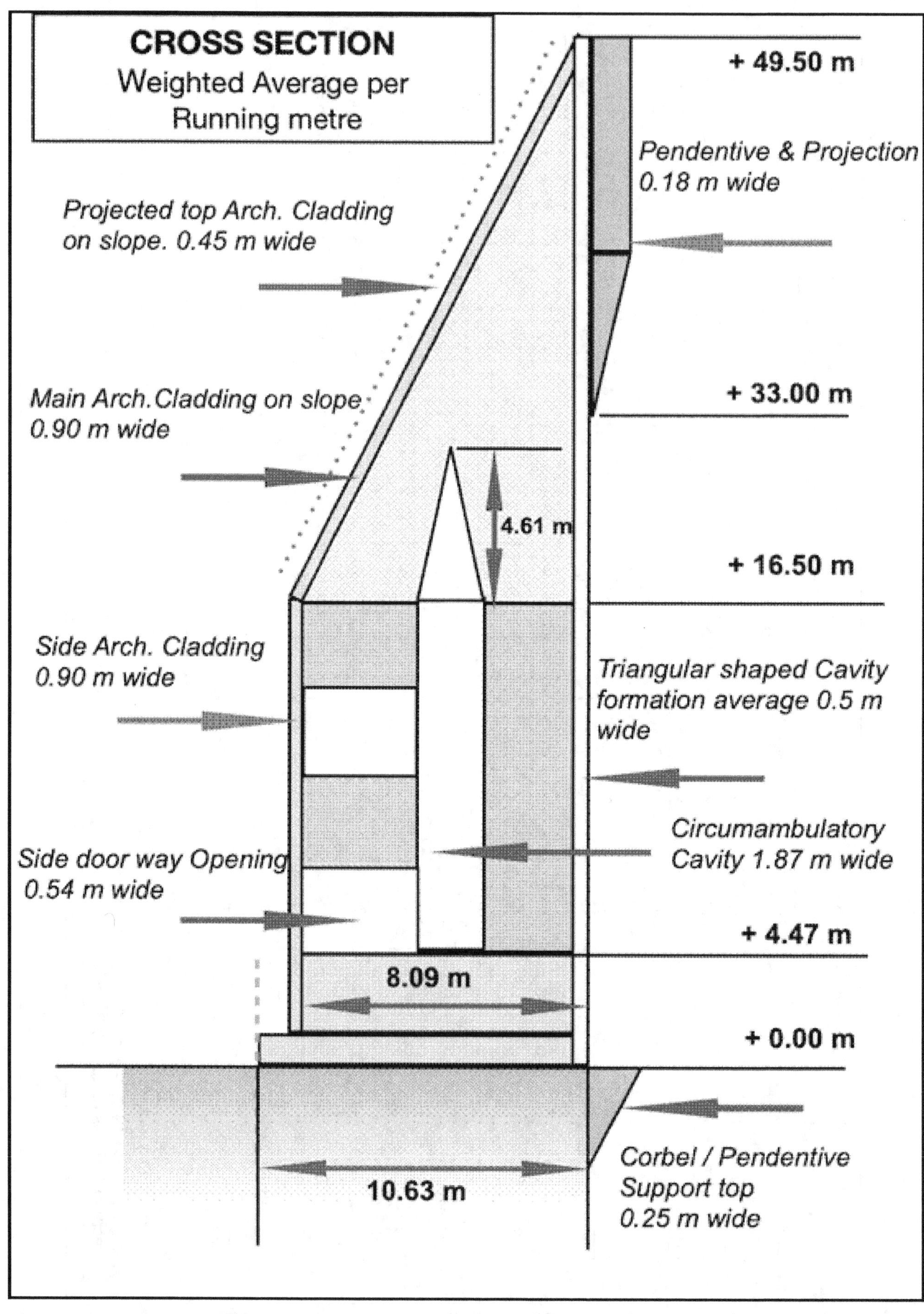
CROSS SECTION
Weighted Average per Running metre
Projected top Arch. Cladding on slope. 0.45 m wide
Main Arch. Cladding on slope. 0.90 m wide
Side Arch. Cladding 0.90 m wide
Side door way Opening 0.54 m wide
Pendentive & Projection 0.18 m wide
Triangular shaped Cavity formation average 0.5 m wide
Circumambulatory Cavity 1.87 m wide
Corbel / Pendentive Support top 0.25 m wide
+ 49.50 m
+ 33.00 m
+ 16.50 m
+ 4.47 m
+ 0.00 m
4.61 m
8.09 m
10.63 m

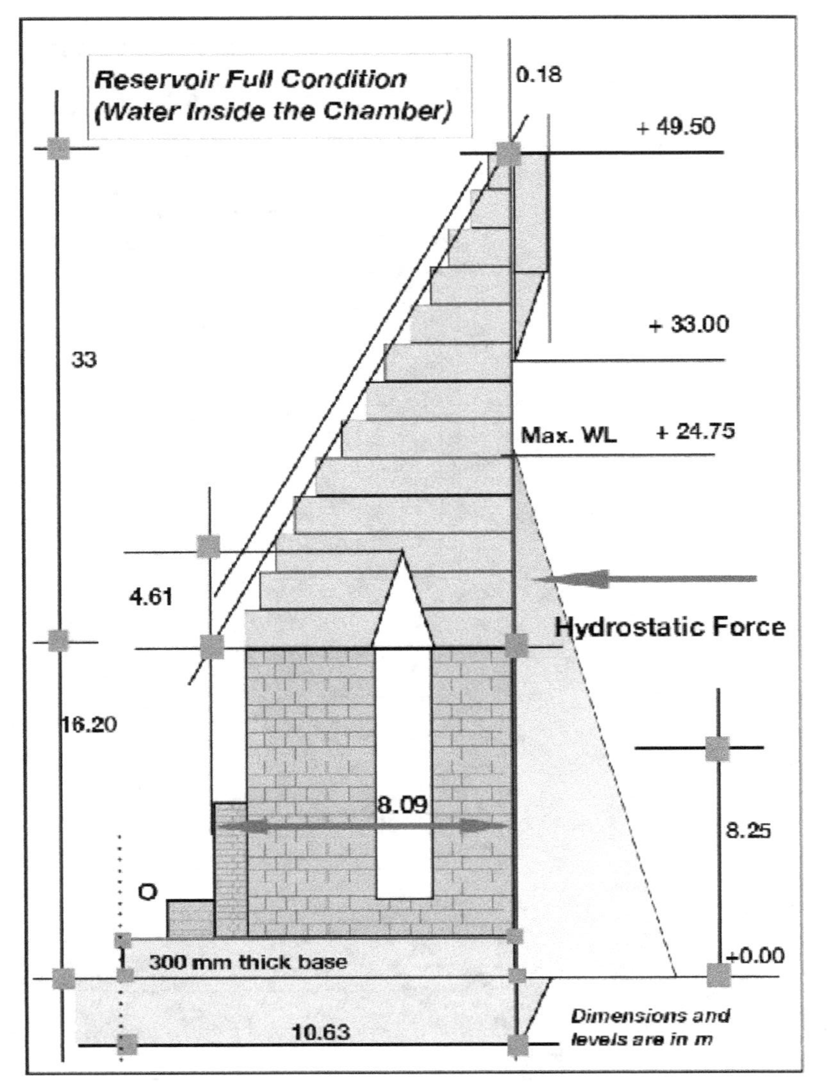

Reservoir Full Condition
(Water Inside the Chamber)
0.18
+ 49.50
+ 33.00
Max. WL + 24.75
33
4.61
Hydrostatic Force
16.20
8.09
8.25
O
300 mm thick base
+0.00
10.63
Dimensions and levels are in m

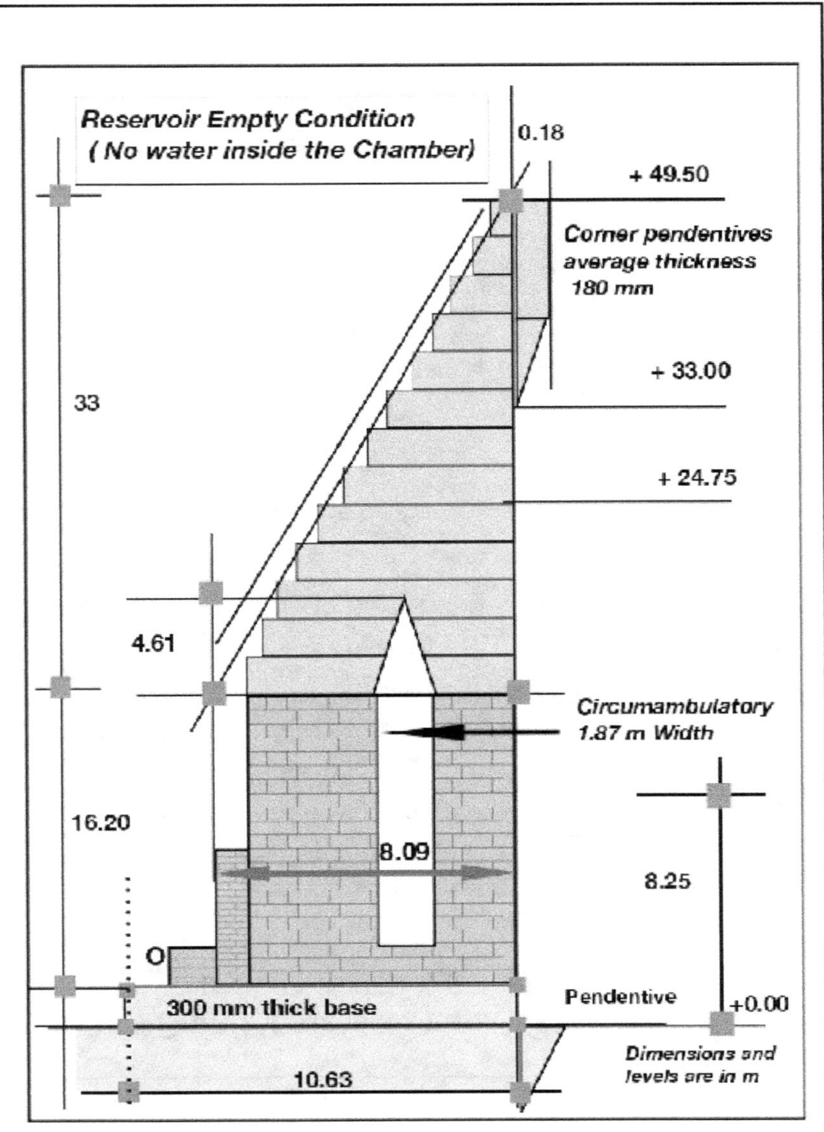

Reservoir Empty Condition
(No water inside the Chamber)
0.18
+ 49.50
Corner pendentives average thickness 180 mm
+ 33.00
+ 24.75
33
4.61
Circumambulatory 1.87 m Width
16.20
8.09
8.25
O
300 mm thick base
Pendentive
+0.00
10.63
Dimensions and levels are in m

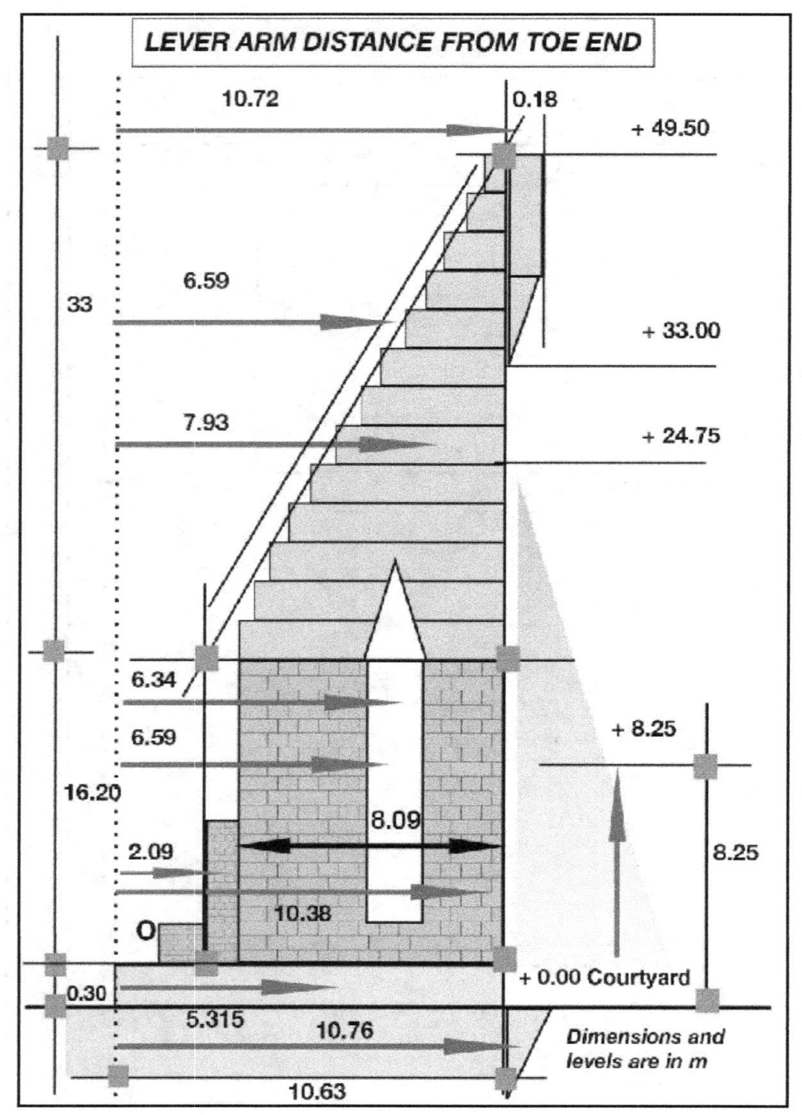

Data for stability analysis

Sl no	Description		Data	Remarks
1	Acceleration due to gravity	g	$9.81\,\text{m/sec}^2$	
2	Density of water	ρ_w	$1000\ \text{kg}/m^3$	
3	Density of granite	ρ_{Gr}	$2700\ \text{kg}/m^3$	
4	Specific weight of water. $\gamma_w = \rho_w \times g$	γ_w	$1000 \times 9.81\ \text{m/sec}^2$ $= 9810\ \text{kgm}/\text{sec}^2$ $= 9.81\ \text{kN}/m^3$	$1\ \text{kg m}/\text{sec}^2$ $= 1\ \text{N}$ and $1000\ \text{N} = 1\text{kN}$
5	Specific weight of granite. $\gamma_{Gr} = \rho_{Gr} \times g$	γ_{gr}	$2.7 \times 9.81\ \text{kN per } m^3$	
6	Total height of wall	H	49.50 m	
7	Base width	b	10.63 m	
8	Sanctum inner width		7.93 m	
9	Maximum water level	h	Ex. no 1 - 24.75 m and Ex. no 2 - empty	
10	Length of wall	L	Per running meter considered for analysis	
11	Coefficient of friction for granite	μ	0.65	

Forces and moments - Reservoir full Condition and maximum water level +24.75 m - Exercise A

Description	Force calculation	FV in kN	FH in kN	Lever arm m	Resisting moments in kN m	Overturning moments in kN m	C/s area in m²
Vertical forces							
Base slab	1m x10.63 x 0.30 x 26.49	84.48		5.32	448.99		3.19
Structure above from +0.30 to +16.50 m lvl	1 m x (8.09) x16.20 x 26.49	3471.73		6.59	22861.32		131.06
Structure above 16.50 m to +49.50 m lvl	1m x 1/2 x (8.09) x 33 x 26.49	3536.02		7.93	28052.29		133.49
Cladding over sloped Vimana Surface	1 m x 33.98 x 0.9 x 26.49	810.12		6.59	5334.62		30.58
Cladding up to +16.50 on outer vert. wall	1m x 16.20 x 0.9 x 26.49	386.22		2.09	807.21		14.58
Less circumambulatory opening- rectangular	1m x 1.87 m x10.98 m x 26.49	-543.91		6.34	-3445.66		-20.53
Less circumambulatory opening - triangular	1m x 1/2 x 1.87 m x 4.61 m x 26.49	-114.18		6.34	-723.34		-4.31
Less triangular cavity inside the Wall	1 m x 0.50 x 49.50 x 26.49	-655.63		10.38	-6805.41		-24.75
Water weight over cavity from +0.00 m lvl	1 m x 0.50 x 24.75 x 9.81	121.40		10.38	1260.12		
Corner pendentives and projection above + 33.00 m lvl	1 m x 0.18 x 16.50 x 26.49	78.68		10.72	843.40		2.97
Water weight over pendentive top from +0.00 m lvl	1 m x 0.25 x 24.75 x 9.81	60.70		10.76	653.13		
Less side door openings	1 m x (2.90 x11.80X1.98) x 75% / 7.93 x 26.49	-168.79		3.95	-666.74		-3.24
Top arch. additional projection on sloped vimana's surface	1 m x 0.45 x 33.98 x 26.49	405.06		6.59	2667.31		15.29
Lateral hydrostatic force	1m x 0.50 x 9.81 x 24.75 x 24.75		3004.62	8.25		24788.11	
Total		7471.88	3004.62		51287.24	24788.11	278.33

Forces and moments - Reservoir empty condition and no water inside the chamber +24.75 m - Exercise B

Description	Force calculation	FV in kN	FH in kN	Lever arm m	Resisting moments in kN m	Overturning moments in kN m	C/s area in m^2
Vertical forces							
Base slab	1m x10.63 x 0.30 x 26.49	84.48		5.32	448.99		3.19
Structure above from +0.30 to +16.50 m lvl	1 m x (8.09) x16.20 x 26.49	3471.73		6.59	22861.32		131.06
Structure above 16.50 m to +49.50 m lvl	1m x 1/2 x (8.09) x 33 x 26.49	3536.02		7.93	28052.41		133.49
Cladding over sloped vimana surface	1 m x 33.98 x 0.9 x 26.49	810.12		6.59	5334.62		30.58
Cladding up to +16.50 on outer vert. wall	1m x 16.20 x 0.9 x 26.49	386.22		2.09	807.21		14.58
Less circumambulatory opening- Rectangular	1m x 1.87 m x10.98 m x 26.49	-543.91		6.34	-3445.66		-20.53
Less circumambulatory opening - triangular	1m x 1/2 x 1.87 m x 4.61 m x 26.49	-114.18		6.34	-723.34		-4.31
Less triangular cavity inside the wall	1 m x 0.50 x 49.50 x 26.49	-655.63		10.38	-6805.41		-24.75
Water weight over cavity from +0.00 m lvl	1 m x 0.50 x 24.75 x 9.81	0.00		10.38	0.00		
Corner pendentives and projection above + 33.00 m lvl	1 m x 0.18 x 16.50 x 26.49	78.68		10.72	843.40		2.97
Water weight over pendentive top from +0.00 m lvl	1 m x 0.25 x 24.75 x 9.81	0.00		10.76	0.00		
Less side door openings	1 m x (2.90 x11.80X1.98) x 75% / 7.93 x 26.49	-168.79		3.95	-666.74		-3.24
Top arch . additional projection on sloped vimana's surface	1 m x 0.45 x 33.98 x 26.49	405.06		6.59	2667.31		15.29
Lateral hydrostatic force	1m x 0.50 x 9.81 x 24.75 x 24.75		0.00	8.25		0.00	
Total		7289.78	0.00		49374.11	0.00	278.33

Exercise A - Reservoir in full condition (Water inside the chamber up to +24.75 m)

Width of the base	10.63	m	
$\sum V$ - Algebraic sum of vertical forces	7471.88	kN	
$\sum H$ - Algebraic sum of horizontal forces	3004.62	kN	
$\sum Mr$ - Algebraic sum of resisting moments	51287.24	kN m	
$\sum Mo$ - Algebraic sum of overturning moments	24788.11	kN m	
Resultant distance $x=(\sum Mr - \sum Mo)/(\sum V)$	3.55	m	
One half of the width of the base b/2	5.32	m	
One sixth of the width of the base b/6	1.77	m	
Eccentricity e = b/2 - x	1.77	m	Maximum
Eccentricity 'e' should be less than b/6 . The resultant precisely intersects the outer border but does not cross the maximum limit			Safe
Maximum stress at toe			
Pn maximum $= \sum V/(b) \times (1+6e/b)$	1404.55	< 1620	kN/m ^{2}
			Safe
Minimum stress at heel			
Pn minimum $= \sum V/(b) \times (1-6e/6)$	1.26	< 1620	kN/m ^{2}
			Safe
FOS for sliding $= \mu \times \sum V/(\sum H)$	1.62	> 1.50	Safe
FOS for overturning$= \sum Mr / \sum Mo$	2.07	> 2	Safe

Exercise B - Reservoir empty condition (No water inside the chamber + 24.75 m)

Width of the base	10.63	m	
$\sum V$ - Algebraic sum of vertical forces	7289.78	kN	
$\sum H$ - Algebraic sum of horizontal forces	0	kN	
$\sum Mr$ - Algebraic sum of resisting moments	49374.11	kN m	
$\sum Mo$ - Algebraic sum of overturning moments	0	kN m	
Resultant distance $x=(\sum Mr - \sum Mo)/(\sum V)$	6.77	m	
One half of the width of the base b/2	5.32	m	
One sixth of the width of the base b/6	1.77	m	
Eccentricity e = b/2 - x	-1.46	m	Maximum
Eccentricity 'e' is less than b/6 and hence safe	1.46 < 1.77		Safe
Maximum stress at toe			
Pn maximum $= \sum V/(b) \times (1+6e/b)$	121.39	< 1620	kN/m ^{2}
			Safe
Minimum stress at heel			
Pn minimum $= \sum V/(b) \times (1-6e/6)$	1250.16	< 1620	kN/m ^{2}
			Safe

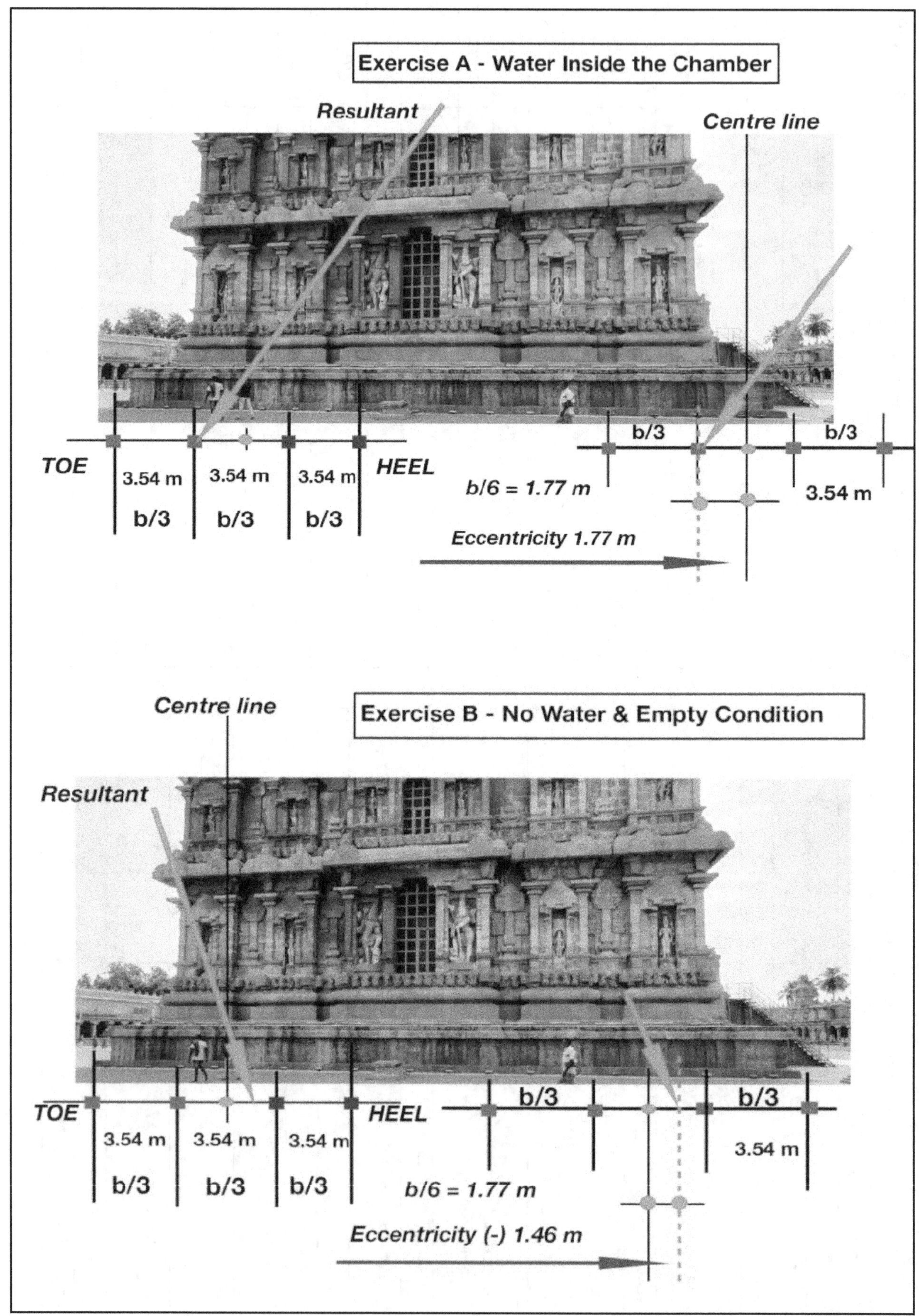

Exercise A - Water Inside the Chamber
Resultant
Centre line
TOE
HEEL
3.54 m
3.54 m
3.54 m
b/3
b/3
b/3
b/3
b/3
b/6 = 1.77 m
3.54 m
Eccentricity 1.77 m

Centre line
Exercise B - No Water & Empty Condition
Resultant
TOE
HEEL
3.54 m
3.54 m
3.54 m
b/3
b/3
b/3
b/3
b/3
b/6 = 1.77 m
3.54 m
Eccentricity (-) 1.46 m

12

Novel Strategy

The square sanctum chamber was dug and extended to a depth of 66 m below the courtyard floor as an underground well, as explained earlier.

Before laying the granite raft foundation and raising the plinth and superstructure, the deep well must have been dug and kept ready. It was extended to 66 m below the plinth as an underground well and projected 49.5 m above the courtyard floor as a vertical sanctum shaft.

To sustain the soil pressure, the deep well's wall had to be solid granite masonry. Granite masonry walls may not be necessary if the soil beneath is of a good mass of rock classification, and if a well has been dug and extended through the large mass of rock strata to form a well, the surrounding solid rock should have served as a wall for the well.

Most likely, the main water canal followed a path that ran alongside the temple's fence as a ground-level water source. If the main canal had been linked by forming a channel at ground level, the needed water could have been drawn from the main canal. This ground-level water source must have been connected to the sanctum well, making it easy for water to flow in by gravity.

The underneath well had both a surface-level water inlet and a drainage outlet at mid-depth or below mid-depth of the well to drain and let off huge volumes of water as and when needed for repeated cycles of operation. Monitoring and control equipment like sluice gates and the like must have been installed in the ground-level channel entry and the outlet location to regulate the flow as required.

As seen in the temple layout design, the Siva Ganga Tank, which is deeper, may have been connected to the deep drainage outlet inside the well to receive a huge volume of water released from the well after each operation. Perhaps the Siva Ganga Tank has deeper drainage outlets beneath the current bed level, connecting to still deeper points away from the tank, to efficiently drain out the large volume of water before each cycle.

The entire system and novel technique adopted from the ancient Tamil engineers were aimed at the optimal utilisation of available natural resources.

The procedure and operation from the engineers were brilliant, easy, and effortless, as elaborately displayed and explained in the sketches and drawings for a complete understanding.

Assuming the vestibule and circumambulatory vacant spaces had been filled with a significant volume of water and reserved ready, the total combined volume is nearly 3535 m³, as calculated and arrived at earlier in Chapter 7, "Cavities."

Size of the Float

The selected wood for the flotation device has a density of 500 kg/m³, which is half the density of water. Gravity pulls half of its volume inside the water when submerged by displacing the equivalent volume of water, which is 50%, while the other half floats above the water's surface. The displaced water moves around the float sides, and its weight is equal to the weight of the wooden flotation device.

The hardwood floating system is long and cylindrical, with a diameter less than the sanctum dimension of 7.93 m, which fits neatly into the 7.93 m × 7.93 m square sanctum well; the enclosed drawings, sketches, and images in detail at the end of this chapter can be referred to side-by-side for a clear and better understanding.

The inner wall of the sanctum must have four triangular vertical cavity formations to secure each projected corner of the Sikhara base for the unit's unrestricted upward movement, as previously computed and explained. Taking into account the diagonal length of the Sikhara's square base, its projection beyond the square sanctum dimension of 7.93 m inside the triangular slot, and clearances from the face of the wall for unrestricted vertical movement, each slot requires approximately 3.88 m², say 4 m², and the total cavity area is 4 × 4 = 16 m², which is 25% of the sanctum's plan area.

Because the selected wood for the flotation system has half the density of water, the space around the float requires a minimum of 50% of the sanctum's area to accommodate the displaced volume of water caused by its weight while sinking.

The sanctum measures 7.93 m x 7.93 m (62.88 m²). 50% of 62.88 m² equals 31.44 m², and the four triangular cavities have already contributed to an area of 16 m². The remaining empty space inside the sanctum to be allocated is 31.44–16 = 15.44 m².

The top plan area of the float is the remaining 47.44 m² to be fixed, which is the difference between the sanctum area of 62.88 m² and the vacant space inside 15.44 m².

47.44 m² denotes the plan area of the float.

When the float is considered to be a long square, its side is the square root of 47.44 m² and equals 6.89 m, and when it is considered to be of a long cylindrical shape, its diameter is 7.77 m.

$3.14 \times d^2/4 = 47.44$ m², where 'd' equals 7.77 m.

The diagonal length of the 6.89 m × 6.89 m square float is 9.74 m, and it cannot be rotated horizontally because it exceeds the inner dimension of the sanctum chamber, 7.93 m.

The 7.77 m circular diameter can fit inside the 7.93 m × 7.93 m square chambers with 80 mm clearance from the wall face, allowing for unrestricted vertical movement, and the Chola engineers must have designed the size accordingly.

Novel Technique

Assuming the entire Sikhara unit has been shifted and moved into the sanctum inside and mounted on the wooden flotation system's deck with its four corners properly aligned and fitted into the triangular cavities already formed in the sanctum's inner wall during construction, as shown in the figure, the four triangular cavity construction had just enough space around the wall surface for the corners to glide vertically without being obstructed.

The Sikhara base is mounted on the float by coinciding its base with the level of the courtyard floor, +0.00 m level. The entire Sikhara unit here could have been a single monolith block or an airtight assembled unit kept ready for the vertical upward movement now as a total single unit.

How could the huge, large-dimensional Sikhara enter the sanctum after the walls were built and the superstructure was raised to 49.50 m in height?

While this important doubt and concern can be discussed and resolved later, let us now focus on the main lifting process that Chola engineers might have employed.

The long cylindrical wooden floating device is 7.77 m in diameter, 66 m high, and has a 3,128 m³ volume of wood. The density of selected wood for the flotation device is 500 kg/m³, which is half the density of water. When submerged inside the well vertically, gravity pulls half of its volume (1564 m³) inside the water, while the other half (33 m) floats above the water's surface. In other words, before it begins to float, the float sinks naturally by displacing 1564 m³ of water equivalent to its weight.

As a result, before gaining buoyancy, the well should have at least 1564 m³ extra free volume to receive and accommodate the equivalent displaced volume of water.

When a well measures 7.93 m × 7.93 m square in size, how can this extra volume of space be created?

Chola engineers have used their superior intelligence to make their plans.

We previously computed and explained that the inner wall of the sanctum must have four triangular cavities to secure each projected corner of the Sikhara base for unrestricted upward movement and each cavity requires roughly 4 m² area and the overall area is 4 × 4 = 16 m².

The engineers designed and extended the four triangular cavity formations in the first half of the 66 m (up to −33 m) in the underground shaft side walls to accommodate the requirement of 1564 m³ additional volume, while the rest of it below could have been a 7.93 m × 7.93 m square chambers without any cavity construction.

The volume of the four cavities in the first half of the 33 m is 16 m² × 33 m = 528 m³, and the shortage quantity of 1564−528 = 1036 m³ has been designed to occupy around the float inside the chamber for the full height at 15.70 m² × 66 m = 1036 m³, indicating that the extended cavities were designed to match the magnitude of the buoyancy as well as the free vertical movement of the corners of the square. For easy vertical movement of the corners up to +49.5 m height, the four triangular-spaced construction provided in the inner wall needed to be extended to the full height of the Vimana superstructure.

The floor area ratio between the sanctum and the circumambulatory, which includes the spaces for the triangular slots, is calculated and shown in the table.

According to the floor area ratio shown above, the circumambulatory floor area was planned and designed by the Chola engineers to be twice as large as the sanctum.

Before the main lifting process begins, the cylindrical float is erected inside the open free well, and water is allowed to enter the well from a ground-level water inlet that connects to the main canal running along the side of the temple layout. The water fills around the float and inside the cavities, and the float is fully submerged until the water rises to the courtyard level.

So far, gravity flow from the ground-level source has raised the water to the level of the courtyard floor. Water cannot rise above this level due to gravity, and no open spaces are left inside the well to receive any further flow. The bottom level of the float is (−) 66 m, while the top level corresponds to the courtyard base level (+) 0.00 m.

The volume required to fill the empty spaces surrounding the float up to the courtyard level is 1564 m³. The weight of the filled-up volume of water equals the weight of the float; the float's weight has just replaced the equivalent volume of water; at this point, the float is about to gain momentum and experience buoyancy.

The float, on the other hand, cannot move any higher because it has only displaced the water equivalent to its weight and has not yet gained the additional buoyant force required to move up along with Sikhara's massive weight. The massive weight of the Sikhara is mounted on the deck, exerting enormous downward pressure on the float, the magnitude of which is unknown and needs to be determined. For further upward movement, the system requires pressured water to flow in from higher elevations to replace the equivalent volume occupied by the wooden float.

So far, filling up to the courtyard level has been as simple as opening the sluice gate at the ground-level inlet and letting the water pour down into the well effortlessly using gravitational force without consuming any volume from the higher-level reserved storage of circumambulatory cavities and rectangular tanks in the annexe building.

The sluice gate at the ground level is closed when the water reaches the courtyard level, and the Sikhara, which is mounted over the float at the courtyard level for upward movement, is ready.

To gain buoyancy and raise the float above the courtyard level along with the massive weight of the Sikhara, the system requires an additional volume of water equal to the total combined weight of the Sikhara and the wooden float.

How can the additional water volume and weight of the Sikhara be determined?

The total storage reserved volume for the entire operation and subsequent use is nearly 3535 m³, which is the combined volume of the circumambulatory and annexe rectangular hall free spaces, as shown in the drawing and illustrated in the previous calculation.

Assume the Sikhara is not mounted on the float and the wooden float is empty to observe its vertical movement from the courtyard base to the Vimana's top, as shown in **Figure 1.**

Figure 2 shows that the well around the float has been filled with 1564 m³ of water from a ground-level water source as a displaced volume equal to the float's weight, and the float is about to gain buoyancy to act in the opposite direction of gravity.

Figure 3 depicts the first stage of operation, which allows a 1,564 m³ volume of water from the reserved storage of the annexe or circumambulatory storage halls to flow down into the well, equivalent to 50% of the float's volume.

When 1564 m³ of water pours down with high pressure into the well, it attempts to occupy the equivalent volume of the wooden float by lifting it from within the well, and the ascending begins, raising the float's top to reach +33 m for its equilibrium from the courtyard base, leaving the balance 33 m beneath inside the well because the courtyard level is one-half for the float. This means that the float's top rises to +33 m and its bottom rises from (−) 66 m to (−) 33 m.

The remaining storage at this stage is 3535–1564 = 1971 m³, and the purpose of this preliminary trial is to observe the float's vertical movement when it is empty and not carrying any weight.

When the weight of the Sikhara is mounted on the float's top, there are three conditions that must be met for the final lifting and erection to achieve equilibrium at +49.50 m.

1. When the total height of the float is 66 m, 50% of the float's height must be maintained by coinciding with the level of +16.50 m.
2. The floating deck's top carries the massive Sikhara or any larger weight as per the design to achieve equilibrium by coinciding with the level of (+) 49.50 m.
3. The most important factor to consider here is that the structure wall construction was designed to withstand a maximum permissible hydrostatic pressure from a normal operating water level of +24.75 m as per stability check and analysis, so the maximum water level that can be allowed to rise inside the sanctum is only +24.75. This must be strictly adhered to meet safety and design standards.

The massive Sikhara or any designed weight should be lifted from +0.00 m level and installed in equilibrium at +49.50 m level by utilising the available water within the remaining 1971 m³ storage by strictly adhering to and meeting the above three conditions.

How much height does this 1971 m³ add to the water level inside the sanctum from the courtyard level (+0.00 m)?

The entire sanctum measures 78.88 m², including the four triangular vertical cavities formed in the inner walls to allow the corners for easy upward movement and each running metre height will consume a volume of 78.88 m³.

When the remaining storage volume of 1971 m³ is allowed to fill inside the sanctuary area at a rate of 78.88 m³ per running metre height, the water level approaches + 24.98 m, which is very close to the level of +24.75 m, which is Vimana's mid-height.

1971 m³/78.88 = 24.98 m, which is very close to the level of 24.75 m, and the minor positive difference is negligible, possibly due to a measurement error.

Surprisingly, the maximum permissible water height inside the sanctum on which the Vimana wall was designed to resist hydrostatic pressure is 24.75 m, and this must be followed to meet safety and design regulations.

This confirms that Chola engineers precisely fixed the mid-height of Vimana +24.75 m as the maximum operating water level that must be maintained during the lifting process, on which they designed the structure while considering the most important safety and design criteria!

The maximum water level that can be raised inside the sanctum is +24.75 m above the courtyard, and the empty cylindrical float is 33 m above the +24.75 m water surface and 8.25 m above the final seating position of +49.5 m at this point, as shown in **Figure 4.**

+24.75 m +33 m = +57.75 m

+57.75 −49.50 = 8.25 m

The float's mid-height level is +24.75 m and its projection from +16.5 m is also 8.25 m.

The preceding study is for the observation trial when the float is empty with its own weight and not carrying any other weight.

At the same time, there are two more requirements for the final process: the flotation deck's top holding the weight of Sikhara or any other load must reach equilibrium at +49.50, and 50% of its float height must be maintained from +16.50 m.

How much weight can be placed on the deck under these conditions?

In other words, how much extra volume of water is required to obtain the magnitude of the buoyant force equivalent to Sikhara's or other granite materials weight to lift from the courtyard base so that the projected height of 8.25 m coincides with the level +49.50 m to reach equilibrium?

When the float is empty, as shown in **Figure 5,** a maximum 8.25 m float length can be forced downwards into the water to reach the equilibrium from +57.75 m by displacing the corresponding volume of the 8.25 m additional submerged height caused by Sikhara's weight in addition to the self-weight of the 8.25 m length of the wooden float that had to be forced down inside the water.

In other words, when the floating system carries the weight of Sikhara or other granite materials from the courtyard level, 8.25 m height of the water level inside the well can be allowed to rise from +16.50 m, enabling the entire system to achieve equilibrium by meeting all three conditions at +49.50 m within the total available storage.

Let us examine the process in detail.

The maximum safe water level is +24.75 m, which is exactly 8.25 m higher than +16.50 m.

The total volume required to fill up to reach the level of +16.50 m is 1564 m³+ 16.50 m × 78.88 m³/m = 2866 m³ and the remaining storage after reaching the level +16.50 m is 3535 m³−2866 = 669 m³.

By meeting all three criteria, the designed system must manage within the remaining storage to raise the water level for a height of 8.25 from +16.50 m and finally position the Sikhara at +49.50 m.

The volume required for 8.25 m height is 8.25 m × 78.88 m³/m and equals 651 m³, which is astonishingly and surprisingly close to the remaining storage figure of 669 m³.

By allowing 651 m³ inside the shaft, the bottom of the float corresponds to the level of (−) 16.5 m, while the top corresponds to the Sikhara's final seating position of +49.50 m with the total weight, and the water level inside the sanctum moves up and corresponds to the mid-height of the Vimana +24.75m.

In a nutshell, as shown in **Figure 6,** the height and volume of the 8.25 m float determine the weight of Sikhara or any other load that Chola engineers have designed, planned, and lifted.

To meet all of the design criteria, the total water volume to be filled inside the well is 50% of the float's volume, 1564 m³ and 24.75 height of sanctum volume and is 24.75 × 78.88 = 1952 m³, totalling 3516 m³, as shown in **Figure 7.**

The total combined volume of vacant spaces designed and created inside the structure is 3535 m³, both inside the circumambulatory and the annexe building vestibule halls, which closely matches the above requirement of 3516 m³.

In conclusion, the Chola engineers designed the open spaces and their corresponding volume within the structure to store the required volume of water to produce the magnitude of the buoyant force that corresponds to the lifting of a massive weight. The detailed calculation reveals that the structure's volume is 3535 m³, and they are astonishingly close. The positive variance in 19 m³ is negligible and may be due to measurement error.

The detailed study conclusively supports and reveals the novel engineering technique brilliantly devised and implemented by the ancient Tamil engineers to lift and install a massive weight by simply combining science and math.

According to the structure's cross-section, water must be drained off through the well below the level of the courtyard after storing a certain volume back inside the circumambulatory and vestibule halls for lifting stones required for subsequent works such as closing the triangular cavities, ornate corbelling, cornices, and so on.

For such a requirement, there must have been a few water outlet points inside the well up to the level of (−) 16.50 m or even lower, connecting to deeper moats and the Siva Ganga Tank.

The Maximum Lifting Capacity

Let us now examine and compute the lifting capacity planned and designed by the engineers in the overall system with the above configuration, as shown in **Figure 8.**

The 7.77 m diameter float has a plan area of 47.39 m².

The volume of 8.25 m height is 8.25 m × 47.39 m² = 390.91 m³ and has a mass of 391 MT.

The weight of the water that has been displaced is 390.91 × 1000 kg/m³ × 9.81 m/s² = 3835 kN and nearly equals 391 MT force.

Because the chosen wooden float system has half the density of water, the weight of the float shares 50% of the displaced weight, with the Sikhara or any weight on the deck sharing the remaining 50%.

50% of 391MT = 195.50 MT, say 195 MT.

Engineers designed the additional float's height of 8.25 m to meet all parameters, which will be immersed in water by displacing the equal volume, and the overall system to carry approximately a mass of 195 MT or a weight of 1913 kN.

Previously, the mass of the Sikhara was roughly estimated to be between 140 and 150 MT.

Figure 195 MT contributes to the mass of the total capstone unit, including the buffer needed to lift the system above +49.5 m prior to final alignment and placement.

The base of Sikhara must be lifted above +49.50 m from the triangular slotted cavities for a 45-degree free horizontal rotation, alignment, and placement on the four corner supporting granite pylons, which are the extension of triangular spherical pendentives from +33 m to +49.50 m, as shown in the detailed drawings and sketches.

All of Sikhara's components are estimated to have a mass between 140 and 160 MT, including the base slab, spherical cover, and four pairs of sacred bulls whereas the mechanism has been designed to carry and hoist a maximum mass of 195 MT (1913 kN weight) in the gravitational field, proving that ancient Tamil engineers had a masterminded application to lift a mass of more than 140 MT in a single-stage lifting operation to finally set it at +49.50 m height.

If the Sikhara's overall weight is assumed to be a maximum of 160 MT force, the maximum water level can be set at a lower height from +24.75 m to that extent, reducing hydrostatic pressure on the wall by allowing the resultant of the forces to pass through within the boundaries of the inner middle third of the base and preventing tension development in the structure.

The reduction of 35 MT from 195 MT to 160 MT corresponds to nearly a 1.4 m drop in the maximum water level, which can be set to 24.75−1.4 = 23.35 m.

The stability check analysis based on fixing the maximum water level as +23.35 m establishes that the resultant forces pass through well within the middle third of the base and the structure is completely safe in both the full and empty conditions by meeting all of the design and safety factors, as shown in the figures and tables.

Ancient Tamil engineers' design expertise, computations, and achievements are astounding here.

They devised, built, implemented, and demonstrated a novel mechanism that could safely and efficiently lift a mass of 140 MT plus in the gravitational field to the Vimana top in a "single-stage lift!"

The term "single-stage lift" here conveys a significant and astounding amount of meaning which is extremely important, informative, hidden and not exposed to date.

By anticipating minor leaks and water wastage through the narrow gaps and cavities in the interlocking system of wall stones during the operation, it appears that the engineers have set the total required volume with some buffers so that the water will flow inside the well from a few orifice/sluice openings to raise the entire system along with the Sikhara block to +49.50 m level as quickly as possible to complete the mission in a few hours of operation for the final installation.

That means the engineers planned, designed, and completed the above Herculean mission in a matter of hours as a single-stage lifting operation is demonstrated by this calculation and its conclusion.

The total volume of the empty spaces inside the circumambulatory and annexe vestibule halls strongly supports the procedure and has been specifically designed, created, and reserved for the total ready storage of 3516 m³ of water.

When everything was ready for a single lifting operation from 0 to 49.50 m high, the massive weight might have reached the summit in hours by activating the sluice gates or opening the orifice of each storage compartment one by one and regulating the flow of 3516 m³ of water into the well.

Around the level of +33 m, which is above the terrace on the eastern face of Vimana, Lord Shiva's image is etched into the massive rock of Mount Kailash.

It was early in the morning before sunrise on the scheduled day.

The emperor Raja Raja Cholan presumably opened the sluice gate after performing religious offerings and adoration on the deity of Lord Shiva at +33 m by pouring holy water brought from the sacred river, the Ganges.

The size of 300 mm × 300 mm or 450 mm × 450 mm sluice/orifice opening can drain the total designed volume of 3516 m³ in a matter of few hours into the well and sanctum shaft.

In that case, the operation could have been completed in a single-stage lifting process a few hours before the sun's midday rays or evening rays hit the earth.

The temple was built in 6.5 years, according to history.

If the historically believed story of building a 6.6 km long ramp to transport huge stones and the Sikhara to the peak is correct, such a massive length and size ramp must have begun concurrently with the foundation work for the main temple.

The Sikhara should have travelled on the long ramp for at least 6.5 months after construction was completed and the tower was made ready in all respects to receive it before being placed in its final location.

Once the Vimana structure was completed, 6.5 months would have seemed excessively long according to the king.

Emperor Raja Raja Cholan might have conveyed to the kingdom's chief engineer when the Tanjore Big Temple was still in the planning and design stages his desire to cover the Vimana as economically and quickly as possible but without compromising the safety and quality.

The ancient Tamil engineers must have held a brainstorming session to discuss the feasibility of incorporating cutting-edge scientific concepts and ideas into the project's design and construction; they ultimately settled on a plan that prioritised the project's safety and quality while also satisfying the king's request.

The entire procedure practically required the mission to be completed in a single day between dawn and dusk. The target was to have the Sikhara over the Vimana by noon on the designated day, at the latest.

Consider this: the monarch directed that the task be completed in less than a half-day!

The king's final directive aimed for the mission to be completed as soon as possible, before the sun's evening rays hit the earth.

The mission, presumably, began before sunrise and ended no later than sunset, before the sun's evening rays hit the earth!

Based on the number of sluice/orifice openings and their larger designed sizes, it's no surprise that the task could have been completed even before noon!

It's a myth that the Vimana's shade doesn't fall on the earth.

It's not as if the Vimana doesn't cast any shadows on the ground.

The ancient Tamil engineers' vow, commitment, and demonstration to the ruler in completing the mission before the sun's midday or evening rays touched the earth on the scheduled day was most likely misinterpreted to traditionally believe and mean that the shade of the Vimana does not cast any shadows on the planet.

While the Sikhara arrived and majestically settled on the summit before the sunset, the holy water from the Ganges, which was ritually poured on Lord Shiva's statue from +33 m level, flowed down and became mixed up in the large volume of water stored in both the annexe and circumambulatory tanks, which finally drained and settled at the nearby tank called "Siva Ganga Tank."

It would be still more interesting to discover and know how the massive block of Sikhara made its entry into the sanctum and got seated on the wooden deck for the vertical journey to the summit.

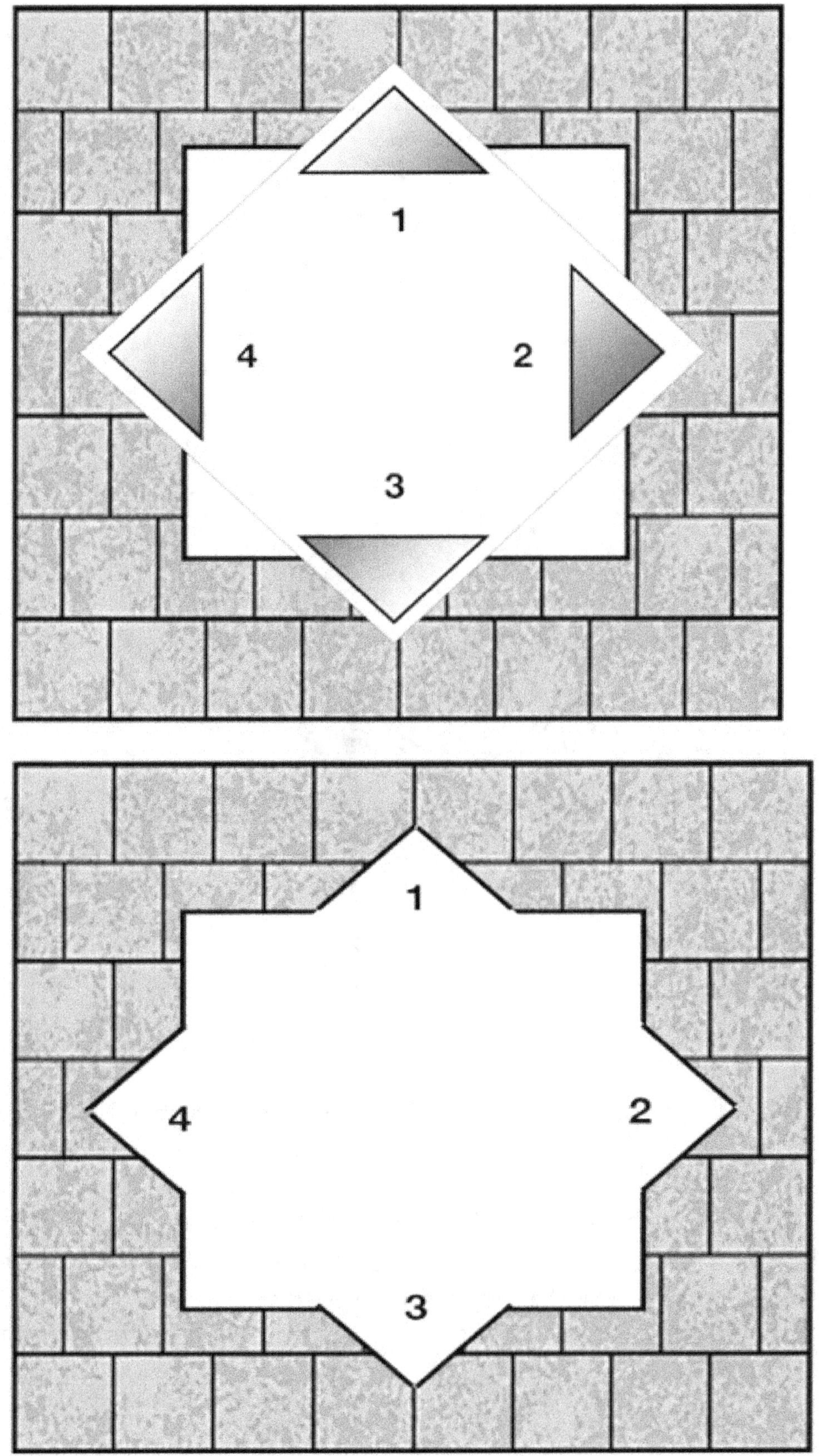

Plan showing four Triangular shaped cavities constructed in the inner Wall

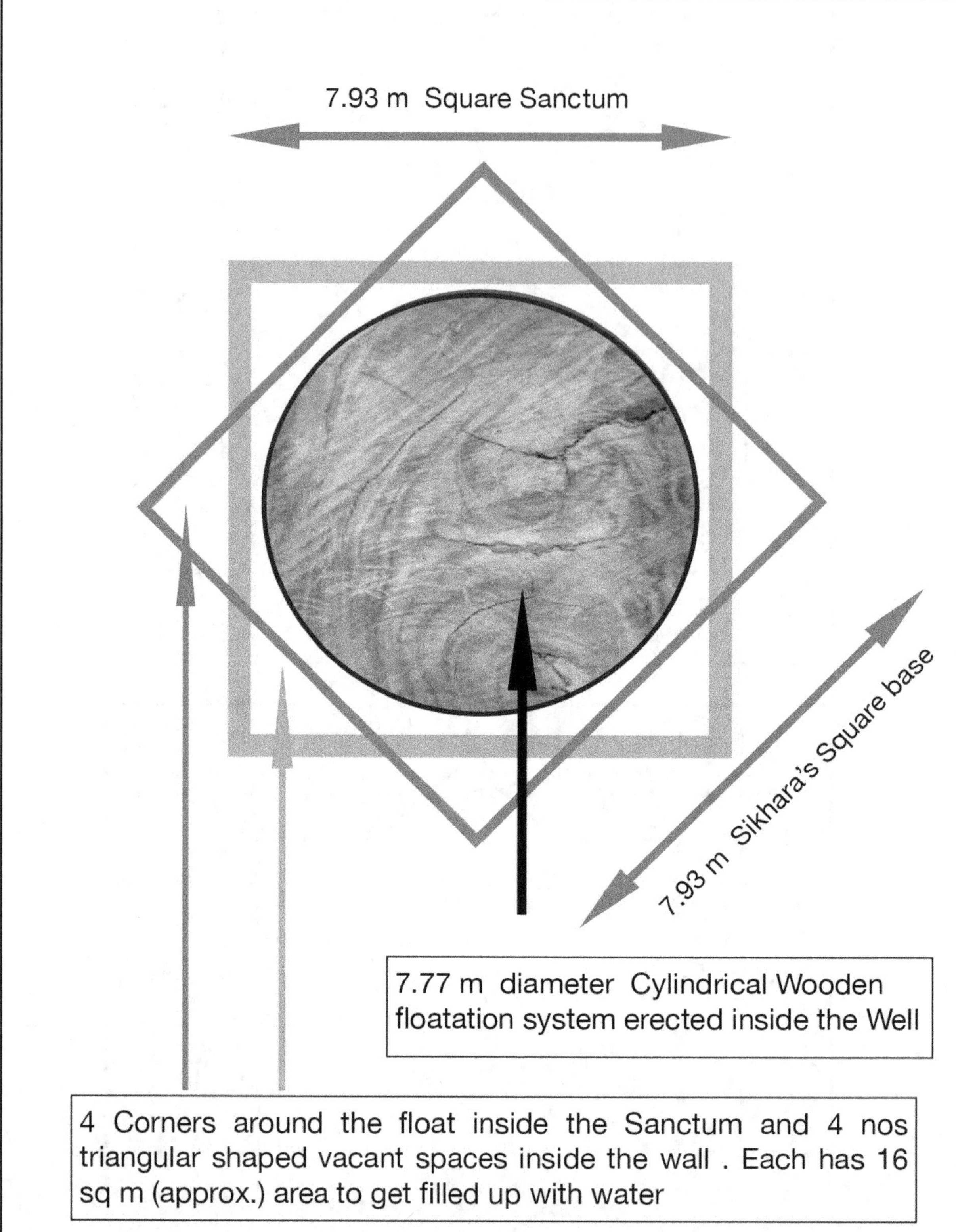

7.93 m Square Sanctum
7.93 m Sikhara's Square base
7.77 m diameter Cylindrical Wooden floatation system erected inside the Well
4 Corners around the float inside the Sanctum and 4 nos triangular shaped vacant spaces inside the wall . Each has 16 sq m (approx.) area to get filled up with water

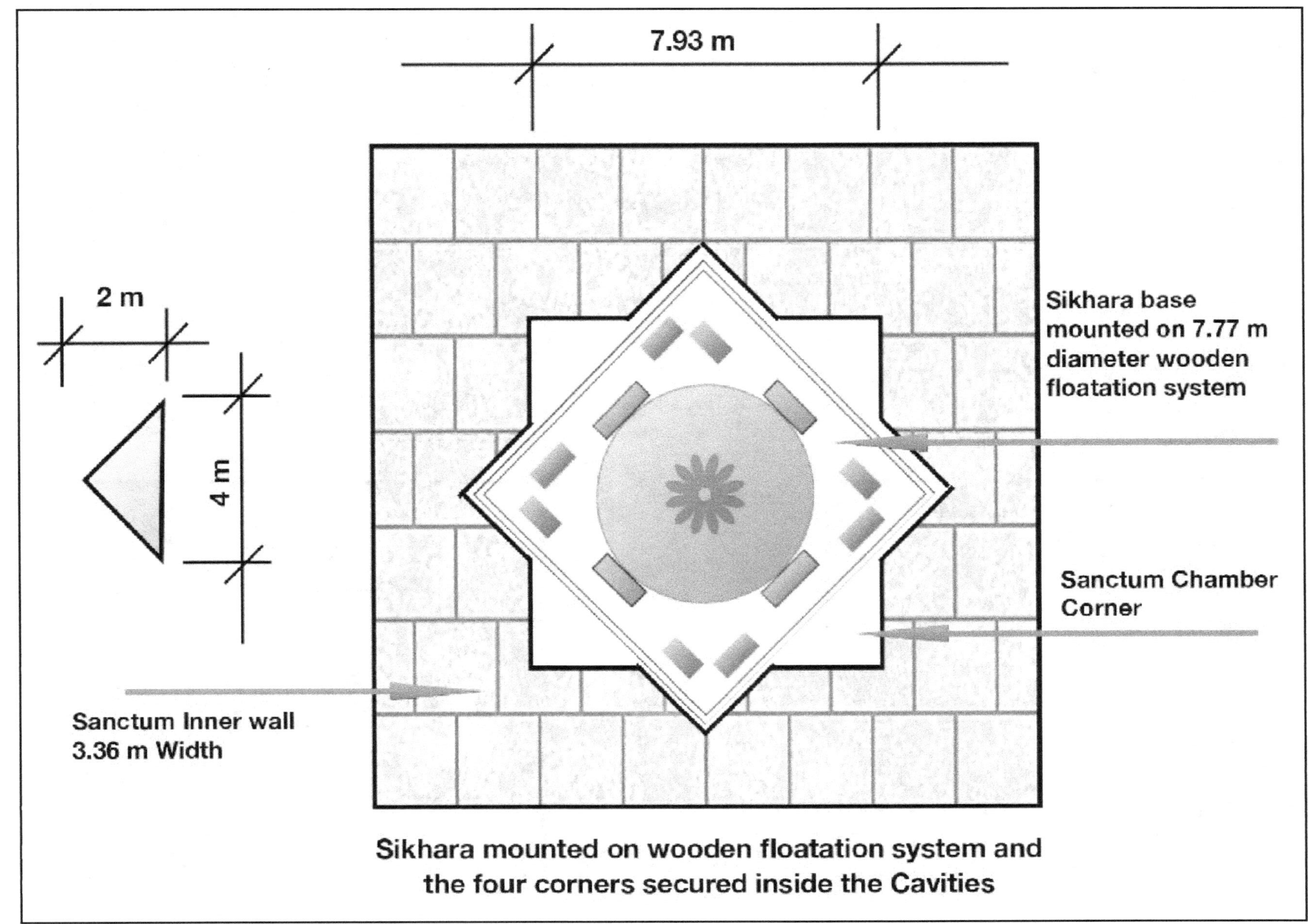

7.93 m
2 m
4 m
Sikhara base mounted on 7.77 m diameter wooden floatation system
Sanctum Chamber Corner
Sanctum Inner wall 3.36 m Width
Sikhara mounted on wooden floatation system and the four corners secured inside the Cavities

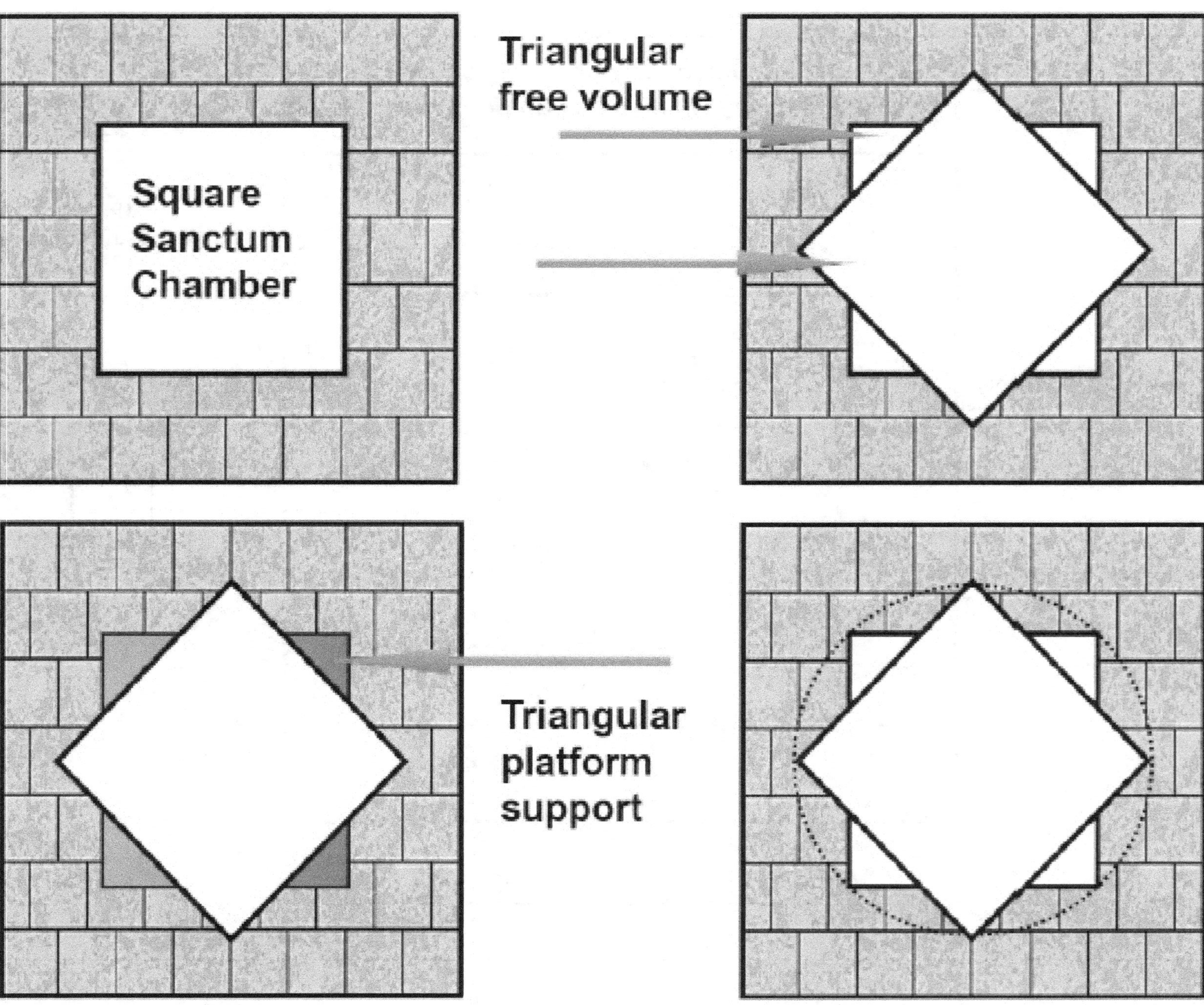

Square Sanctum Chamber
Triangular free volume
Triangular platform support

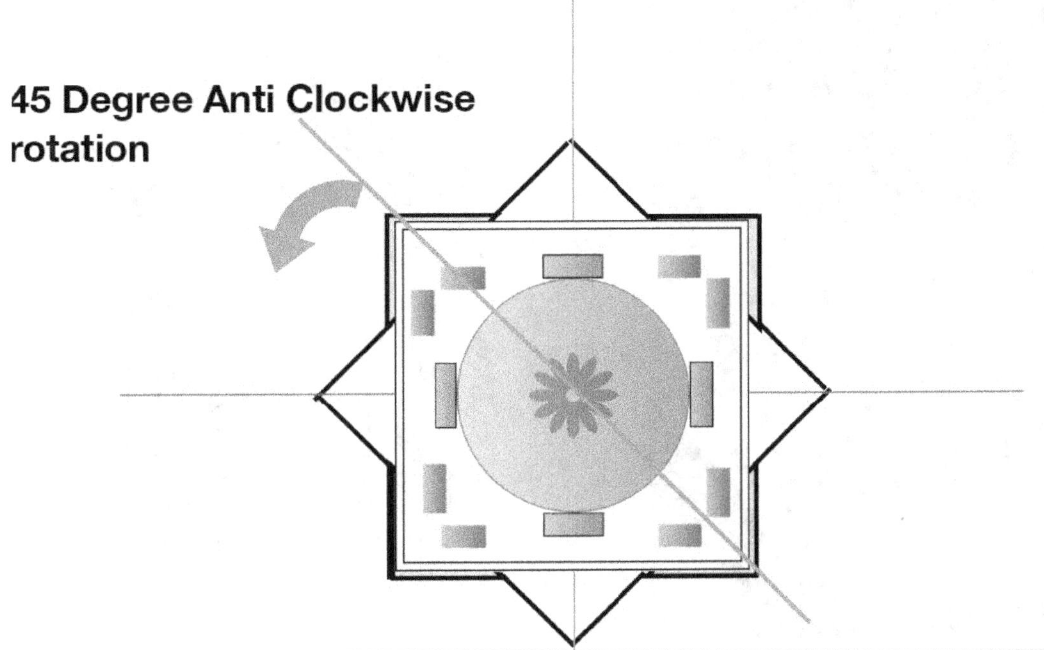

45 Degree Anti Clockwise rotation to Secure inside the Triangular Cavities

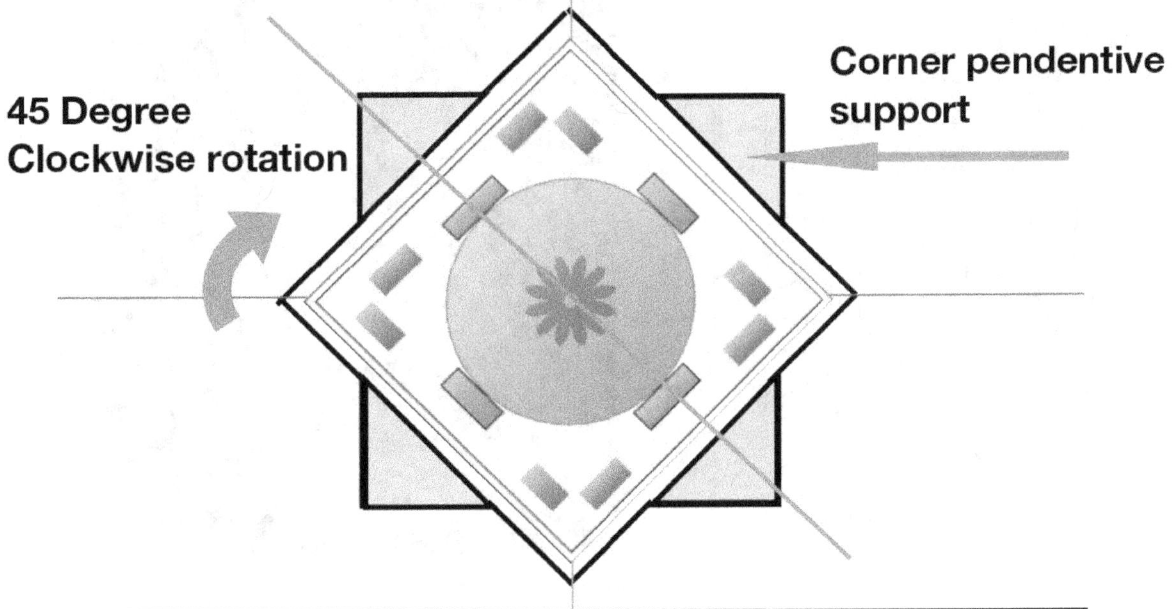

45 Degree Clockwise rotation to rest on the Corner Supports

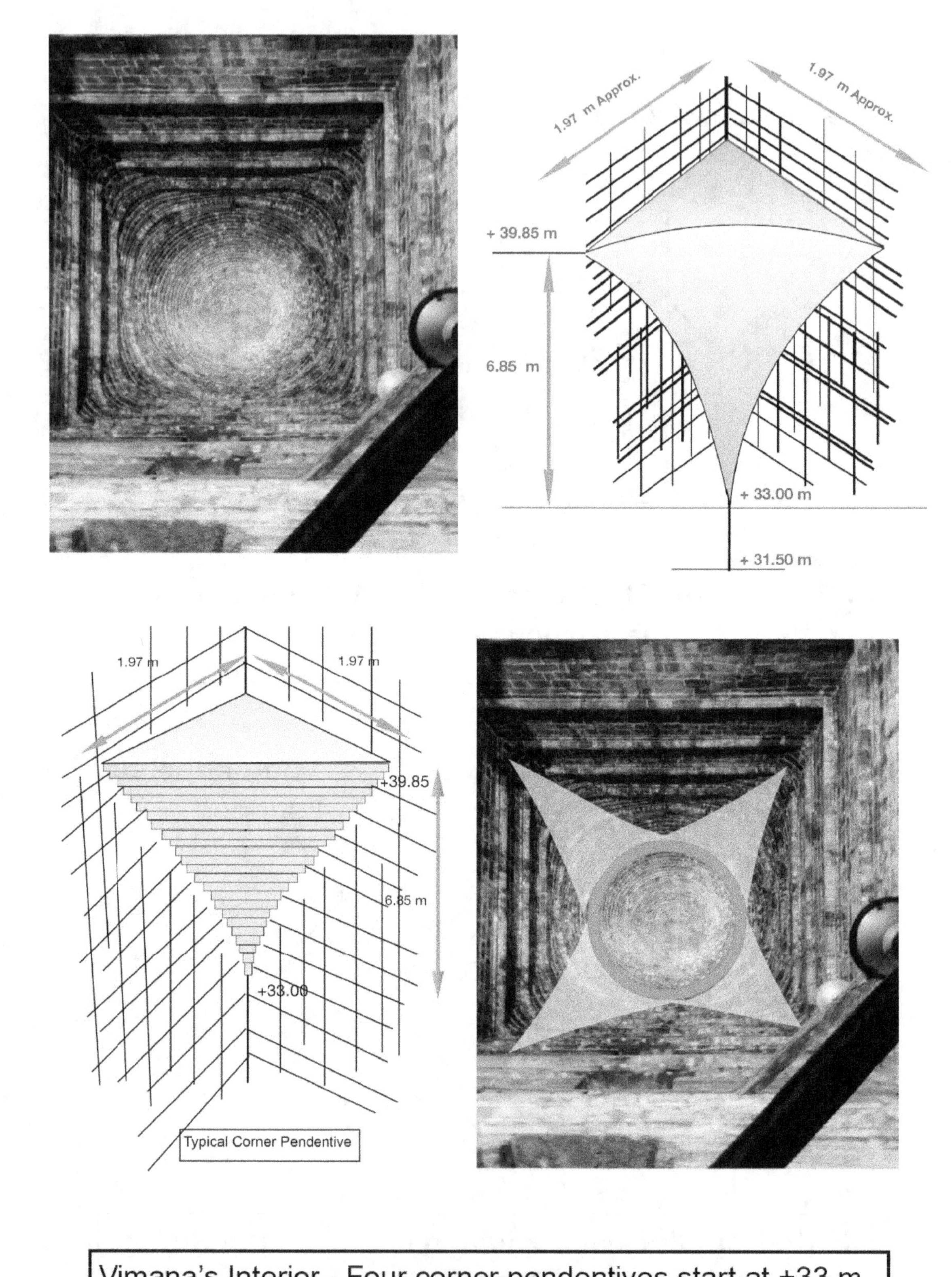

Vimana's Interior - Four corner pendentives start at +33 m and reach +49.50 m to support the square Sikhara slab.

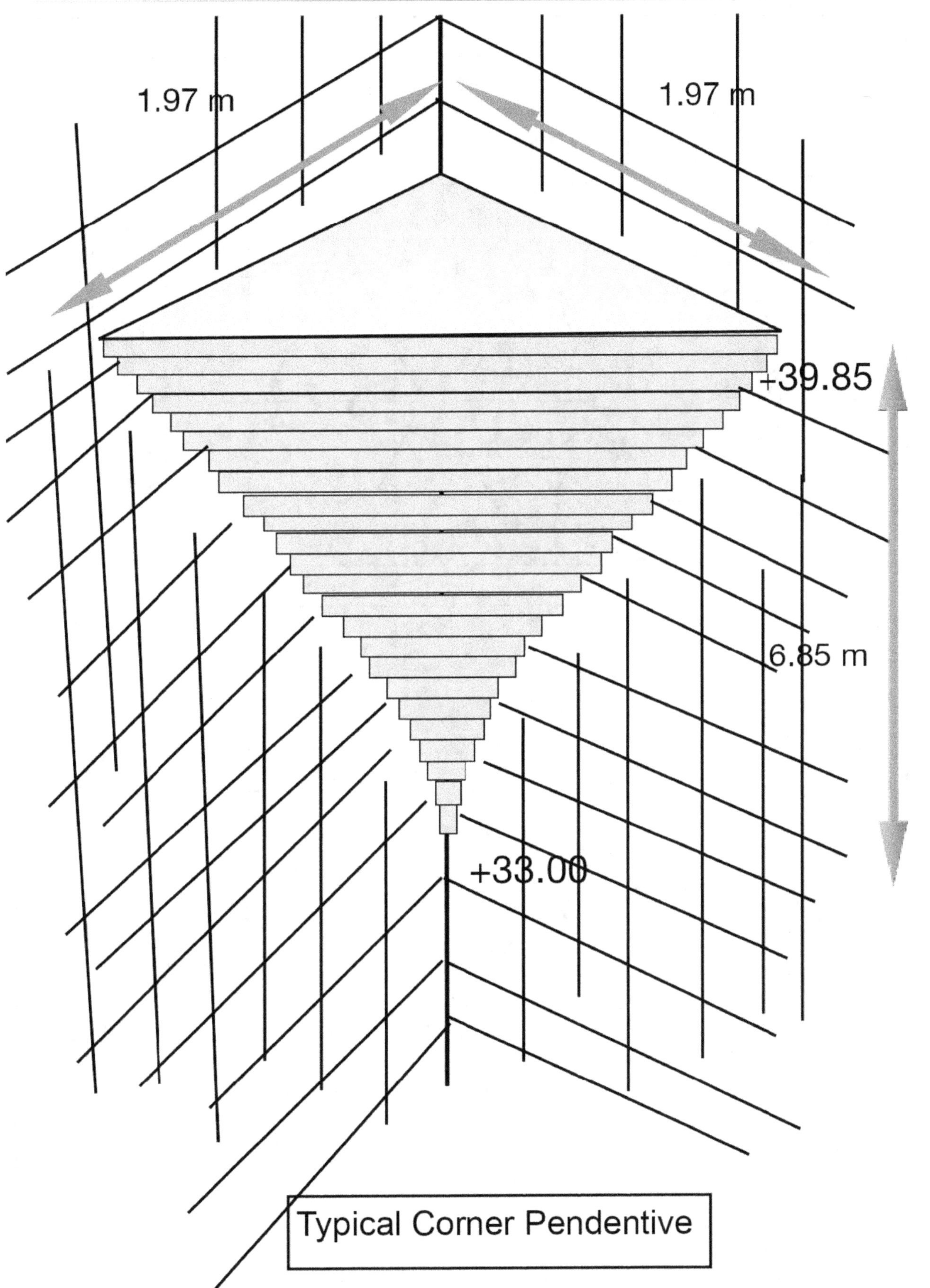
1.97 m
1.97 m
+39.85
6.85 m
+33.00
Typical Corner Pendentive

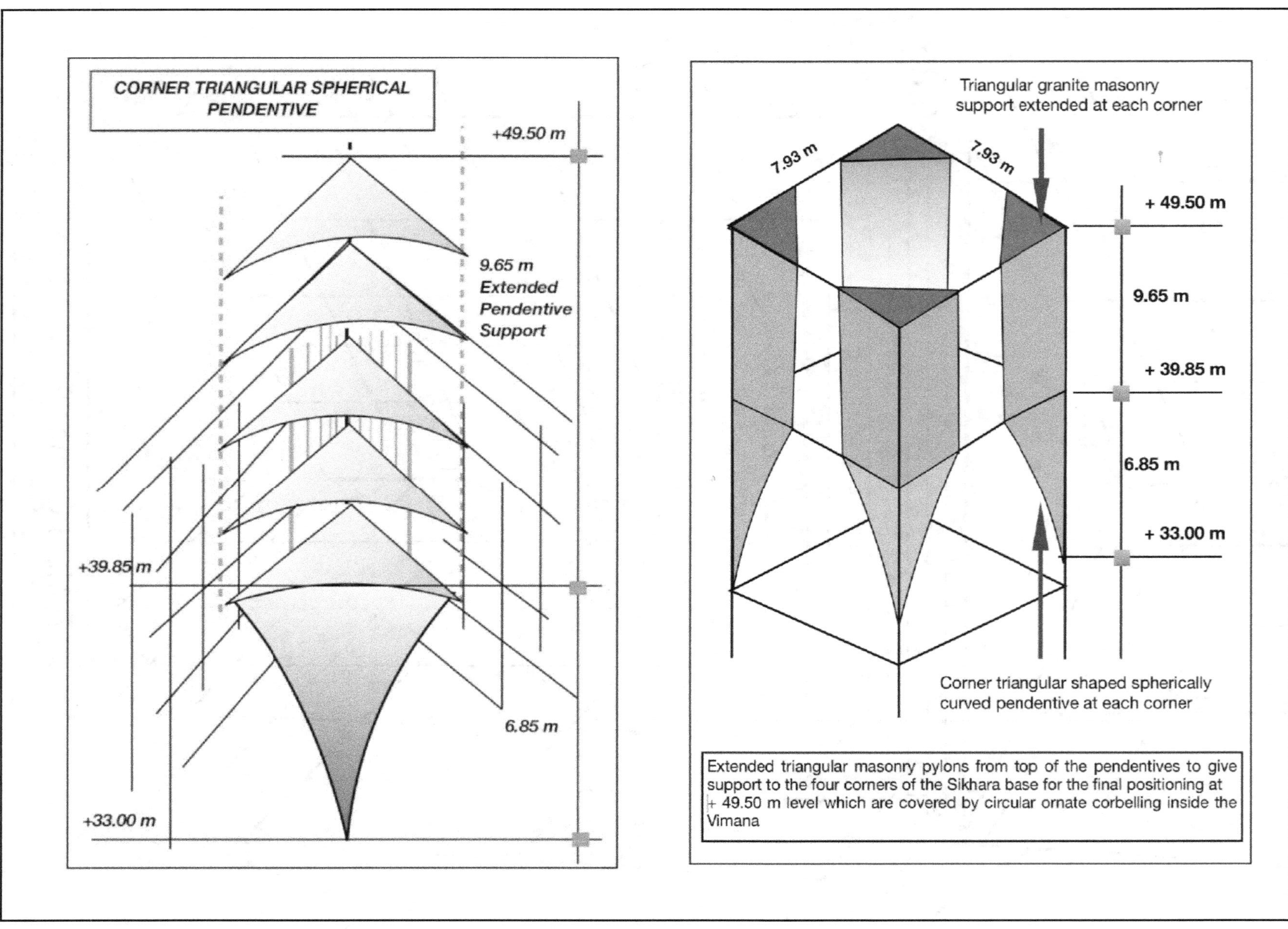
CORNER TRIANGULAR SPHERICAL PENDENTIVE
+49.50 m
9.65 m Extended Pendentive Support
+39.85 m
6.85 m
+33.00 m
Triangular granite masonry support extended at each corner
7.93 m
7.93 m
+ 49.50 m
9.65 m
+ 39.85 m
6.85 m
+ 33.00 m
Corner triangular shaped spherically curved pendentive at each corner
Extended triangular masonry pylons from top of the pendentives to give support to the four corners of the Sikhara base for the final positioning at + 49.50 m level which are covered by circular ornate corbelling inside the Vimana

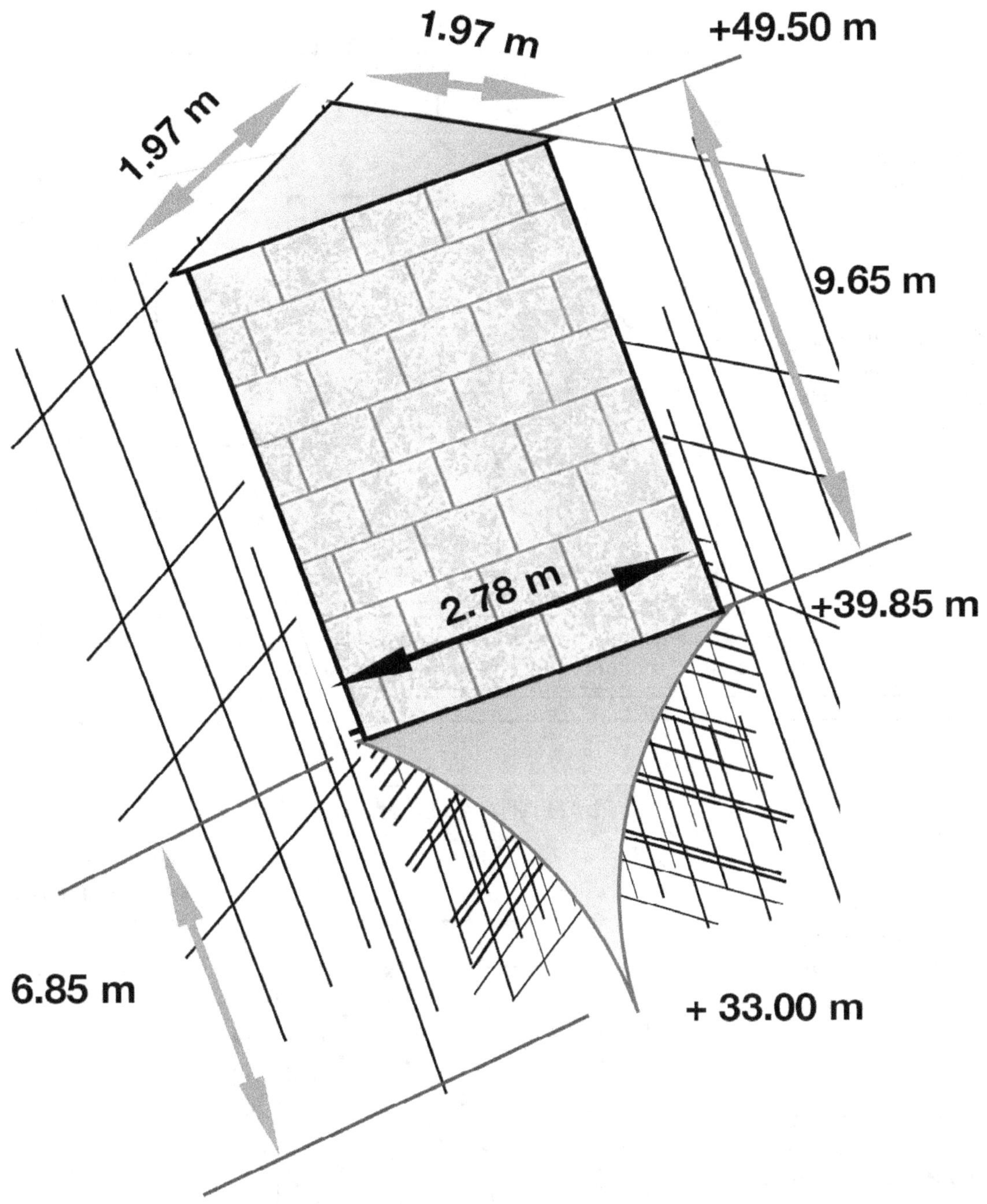

Typical Triangular shaped spherically curved corner pendentives extended from +39.85 m to + 49.50 m level to give support to the four corners of the Sikhara base.

Pendentive Structural features receive and transfer the total load of the Sikhara to the four corners which are hidden behind the extensive ornate circular corbeling inside the Vimana .

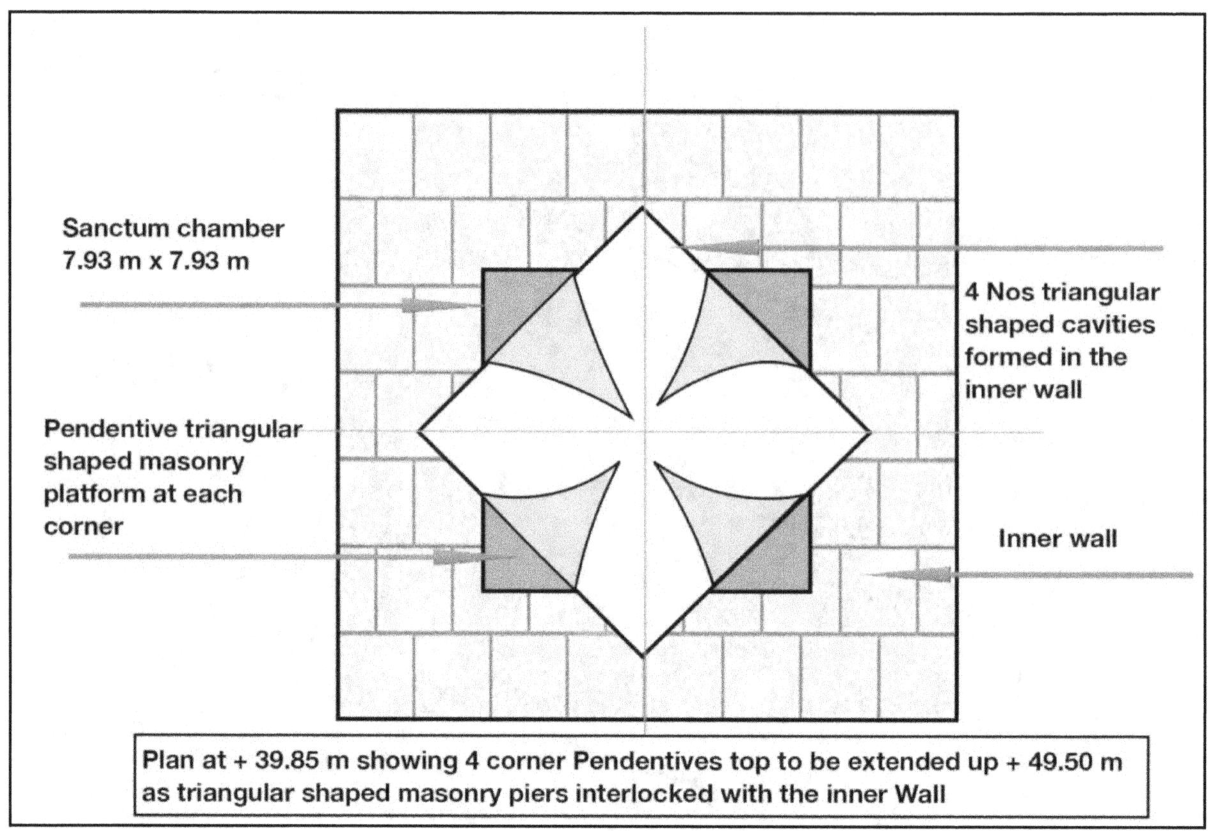

Plan at + 39.85 m showing 4 corner Pendentives top to be extended up + 49.50 m as triangular shaped masonry piers interlocked with the inner Wall

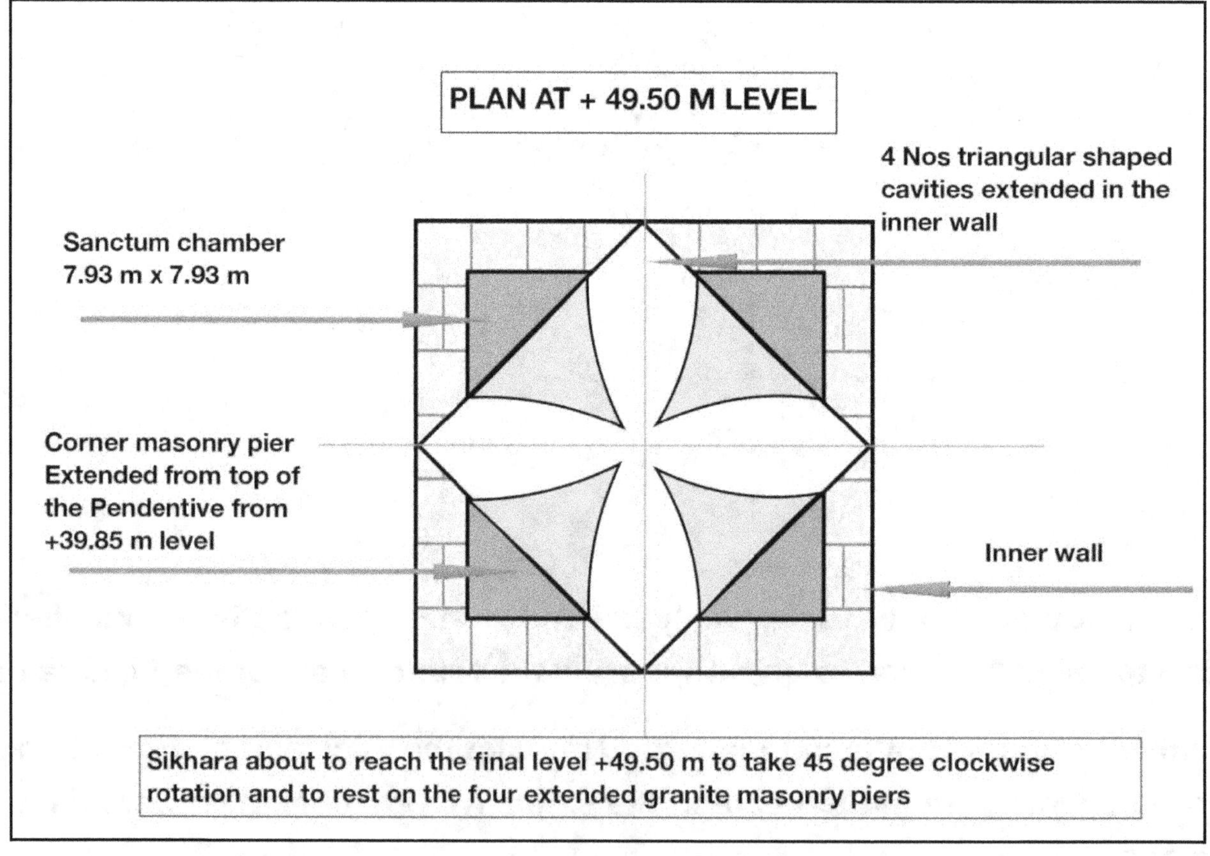

Sikhara about to reach the final level +49.50 m to take 45 degree clockwise rotation and to rest on the four extended granite masonry piers

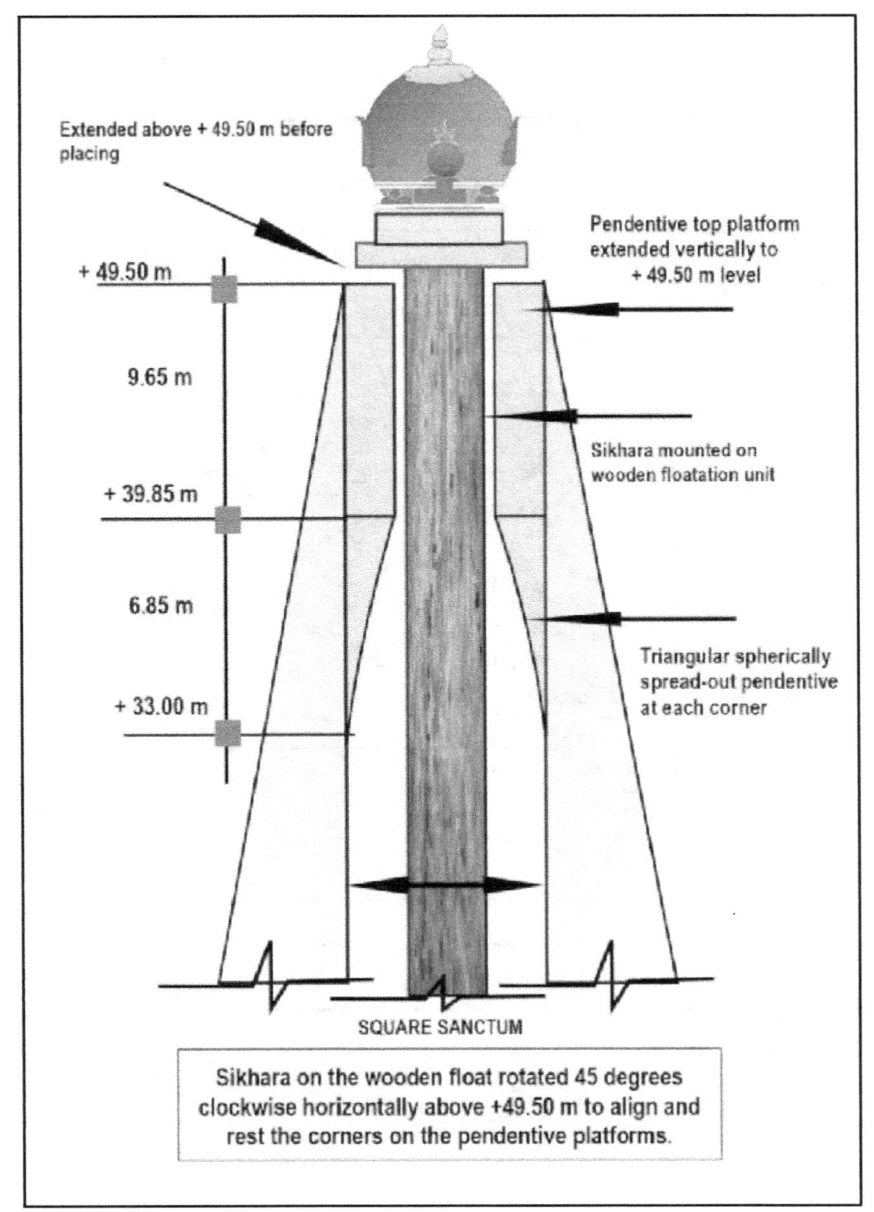

Extended above + 49.50 m before placing
Pendentive top platform extended vertically to + 49.50 m level
+ 49.50 m
9.65 m
Sikhara mounted on wooden floatation unit
+ 39.85 m
6.85 m
Triangular spherically spread-out pendentive at each corner
+ 33.00 m
SQUARE SANCTUM
Sikhara on the wooden float rotated 45 degrees clockwise horizontally above +49.50 m to align and rest the corners on the pendentive platforms.

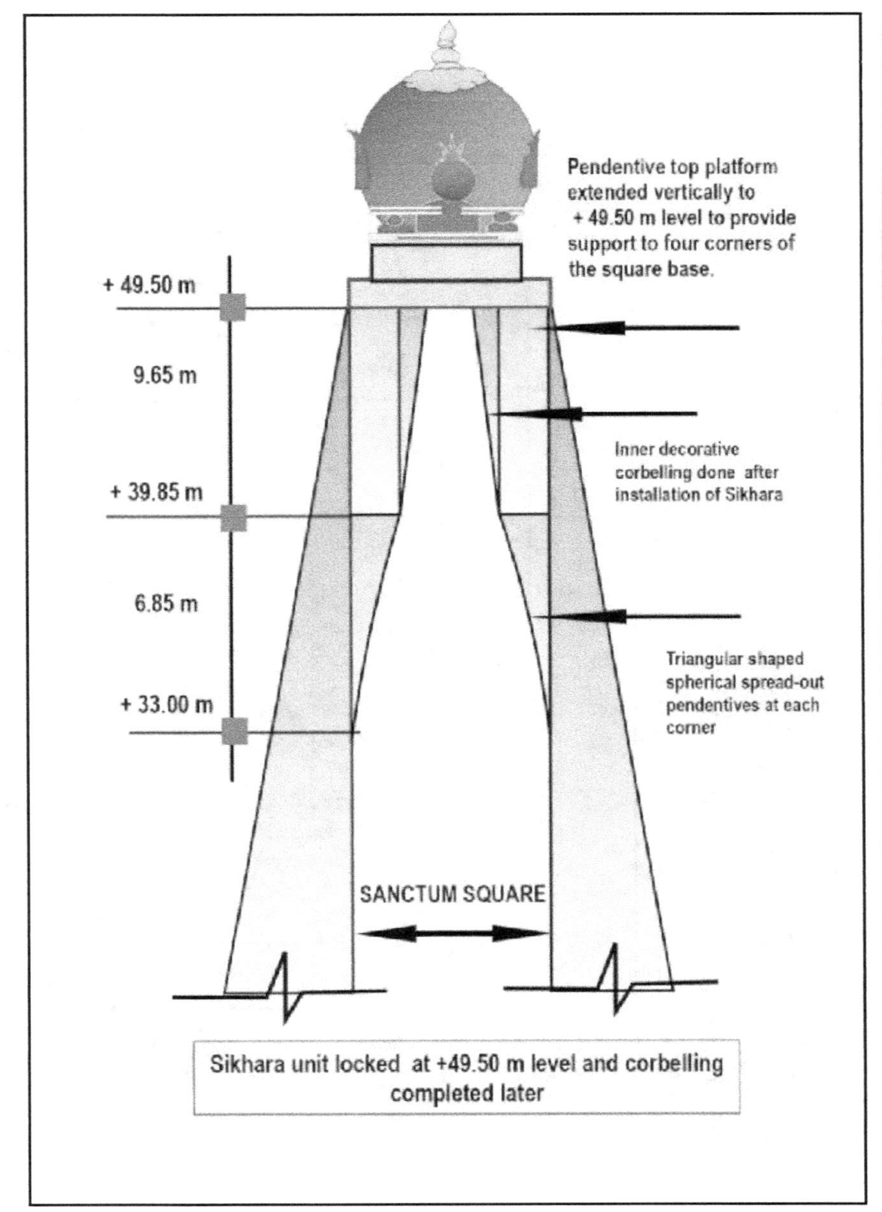

Pendentive top platform extended vertically to + 49.50 m level to provide support to four corners of the square base.
+ 49.50 m
9.65 m
Inner decorative corbelling done after installation of Sikhara
+ 39.85 m
6.85 m
Triangular shaped spherical spread-out pendentives at each corner
+ 33.00 m
SANCTUM SQUARE
Sikhara unit locked at +49.50 m level and corbelling completed later

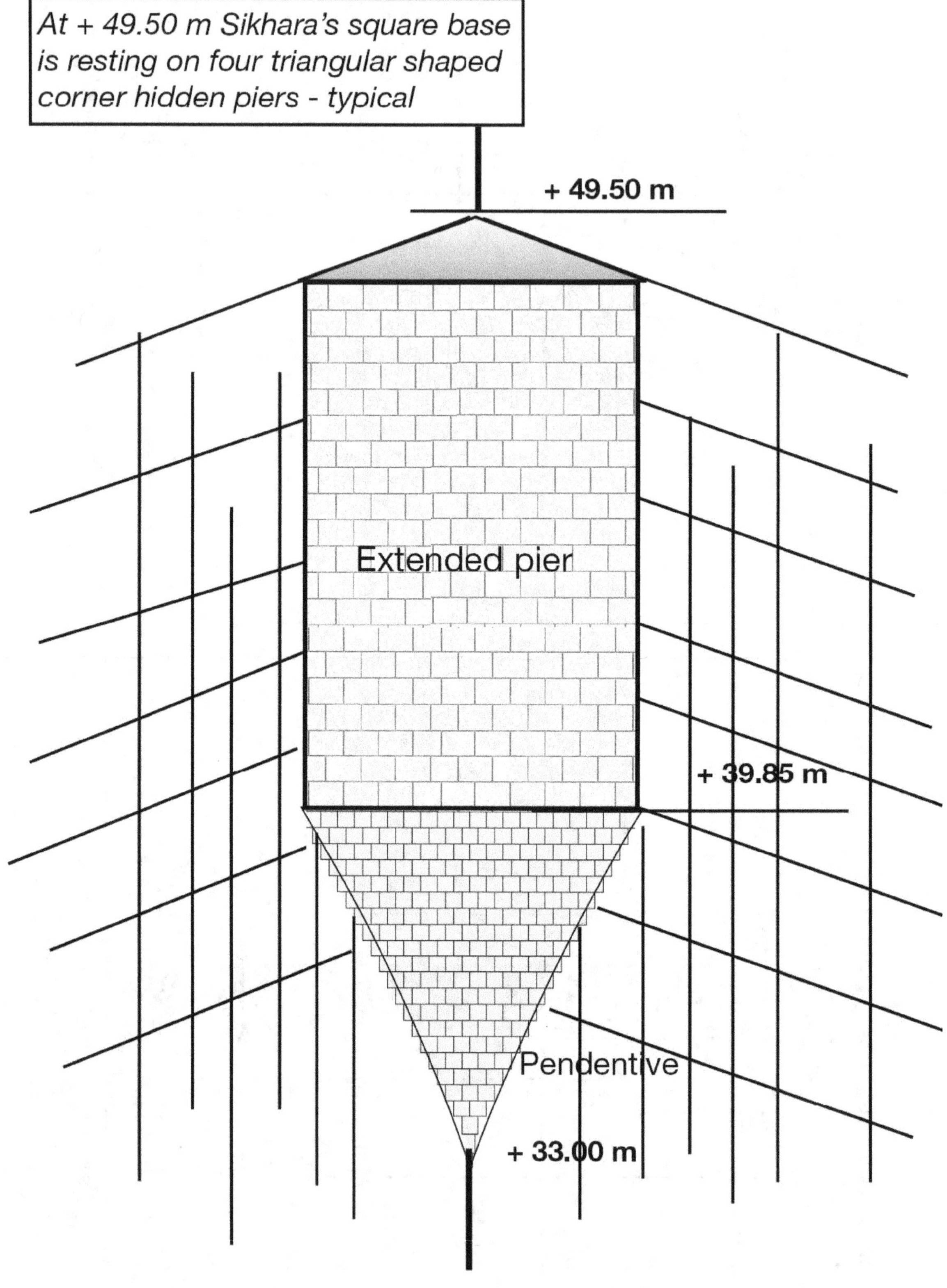
At + 49.50 m Sikhara's square base is resting on four triangular shaped corner hidden piers - typical
+ 49.50 m
Extended pier
+ 39.85 m
Pendentive
+ 33.00 m

Four corner extended pendentive supports at +49.50 m.
Sikhara to rotate 45° clockwise horizontally and align for final positioning

Lifted and majestically seated at the summit +49.50 m level

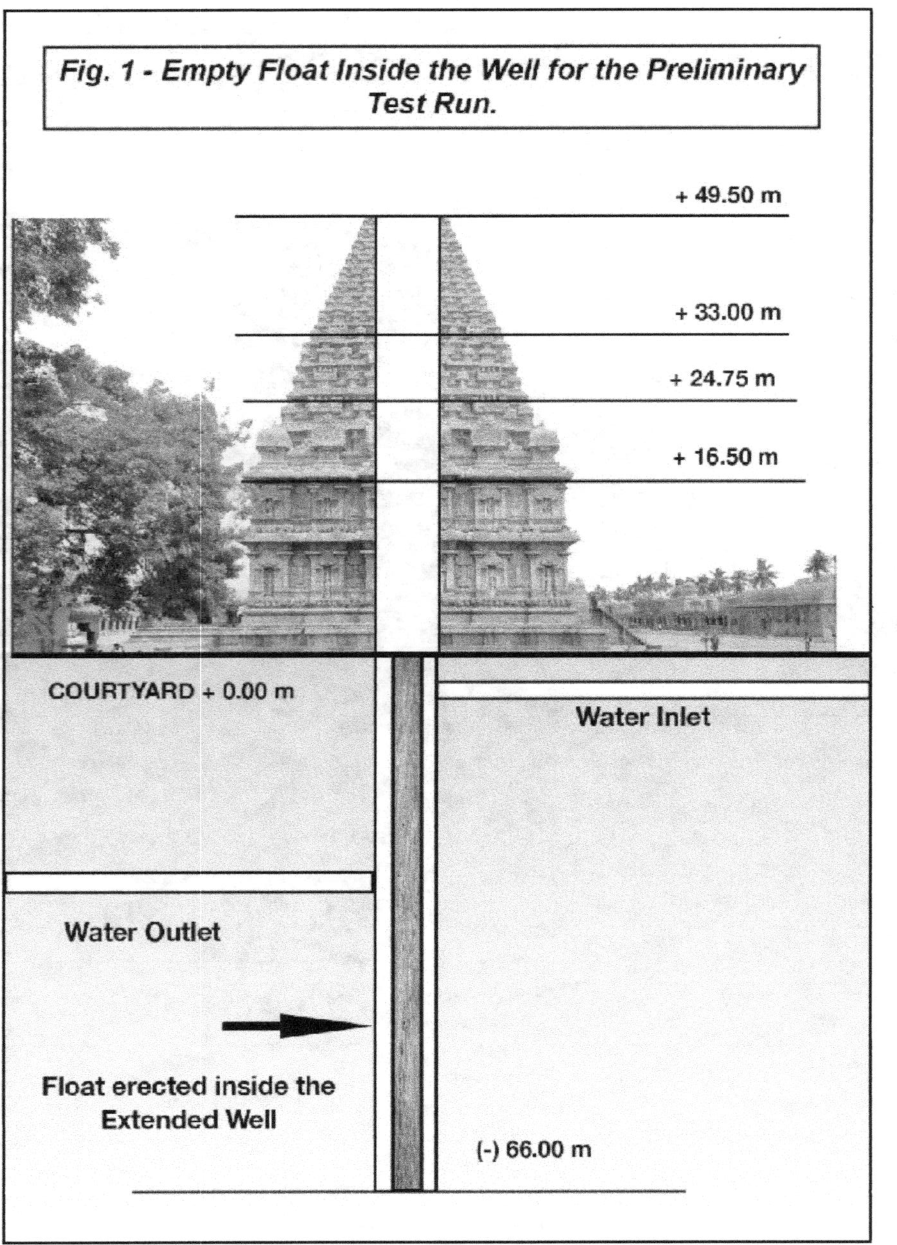

Fig. 1 - Empty Float Inside the Well for the Preliminary Test Run.

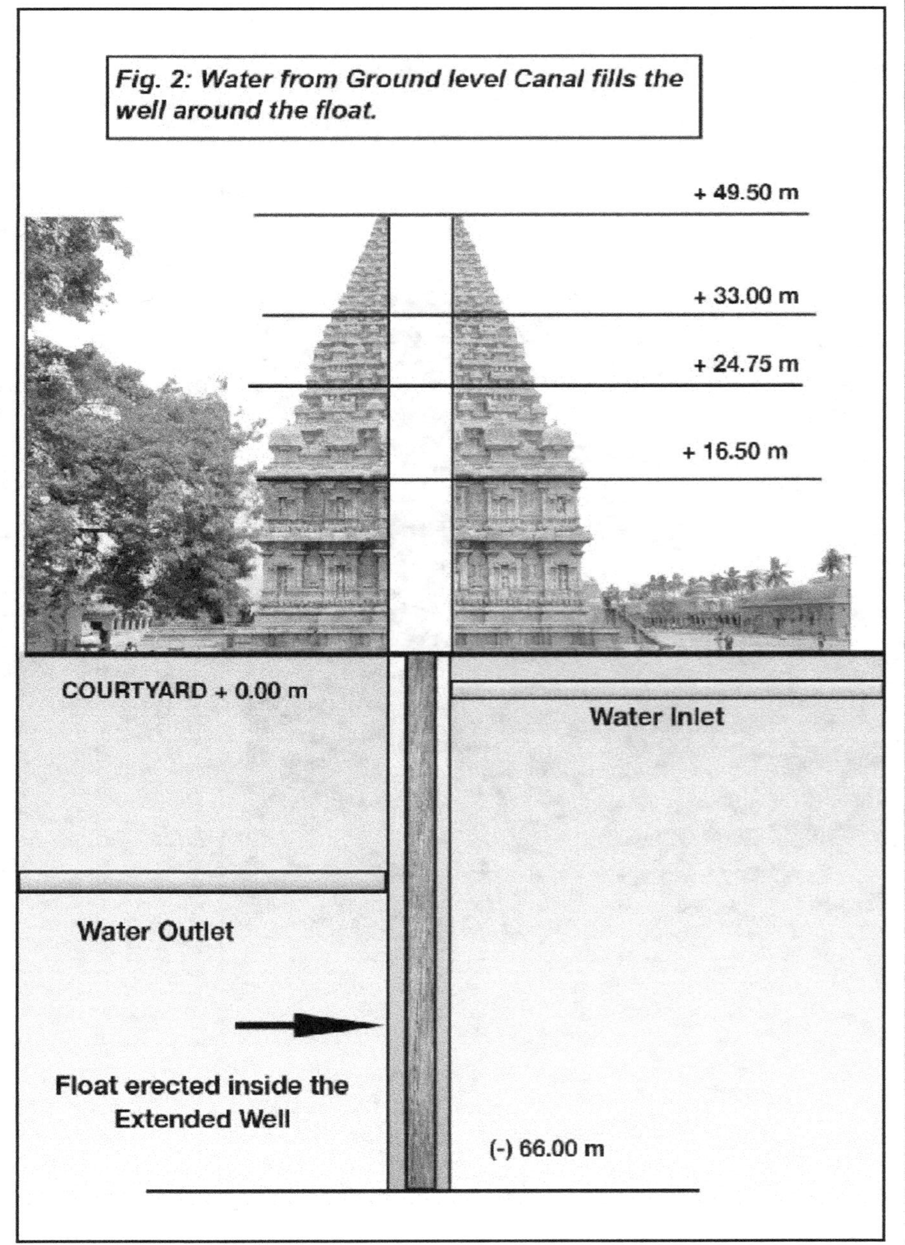

Fig. 2: Water from Ground level Canal fills the well around the float.

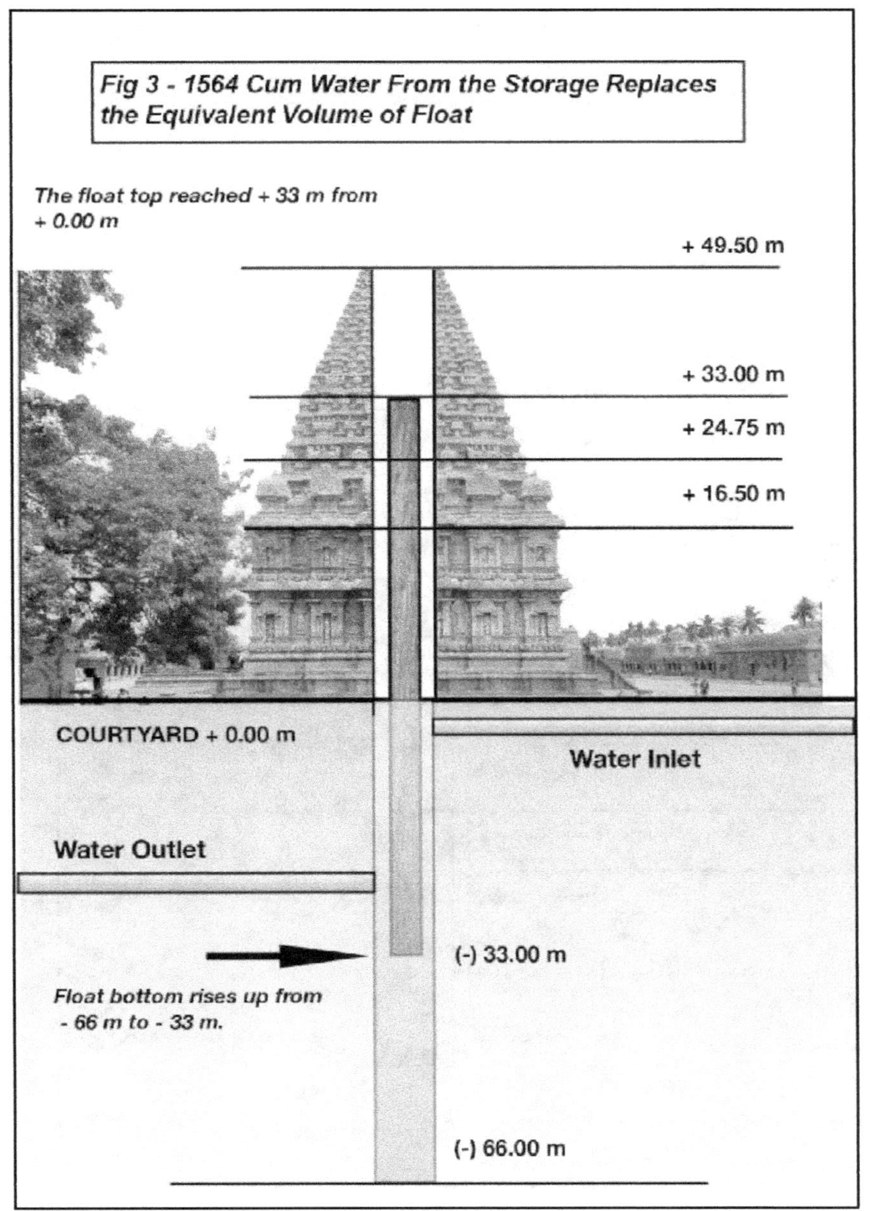

Fig 3 - 1564 Cum Water From the Storage Replaces the Equivalent Volume of Float

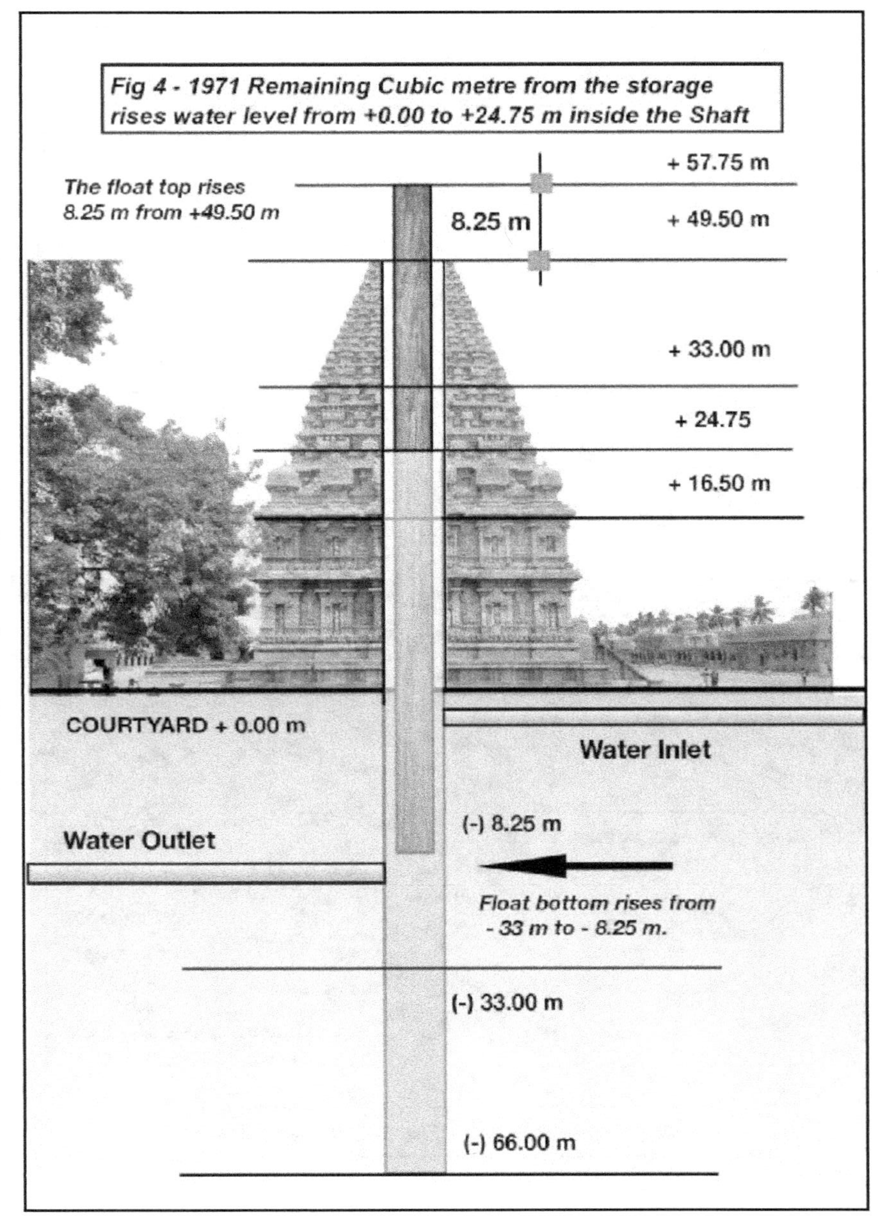

Fig 4 - 1971 Remaining Cubic metre from the storage rises water level from +0.00 to +24.75 m inside the Shaft

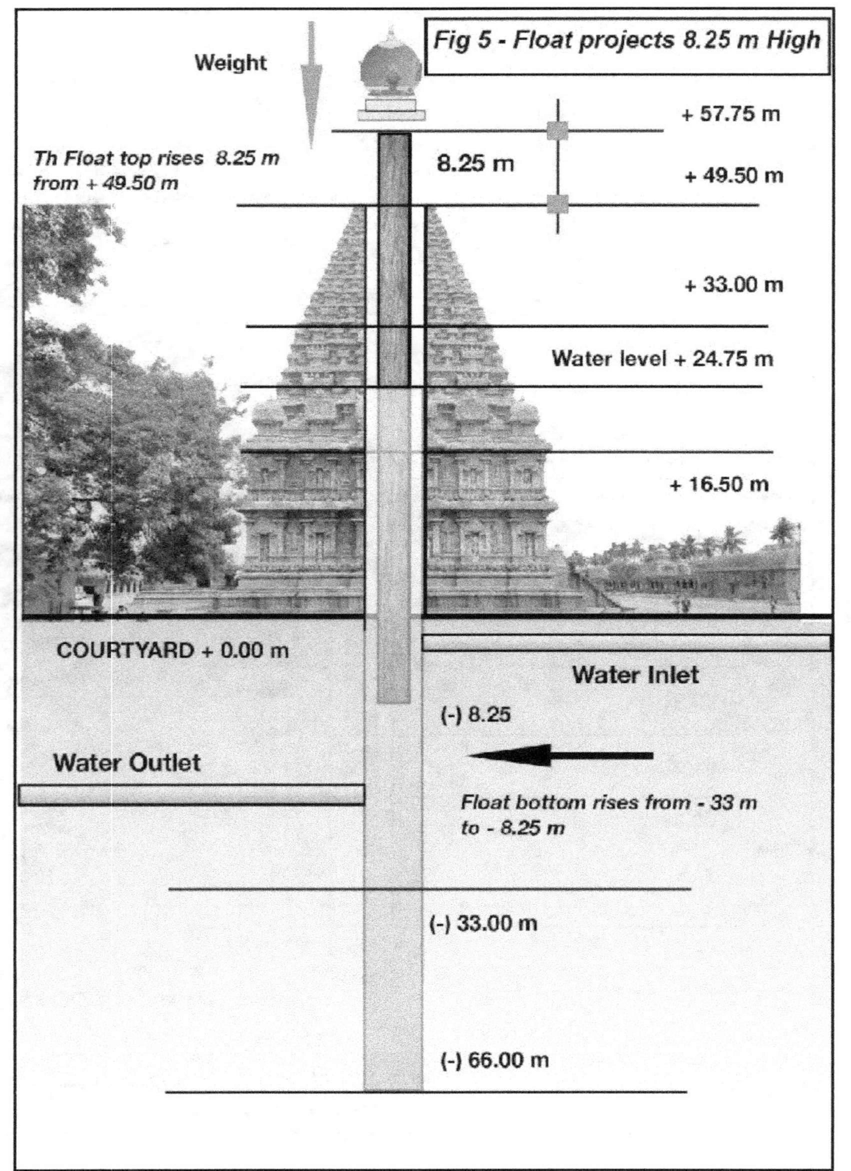
Fig 5 - Float projects 8.25 m High
Weight
Th Float top rises 8.25 m from + 49.50 m
8.25 m
+ 57.75 m
+ 49.50 m
+ 33.00 m
Water level + 24.75 m
+ 16.50 m
COURTYARD + 0.00 m
Water Inlet
Water Outlet
(-) 8.25
Float bottom rises from - 33 m to - 8.25 m
(-) 33.00 m
(-) 66.00 m

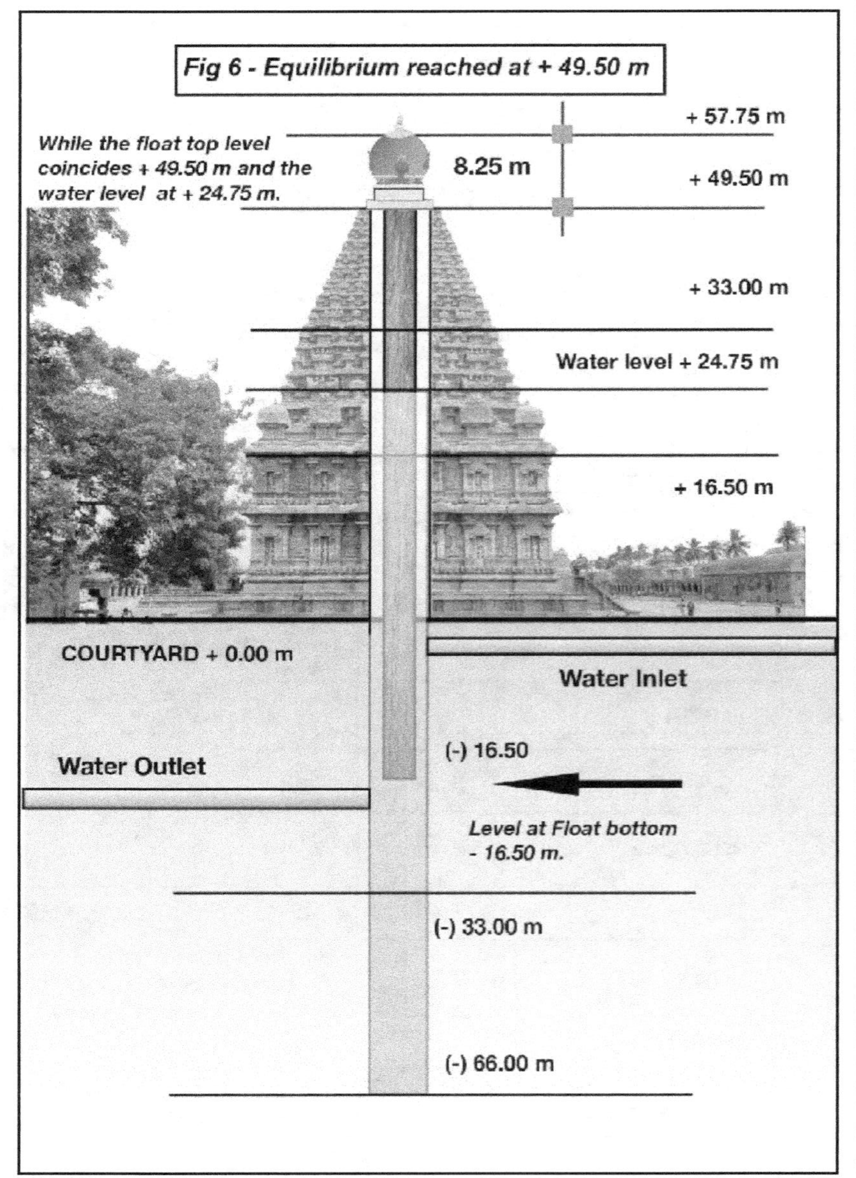
Fig 6 - Equilibrium reached at + 49.50 m
While the float top level coincides + 49.50 m and the water level at + 24.75 m.
8.25 m
+ 57.75 m
+ 49.50 m
+ 33.00 m
Water level + 24.75 m
+ 16.50 m
COURTYARD + 0.00 m
Water Inlet
Water Outlet
(-) 16.50
Level at Float bottom - 16.50 m.
(-) 33.00 m
(-) 66.00 m

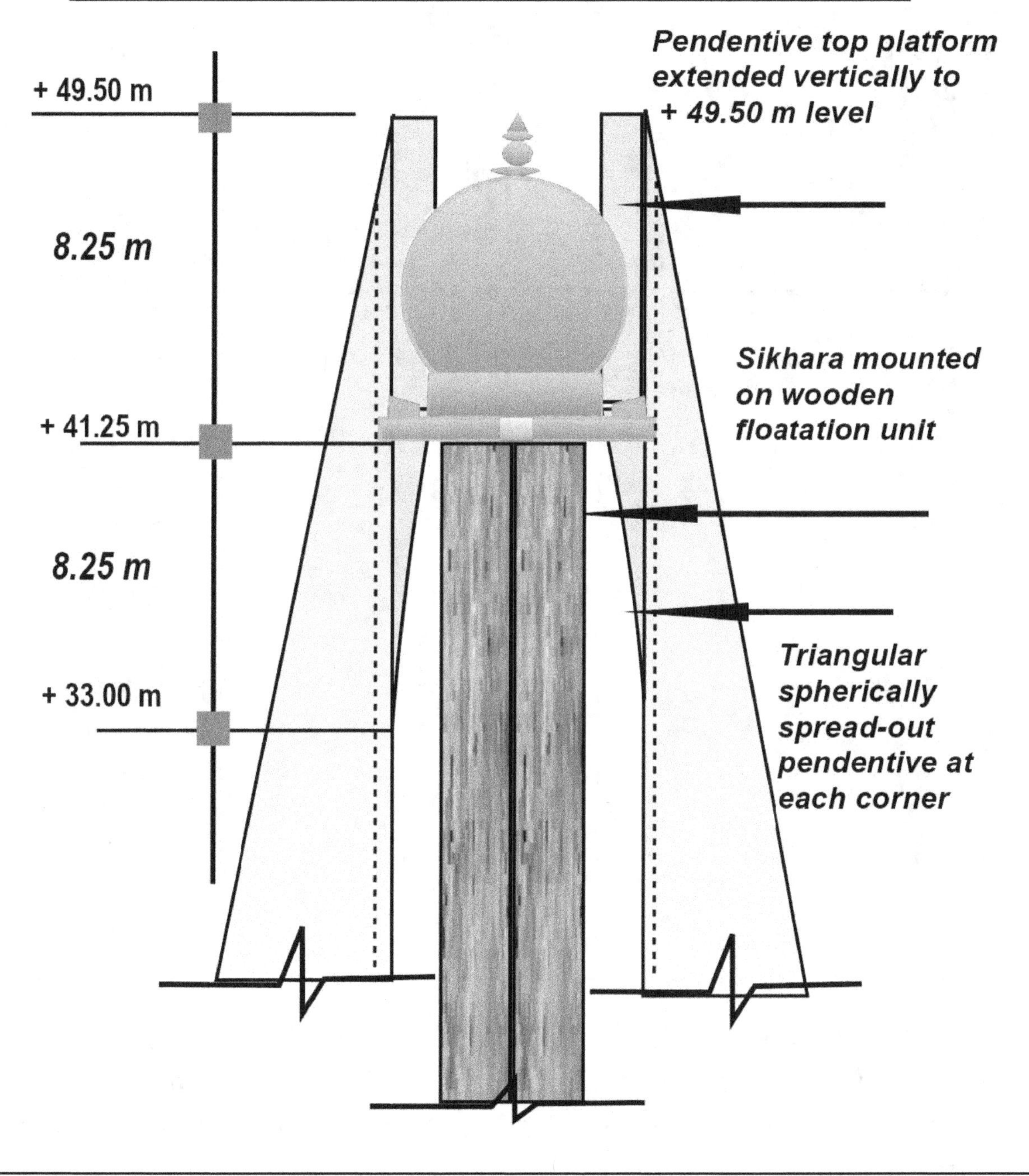

Sikhara on the wooden float rotated 45 degrees clockwise horizontally above +49.50 m to align and rest the corners on the pendentive platforms.

8.25 M HIGH LIFT INCLUDES THE MASSIVE WEIGHT PLUS THE WEIGHT OF 8.25 M HIGH WOODEN FLOATATION UNIT

+ 49.50 m
8.25 m
+ 41.25 m
8.25 m
+ 33.00 m

Pendentive top platform extended vertically to + 49.50 m level

Sikhara mounted on wooden floatation unit

Triangular spherically spread-out pendentive at each corner

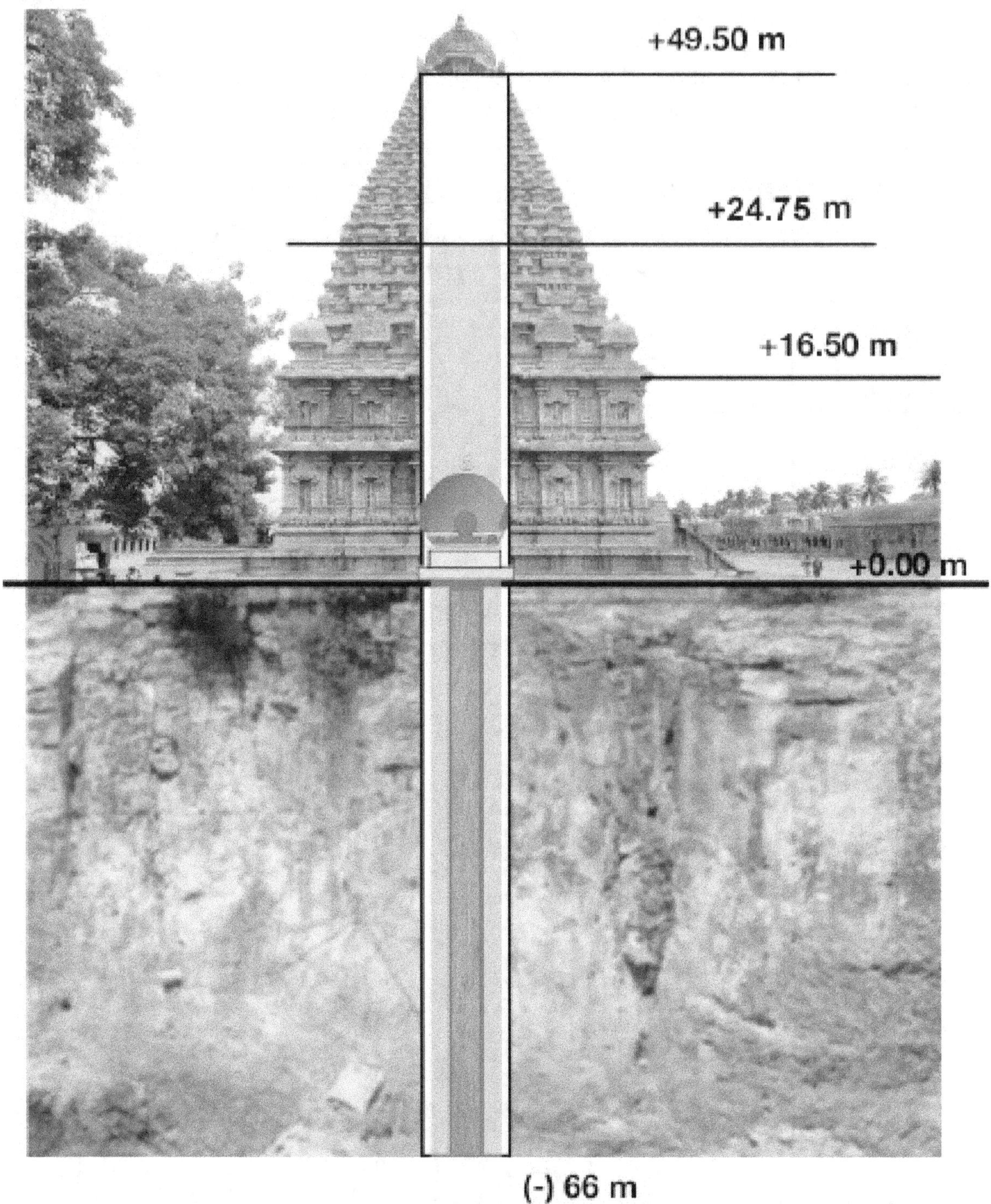

The process requires 3516 m3 of water to flow down from higher storage to lift the massive weight from the Courtyard +0.00 m to the Summit +49.50 m level. The system attains equilibrium when the water level reaches and stops at +24.75 m

Mount Kailash at + 33.00 m level

The Emperor Raja Raja Cholan presumably started the operation after performing religious offerings and adoration on the deity of Lord Shiva at + 33 m level on the scheduled day by pouring holy water brought from the sacred river, the Ganges .

Siva Ganga Tank

While the Sikhara arrived and majestically seated on the summit before the Sun's evening rays hit the earth, the holy river Ganges water that flowed from Lord Shiva's statue and became mixed up in the large volume of water stored in the Annexe and Circumambulatory free spaces has finally drained and settled at the near by tank called " **Siva Ganga Tank** "

Sanctum vs Circumambulatory - Floor area ratio		
Sanctum's floor space	7.93 m x 7.93 m	62.88
Area allocated to triangualr shaped cavities	4 Nos x 1/2 x2 m x 4 m	16.00
A Total sanctum area	62.88 + 16	78.88 m^2
Circumambulatory area all around (1.87 m wide passage)	16.52 m x 4 sides x 1.87 m	123.57
Side openings connecting to circumambulatory	3 Nos x 3.97 x 1.98	23.58
Front main entrance	1 No x 2.54 x 3.97	10.08
B Total circumambulatory	123.57 + 23.58 + 10.08	157.23 m^2
Floor area ratio	78.88 : 157.23	1:2

Lift designed

Displaced volume of water is 8.25 m height of the wooden float's volume

8.25 m x 47.39 m^2 = 390 m^3 and 390 m^3 x 1 MT per m^3 = 390 MT of mass

Weight = 390 MT x 1000 x 9.81 = 3826 kN

Density of the wooden float = 500 kg / m^3 (half the density of water)

Mass consumed by the wooden float = 50% x 390 MT = 195 MT (1913 kN weight)

Remaining 50% = 390 - 195 = 195 MT (1913 kN weight)

195 MT of mass contributes to the lifting of Sikhara or any other material designed by the Chola engineers!!

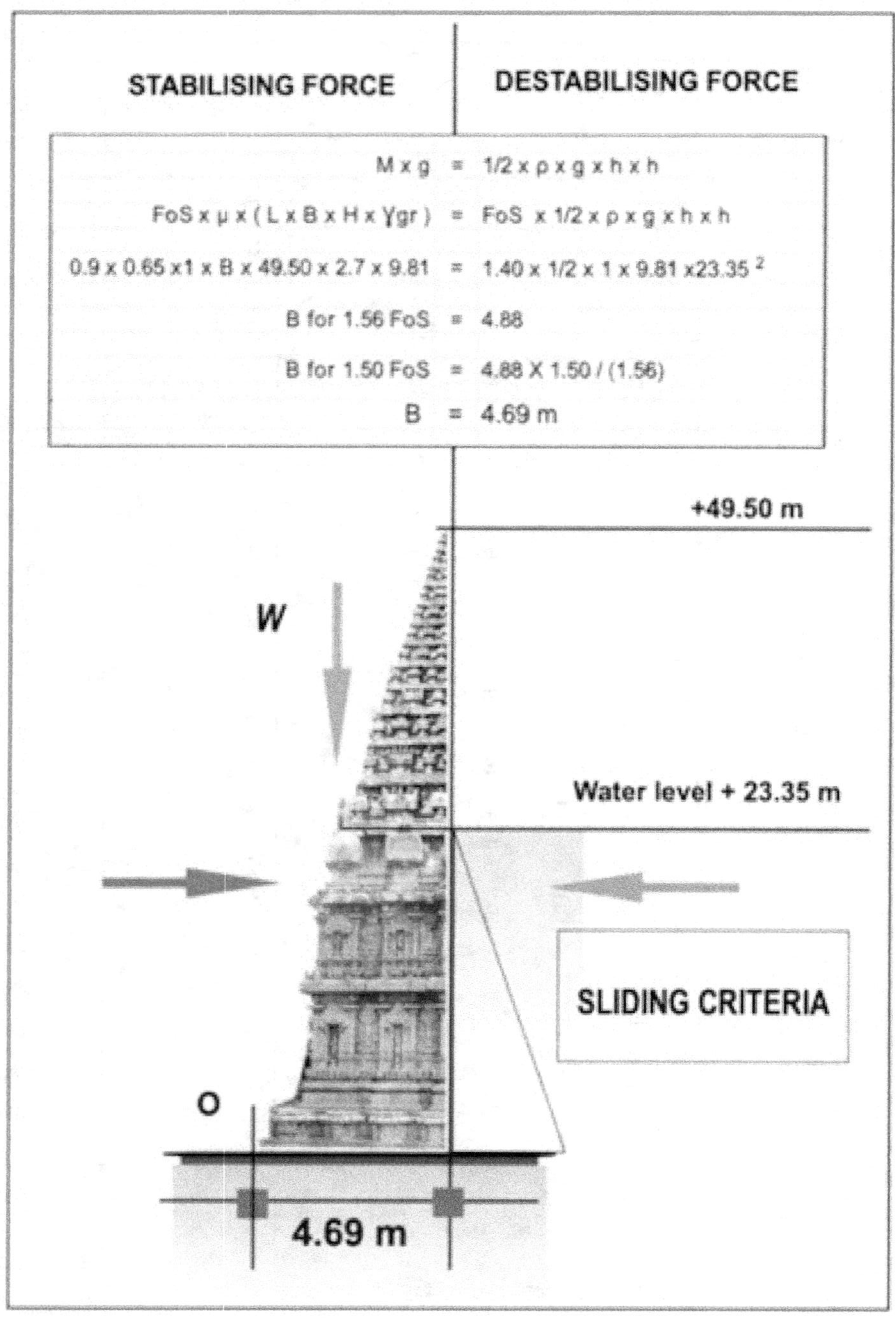
STABILISING FORCE
DESTABILISING FORCE
M x g = 1/2 x ρ x g x h x h
FoS x μ x (L x B x H x Υgr) = FoS x 1/2 x ρ x g x h x h
0.9 x 0.65 x 1 x B x 49.50 x 2.7 x 9.81 = 1.40 x 1/2 x 1 x 9.81 x 23.35 ²
B for 1.56 FoS = 4.88
B for 1.50 FoS = 4.88 X 1.50 / (1.56)
B = 4.69 m
+49.50 m
W
Water level + 23.35 m
SLIDING CRITERIA
O
4.69 m
STABILISING MOMENT
DESTABILISING MOMENT
M x g x B/2 = 1/2 x ρ x g x h x h x h/3
FoS x (L x B x H x Υgr) x B/2 = FoS x 1/2 x ρ x g x h x h x h/3
0.9 x 1 x B x 49.50 x 2.7 x 9.81 x B/2 = 1.40 x 1/2 x 1 x 9.81 x 23.35 ³ / 3
B for 1.56 FoS = 7.03
B for 1.50 FoS = 7.03 X 1.50 / (1.56)
B = 6.76 m
+49.50 m
W
Water level + 23.35 m
OVERTURNING CRITERIA
O
6.76 m

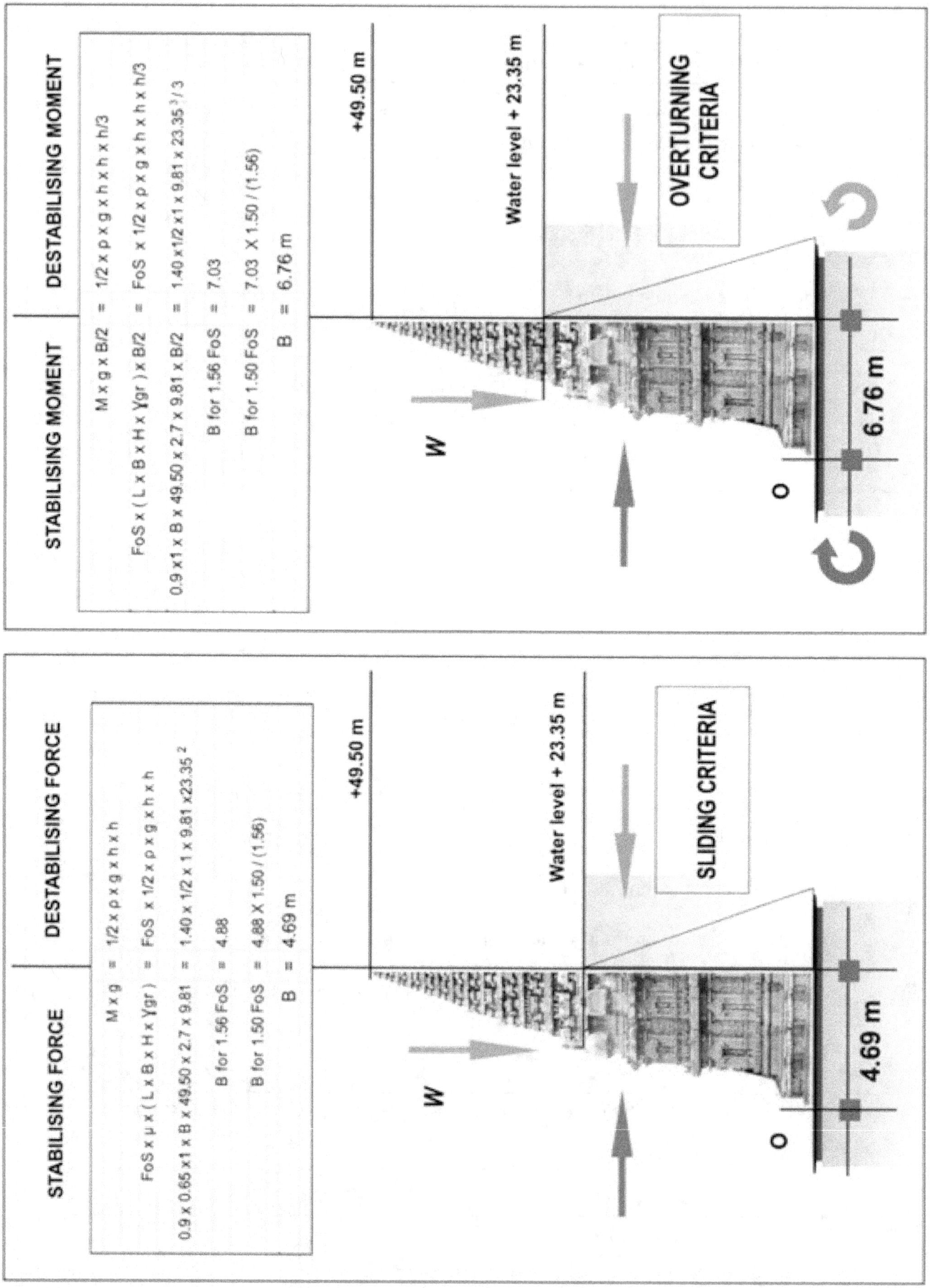

Forces and moments - Reservoir full condition and maximum water level +23.35 m - Exercise A

Description	Force calculation	FV in kN	FH in kN	Lever arm m	Resisting moments in kN m	Overturning moments in kN m	C/s area in m^2
Vertical forces							
Base slab	1m x10.63 x 0.30 x 26.49	84.48		5.32	448.99		3.19
Structure above from +0.30 to +16.50 m lvl	1 m x (8.09) x16.20 x 26.49	3471.73		6.59	22861.32		131.06
Structure above 16.50 m to +49.50 m lvl	1m x 1/2 x (8.09) x 33 x 26.49	3536.02		7.93	28052.29		133.49
Cladding over sloped vimana surface	1 m x 33.98 x 0.9 x 26.49	810.12		6.59	5334.62		30.58
Cladding up to +16.50 on outer vert. wall	1m x 16.20 x 0.9 x 26.49	386.22		2.09	807.21		14.58
Less circumambulatory opening- rectangular	1m x 1.87 m x10.98 m x 26.49	-543.91		6.34	-3445.66		-20.53
Less circumambulatory opening - triangular	1m x 1/2 x 1.87 m x 4.61 m x 26.49	-114.18		6.34	-723.34		-4.31
Less triangular cavity inside the wall	1 m x 0.50 x 49.50 x 26.49	-655.63		10.38	-6805.41		-24.75
Water weight over cavity from +0.00 m lvl	1 m x 0.50 x 23.35 x 9.81	114.53		10.38	1188.84		
Corner pendentives and projection above + 33.00 m lvl	1 m x 0.18 x 16.50 x 26.49	78.68		10.72	843.40		2.97
Water weight over pendentive top from +0.00 m lvl	1 m x 0.25 x 23.35 x 9.81	57.27		10.76	616.18		
Less side door openings	1 m x (2.90 x11.80X1.98) x 75% / 7.93 x 26.49	-168.79		3.95	-666.74		-3.24
Top arch. additional projection on sloped vimana's surface	1 m x 0.45 x 33.98 x 26.49	405.06		6.59	2667.31		15.29
Lateral hydrostatic force	1m x 0.50 x 9.81 x 23.35 x 23.35		2674.32	7.78		20815.10	
Total		7461.58	2674.32		51179.01	20815.10	278.33

Forces and moments - Reservoir empty condition and no water inside the chamber + 23.35 m - Exercise B

Description	Force calculation	FV in kN	FH in kN	Lever arm m	Resisting moments in kN m	Overturning moments in kN m	C/s area in m²
Vertical forces							
Base slab	1m x10.63 x 0.30 x 26.49	84.48		5.32	448.99		3.19
Structure above from +0.30 to +16.50 m lvl	1 m x (8.09) x16.20 x 26.49	3471.73		6.59	22861.32		131.06
Structure above 16.50 m to +49.50 m lvl	1m x 1/2 x (8.09) x 33 x 26.49	3536.02		7.93	28052.29		133.49
Cladding over sloped vimana surface	1 m x 33.98 x 0.9 x 26.49	810.12		6.59	5334.62		30.58
Cladding up to +16.50 on outer vert. wall	1m x 16.20 x 0.9 x 26.49	386.22		2.09	807.21		14.58
Less circumambulatory opening- rectangular	1m x 1.87 m x10.98 m x 26.49	-543.91		6.34	-3445.66		-20.53
Less circumambulatory opening - triangular	1m x 1/2 x 1.87 m x 4.61 m x 26.49	-114.18		6.34	-723.34		-4.31
Less triangular cavity inside the Wall	1 m x 0.50 x 49.50 x 26.49	-655.63		10.38	-6805.41		-24.75
Water weight over cavity from +0.00 m lvl	1 m x 0.50 x 23.35 x 9.81	0.00		10.38	0.00		
Corner pendentives and projection above + 33.00 m lvl	1 m x 0.18 x 16.50 x 26.49	78.68		10.72	843.40		2.97
Water weight over pendentive top from +0.00 m lvl	1 m x 0.25 x 23.35 x 9.81	0.00		10.76	0.00		
Less side door openings	1 m x (2.90 x11.80X1.98) x 75% / 7.93 x 26.49	-168.79		3.95	-666.74		-3.24
Top arch. additional projection on sloped vimana's surface	1 m x 0.45 x 33.98 x 26.49	405.06		6.59	2667.31		15.29
Lateral hydrostatic force	1m x 0.50 x 9.81 x 23.35 x 23.35		0.00	7.78		0.00	
Total		7289.78	0.00		49373.99	0.00	278.33

Exercise A - Reservoir in full condition (Water inside the chamber up to +23.35 m)

Width of the base	10.63	m	
$\sum V$ - Algebraic sum of vertical forces	7461.58	kN	
$\sum H$ - Algebraic sum of horizontal forces	2674.32	kN	
$\sum Mr$ - Algebraic sum of resisting moments	51179.01	kN m	
$\sum Mo$ - Algebraic sum of overturning moments	20815.10	kN m	
Resultant distance $x=(\sum Mr -\sum Mo) / (\sum V)$	4.07	m	
One half of the width of the base b/2	5.32	m	
One sixth of the width of the base b/6	1.77	m	
Eccentricity e = b/2 - x	1.25	m	
Eccentricity 'e' is less than b/6 and hence safe	1.25 < 1.77		Safe
Maximum stress at toe			
Pn maximum $= \sum V /(b) \times (1+6e/b)$	1195.46	< 1620	kN/m^2
			Safe
Minimum stress at heel			
Pn minimum $= \sum V /(b) \times (1-6e/6)$	208.42	< 1620	kN/m^2
			Safe
FoS for sliding $= \mu \times \sum V / (\sum H)$	1.81	> 1.50	Safe
FoS for overturning$= \sum Mr / \sum Mo$	2.46	> 2	Safe

Exercise B - Reservoir empty condition (No water inside the chamber up to +23.35 m)

Width of the base	10.63	m	
$\sum V$ - Algebraic sum of vertical forces	7289.78	kN	
$\sum H$ - Algebraic sum of horizontal forces	0	kN	
$\sum Mr$ - Algebraic sum of resisting moments	49373.99	kN m	
$\sum Mo$ - Algebraic sum of overturning moments	0	kN m	
Resultant distance $x =(\sum Mr -\sum Mo) / (\sum V)$	6.77	m	
One half of the width of the base b/2	5.32	m	
One sixth of the width of the base b/6	1.77	m	
Eccentricity e = b/2 - x	-1.46	m	
Eccentricity 'e' is less than b/6 and hence safe	1.46 < 1.77		Safe
Maximum stress at toe			
Pn maximum $= \sum V /(b) \times (1+6e/b)$	121.40	<1620	kN/m^2
			Safe
Minimum stress at heel			
Pn minimum $= \sum V /(b) \times (1-6e/6)$	1250.15	< 1620	kN/m^2
			Safe

Eccentricity for water level +23.35 m
Water level +23.35 m
B/6 = 10.63/6 = 1.77 m
B/3
B/3
Eccentricity less than B/6 = 1.25 m and Safe

Eccentricity in Empty Condition
B/6 = 10.63/6 = 1.77 m
B/3
Eccentricity less than B/6 = 1.46 m and Safe

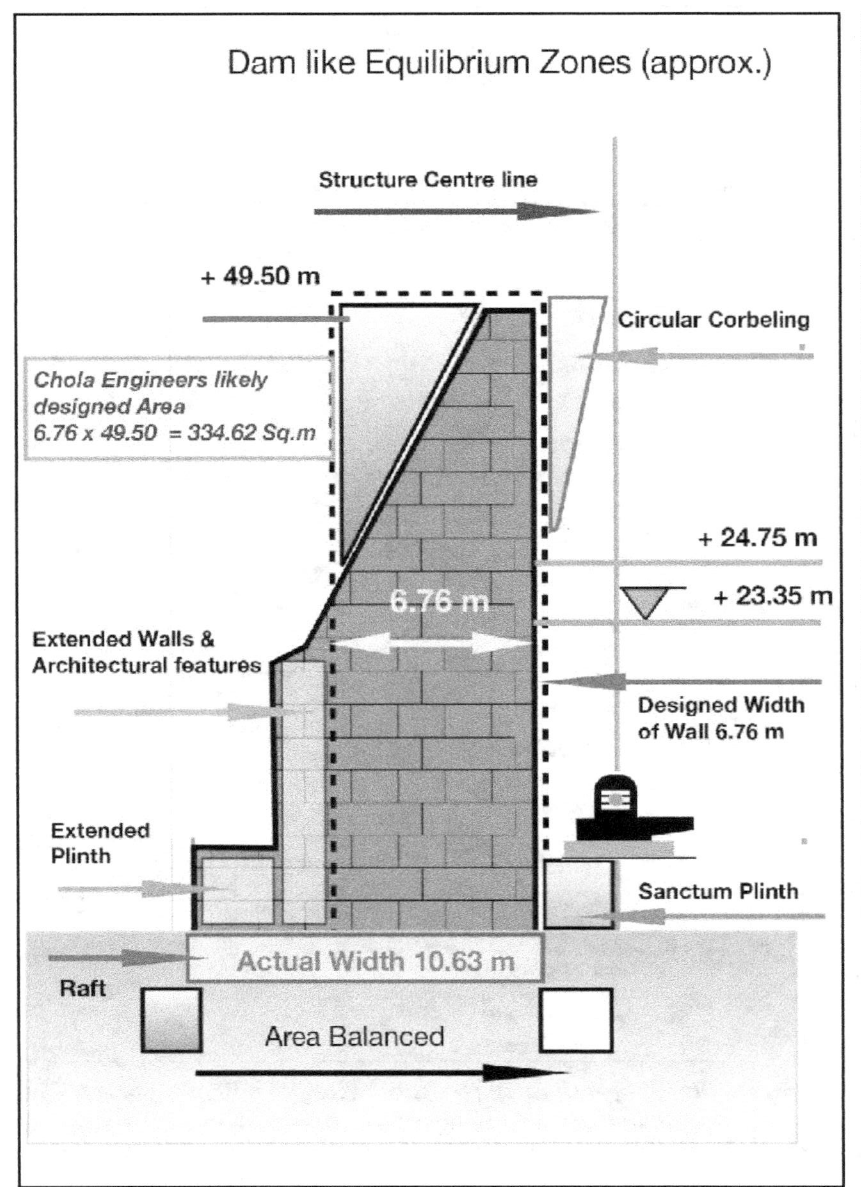

Dam like Equilibrium Zones (approx.)
Structure Centre line
+ 49.50 m
Circular Corbeling
Chola Engineers likely designed Area 6.76 x 49.50 = 334.62 Sq.m
+ 24.75 m
+ 23.35 m
6.76 m
Extended Walls & Architectural features
Designed Width of Wall 6.76 m
Extended Plinth
Sanctum Plinth
Actual Width 10.63 m
Raft
Area Balanced

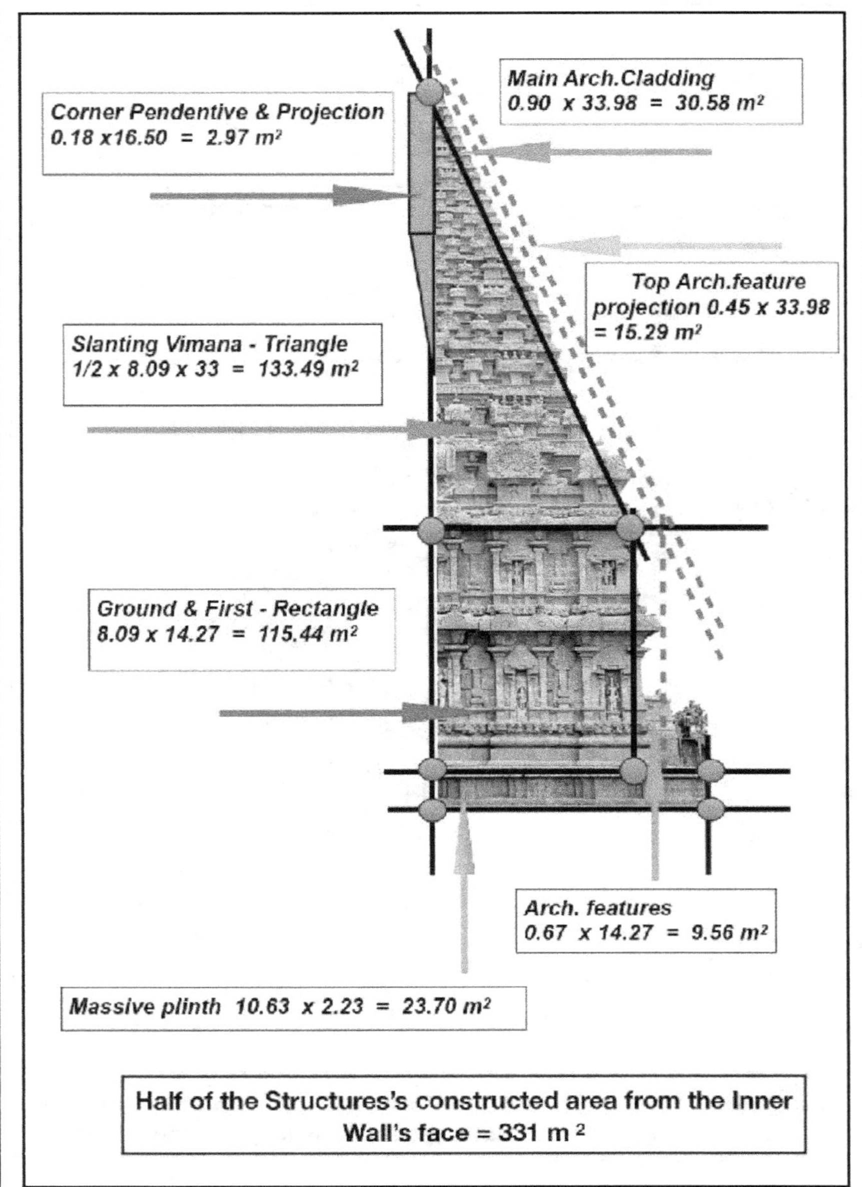

Corner Pendentive & Projection 0.18 x16.50 = 2.97 m²
Main Arch.Cladding 0.90 x 33.98 = 30.58 m²
Top Arch.feature projection 0.45 x 33.98 = 15.29 m²
Slanting Vimana - Triangle 1/2 x 8.09 x 33 = 133.49 m²
Ground & First - Rectangle 8.09 x 14.27 = 115.44 m²
Arch. features 0.67 x 14.27 = 9.56 m²
Massive plinth 10.63 x 2.23 = 23.70 m²
Half of the Structures's constructed area from the Inner Wall's face = 331 m²

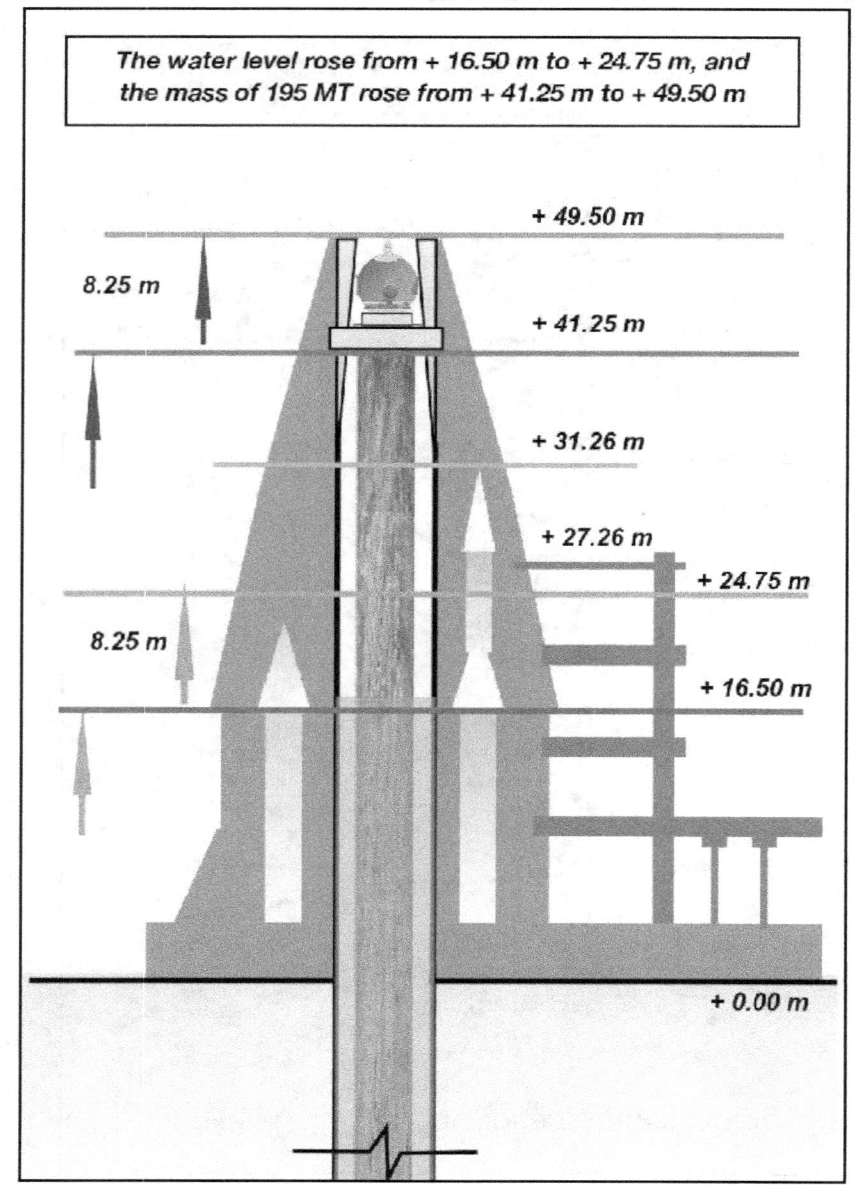

The water level rose from + 16.50 m to + 24.75 m, and the mass of 195 MT rose from + 41.25 m to + 49.50 m
+ 49.50 m
8.25 m
+ 41.25 m
+ 31.26 m
+ 27.26 m
+ 24.75 m
8.25 m
+ 16.50 m
+ 0.00 m

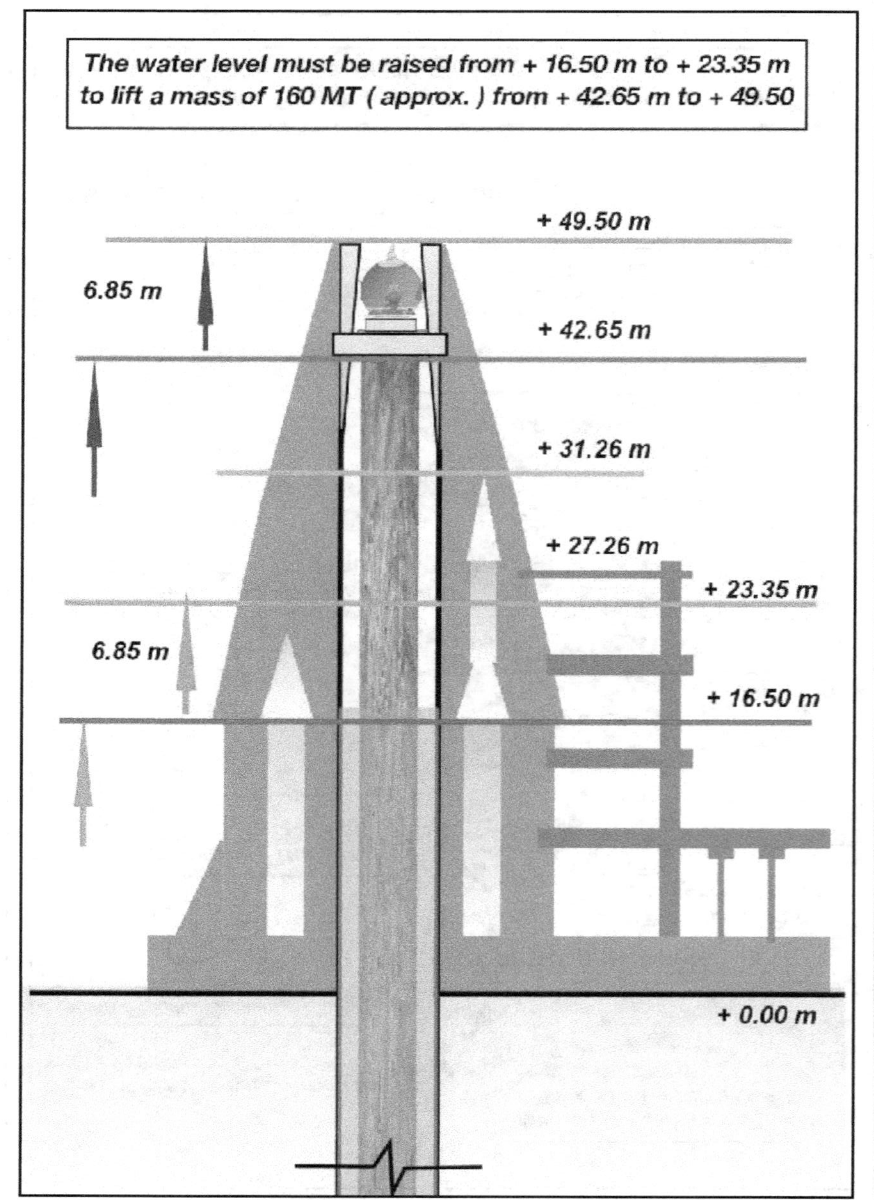

The water level must be raised from + 16.50 m to + 23.35 m to lift a mass of 160 MT (approx.) from + 42.65 m to + 49.50
+ 49.50 m
6.85 m
+ 42.65 m
+ 31.26 m
+ 27.26 m
+ 23.35 m
6.85 m
+ 16.50 m
+ 0.00 m

13

Logical Shifting

How the Sikhara gained access to the sanctum chamber will be more interesting.

The entire massive block reportedly weighs 81 MT. Referring to ASI drawings and dimensions, the detailed computation shows the combined weight to be around 140 MT of force.

A single monolithic block of rock or interlocking components assembled at ground level inside the sanctuary before the vertical lifting operation are the only two possibilities that can be considered.

If it was a monolith carved from a massive block of granite, it is justifiable and certain that no rainwater leakage has occurred to date. On the other hand, if the unit was made of assembled components, perfect assembly and interlocking at the top level would have been impossible and difficult to achieve.

While the soil parameters and the process did not support it technically, logically, and practically, a sufficient working area around the summit level's 32 m periphery cannot be made available to pull, lift, tilt, and install the massive weighted elements. The available space around the Sikhara block is so limited that a large number of elephants and other resources cannot be deployed and employed.

Only 8 to 12 elephants can practically stand within a 32-m periphery at the top, which has been analysed previously. An elephant can only carry 300 kg on average, therefore lifting even 81 MT takes around 250 elephants working simultaneously at the summit, which seems unfeasible given the restricted space. An African bush elephant's height is between 3 and 4 m. The trunk is 1.8–2m long.

How can an elephant with these physical characteristics lift above 9 to 10 m to align and arrange the granite components on the profile of the Sikhara?

The Chola engineers must have assembled the entire unit as a single monolithic block at ground level before lifting and installing it at the summit as a perfect assembly to the final equilibrium position at the top with the restricted areas is more complex and difficult.

Because the traditional method of laying the massive ramp and employing a large number of elephants became technically and practically impractical, the only option was to gradually move the massive unit from the side of the Vimana beneath the ground far below the foundation level to enter the sanctum shaft before its vertical rise.

While designing and profiling the entire dome unit, they devised a masterful technique for moving the entire unit inside the sanctuary using a safe, well-planned scientific approach and understanding. They carefully moved the unit from the assembly yard for alignment and positioning beneath the sanctuary as an initial operation before processing for the vertical movement, as explained below.

The Sikhara is a spherical dome supported by the stem or Griva wall. According to the ASI measurement, as documented and used in the earlier computations, the outer diameter of the dome is 5.39 m, the height is 5.87 m, and the stem wall height is 1.91 m, resting on a square base of granite block of 7.93 m × 7.93 m. It is evaluated by taking into account the monolithic spherical dome and stem wall structure of a cupola resting on a square base.

As calculated and shown in the table "Mass of the total Sikhara unit," the total volume of the spherical dome, vertical drum, and horizontal slab, including the four pairs of holy bulls, is 250 m³, while the volume of solid granite is 51.52 m³.

The total volume of free space inside is 250–51.52 and equals 198.48 m³.

The base slab has a circular through-opening with a diameter of approximately 850 mm, which serves as the container's mouth from the bottom. When this aperture at the slab's bottom is plugged and closed, the entire unit transforms into a hollow spherical granite ball, a granite balloon, or a granite drum, and it operates as an airtight sealed granite container having a mass of material of approximately 140 MT by trapping an air volume of 198 m³ inside.

The law of physics is that a liquid maintains something floating, providing lightness to any heavily immersed object inside the water, through the power of buoyancy. According to science, one trapped litre of air has the potential to lift and float a kilogram of weight under water against gravity.

When the bottom mouth of the dome unit is sealed, it transforms into an airtight hollow spherical granite vessel that floats in water. A hollow object is generally light in weight inside the water, so the amount of water displaced is usually sufficient to match the object's weight, and it floats.

Ancient Tamil engineers were clever to create a granite dome with a lower mass-to-volume ratio than water for this reason.

The overall mass of the unit is 51.52 m³ × 2.70 MT/ m³= 139.11 MT, and the total volume of the unit is 250 m³.

The actual designed density = 139.11/250 = 0.56 MT/m^3.

The density of water is 1 MT/ m^3, whereas the density of the spherical granite dome here is 0.56 MT/m^3, resulting in a net positive buoyant force and it floats on water. The secret of floating is that the density of the object should be smaller than the density of water. Even if the entire unit is immersed, the downward pull of gravity is reversed upwards due to positive buoyancy caused by the lower mass–volume ratio.

In science and engineering, the weight of an object is the force acting on the object due to gravity.

When an object is submerged in fluid, it will experience buoyancy; the fluid will push it upward with a force equal to the weight of the displaced fluid. So the apparent weight of an object that is fully submerged in a fluid is its actual weight on the gravitational field minus the buoyancy.

The massive Sikhara unit weighing 140 MT force is tightly plugged to make it airtight and filled with 198 m^3 air. When fully immersed, the unit will try to displace more than 140 m^3 of mass of water, and the trapped air weighs much lesser than the water it displaces, so the water pushes up harder than the air pushes down, allowing the Sikhara to remain buoyant and float on the surface. The buoyancy is strong enough (more than 140 MT force) to hold up the weight of the Sikhara without sinking.

The airtight Sikhara unit as a whole will float like a diver's air-lifting bag used in marine work. A lifting bag is a type of diving equipment that consists of a sturdy, airtight bag with straps used to move heavy objects underwater utilising the bag's buoyancy. The diver can either move the heavy object horizontally underwater or send it to the surface unattended in the marine works.

Therefore, the Sikhara was designed in such a manner that it can get submerged in water; the buoyancy of the immersed granite drum with trapped air inside forces it up, allowing the unit to float and be dragged horizontally underwater to enter the sanctum through a predefined and preformed large underground passage comparable to an underground arched tunnel.

Sikhara needs a large-sized entrance underneath the structure to enter the sanctum shaft. This opening may have been provided either on one side or in one of the corners so the square base can enter diagonally and rest on the four triangular cut cavities platform made in the walls of the well.

How can an entrance for this requirement be provided while the Vimana is already being built vertically to a large height?

A large underground passageway, comparable to an arched tunnel, could have been created from the outside of Vimana to connect to the adjacent Siva Ganga Tank, with an opening and closing system similar to a sturdy shutter or gate.

The arch is extremely strong in the face of the enormous compressive load from the superstructure. The limestone rock mass beneath the raft may have been bored from the side of the Vimana far below the level of the raft at $(-)16.50$ m or down below to accommodate the total dimensions of the Sikhara with allowances for free and easy horizontal movement and alignment inside the tunnel, as shown in the typical drawing. The access might have been carefully created and constructed as a covered underground tunnel through the rock layers for the length of the raft foundation, with the rest of the tunnel length done by the open cut and cover method.

To complete this mission, the engineers had to create a large body of water nearby.

This requirement and the feature can be seen in the surrounding layout of the temple, where the deep Siva Ganga Tank was built to connect to the underground passage roughly at $(-)$ 16.50 m or down below. All of these amenities in the area suggest that the Siva Ganga Tank was used as an assembly yard during the phase of construction for the Sikhara as well as for conducting a few preliminary test runs before horizontal floating movement to reach beneath the sanctum shaft through the underground tunnel.

When everything was ready, the unit was submerged and suspended underwater after a few test runs and observations in the tank, then horizontally floated through the underground tunnel built around the level of $(-)16.50$ m below the raft foundation connecting Siva Ganga Tank to make the entry inside the sanctum shaft for further alignment and positioning before the vertical journey. Niches may have been created to prevent overturning or colliding tunnel sidewalls during flotation.

The unit entered the sanctum shaft through a large arch opening after floating through the tunnel from the Siva Ganga Tank. The opening featured a sturdy shutter for frequent opening and closing, a gate-type structure, or a granite stone wall covering before the vertical lifting operation to withstand significant water pressure, which may have been predefined and provided at the north side or in one north side corner of the structure connecting Siva Ganga Tank with the short travel distance.

The massive block entered the sanctum chamber either sideways or diagonally through this large corner entry to align and secure its four projected corners on the triangular cut cavity formations made in the side wall at the tunnel floor level.

Taking advantage of the flotation and lightness of the unit from the law of buoyancy, upon entering the well, a group of highly trained manpower handled and aligned the four corners of the base slab to precisely rest on the four triangular supports specially made inside the triangular slots for a temporary halt before the vertical movement. With the surrounding clearances, these triangular cut formations fit and secure the four corners of the Sikhara base.

The complete unit has been floated in the water, and its apparent weight was less since the block's vertical weight was well balanced by the upward buoyant force. The whole thing was suspended in water and did not come into contact with any hard surface; therefore, friction also was zero, and more workers were not needed for the alignment and positioning at the tunnel base level.

On entry below the sanctum, the unit must be raised to ground level after the tunnel gate mechanism is closed or the large opening of the structure needed to be covered with granite masonry and temporarily supported with a large number of sand-filled gunny bags to sustain the huge hydrostatic pressure from the large height of water column.

At the courtyard base, four-corner spherical triangular pendentive-like corbel supporting platforms similar to the arrangements at +39.85 m level have been created at the corners of the inner face of the wall, with the top level matching the courtyard base.

Water is released into the well from a ground surface source through a channel, or it could have been from the vestibule and circumambulatory storage, so the water level rises inside the chamber and the unit vertically travels up with its four corners secured inside the triangular cut cavities due to buoyancy. This was done for vertical lifting from the level of the tunnel floor to the base of the courtyard.

A circumferentially carved cut in the inner wall could have been designed and made at the courtyard level. The size of this horizontal cavity must accommodate the projected length of the corners as well as Sikhara's base slab thickness, with clearances for obstruction-free horizontal clockwise and anti-clockwise movement. When the unit reaches the courtyard level, the corners of the square base are moved away from the vertical triangular recesses for a 45-degree horizontal clockwise movement, as shown in the drawing. This will allow the four corners of the square base to align and come to a halt on the four-corner pendentive platforms for a brief period.

The Sikhara unit must rotate counter-clockwise for the same 45 degrees by rising from the top of corner platform in order to properly align and secure the four corners inside the triangular-shaped cavities and mount on the wooden deck for a further vertical movement. Further vertical movement will be as a single stage lift that will be directly to the top final seating level +49.50 m from the courtyard floor base without any intermediate halts. To make things easier, four platforms comparable to corbelling supports may have been created and constructed inside the triangular cut cavities for a specific height, with the top aligning with the courtyard.

This is comparable to pendentive corner platforms that support the Sikhara's four corners so that the unit can float and the corners made to move backwards counter-clockwise in a circular horizontal motion through circumferential cut grooves with the use of buoyancy and less labour.

As a result, a brief period was required to construct pendentive supports like arrangements inside the triangular cut cavities, as well as the erection of the long cylindrical wooden flotation system inside the well, so that the Sikhara unit could be properly mounted on the float after the backward rotation prior to vertical movement.

The entire water inside the underground well had to be drained through an outlet located underneath the level of the tunnel or down below to facilitate the installation of the flotation system for the depth of 66 m. The wooden parts of the flotation system could have entered the beneath sanctum shaft via the same tunnel entry used by the Sikhara previously.

To withstand the tremendous hydrostatic pressure and for further processing, the shutter or tunnel arch opening constructed through the limestone rock mass far below the foundation level should have been properly closed and sealed.

In its initial phase, the Sikhara unit travelled horizontally from the Siva Ganga Tank assembly yard to underneath the shrine via an underground passage.

How was the immense weight handled and positioned within the sanctuary before its vertical movement?

How were only a few highly skilled personnel able to position and lock the unit in equilibrium at +49.50 m altitude?

The subsequent topic will address these issues.

Mass over volume of the total Sikhara unit
Monolithic spherical diameter 5.39 m, height 5.87 m , Griva 1.91 m high and slab 0.47 m thick.

Description	Unit	Spherical shell or Dome	Griva or Drum	Slab	Holy bulls	Total
Total outer volume	m^3	173.00	43.50	29.50	4	250.00
Surface area	m^2	131.09	32.33	62.88		
Average wall thickness	mm	100	150	470		
Granite volume	m^3	13.11	4.85	29.55	4	51.51
Granite density	MT/m^3	2.7	2.7	2.7	2.7	
Total mass	MT	35.39	13.09	79.79	10.80	**139.08**
Trapped air or voids inside	m^3	159.89	38.65			198.54
Overall density of the unit with the trapped air inside		**139.08/250 = 0.56 MT /m^3**				

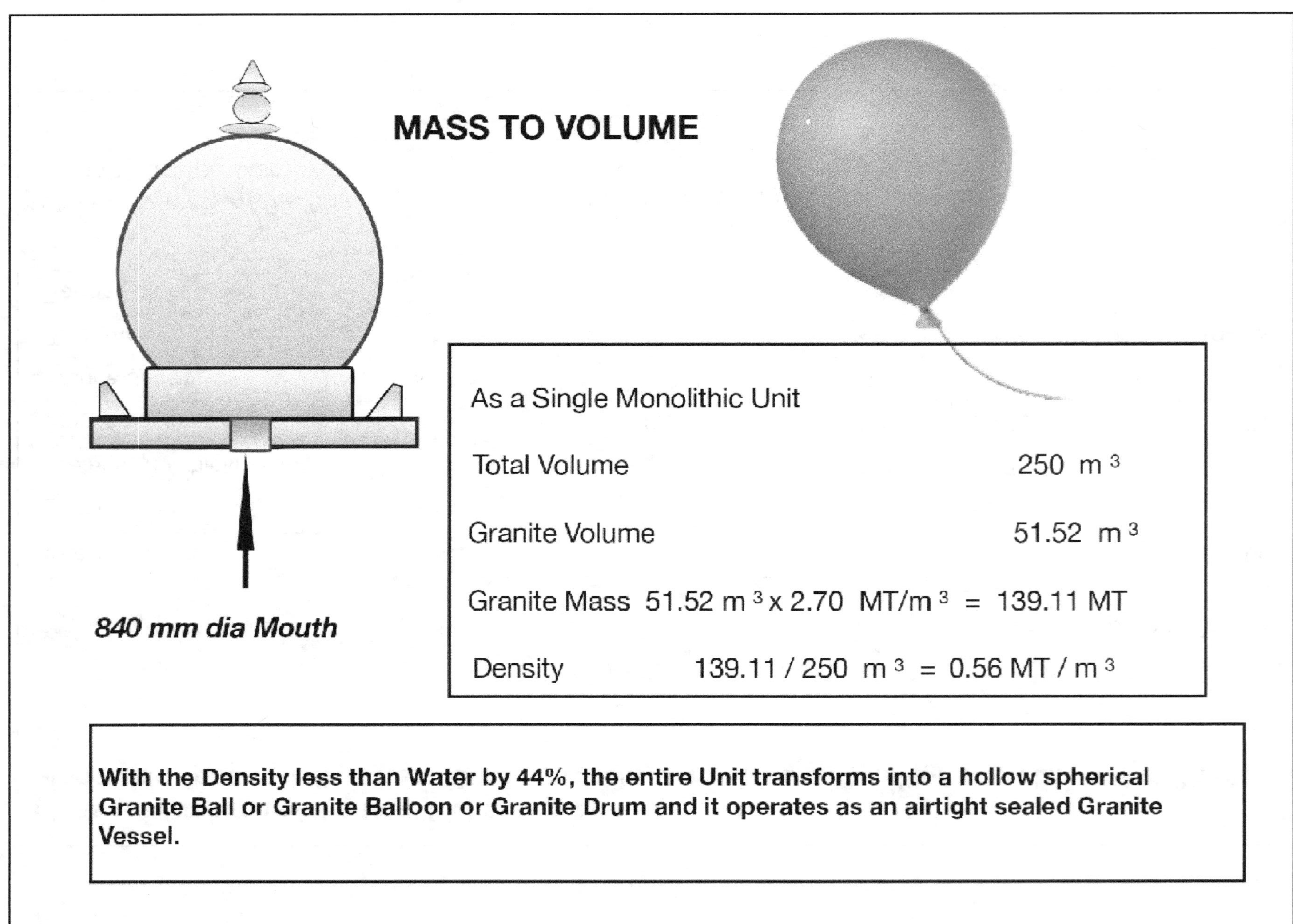

With the Density less than Water by 44%, the entire Unit transforms into a hollow spherical Granite Ball or Granite Balloon or Granite Drum and it operates as an airtight sealed Granite Vessel.

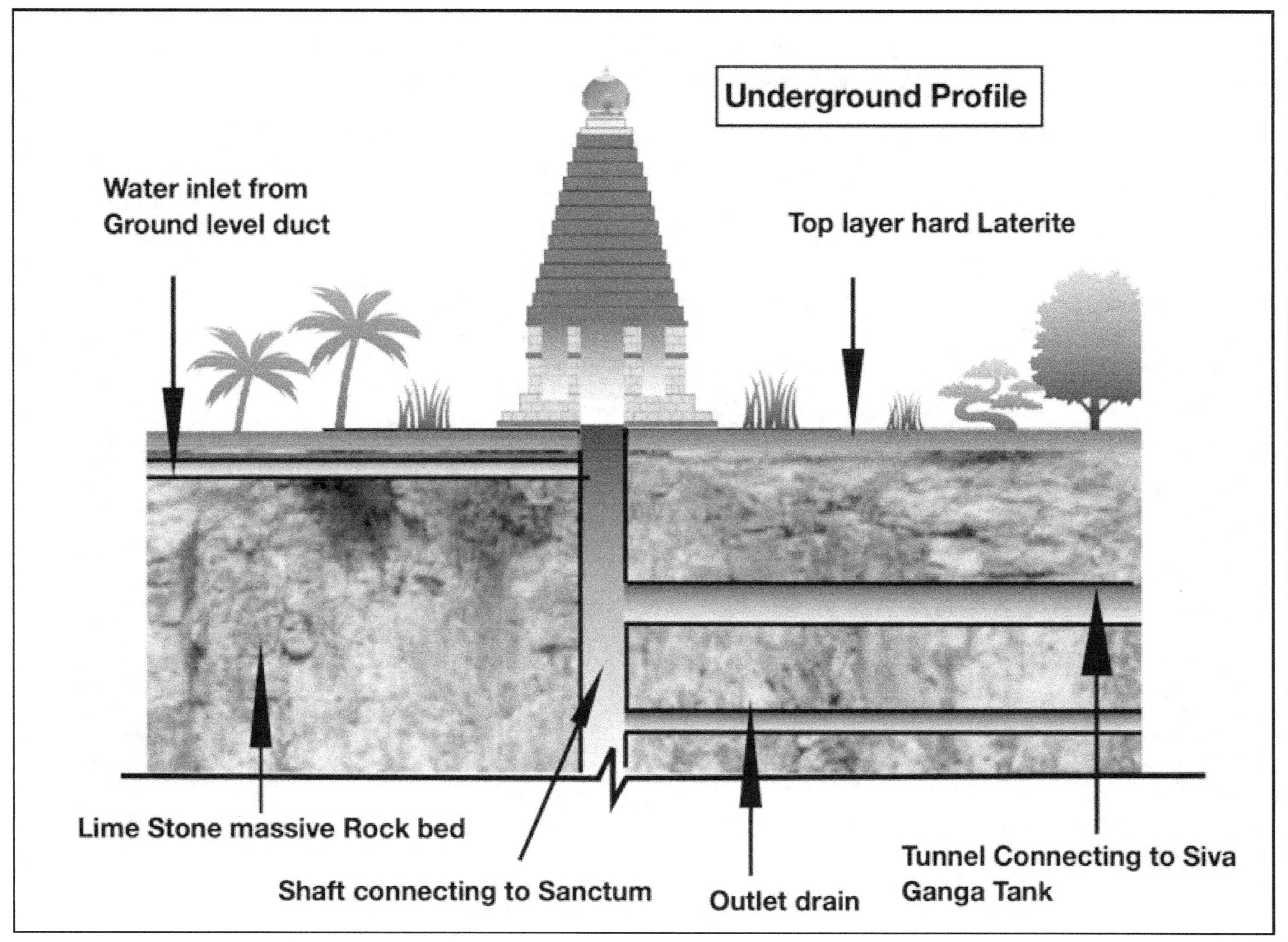

Underground Profile
Water inlet from
Ground level duct
Top layer hard Laterite
Lime Stone massive Rock bed
Shaft connecting to Sanctum
Outlet drain
Tunnel Connecting to Siva
Ganga Tank

With the Mass to Volume ratio 44% lower than Water, the massive Sikhara has been designed to float

Typical underground tunnel connecting Siva Ganga Tank and underneath Sanctum shaft

Less dense than water, the entire granite block gains ability to float and reach underneath the sanctum shaft via tunnel from Siva Ganga Tank

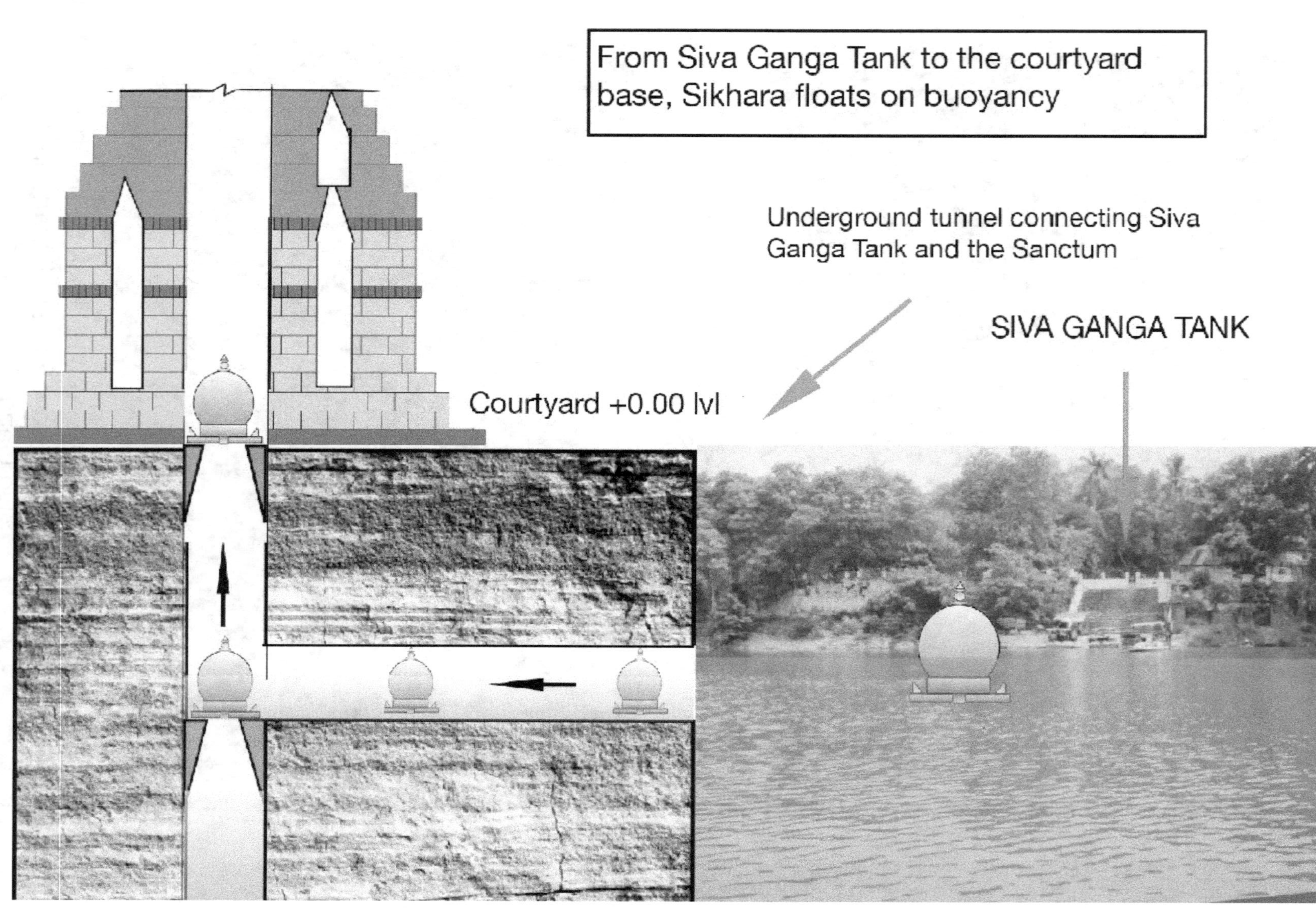
From Siva Ganga Tank to the courtyard
base, Sikhara floats on buoyancy
Underground tunnel connecting Siva
Ganga Tank and the Sanctum
SIVA GANGA TANK
Courtyard +0.00 lvl

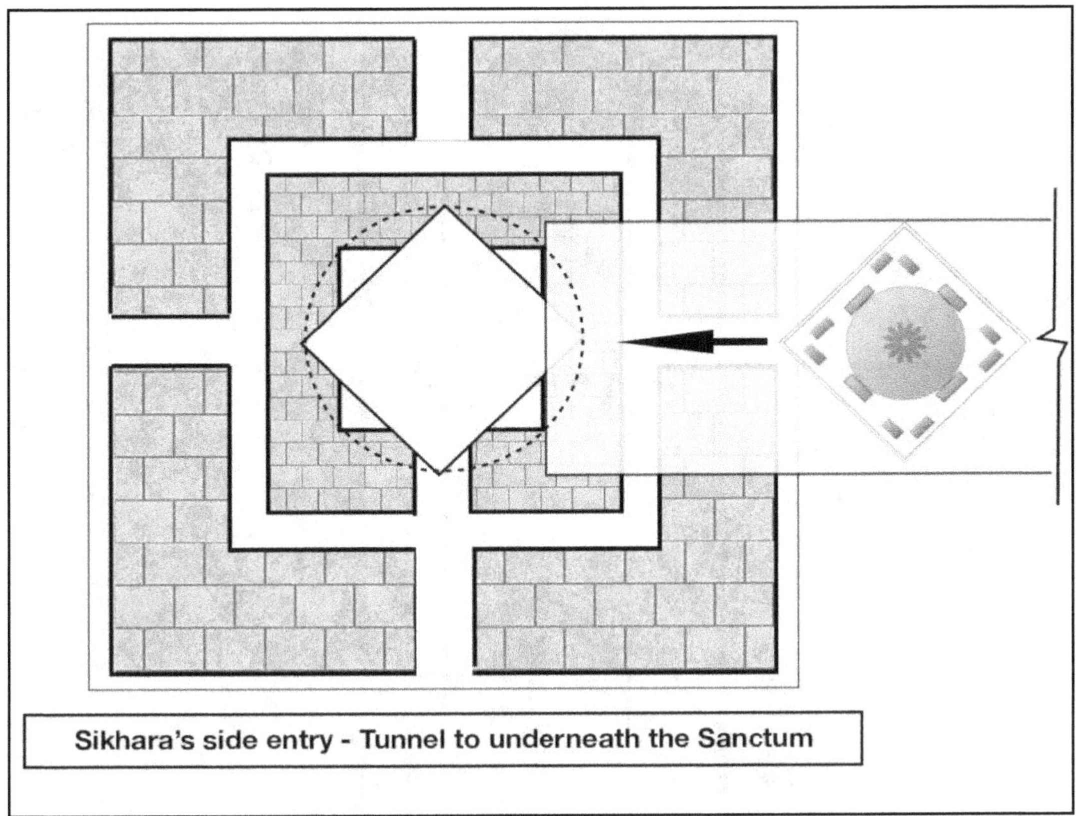

Sikhara's side entry - Tunnel to underneath the Sanctum

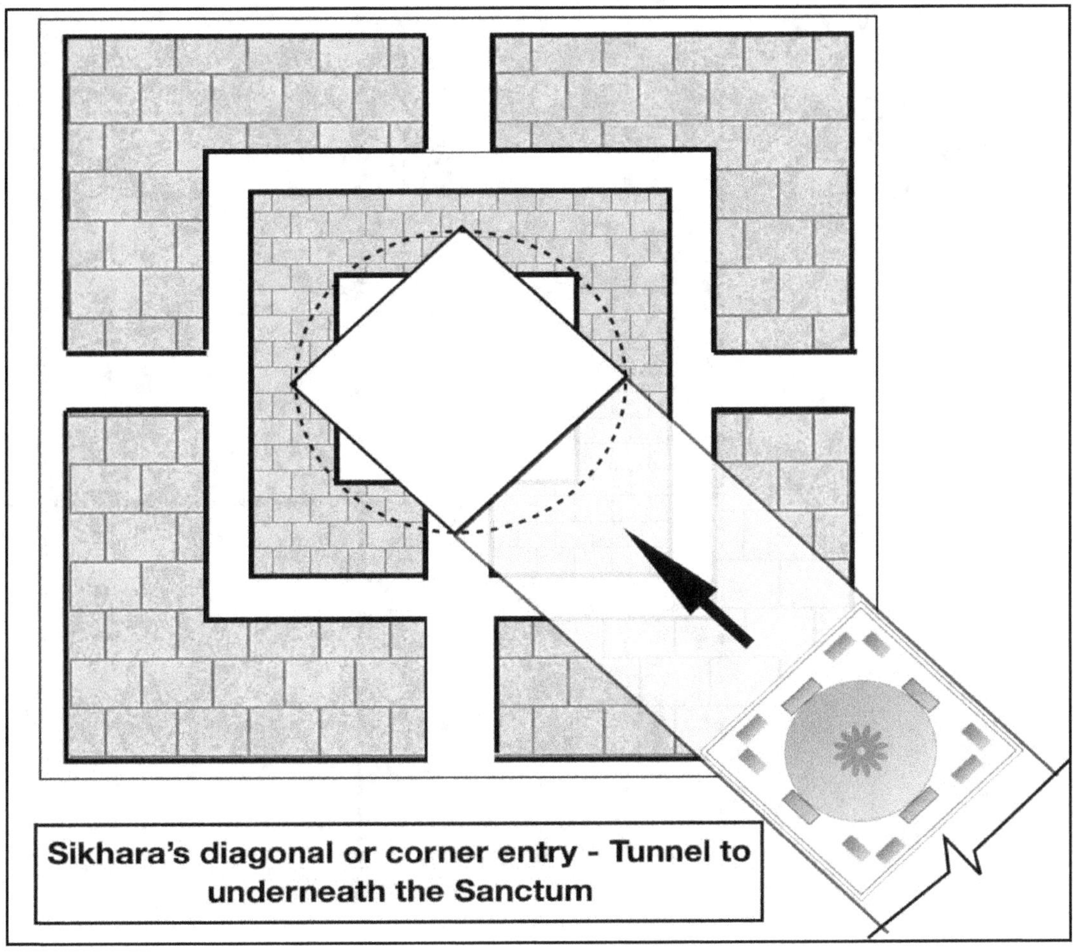

Sikhara's diagonal or corner entry - Tunnel to underneath the Sanctum

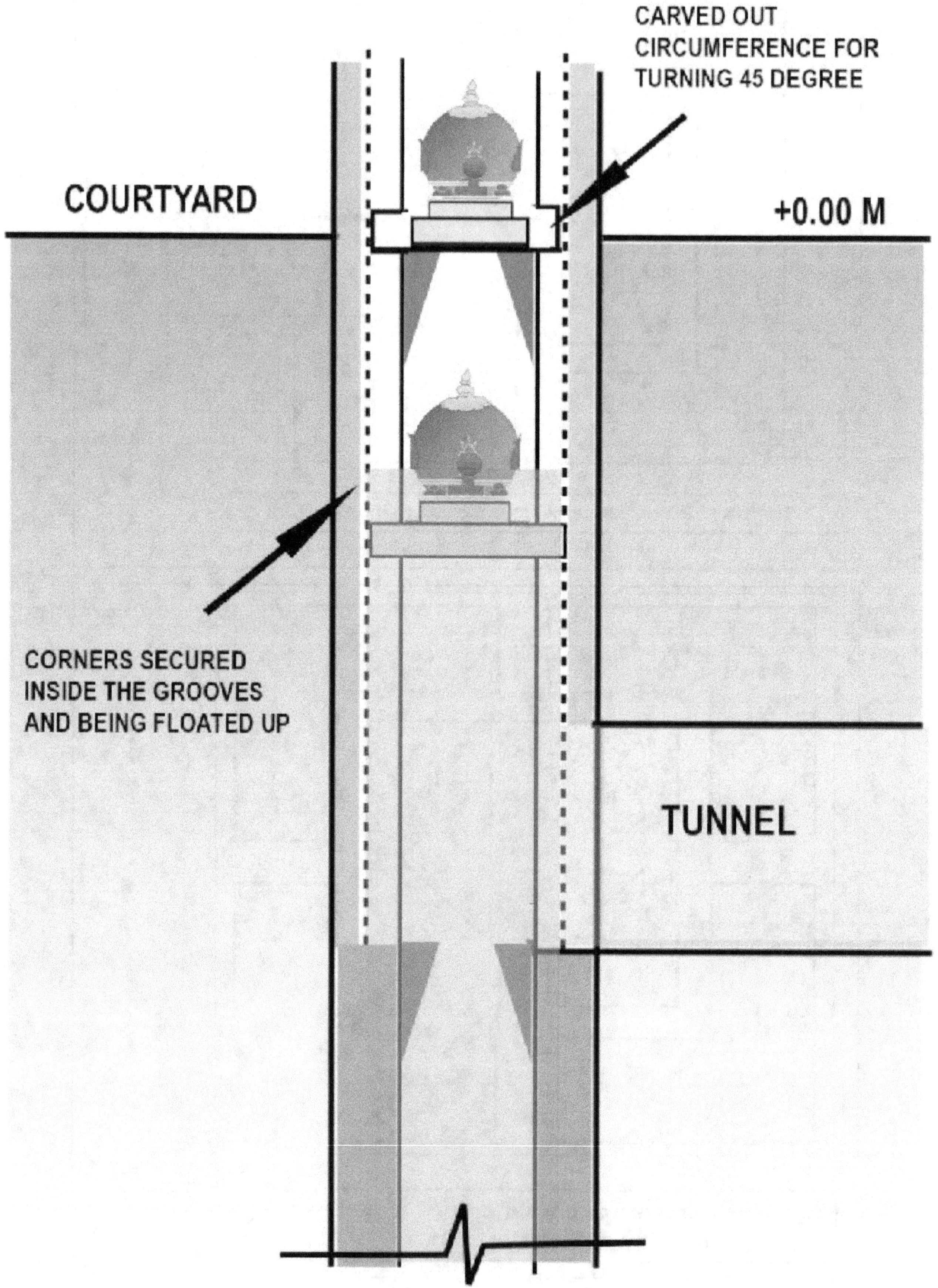

COURTYARD
CARVED OUT CIRCUMFERENCE FOR TURNING 45 DEGREE
+0.00 M
CORNERS SECURED INSIDE THE GROOVES AND BEING FLOATED UP
TUNNEL

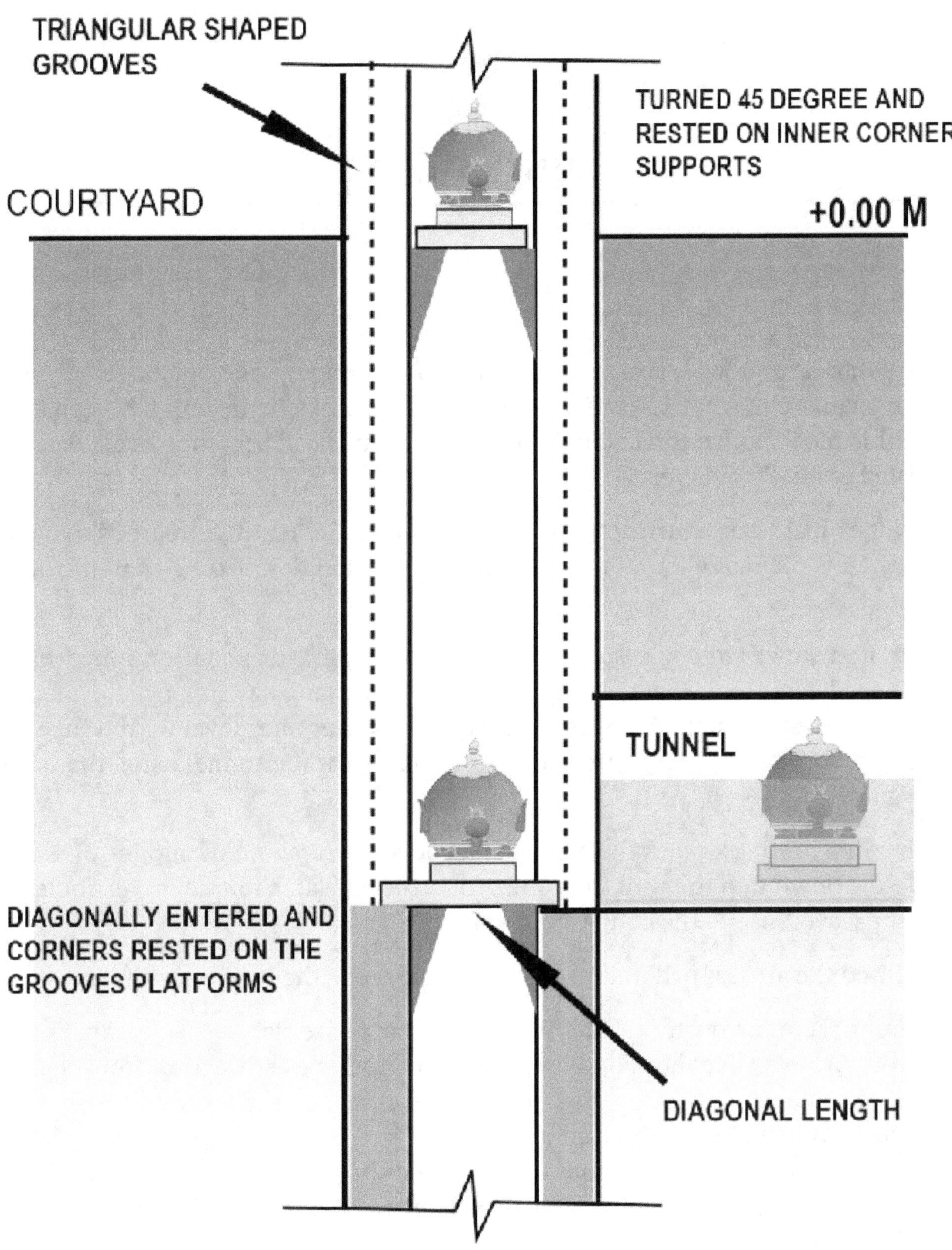

TRIANGULAR SHAPED GROOVES
TURNED 45 DEGREE AND RESTED ON INNER CORNER SUPPORTS
COURTYARD
+0.00 M
TUNNEL
DIAGONALLY ENTERED AND CORNERS RESTED ON THE GROOVES PLATFORMS
DIAGONAL LENGTH

14

Manoeuvring

The entire Sikhara unit was designed, profiled, and built by ancient engineers to hold 198 m³ of air against a mass of 140 MT. As previously researched, the unit has been designed as a monolithic block with a total volume of 250 m³ to function as a submarine vessel or an airtight-sealed granite container.

The entire block mass was constructed as an airtight container and submerged to be floated by the buoyancy of liquid into the extended underground sanctum shaft through the underground passage.

The unit floated slowly into the square chamber through a diagonal entrance from one corner or the side, its four corners precisely fitting into triangular supports formed within the side walls. When the shutter or gate was closed and the water level within the well was raised, the unit was able to ascend from the bottom level of the tunnel using the triangular notches as guides.

To raise the Sikhara block from the tunnel floor level, the required amount of water was allowed to flow down into the well from the ground-level water source or vestibule storage until the water level rose to the courtyard level.

The water lifted the air-trapped unit to the courtyard using the buoyancy theory.

A circumferential cut furrow for the depth of the Sikhara base slab, with clearances to freely move and rotate the corners horizontally in the circumferential direction from the vertical grooves, may have been created at the courtyard level, inside the structure base as shown in the sketches. When the unit arrived at the courtyard level, the four-corner bases were lifted from the vertical grooves and rotated 45 degrees horizontally for a distance of 3.11 m along the circumferential cut furrow, allowing them to be properly aligned and set on the four-corner pendentive-like platforms before being mounted on the wooden flotation deck for its vertical journey.

How was the enormous weight of the unit handled, and how many workers were deployed?

The previous calculation showed that the entire dome unit was designed to have a density of around 560 kg/m³, resulting in a net positive buoyant force when immersed. The complete unit has been designed to float like a granite ball on water. The block's vertical weight due to gravitational pull is lower than the upward buoyant force. The whole thing was just designed to float on water without touching any hard surface; therefore, friction is also zero, and more workers were not needed for handling and making a horizontal rotation.

However, the water does exert some hydrodynamic resistive force called "drag" on the submerged wall surface while making a rotation by opposing the movement. This resistance is much less in calm static water than the friction involved in dragging an object across the ground. This is manageable when the entire unit only needs to be rotated about the vertical axis for 45 degrees in a circular motion to a distance of 3.11 m at a very slow pace without displacing any mass of water for final positioning and seating.

How did the workers move the huge unit inside and how large was the workmen force deployed at the courtyard level to handle the task?

Inland waterway and canal barges, which were historically designed during ancient times for humans to push or pull and were generally around 150 MT, with a maximum capacity of 180–200 MT, can be imagined.

It is easy to understand, and the best way to demonstrate how it works is to use a coracle as an example. A coracle is a small, round, light boat that has been traditionally used for fishing and transportation for a long time.

The picture shows a typical coracle with people and two-wheeler bikes on board. An elderly driver is able to effortlessly pull it with less force even if it is fully laden with 13 persons and 13 two-wheeler bikes, adding up to roughly 2.5 to 3 MT of weight.

The dome unit is mounted on the wooden float in our case, and the wood is floating and suspended in water; there is no friction, and the water is static and calm, with no wind or current. A skilled adult can easily pull and adjust more than a 3 MT weight that floats on the water's surface in the absence of static and kinetic friction, as explained above.

The total mass is 140 MT, which is freely floating on the water's surface with no friction. The entire operation of pulling and moving for a very slow circular horizontal rotation requires only a few highly qualified, trained, and strategically located workers who can perfectly pull and arrange the four corners seated on the respective slots of the triangular spherical pendentive platform that corresponds to the courtyard level.

It is not necessary for all workers to stand around the Sikhara inside the well for this process because there is insufficient working space around the sides. This action can be performed by tying the unit and the corner holy bulls to a sturdy wooden wheel and long rope arrangement that allows the strategically located trained personnel to gradually pull, rotate to a 45-degree clockwise circular movement, position the corners on the slots, and then return the corners to the triangular grooved supports by making an anti-clockwise movement before mounting the Sikhara on the wooden float.

After draining out the water from the well, a 66-m wooden flotation system is erected inside to attach the Sikhara on top of it. Before mounting the unit on the deck of the long cylindrical float mechanism as explained above, the unit must be twisted anti-clockwise 45 degrees to secure the four corners back on the central triangle cut-slot platform made in the walls using the buoyant force and lightness of the unit in the water.

The entire system, including the weight of the Sikhara, is now ready to move up after gaining positive buoyancy. To achieve positive buoyancy and flotation, the required volume of water is allowed to enter the well from higher-level storage to move up the wooden float. At this point, except for the dome unit which is fixed on the deck above the water surface by just touching the courtyard floor, the entire wooden flotation system will be inside the well and submerged in water.

When the Sikhara reached a height of +49.50 m, how did the crew manage with the tremendous weight of the dome unit and the wooden flotation?

There is no difference in the technique, but both the weight of the wooden flotation device and Sikhara had to be managed.

Due to the effect of gravity, the Sikhara's 140 MT mass weighs nearly 1373 kN.

7.77 m in diameter and 66 m in length, the wooden flotation unit has a total volume of 3128 m³ and a mass of 1564 MT. Half the density of water, the flotation weighs roughly a total of 15343 kN.

When immersed, it displaces 1564 m³ of water, and the weight of the displaced water equals its own weight, with the buoyant force balancing the gravitation effect to bring the system into equilibrium.

Because of the dome's weight or other granite materials, an extra 8.25-m flotation height is lowered inside the water, resulting in a total submerged height of 41.25 m, while the net projection above the maximum water level is raised to 24.75 m by attaining equilibrium.

When the system reaches +49.50 m, and just above the vertical triangular grooves for the final setting and installation, the float along with Sikhara on top must be turned 45 degrees about its vertical axis for a distance of 3.11 m in a clockwise orientation at an extremely slow pace with a very low velocity, so water skin friction is ineffective.

The flotation system's external surface is cylindrical in shape and may have been shaped, smoothened, and coated with oil and lubricants to reduce drag or skin frictional resistance. However, the friction resistance from water or drag resistance cannot be completely reduced, and it can be managed. This means that with the slow velocity towards zero, the drag effect can be significantly nullified. However, if necessary, a few extra workers can be factored in and considered during the final alignment and locking.

With the load on top of the flotation unit, the weight has pushed down an extra height of 8.25 m inside the water. The net length protruding over the water surface is only 24.5 m, the system is still on flotation, and the forces of gravity and buoyancy are balancing each other.

The whole system is suspended in water with no static friction, and the mass of the protruding part above the water surface +24.75 m level, as well as the mass of the submerged part, must be managed.

Wooden float's mass = 66 m × 47.39 m^2 × 0.50 MT = 1564 MT

The total mass to be handled and managed, including the Sikhara of 140 MT, is approximately 1704 MT. This is analogous to a ship with a mass of 1704 MT floating on water in the gravitational field and requiring manual pulling and adjustment for a horizontal circular motion to 45 degrees about the vertical axis for a distance of 3.11 m. This is possible manually at a very slow velocity by performing a circular motion because there is no need to move a large mass of water and no static or kinetic friction to oppose the motion, both of which are negligible.

Similar to the coracle example described, only a few workers are needed to pull and adjust the entire weight from the triangular cut slots 45 degrees horizontally to secure and lock the corners on the extended spherical pendentive platforms at +49.50 m level.

Newton's second law of motion, which states that force is equal to mass multiplied by acceleration, plays a role in this situation. The law states that the effect can be determined by applying the law.

F = m × a

The coracle example described previously demonstrated that an elderly driver can efficiently and effortlessly pull a weight of 2.5 to 3 MT on water.

Even when there is friction, an average person can effectively exert a pulling or pushing force of 40 kg at the ground surface, which is equivalent to applying a force of 400 Newtons. The force that can be produced by stationing four trained workers at the top +49.50 m level in each corner with the same efficiency is

4 corners × 4 workers × 400 N = 6400 Newtons approximately.

Mass involved = 1704 MT × 1000 = 1704,000 kg.

Newton's second law states,

Acceleration 'a' = F/m = 6400 /1704000= 0.0038 m/sec²

The total time required to pull or turn the weight to a 45-degree horizontal angle for a distance of 3.11 m with the manual force exerted by 16 workers at an acceleration of 0.0038 m/sec² is calculated as follows.

In physics, the third equation of motion states that $V^2 - U^2 = 2\,a\,s$, where 'V' is the final velocity, 'U' is the initial velocity, 'a' is the acceleration, and 's' is the distance displaced.

Here the system was at rest before making the horizontal movement, and hence the initial velocity is zero and the equation becomes $V^2 = 2\,a\,s$.

$V^2 = 2 \times 0.0038 \times 3.11$

$V = \sqrt{(2 \times 0.0038 \times 3.11)}$

$V = \sqrt{(0.023636)}$

$V = 0.154$ m/sec.

Total time required = 3.11 m/ 0.154 = 20.19 seconds.

Amazingly, the whole floating mass can be turned 45 degrees to set and align for the final position in less than a minute.

As a result, it is required to deploy strategically only minimally trained and highly skilled workers at the top who can apply the required pulling force manually to rotate the entire weight and rest the base on the respective corner supports.

The spread-out triangular and spherically curved pendentives were designed to extend vertically up to an elevation of +49.5 m as four triangular corner piers of masonry from +33 m level to finally receive the four corners of the Sikhara's base, as shown in the drawings. These pendentive supports receive the outward forces from the dome and transfer the complete load by concentrating it at the four corners of the structure, allowing the dome roof of the Sikhara to be adapted for a square sanctum.

Vimana interior views reveal pendentives that rise to a height of 6.85 m from +33 m, while the entire height above +39.85 m has been covered and ornamented with successive layers of corbelling for aesthetic purposes.

If there was insufficient space at the top for more workers to stand and function efficiently, the Sikhara's dome and drum elements could have been attached with strong wooden wheels positioned horizontally and vertically with ropes as described previously to allow the workers to easily do the pulling action from the ground or intermediate level for making a 45-degree horizontal turn so that the four corners can be perfectly aligned to take the seat of the respective slots at the line, level, and equilibrium.

Newton's second law and the equation of motion have played a major role in determining and deploying the minimum workmen forces at the top for the hassle-free completion of the novel technique, and in this manner, the Sikhara was finally installed at the summit of the Vimana.

The four vertical triangular cavities that guided the corners of the square base for harmonised vertical movement were filled, and the Vimana's inner walls were later covered and adorned with circular corbelling works interlocking with cavity fill works.

How did the large-sized Lord Shivalinga deity get into the shrine, which had a narrow entrance?

This must be the last activity, and learning the underlying scientific truths will be more exciting in the following chapter!

A typical Coracle carrying nearly 3 Tons of load is effortlessly handled and manoeuvred by an elderly driver

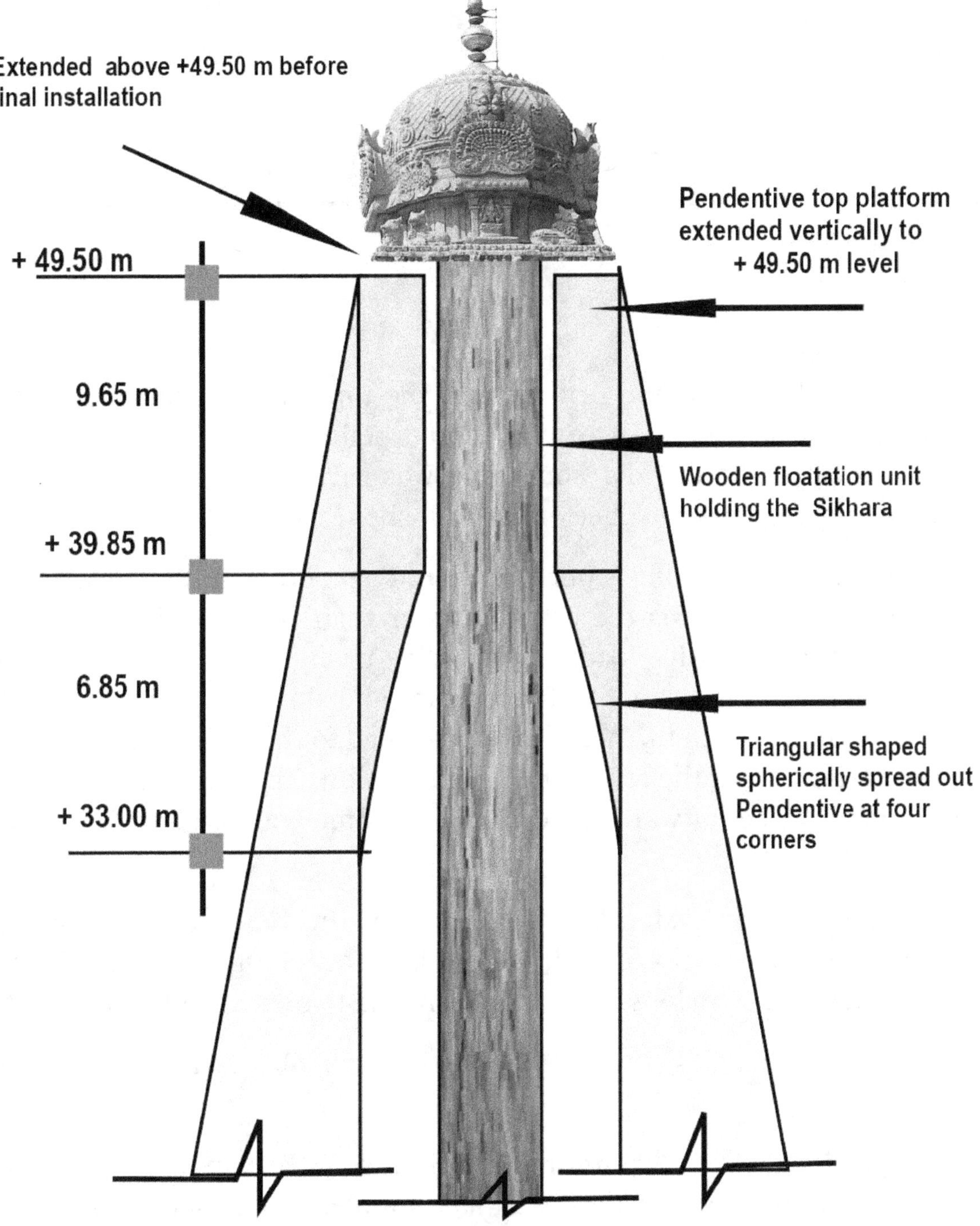

Few highly skilled trained workers strategically located at + 49.50 m around the Sikhara to make a 45-degree horizontal rotation and place the corners on the pendentives platform.

15

Lord Shiva's Entry

After the Sikhara had reached and ornamented the top, the vertical cavities made in the inner wall were filled and the ornate circular corbelling work was completed. As seen in the previous images, the circular corbelling was carried out in the interior structure, concentrically extending from the face of the wall above the level +39.85 m.

In this case, the circular corbelling is purely decorative; it is an architectural technique used to span a space or void towards the centre, rather than acting as load-bearing elements to support the Sikhara's massive load. The massive triangular and spherically spread-out pendentives receive the total weight of the drum and dome through the four extended granite masonry pylons, which further transfer the load to the pillars beneath, as previously described and clarified from the structural configuration. The pendentives are designed in engineering to receive the outward force from the dome weight and concentrate it at the four corners.

The same wooden flotation system and technique had to be used to lift the stones from ground level for the above works of cavity filling and corbelling, and once the major lifting work was completed, the 66 m long wooden system had to be dismantled to backfill the well.

The main and final challenge is to move the massive Lord Shiva statue inside the sanctuary for installation.

The massive statue is said to weigh around 25 MT, and the bottom resting pedestal is about 5 m in diameter. The Vimana structural wall has completely encased the structure, making it impossible to move the unit through the narrow main entranceway.

Cholas discovered Newton's laws of motion, as well as the laws of fluid pressure and behaviour, and used them to design a structure in the style of a gravity dam.

So far, the Chola engineers' scientific theories and plans have been observed to be exceptional and clever.

How did the massive Shivalingam, weighing 25 MT, get inside the sanctum and sit majestically?

There were no other options for the massive statue except to follow the Sikhara's path and use the same underground tunnel route to enter inside the sanctum shaft and be lifted up to Its final position.

When the Cholas were already aware of Newton's laws and the properties and behaviour of fluids, it appears that they had two scientific mechanisms and options for lifting and positioning the huge Shivalingam statue.

The first is from Archimedes' scientific theory.

Wood floats on water, and Archimedes' principle of buoyancy states that the amount of water displaced equals the weight of the wood, as previously discussed.

Using the aforementioned scientific logic, the enormous Lord Shiva unit may have been built and erected on a temporary sturdy wooden flotation platform at the Siva Ganga Tank, bed as shown in the sketches and drawings.

Similar to the dome shifting, the entire setup would have floated via the underground tunnel to reach the sanctuary enclosure beneath, but here the huge weight is sitting on the wooden float. When the shutter at the tunnel terminal was closed, the requisite amount of water was allowed to flow down into the well from higher-level circumambulatory or annexe vestibule storage until the wooden flotation bearing the heavy statue reached the plinth level for final alignment and positioning.

Constructional features and arrangements, such as an enlarged pendentive platform extending from the four corners to receive and support the large Shivalingam, must have been made at the tunnel entry and at the plinth final level, as shown in the figure, similar to the provisions made at the courtyard base while lifting the Sikhara.

The same buoyancy theory of fluid was employed in the above first choice.

According to history, the Chola dynasty and its engineers lived and worked with water and its properties; therefore, the fascinating hypothesis of a second alternative cannot be ruled out from them.

A total of six wells, each measuring 1.5 to 1.8 m in diameter and reaching a depth of 15 to 18 m, were located all around the temple's main Vimana. All of these wells had to be linked to the underground sanctum shaft, or the plan may have featured a single larger diameter well with a direct conduit connection to the underground shaft during construction.

Pascal's scientific concept of fluid mechanics was published in 1663.

Regardless of the shape of the container, "the force exerted to a confined liquid is transferred uniformly in all directions through the liquid," says this law.

By applying a small force on one end, the input is multiplied, and the output is very large, allowing much more weight to be lifted on the other end.

It is mathematically defined and illustrated in the given diagram.

$$F1/A1 = F2/A2$$

A 100-kilogram baby calf standing on a 1 m² piston can give an output to lift a 6400 kg adult elephant that is standing in a 64 m² area equivalent to the sanctum square space, as explained and shown in the drawing.

A typical application of Pascal's principle for liquids is the automobile lift seen in many service stations (the hydraulic jack). Applying hydraulic pressure in a confined incompressible fluid through a tube at one end lifts a large truck at the other end using the same technique in the automobile industry.

In physics, it is because of its fluid qualities, and the law is called Pascal's principle or principle of transmission of fluid pressure in hydraulics, which was established in 1653 and published in the year 1663. Hydraulics is employed by modern devices ranging from very small to very large. For example, there are hydraulic pistons in almost all construction machines where heavy loads are involved.

In our case, imagine that both the exterior and main sanctum wells are connected far below the level of the foundation by a water-flowing, leak-proof duct that is closed like a confined conduit and a strong wooden platform with pistons at each end.

By floating and mounting the statue on the air- and water-tight sturdy wooden platform that acts as the main piston at the extended sanctum shaft and letting a few baby elephants use their weight on the wooden piston platform at the external shaft, the piston carrying the huge statue will naturally rise to the level of the plinth for the final installation.

If the statue had been moved by the force of buoyancy from the Archimedes principle, there was every chance that Pascal's hydrostatic pressure principle would have been used by the Chola engineers for the final lifting and alignment and to set the statue at the ideal balance on the floor.

As an additional option, the cross-section depicts a circumambulatory and an annexe with a space-like water storage tank and a closed conduit system. These empty areas were designed to store a large volume of water at varying heights and compartments to generate enormous fluid pressure from larger heights at the base of the float to lift the massive weight of granite sitting on its deck from the tunnel-floor level to the plinth platform.

When the annexe's tank is filled to the 24.75 m water level, the pressure at the courtyard's base and below is extremely high, allowing it to hold and gradually lift heavy loads. The vertical cavities, which contain a large volume of water at varying heights inside, strongly support the fact that they were created and connected in the manner of a closed confined container and conduits beneath the courtyard level in accordance with Pascal's law!

Water is incompressible and the pressure applied at one point in such a confined atmosphere is transmitted equally at other points.

The water's surface pressure is nil at +24.75 m level, but very high at the courtyard-floor level due to the large depth of the fluid's weight in the gravitational field. The cross-section shows that the rectangular hollow shaft has been extended from +24.75 m to +31.60 m, measures 1.9 m × 3.8 m, and holds 49.46 m³ of water. When this 49.46 m³ of 6.85 m height water column applies its weight to the 24.75 m water surface, the water pressure at the base rises by 67.20 kN/m² or 67.20 kilo Pascal, which is equivalent to 6.85 MT of force per square metre.

It's like Pascal's barrel principle.

He proved that hydrostatic pressure depends not on the weight of the fluid but on the elevation difference. He demonstrated this principle by attaching a thin tube to a barrel full of water. When a thin tube is inserted into a barrel and water is poured into the top, the hydrostatic pressure from the elevation causes the barrel to explode, as shown in the sketch "Pascal's barrel."

Pascal conducted this experiment in the year 1646, and the principle is stated mathematically as

$$P = \rho \times g \times h$$

Where 'P' is the difference in hydrostatic pressure between two points in a fluid column due to the fluid's weight, 'ρ' is fluid density in kg/m³, 'g' is the acceleration due to gravity in m/s², and 'h' is the height of fluid above the location of measurement or the difference in elevation between the two points within the fluid column in m.

The intuitive reason for this formula is that the difference in pressure between two elevations is due to the weight of the fluid between the elevations. Alternately, the result might be understood as a pressure change induced by the change in potential energy per unit volume of the liquid due to the gravitational field.

Assume the statue is mounted on a piston at the level of the courtyard base and must be lifted up from the courtyard's floor level for the final seating level.

At this point, the water column pressure from a height of 25 m at the courtyard's floor level due to gravitational acceleration is

P = 1000 × 9.81 × 25 = 245.25 kN/m², or the mass of 25 m height of the water column is applying a 25 MT force on a square metre area at the courtyard base level.

To verify the pressure in terms of MT force/m², the calculation is 245.25 /9.81=25MT/m².

Even assuming the Sikhara's weight of 25 MT was placed on a sturdy wooden piston of 5 m diameter, the pressure required to hold the weight at the bottom of the piston is 25 MT/19.63 m² and equals 1.27 MT/m² excluding the additional pressure required to hold the weight of the piston.

The finding shows that a 25 m water height can generate enough pressure at the courtyard base to hold and move a massive weight to push the piston of 5 m diameter. The pressure will still be more at the tunnel's bottom, allowing the statue to gradually rise to the required higher level. It functions similarly to a hydraulic lift, except that the weight of the water and its pressure from a large height do the lifting.

The statue of Lord Shiva was supposed to be assembled, mounted on a wooden platform, and floated underneath the sanctum via an underground passage from the Siva Ganga Tank.

The wooden float holding the massive statue was required to temporarily halt after entering the sanctum shaft (similar to the dome unit), and the entire setup was made to rest directly on the pendentive-like corbel supports. It is believed that there were already built corner triangular spherical pendentives or corbels here that match the tunnel's floor level, which may have provided support for the temporary halt.

Before beginning the vertical movement, the Sikhara's centre was transferred down from its square base level +49.50 m through a suspended vertical reference line or plumb line, with the pointed tip precisely meeting the centre of Shivalinga statue to ensure the perfect vertical alignment for the final positioning, and the wooden platform's contact with the inner wall surfaces was made air- and water-tight as it must function like a sturdy piston.

Using Pascal's concept, the water level from the elevated storage compartments was flowed down, monitored and maintained to create the appropriate intended pressure at the base of the wooden piston-like platform carrying the huge statue. The statue must have taken a very gradual perfect vertical upward movement from the tunnel base level in line with the pressure created from the large depth of the water column till it reaches the plinth platform for the final positioning.

The entire assembled statue unit appears to be resting on a solid square base slab that is tightly interlocked, similar to the arrangement made for the Sikhara's base. When the weight gradually raised from the tunnel's base level, the wooden circular platform's top, which carried the entire assembly and functioned like a piston, was monitored and stopped to coincide with the bottom level of Shiva's seating position, +4.47 m.

The enormous pressure from the large height of water ensured enough holding support to sustain the huge weight, the pendentives or corbelling-like projections constructed at the corners and from the sides of the inner wall for a height of 4.47 m from the courtyard base level were supposed to have finally ensured the four supporting corner platforms for the square base slab.

The statue uses Pascal's principle to reach the plinth top level for the final seating position, and it must ensure that the alignment and installation are perfect by exactly coinciding with the centre projected from the Sikhara's base from the top.

The sides of the supporting piston platform are made air- and water-tight with granite side walls all around its sides; it is difficult to handle, turn, and position such a massive weight for the final alignment. When the statue reaches the plinth platform, it takes up the majority of the sanctum plan area, and there is also very little working space inside, making the task extremely difficult.

However, the Chola engineers had excellent fluid statics and dynamics awareness, and under such conditions, the possibility of using hydrodynamic lubrication theory by using the huge pressure from the large height of the water column cannot be ruled out.

The term "hydrodynamic lubrication" refers to a situation in which two rubbing surfaces are separated by a thin film of lubricant layer to reduce friction with the help of liquid.

In this case, the goal of hydrodynamic lubrication is to penetrate water into the contact zone between the two rubbing solids by creating a narrow gap between the piston and the granite wall, ensuring a thin liquid film when water flows at high pressure from a higher altitude. This film protects the surfaces from direct contact and reduces friction between the solids that are in direct contact.

Before the massive statue's final alignment and positioning, pressurised water was allowed to flow from a higher altitude from the annexe and circumambulatory storage to hit the base and the sides around the base to hold and balance the weight. The high pressure from the large height of water builds up at the base, and the water flows through the narrow gap, forming a thin squeezed fluid layer that provides enough force to hold, balance, and hang the massive weight on the liquid surface without making contact with the side hard granite wall surfaces.

Because pressurised water flows between the base and the side wall, creating a mechanical hydrostatic bearing that is nearly frictionless, any mass, no matter how heavy, can be moved on the liquid surface as if it weighed nothing at all.

The mass can weigh thousands of kilograms, but the efficient bearing allows it to rotate and align horizontally with the force of a few workers' hands.

It is astonishing that the ancient Tamil engineers were aware of such advanced complex physics and precision engineering.

As a result, aside from the application of Pascal's principle, the lubrication bearing theory also cannot be ruled out because the efficient bearing allows the massive weight to be handled and moved by hand during the final installation and positioning. Furthermore, the large dimensional Shivalinga statue cannot enter through the narrow sanctums' opening, and the only way is through an underground tunnel from the Siva Ganga Tank to rise vertically inside the shaft at a slow pace for the perfect final alignment and positioning using the above scientific principles and the efforts of a few workers.

The 66-meter-deep shaft beneath the sanctum may have been backfilled with rock boulders or sand after the final installation of the Shivalinga statue. Alternatively, the depth of the underground well may have been refilled and shortened to a significant extent up to the level of the tunnel base before lifting the statue to accommodate only the designed size of the piston that suits the holding and lifting weight.

We set out on a journey to investigate the method of the Sikhara's movement to the summit from the earth's surface, as well as the precise shifting and installation logic used by the Chola engineers a thousand years ago.

One study leads to another. Surprisingly, the investigation researched, captured, and presented other advanced scientific ideas and concepts that existed a thousand years ago, such as Newton's classic mechanics, Pascal's principle, and the application of lubrication theory from the ancient Tamil engineers in the construction of the Tanjore Big Temple.

Finally, similar to the Sikhara, Lord Shiva's statue was floated horizontally from the Siva Ganga Tank assembly yard to enter beneath the shrine via an underground passage using the same principle as Archimedes. Using Pascal's principle and lubrication-bearing scientific concepts, the massive weight climbed up from the tunnel base to take the perfect final seating position at the plinth.

The width of the base of the Vimana determines the style of a dam design based on Newton's laws of motion and gravity. The open storage volume of the circumambulatory and annexe levels validates the Archimedes principle and the buoyancy concept. Pascal's theory is revealed by the Vimana's total height, the confined water storage up to the mid-height of the Vimana, the extended shaft up to 31.60 m level, and its hydrostatic pressure. The Sikhara's flotation from the Siva Ganga Tank is clearly established by the factor of lower mass–volume ratio than water's adopted in its design.

It took a lot of hard and precise engineering effort and determination for Raja Raja Cholan and his engineers to reach the summit of the 216 feet for the inspired climax that corresponded to the total Tamil combination letters.

The overall Tamil alphabet contains 247 characters, so why not make Vimana 247 feet tall instead of 216?

How could the king miss those 247 numbers?

When a Tamil emperor decided to build the tallest Vimana over the sanctum, he must have picked 247 feet only as the maximum height by considering the total 247 Tamil characters.

How did this slip from the king's decision? In the next section, we'll look at this issue.

Lord Shiva mounted on Wooden float System for gaining flotation

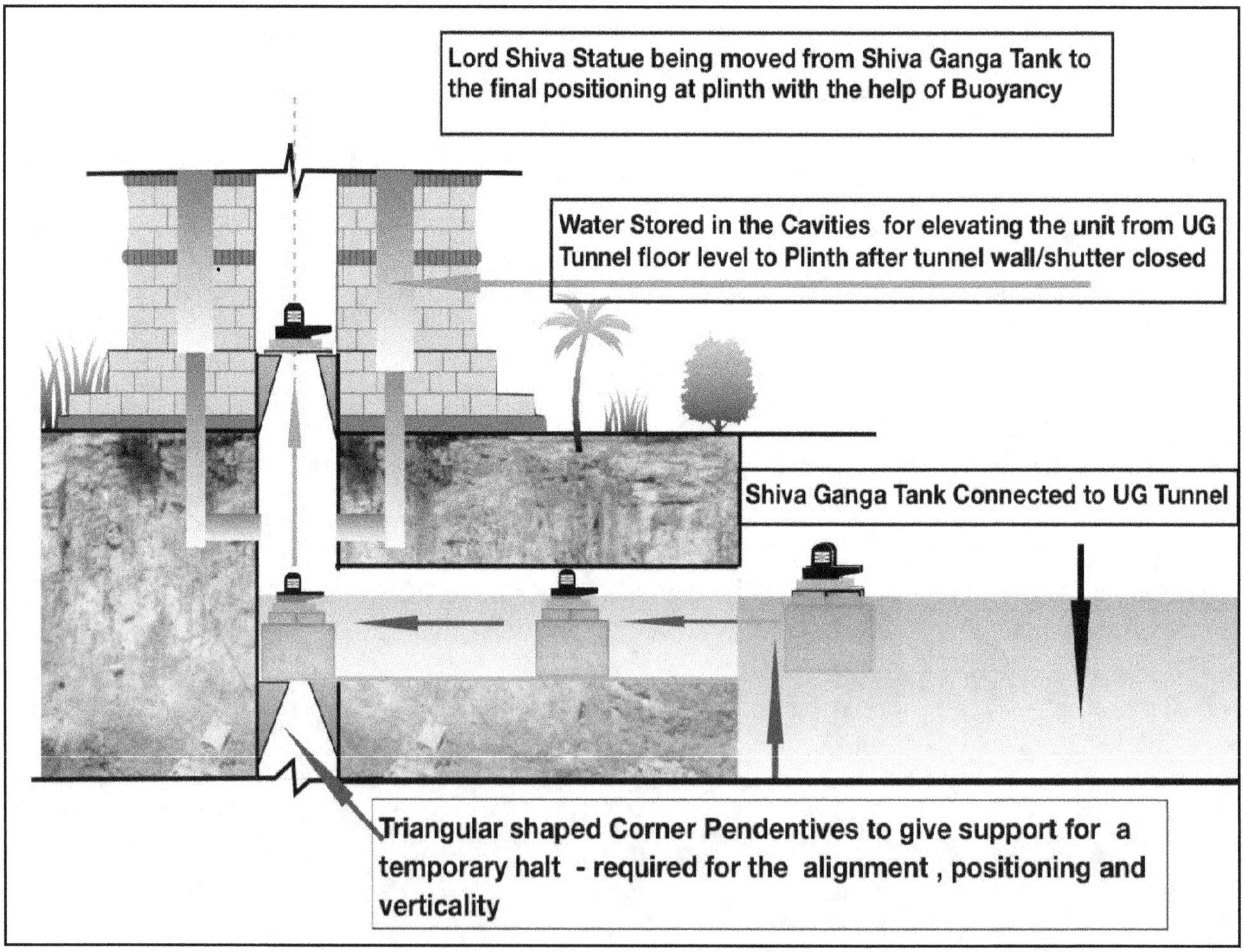

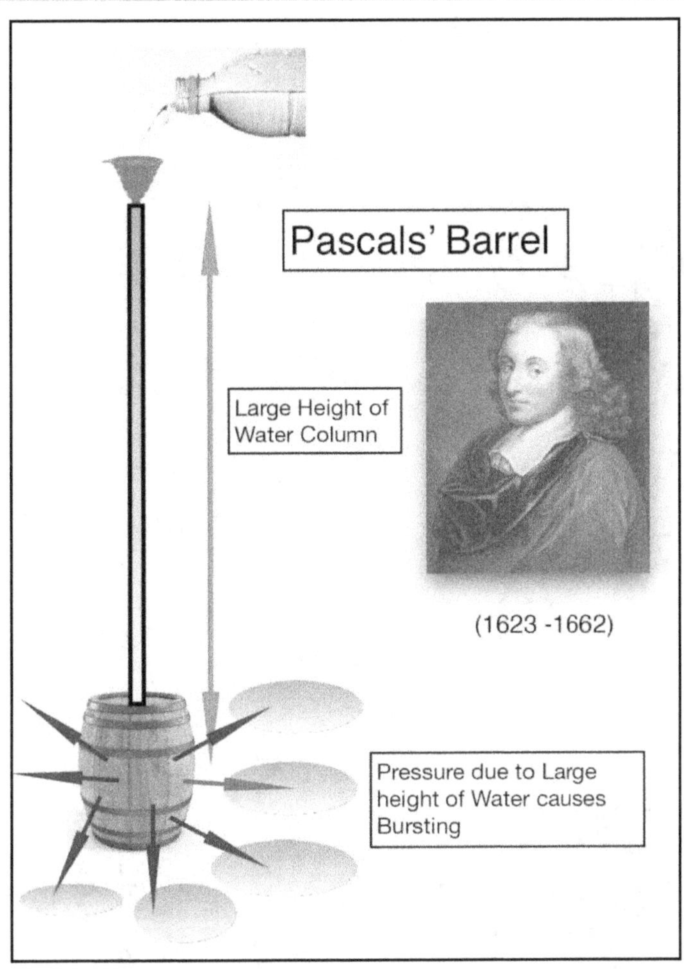

Pascals' Barrel
Large Height of Water Column
(1623 -1662)
Pressure due to Large height of Water causes Bursting

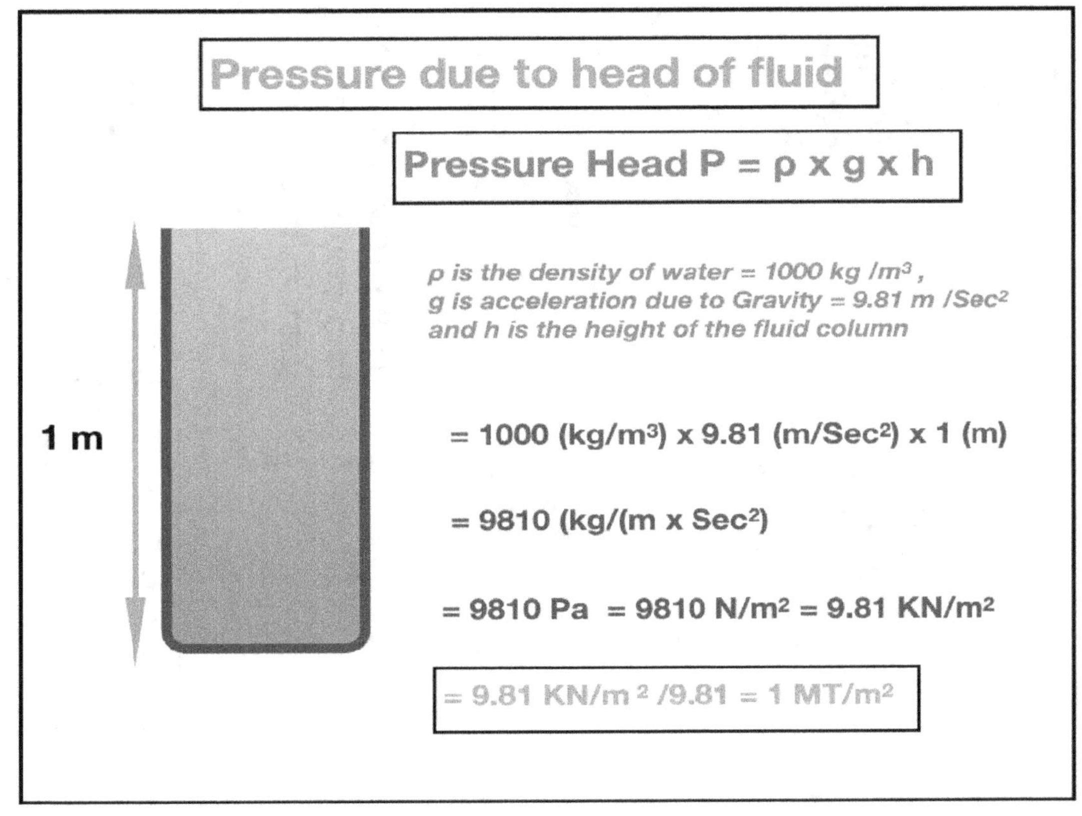

Pressure due to head of fluid

Pressure Head P = ρ x g x h

ρ is the density of water = 1000 kg /m³ ,
g is acceleration due to Gravity = 9.81 m /Sec²
and h is the height of the fluid column

= 1000 (kg/m³) x 9.81 (m/Sec²) x 1 (m)

= 9810 (kg/(m x Sec²)

= 9810 Pa = 9810 N/m² = 9.81 KN/m²

= 9.81 KN/m² /9.81 = 1 MT/m²

1 m

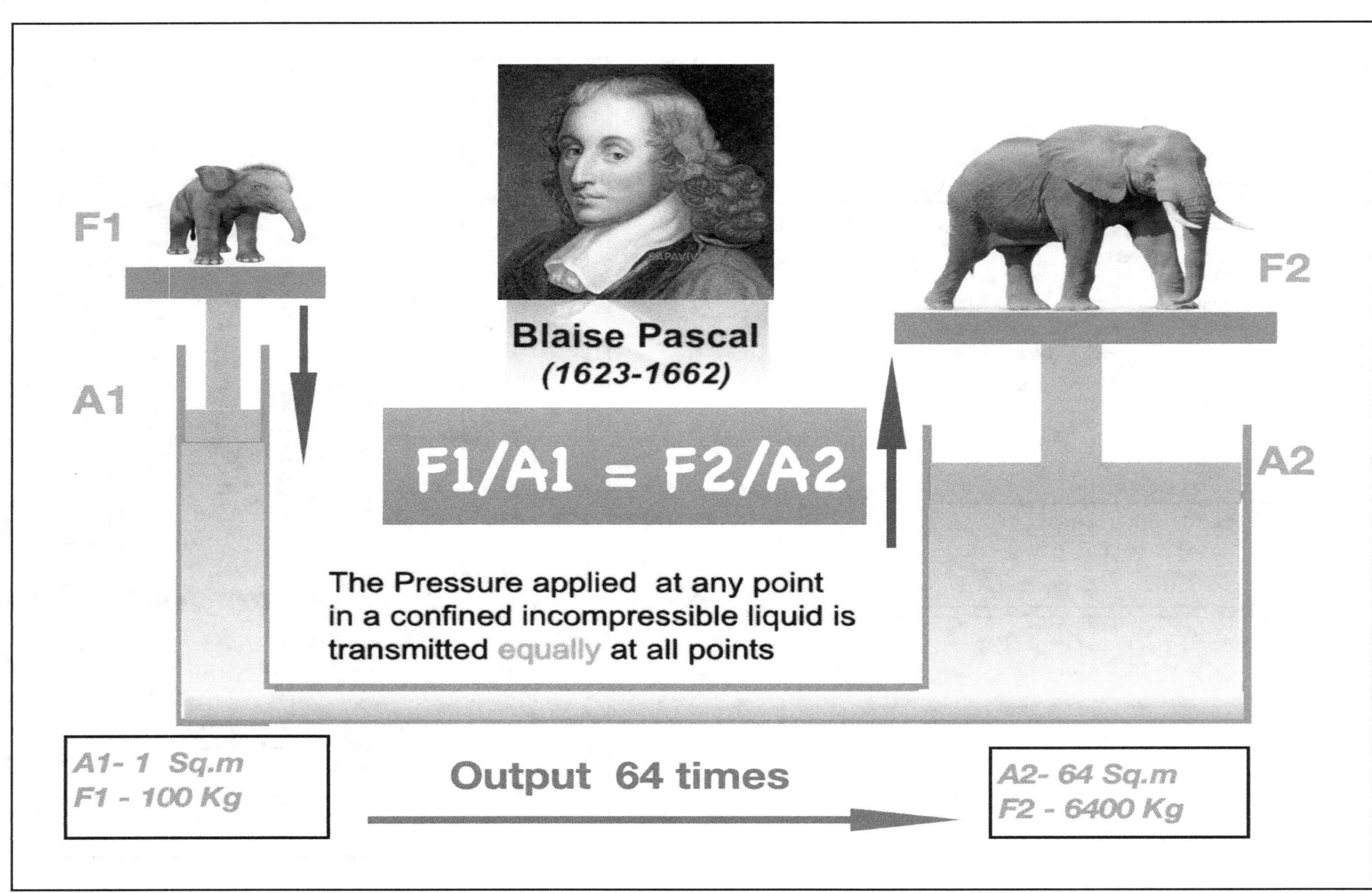

F1
A1
Blaise Pascal
(1623-1662)
F1/A1 = F2/A2
The Pressure applied at any point in a confined incompressible liquid is transmitted equally at all points
F2
A2
A1- 1 Sq.m
F1 - 100 Kg
Output 64 times
A2- 64 Sq.m
F2 - 6400 Kg

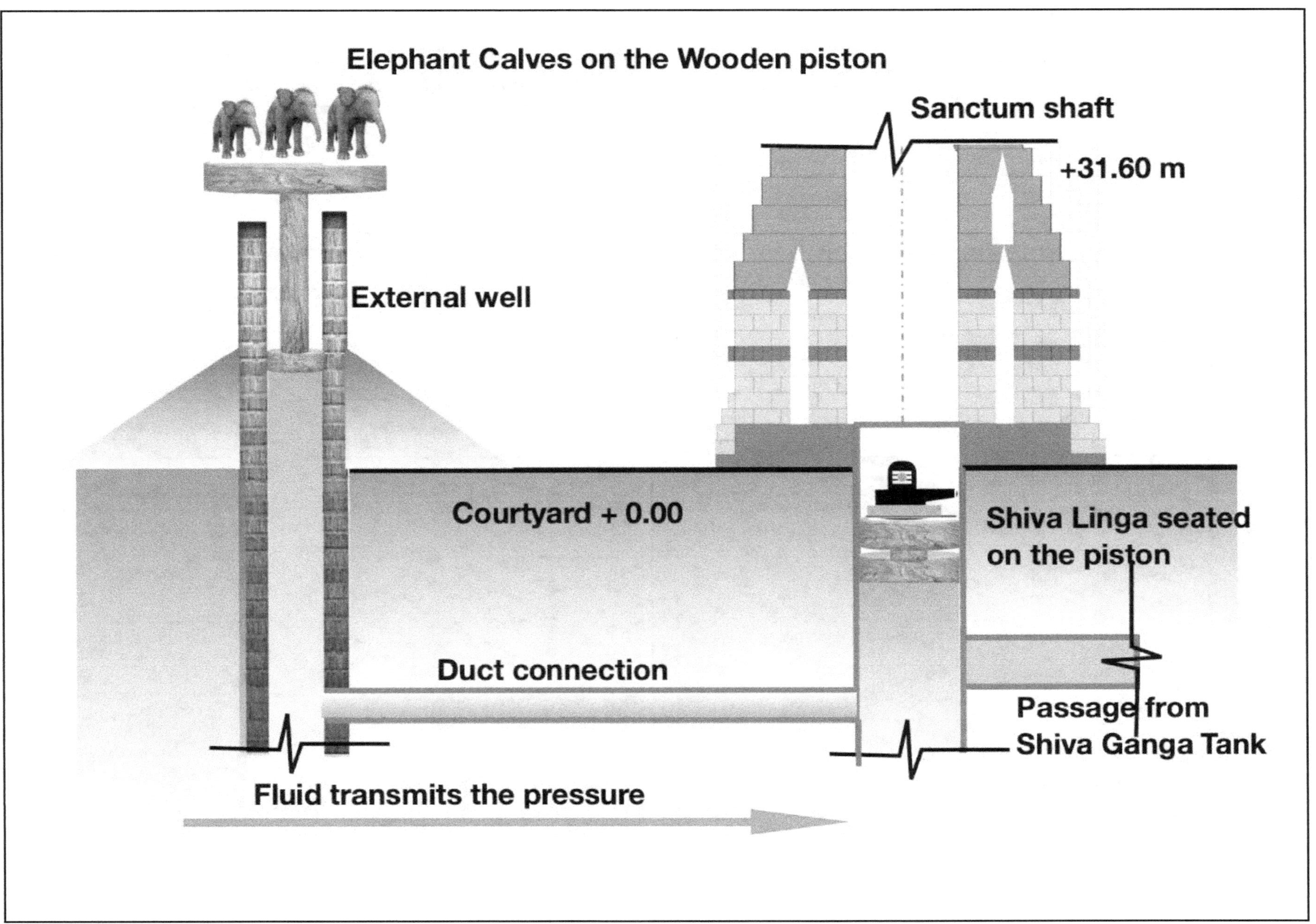

Elephant Calves on the Wooden piston
Sanctum shaft
+31.60 m
External well
Courtyard + 0.00
Shiva Linga seated on the piston
Duct connection
Passage from Shiva Ganga Tank
Fluid transmits the pressure

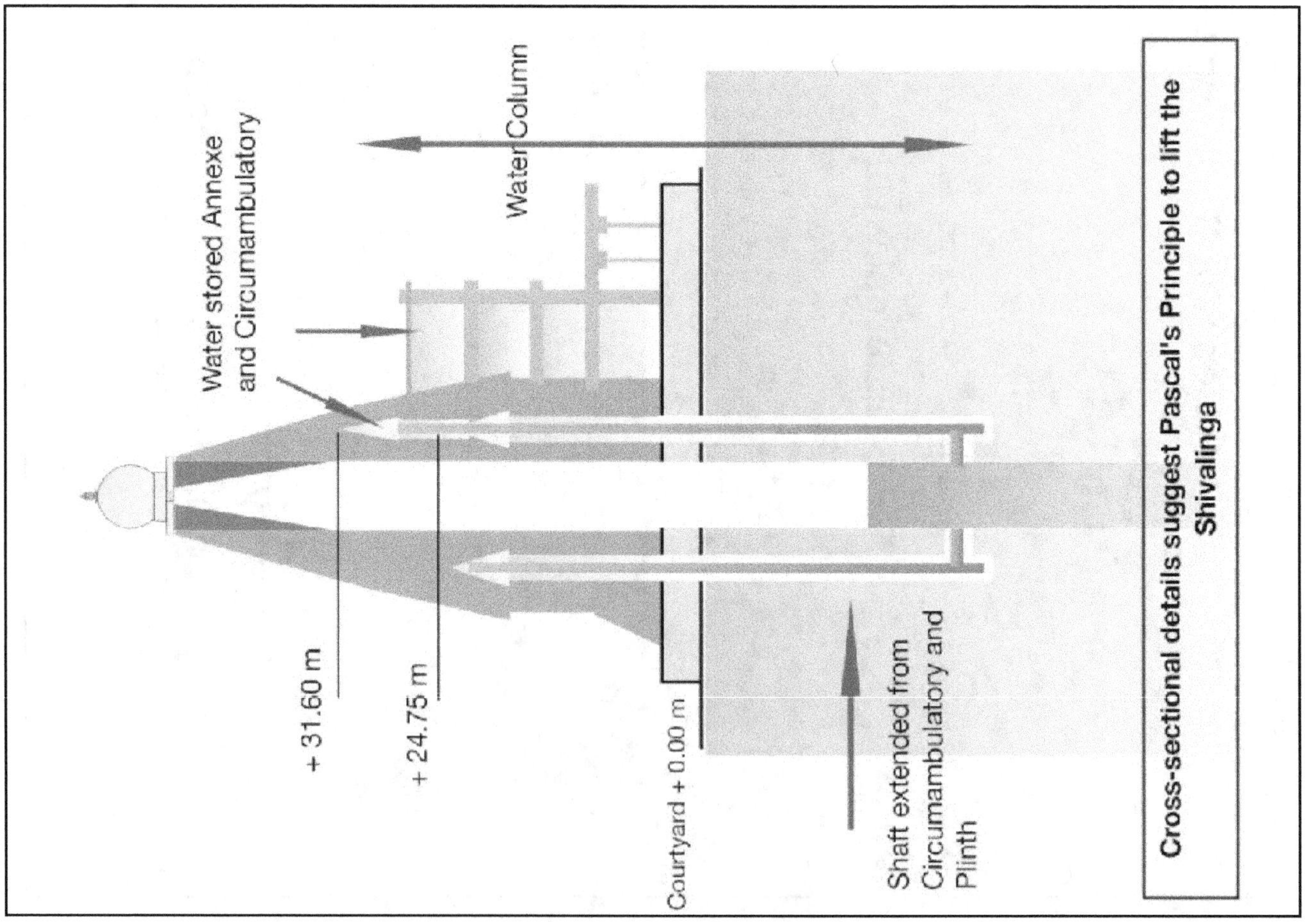

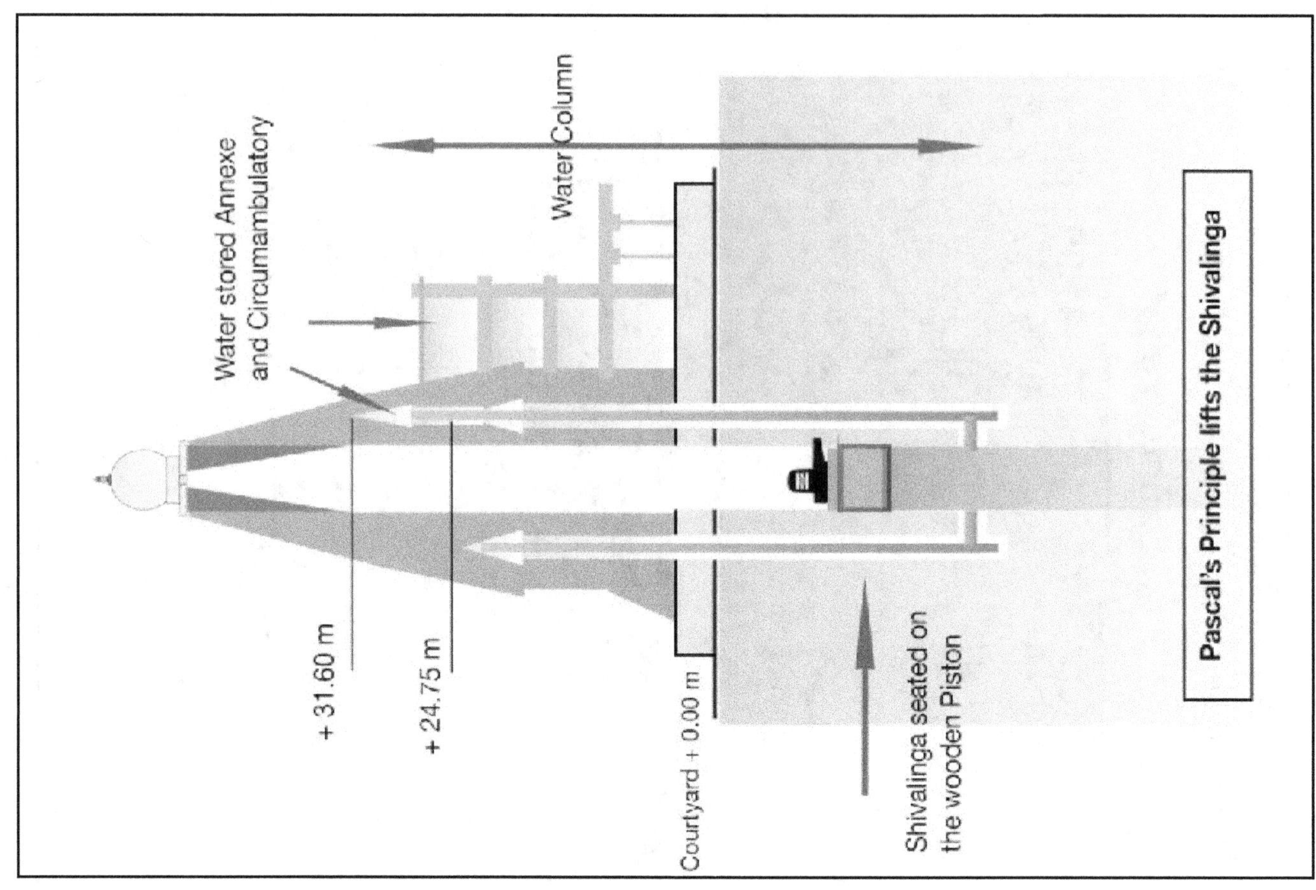

Pascal's Principle lifts the Shivalinga

Cross-sectional details suggest Pascal's Principle to lift the Shivalinga

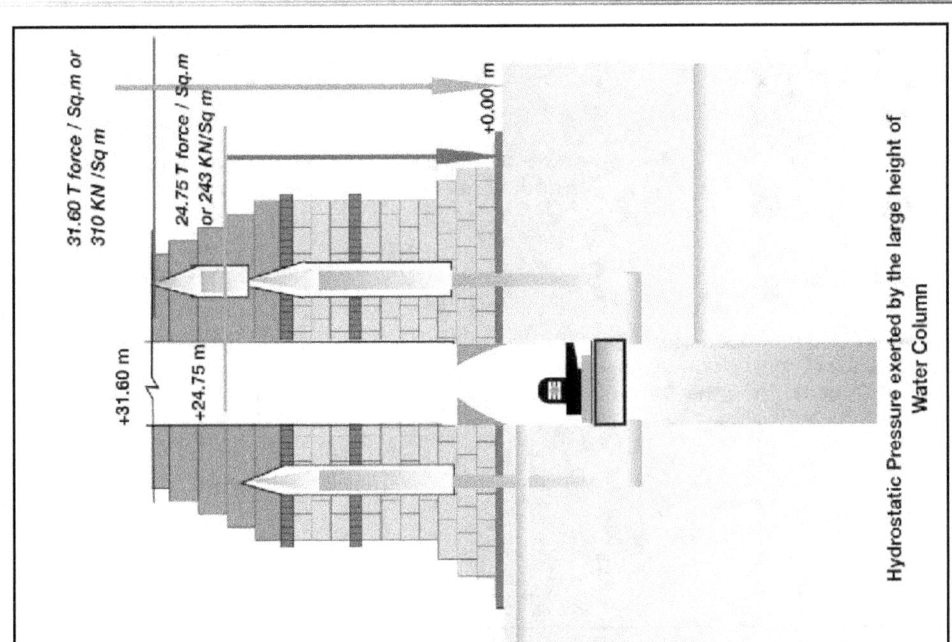

Hydrostatic Pressure exerted by the large height of Water Column

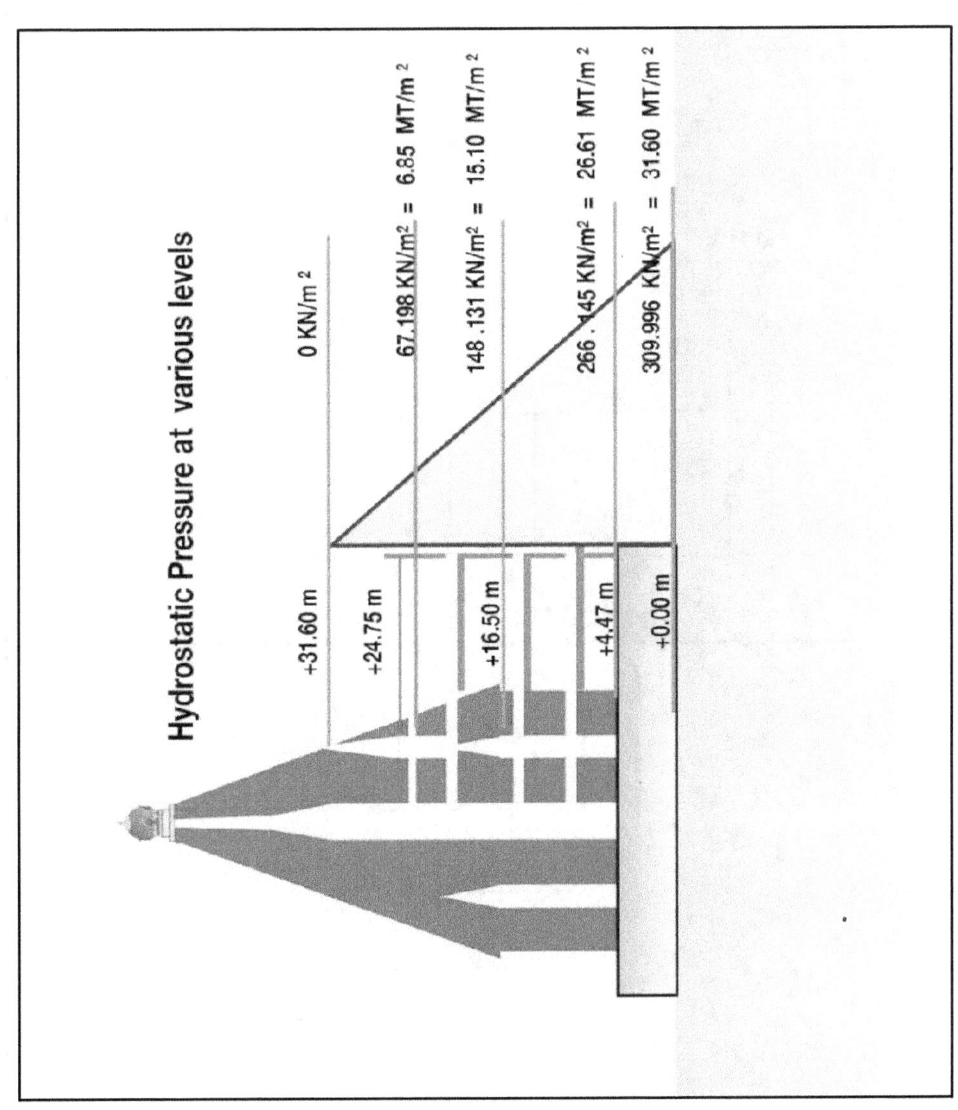

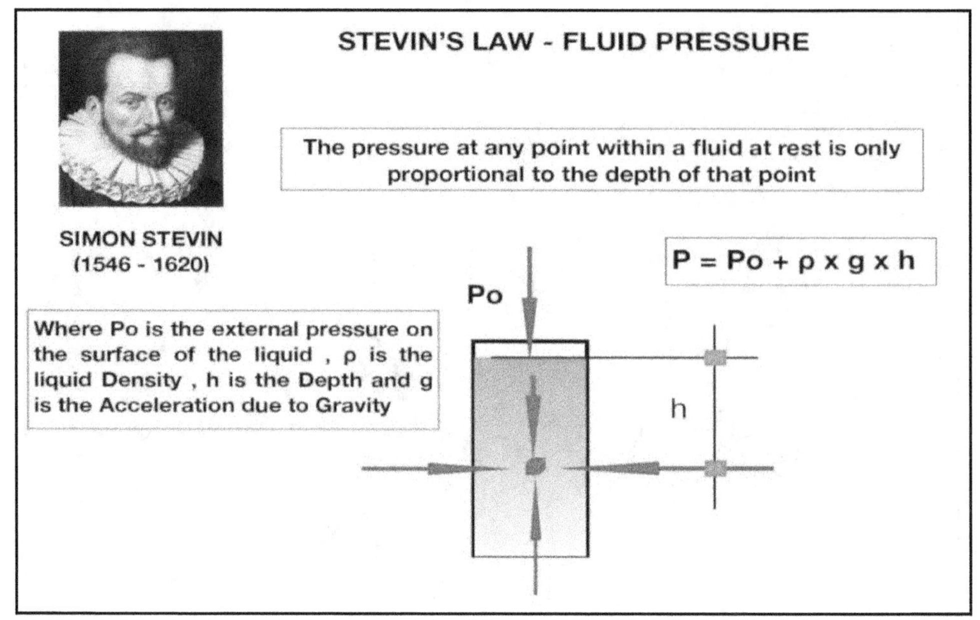

$$P = Po + \rho \times g \times h$$

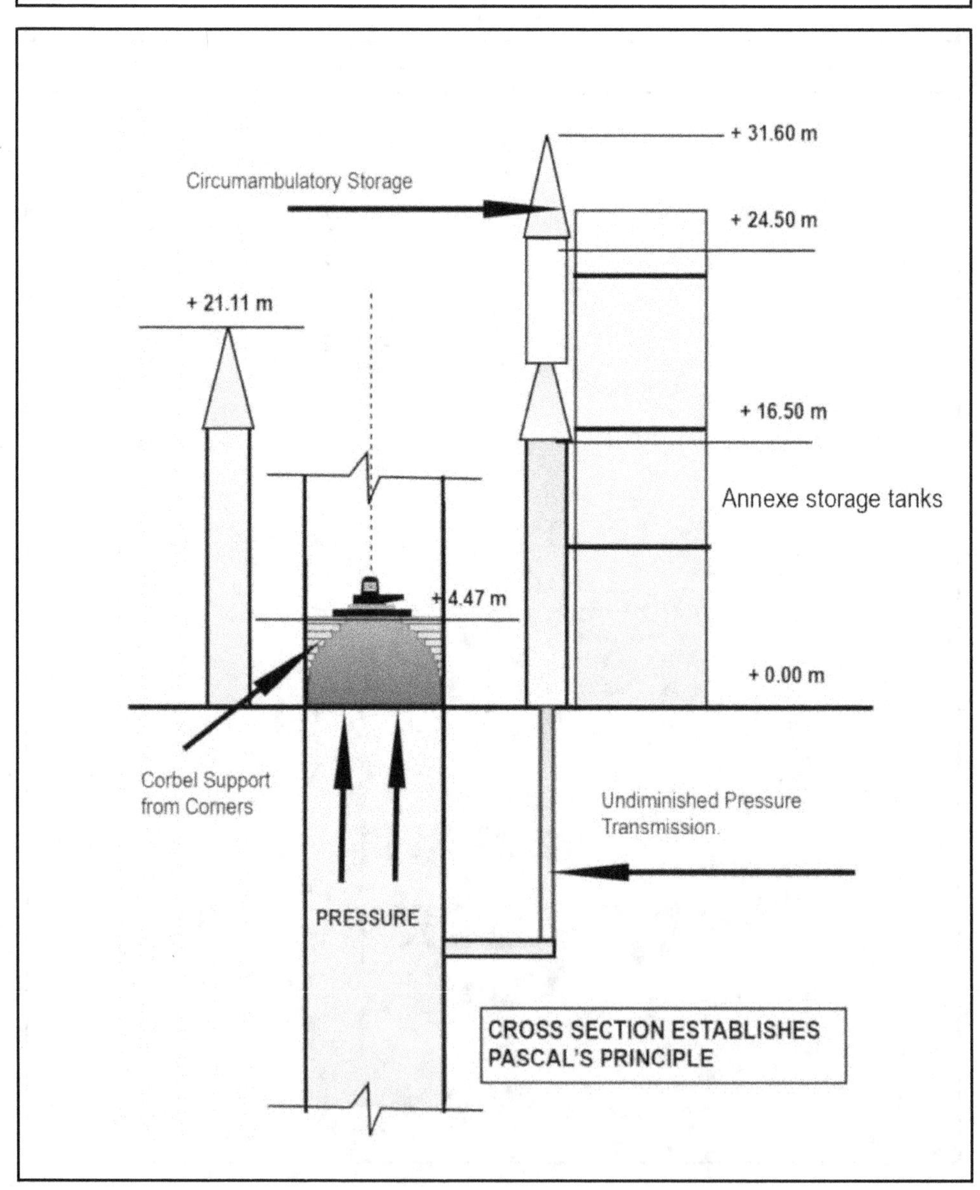

16

Why Not 247?

Why not have a 247-foot tall Vimana instead of 216 as the Tamil language has a total of 247 letters?

And how did it slip through the king's mind?

Tamil comprises 12 vowels, 18 consonants, and 216 combined letters. Including the three-dotted unique character letter, the Tamil language overall has a total of 247 letters.

When the Tamil monarch Raja Raja Cholan decided to construct the tallest Vimana right over the sanctum for Lord Shiva, he must have chosen the maximum height of 247 feet rather than 216 feet.

Was the 247-foot-tall Vimana his plan A?

History did not disclose itself anywhere, not even through any of the inscriptions from the king.

Assume that the king's original vision called for a height of 247 feet rather than the current 216 feet which is 247–216 = 31 feet = 9.46 m of added height.

In the current profile, the Vimana has an inclination from +16.50 m to +49.50 m for a vertical height of 33 m above the first floor, as indicated in the sketch, which takes into account the 216-foot-high Vimana that was built.

The outer gradient is provided at 9.99 m/33 m, which is at a rate of 0.3 m per running metre height when considering a 216-foot-tall Vimana.

The slanting pyramid has a total vertical height of 33 m.

It is 247 × 33/216 = 37.74 m proportionally for a height of 247 feet.

In the case of 247 feet, the proportionate extra height is 37.73–33 = 4.74 m.

The square's Sikhara base measures 7.93 m × 7.93 m for the presently laid one.

The base slab size must be 7.93 m - 4.74 m × 0.3 × 2 times = 5.086 m when the Vimana must extend for 4.74 m additionally to meet the criteria of rising to 247 feet.

As a result, the square Sikhara's base must be around 5.09 m × 5.09 m or approximately a 5 m × 5 m size at the top.

Suppose King Raja Raja Cholan had planned to raise the Vimana to 247 feet as plan A. In that case, his engineers must have produced and had ready somewhere nearby a similar Sikhara square base block with dimensions of roughly 5 m × 5 m with a thickness nearly matching.

Whether his engineers planned for plan A and had a 5 m × 5 m slab ready?

Yes, it appears that the king's plan A was to build a total height of 247 feet.

A slab of similar and nearby size was kept on reserve, presumably for the originally planned height of 247 feet.

As shown in the image, a massive granite slab is lying beneath the figure of King Serboji II in the Tanjore Palace museum, which is presumed to have been designed and kept for plan A.

The dimensions of this granite slab are 5.08 m × 5.62 m, with a thickness of 0.52 m and a weight of roughly 40 MT it was most likely cut and kept ready for the final dressing by the engineers for the originally planned height of 247 feet.

The current square section bottom slab of the Sikhara measures 7.93 m × 7.93 m, has a thickness of 0.47 m for the current constructed height of 216 feet and weighs nearly 81 tonnes.

The size of around 5 m × 5 m and the thickness of 0.52 m closely match and are in line with the design requirements for a height of 247 feet.

Due to the increased height and weight of the Vimana from 216 to 247 feet, there may have been certain technical and dimensional constraints experienced by the engineers in the design calculations and construction.

The structure was designed in the style of a gravity dam demanding no tension to develop at the base.

For overall safety and stability, the resultant should pass through within the middle third of the base in a dam structure, with an eccentricity of less than one-sixth of the width of the base and normal stresses not exceeding the maximum allowable SBC of the soil, as elaborately exercised earlier.

The stability check and analysis have already cautioned that for a height of 49.50 m and a maximum water level of +24.75 m, the resultant forces on the structure base experienced the maximum permissible eccentricity limit by preciously intersecting the outer boundary of the inner middle third, and any further cross over will produce negative stress, which is not permitted in a gravity dam type of structure.

The results of the calculation and stability analysis for a height of 247 feet may have posed certain technical and engineering limitations for the Chola engineers in terms of eccentricity exceeding the middle third of the base, causing negative stress, which may be due to additional pressure from the increased depth of the water column and the weight of the structure, by failing to meet the required minimum safety factors, and enormous stresses exceeding the maximum SBC of the soil beneath the foundation.

To meet all of the above engineering standards and limitations, as well as to ensure overall stability, the Chola engineers appear to have suggested and recommended to the king that the height be limited to a maximum of 216 feet!

The above size of around 5 m × 5 m × 0.52 m, which is similar to the shape of the actual installed Sikhara base of 7.93 m × 7.93 m × 0.47 m, strongly establishes that the current Sikhara base may be a solid monolithic slab with a weight of around 81 MT force, with the other components such as the vertical drum, spherically curved dome surface, and the four pairs of holy bulls weighing the remaining 59 MT. These remaining parts could have tightly interlocked air- and water-tight segments assembled as a single monolithic unit to hold the designed volume of air inside, allowing for easy flotation from the surface of the water in the Siva Ganga Tank, as well as handling and manoeuvring the unit inside the sanctuary with fewer workers, as described previously.

Why not have 247 Feet ?

216 Feet
247 Feet
12 Vowels , 18 Consonants , 216 Combinations & 247 Total letters
TAMIL LETTERS

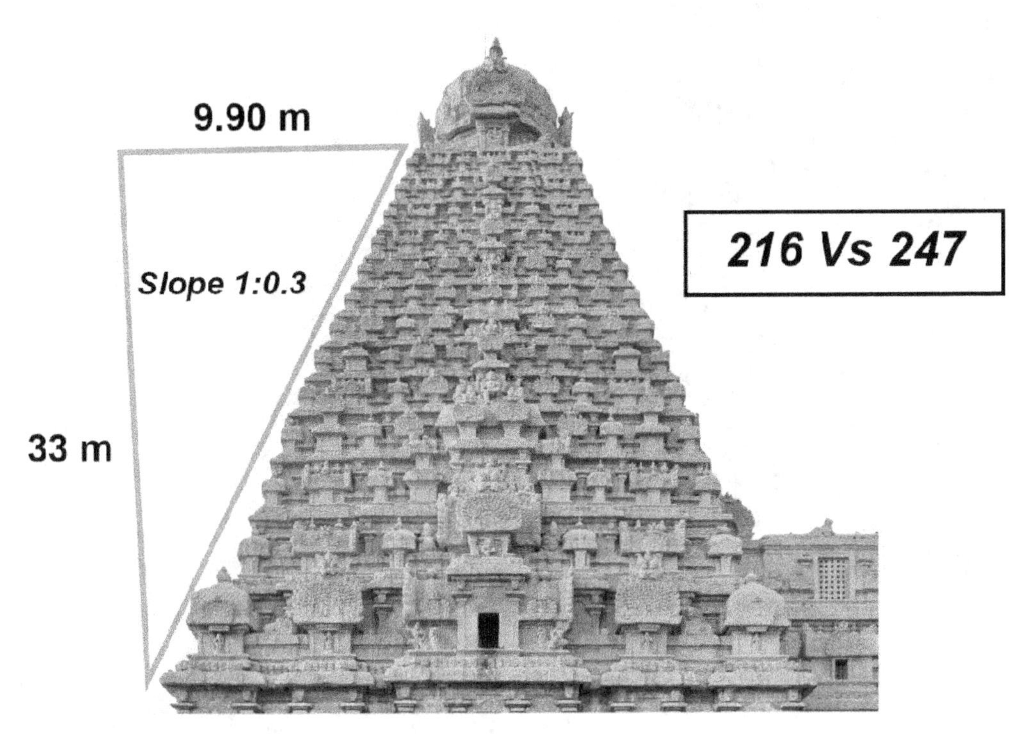

Vimana's height for 216 Nos of Tamil Alphabets			33	m
For 247 nos of Tamil Alphabets	= 33 m x 247/(216)	=	37.74	m
Difference in Height	= 37.74 - 33	=	4.74	m
Gradient provided for every running metre Height in the standing Structure	= 9.99 m / 33m	=	0.30	m
Reduction in size from both the ends	= 2 x 4.74 x 0.3	=	2.84	m
Size of Sikara for 216 Nos of Tamil Alphabets	7.93 m x 7.93 m Square		7.93	m
Net size required for 247 Nos	7.93 m - 2.84	=	5.09	m

An approximate size of 5.09 m x 5.09 m is required proportionately

Size lying in Tanjore Museum	5.08 m x 5.62 m

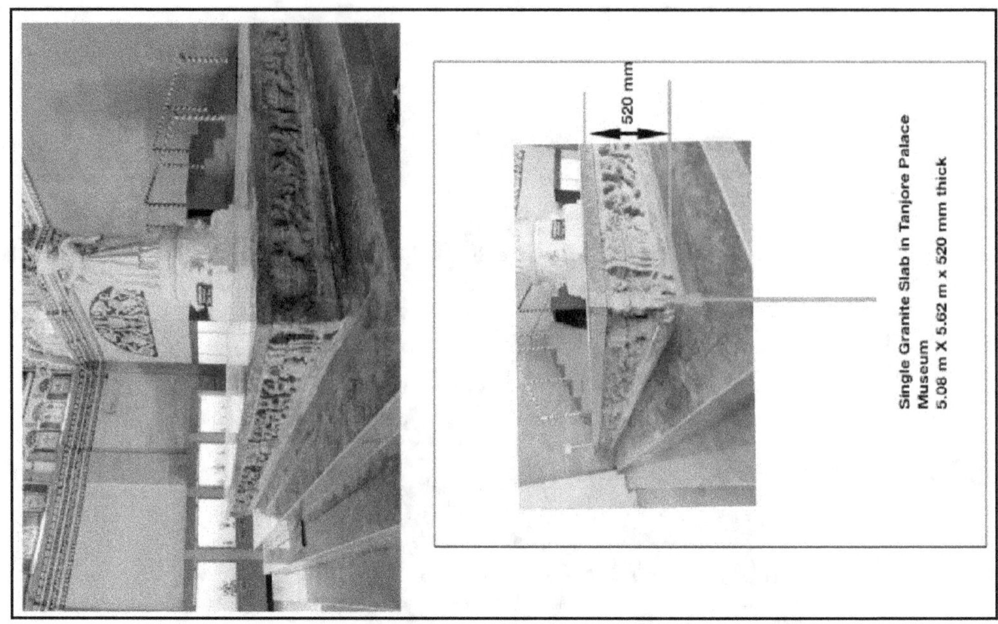

520 mm
Single Granite Slab in Tanjore Palace Museum
5.08 m X 5.62 m x 520 mm thick

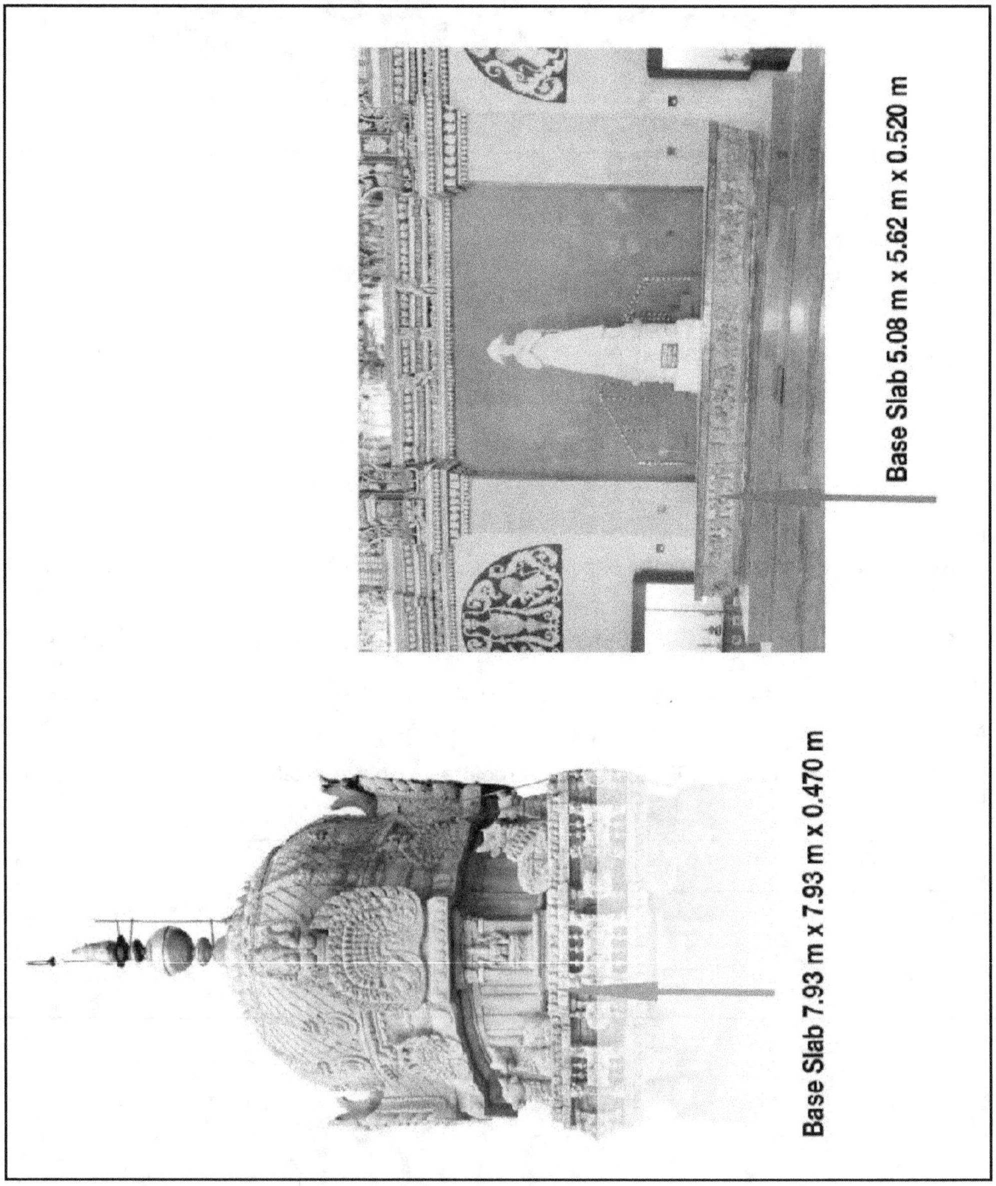

Base Slab 5.08 m x 5.62 m x 0.520 m
Base Slab 7.93 m x 7.93 m x 0.470 m

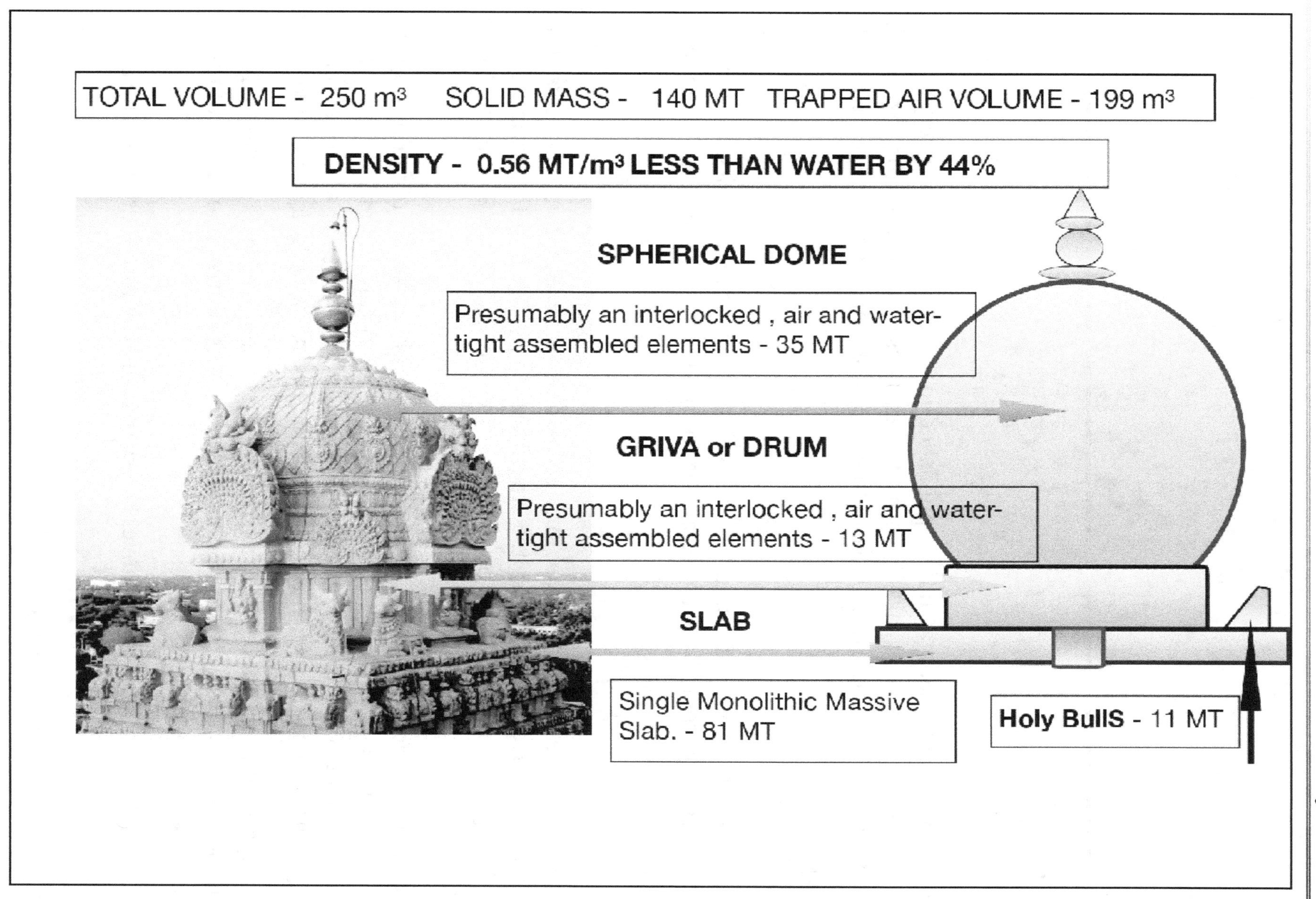

TOTAL VOLUME - 250 m³   SOLID MASS - 140 MT   TRAPPED AIR VOLUME - 199 m³
DENSITY - 0.56 MT/m³ LESS THAN WATER BY 44%
SPHERICAL DOME
Presumably an interlocked , air and water-tight assembled elements - 35 MT
GRIVA or DRUM
Presumably an interlocked , air and water-tight assembled elements - 13 MT
SLAB
Single Monolithic Massive Slab. - 81 MT
Holy BullS - 11 MT

17

G & g

Newton's law of universal gravitation, published in 1686, asserts that every particle in the universe attracts every other particle with a force that is proportional to the product of their masses and inversely proportional to the square of the distance between their centres.

$$F\alpha \frac{M1 \times M2}{r^2}$$

The universal gravitational constant 'G' was needed to make this equal-sided formula so that the force of gravity would be equal regardless of the mass or distance between them.

$$F = \frac{G \times M1 \times M2}{r^2}$$

To prove his inverse-square law, Newton needed a precise measurement of this constant 'G'. Scientist Henry Cavendish did the first experiment in 1797, a hundred years after Newton's theory. Using the torsion balance method, he came up with a value of about 6.67×10^{-11} N m^2/kg^2.

The acceleration due to gravity (g) was derived from observations of falling objects. Galileo observed that all objects fall at the same rate of speed regardless of the mass of the object. Over time, scientists were eventually able to put a value on the acceleration due to the earth's gravity as 9.81 m/sec^2, and the magnitude of this value 'g' is computed as follows.

Let 'M' represent the mass of the earth and 'm' represent the mass of the body. The whole mass of the earth is considered to be concentrated at its centre. The radius of the earth 'r' is about 6378 km, say 6400 km.

According to Newton's theory of universal gravitation, the force acting on the body is given by

$$F = \frac{G \times M1 \times M2}{r^2}$$ which is Equation No 1

When a body is at rest on the earth's surface, it is influenced by the gravitational force of the earth.

According to Newton's second law of motion, the force acting on a body is defined by the product of its mass and acceleration (called weight),

$F = m \times a$

If the acceleration due to gravity at a particular place is 'g', the above equation is modified to $F = mg$, which is Equation No. 2.

By replacing F in equation 2 with 'mg' and equating it to the value in equation 1, G M m / r², the new equation becomes

$$m \times g = \frac{G \times M \times m}{r^2}$$ and the final relationship is arrived as

$$g = \frac{G \times M}{r^2}$$

The smaller object's radius is insignificant compared to that of the earth's radius.

To determine the exact value of the earth's gravitational acceleration 'g' using the above equation, the universal gravitational constant 'G,' the mass 'M,' and the earth's radius 'r' must be known and plugged in the equation; the exact awareness of these fundamental physical data were surprisingly known to the Tamil engineers 1000 years earlier.

Henry Cavendish discovered the first reliable measurement of G, the value of the universal gravitational constant experimentally in 1798, after 100 years of Newton's theory, whereas the Chola engineers discovered and weighed the mass of the earth long before!

The attached pictorial sketches provide a clear illustration of the above calculation.

The fact that the results of all calculations were so accurate shows that the ancient Tamil engineers had a deep understanding of how the physical universe works and the law of the universal gravitational component.

Their knowledge of the relationship between the earth's gravitational pull 'g' and the law of universal gravitation 'G' is remarkable!

Otherwise, how could they have obtained the exact number of the earth's gravitational force 'g' and used the value 9.81 m/sec² exactly in the formulas and calculations?

The granite stones used in the temple tower construction range in size and weight from 0.5 to 15 tonnes. Lifting the heavy stones above ground level by defying the earth's gravity was a Herculean task thousands of years ago, in the absence of any high-end types of machinery.

The Chola regime must have had a full-fledged gravity research foundation that progressed to antigravity technology and was finally able to measure the earth using the technology at their fingertips. They could not have designed and provided the exact dimensions of base width and profiled the Vimana tower in the style of a gravity dam without an in-depth knowledge of the precise gravitational acceleration number of 9.81 m/sec².

Be it Newton's second law formula, $F = m \times a$, Pascal's law of fluid pressure, $P = p \times g \times h$, Archimedes' theory of buoyancy, $Fb = p \times g \times V$, or stability check calculations, 'g' played a significant role and the result cannot be obtained so accurately without the precise application of the earth's gravity value as 9.81 m/sec² in the formulas.

Without the value of 9.81 m/sec², they could not have designed and correctly selected the size of the float, its density, and volume to calculate the precise value of the force acting upon a specific mass in the gravitational field. The total volume of cavities designed and created inside the structure that matches the exact requirement of the total volume of water required for the novel strategy using the Archimedes principle justifies their brilliance and advancement in their awareness of gravitational acceleration and its number, 9.81 m/sec².

For centuries, the world has been perplexed by the Tanjore Big Temple mystery. The solutions in this book are not made up or imagined! The conclusion of this research is firmly supported by all of the scientific facts, engineering data, and evidence present in the temple tower and the surrounding area!

A comprehensive examination of the overall plan, cross-section, structural components, cavity volume, interiors, shapes, dimensions, and surroundings of the temple towers, all of which contributed to and supported the masterful efforts of the Chola engineers, as described in great detail in this volume, will provide conclusive evidence for the claims made here.

The huge Vimana took its cues from the fields of science and mathematics!

Science completely ignores the size!

As previously stated, whether something is small or large, simple or complex, it obeys and delivers on time and every time as long as the laws of physics are truly, faithfully, and unwaveringly mastered!

As an engineer, I understand how simple scientific theories and engineering concepts were secretly blended and hidden in the Vimana tower's design and construction.

The ancient Tamil engineers devised a brilliant technique and novel strategy to merge science and arithmetic in their engineering to safely and successfully move and install a massive weight far exceeding 81 tonnes on the summit, irrespective of the Sikhara being a single monolithic block or an interlocked airtight assembled one.

The Vimana's interior and surroundings strongly support this book's technical analysis and research findings by demonstrating the ancient Tamil engineers' integration of advanced scientific ideas into construction one thousand years ago.

Hard limestone rock layers below the ground level, the width of Vimana base, wall thickness visible at the plinth base following a right triangular profile, annexe structure holding the exact large empty volume inside the vestibule halls connected to the central tower, the lower mass-to-volume ratio of the dome unit, circumambulatory and its large extended voids, wells around the tower, the connection that leads to the Siva Ganga Tank by an underground passage and the huge Siva Ganga Tank just adjacent to the layout have all made substantial contributions scientifically towards the accomplishment of the mission.

Only the underground shaft that goes down 66 m deep from the courtyard and the tunnel that leads to the Siva Ganga Tank are buried.

We climbed to the top of the Vimana in the footsteps of Sikhara, using the laws of physics and engineering analysis to find answers to a mystery that has stumped scientists and explorers for centuries.

Without you, I could not have done it!

If my observations through this research mission or journal are determined to be trustworthy after this point, it is due to the continuous cooperation work of everyone involved, as well as the readers who have been patient enough to grasp a thorough understanding of the relevant scientific concepts, calculations, and engineering analysis that accompanied the Sikhara's journey to the summit.

Thank you for reading and comprehending this engineering observation with patience.

Any criticism or disagreement is my responsibility, and I will keep putting in extra effort in my quest of finding a perfect solution.

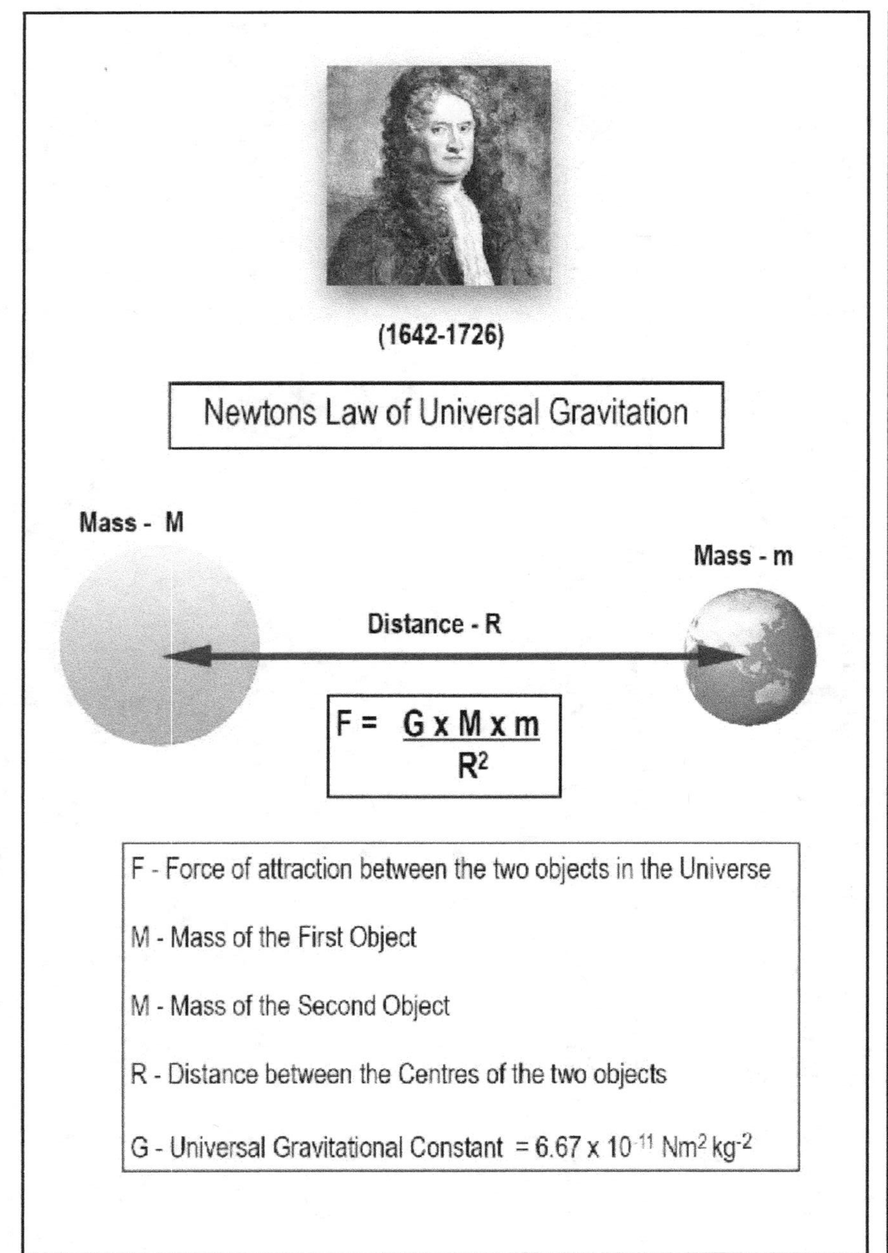

(1642-1726)
Newtons Law of Universal Gravitation
Mass - M
Mass - m
Distance - R
F = G x M x m / R²
F - Force of attraction between the two objects in the Universe
M - Mass of the First Object
M - Mass of the Second Object
R - Distance between the Centres of the two objects
G - Universal Gravitational Constant = 6.67 x 10⁻¹¹ Nm² kg⁻²

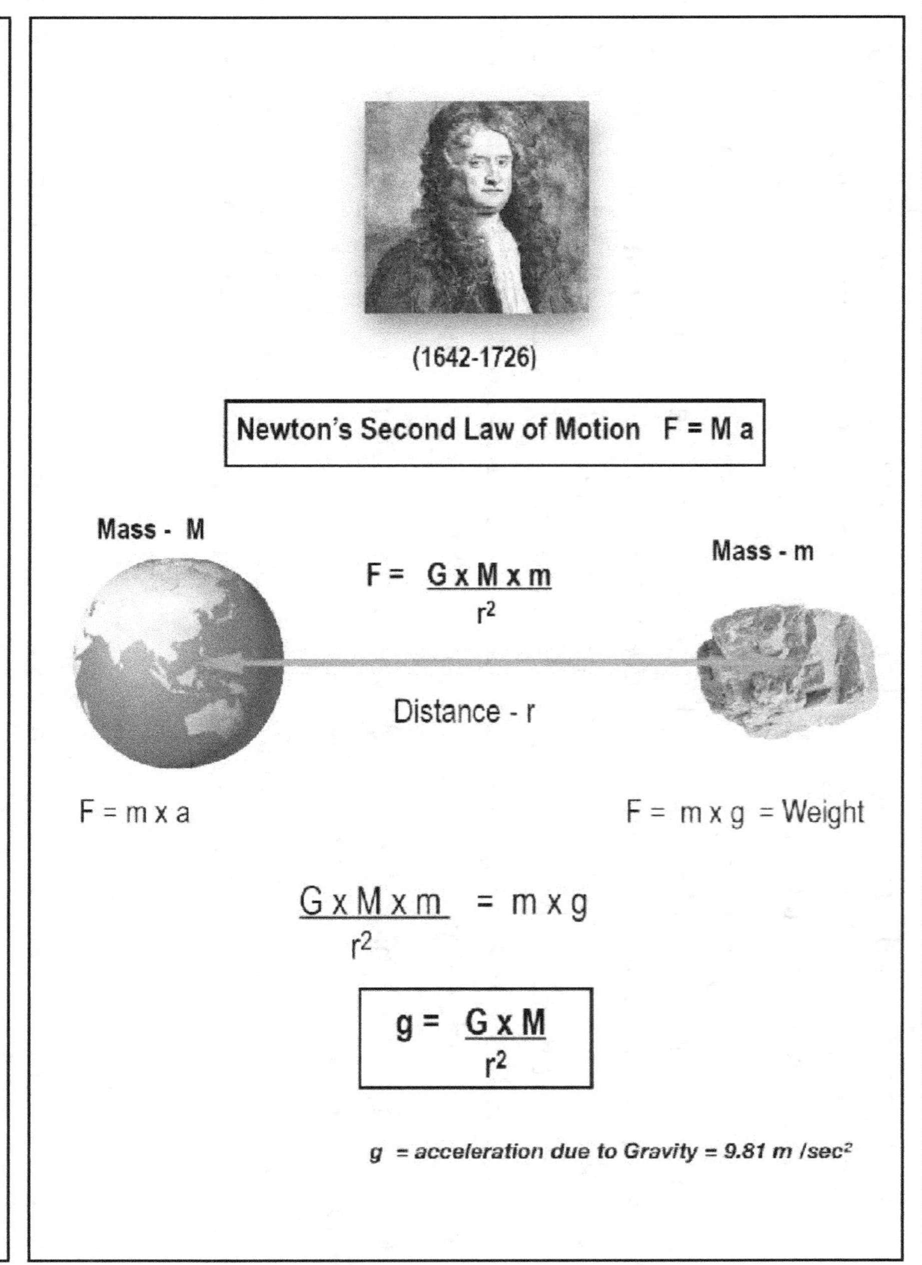

(1642-1726)
Newton's Second Law of Motion   F = M a
Mass - M
Mass - m
F = G x M x m / r²
Distance - r
F = m x a
F = m x g = Weight
G x M x m / r² = m x g
g = G x M / r²
g = acceleration due to Gravity = 9.81 m /sec²

Gravitation - Newton's 2nd Law of motion

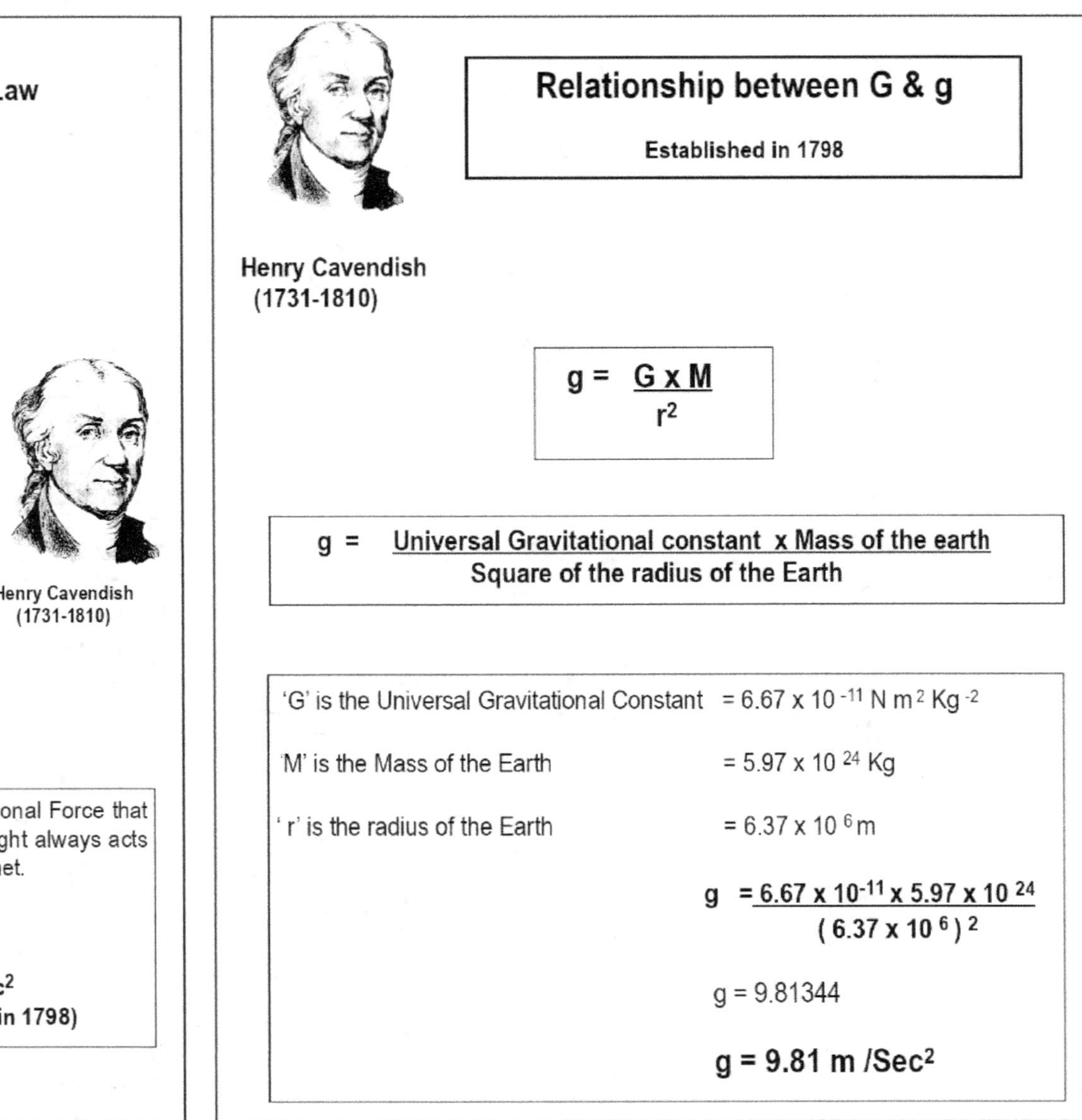

Sir Isaac Newton
(1642-1726)

$$F = m \times a$$

(Established in 1687)

Mass 'm'

Gravity 'g'

Weight = m x g

Weight

Weight = Mass X Gravity

$$W = m \times g$$

Henry Cavendish
(1731-1810)

The **Weight** of an object is the Gravitational Force that the planet exerts on the Object. The weight always acts downward towards the centre of the planet.

m is the mass of the body

g is the gravity acceleration **9.81 m / Sec^2**
(arrived approx. by Henry Cavendish in 1798)

Relationship between G & g

Established in 1798

Henry Cavendish
(1731-1810)

$$g = \frac{G \times M}{r^2}$$

$$g = \frac{\text{Universal Gravitational constant} \ \times \text{Mass of the earth}}{\text{Square of the radius of the Earth}}$$

'G' is the Universal Gravitational Constant $= 6.67 \times 10^{-11}$ N m^2 Kg^{-2}

'M' is the Mass of the Earth $= 5.97 \times 10^{24}$ Kg

' r' is the radius of the Earth $= 6.37 \times 10^{6}$ m

$$g = \frac{6.67 \times 10^{-11} \times 5.97 \times 10^{24}}{(6.37 \times 10^{6})^2}$$

$$g = 9.81344$$

$$g = 9.81 \text{ m /Sec}^2$$

18

The Granite Lab

The Tanjore Big Temple was built much earlier, between 985 and 1014 AD, under the reign of Raja Raja Cholan-I and was finished in 6.5 years. The emperor's proposal for a temple, as well as its basic engineering design, must have been completed at the end of the 10th century, at least.

The design calculations were optimal and follow International Engineering Standards. Their design met the specifications by taking into account the precise values and constants of physics and engineering parameters. What distinguished their design was the identification and elimination of all potential sources of danger that could compromise the structural stability.

Chola engineers, for example, planned and delivered the exact cross-sectional area and profile of the wall to ensure that the required base width, mass, and force were in full compliance with the gravity dam style. This is required to counteract the lateral hydrostatic force generated by the water column's 24.75 m height, which is the mid-height of Vimana and may be the maximum operating overflowing water level maintained by the engineers in the methodology and procedure.

While the required average wall thickness is 6.76 m as per the design to sustain the hydrostatic force of 23.35 m height of the water column, the overall base width of the wall has been set at 10.63 m to account for any failure mechanisms to meet any problematic situation when the water level unexpectedly rises for the Sikhara's height of 8.25 to the level +31.60 m. Considering the heavy-weighted granite construction material that must be produced and transported away from the Tanjore location, it is astounding to note the design output that demonstrates their most economical and optimal design by ensuring the required optimum safety factors and cross-sectional area.

The cross-sectional area gives the required mass and weight to sustain the lateral hydrostatic pressure from a height of 23.35 m from the level of the courtyard base.

The design calls for 6.76 m × 49.5 m = 334.62 m² with an average width of 6.76 m.

The existing structure has a physical area of 331 m², which is strikingly close to the 335 m² specified by design and engineering criteria. The difference of 4 m² is insignificant and may be due to measurement error. The precise safety margin has been factored into the design by the engineers to ensure that the weight of the structure and the lateral hydrostatic pressure from water are balanced to meet any potentially problematic circumstances.

The discovery confirmed that the large height of the water column played a major role in the structure's design and that the filled water column created pressure and buoyancy to lift the massive weights against gravity.

Pascal's law of fluid properties and behaviour, Stevin's law of hydrostatic paradox, and Newton's second law of motion were all used in the design by the Chola engineers 700 years before the aforementioned renowned scientists.

When it comes to understanding how forces, reactions, pressures, and moments behave, who taught the ancient Tamil engineers?

To compute an object's acceleration due to the earth's gravitational attraction, they needed the value of universal gravitational constant 'G' as 6.67×10^{-11} N m²/kg². It is astounding how they knew this exact number!

How did they know about engineering design requirements like the centre of gravity, friction, sliding, reactions, overturning, and the overall stability and safety factors?

How did they know to follow the Rule of the Middle Third in a dam design and stability analysis?

Who taught them shape, quantity, areas, volumes, sums, and differences?

Ancient Tamil civilisation must have inherited and practised the aforesaid knowledge from their forebears.

The Cholas merged their cutting-edge scientific discoveries with engineering design to create a new type of art. The Chola era's unique innovations, styles, and adventures continue to astonish us now. They aimed to transform the way the world thought.

The Cholas lived long before famous scientists like Galileo, Copernicus, Kepler, Newton, Pascal, Cavendish, etc.

While Archimedes discovered and published the law of buoyancy in the third century, the Newtonian law of motion was developed only in the 17th century, in the year 1686.

In 1798, a century later, Henry Cavendish arrived at and published the precise value of the universal gravitational constant 'G' and the mass of the earth as a result of his extensive experiments.

By the end of the 16th century, mathematician and military engineer Simon Stevin introduced and contributed to the field of science that the hydrostatic pressure in liquid solely depends on its depth.

The concept of liquid pressure and how it is transmitted by fluids was developed and published in 1647 by mathematician and philosopher Blaise Pascal.

Other great scientists of the 15th and 16th centuries included Nicolas Copernicus, Johannes Kepler, and Galileo Galilei, who evaluated theories of universal planetary motion and gravitation and made significant contributions to science.

It should be noted that many of the main scientific discoveries and theories originated between the 14th and 17th centuries. This was evident in Europe during the Renaissance and Scientific Revolution.

After a second Danish team landed on the Indian mainland in 1620, trade agreements were made to keep Danish colonies in India. One of these deals was made with Ragunatha Nayakar, the ruler of the Tanjore Kingdom; it included the town of Tharangambadi, which is just 100 km from Tanjore.

The Danish team exported a lot of tea, cotton, and other goods from India to London during the treaty. Tharangambadi's "Danish" fort, built around 1620, is now a museum run by Tamil Nadu's Department of Archaeology.

Renaissance-era scientific ideas and equations are astonishingly similar to those used by the Chola rulers and engineers 700–800 years ago to build the Tanjore Big Temple.

The Renaissance is a period in European history when Europeans mapped every continent to find learnings and scientific concepts and answers. Intercultural interaction expanded, and technological breakthroughs and intellectual ideas were exchanged through numerous libraries.

Did a foreigner visit the temple during the Renaissance or Commercial Treaty?

Because a foreigner's statue is on Vimana's north side. The statue depicts a foreigner with a cap and a half-sleeved shirt, possibly a European who visited the temple during renovations.

The Chola regime's scientific advances, ideas, and intellectual property knowledge were most likely copied and passed down during the Renaissance and treaty periods.

The ruler Ragunatha Nayakar refurbished and altered the annexe building and the main Vimana during this period, as physically visible in the annexe vestibule hall outer walls.

Isaac Newton was the greatest pioneer of the Renaissance era and he was a man of talent, especially in science and mathematics for a multitude of reasons. Two of the numerous explanations include his discovery of gravity and his three laws of motion.

Gravity is a universal force that exists everywhere and Newton is well known for discovering gravity.

The unpublished notes written in 1680 by Isaac Newton reveal that he attempted to uncover the secrets of the pyramids in Egypt while establishing his theory of gravity.

Newton, who examined the pyramids in the late 17th century, believed that how pyramids were created would unveil other truths about the earth. He believed that Egyptians had been able to measure the earth and believed that if he found how they had measured the pyramids, he would also be able to estimate the circumference of the earth. He was desperately attempting to work out the unit of measurement the ancient Egyptians used when erecting the pyramids.

His wide-ranging research took him to strange places far outside of Egyptian pyramids in search of proof for his theory of gravitation, as is evidenced in some half-burnt fragmentary manuscript notes.

The Tanjore Big Temple Vimana resembles a pyramid in every respect.

Did he conduct a similar exercise on Tanjore Big Temple? Newton's half-burnt writings indicate some measurements strikingly near to the dimensions of the main Vimana, a copy of which is shown here.

Who was the foreign visitor to the temple wearing the cap and half-sleeved shirt whose image is featured on the north side of Vimana, and what information did he take with him?

Tamil engineers from the Chola Empire on the other hand meticulously studied and determined precisely the value of the universal gravitational constant 'G' and arrived at the earth's gravity acceleration of 9.81 m/sec^2 and the concept of forces, which they applied to the engineering formulas and design calculations 700–800 years ago before the discoveries from the western world.

Cholas discovered advanced scientific concepts and ideas before the great scientists and cleverly applied them in the Big Temple construction.

The Sikhara is not 81 MT, as commonly stated and believed. The research findings strongly establish that a massive weight far exceeding 81 MT climbed against gravity and reached the summit in a matter of hours!

The mission presumably began before sunrise and ended before noon or at the very least before the sun's evening rays hit the earth!

The research findings solidify the legacy of the Cholas' exceptional and advanced science and engineering intelligence, which will greatly enhance the Tamils' international reputation.

It is the responsibility of countries worldwide, not just 1.3 billion Indians, to preserve and enrich the Tamil legacy.

It is more than just a large Vimana and a massive Sikhara from the great Tamil emperor. Advanced scientific theories and concepts were secretly combined with precision engineering and hidden in the temple Vimana, which has stood majestically in front of us for over a thousand years.

To reach the summit, the system only required a 66-m deep underground well rather than a 6600-m ramp!

It took 350 truckloads of water rather than 6 million m³ of stone and sand ramp.

Ramp and elephants is an imagined and made-up solution that may be due to ignorance and misunderstanding. It is a fabricated story designed to conceal and hide the Cholas' advanced scientific ideas, discoveries, and extraordinary engineering brilliance that predated major scientists!

The great emperor Raja Raja Cholan was a courageous, determined, and powerful ruler who dared to imagine the impossible; his engineers, architects, and artisans were masters of science, invention, engineering, and creativity who defied all human limitations and built and shaped such an impressive historical granite monument by adorning it with a majestic Sikhara at the start of 11th century.

The temple was built by the emperor Raja Raja Cholan, who abundantly donated. All his sisters and family donated a lot. Donations from the general public poured in, and the outstanding ruler recorded the facts of all such donations on the plinth of the temple Vimana, where they can be seen by all.

All of our forebears contributed generously, thus we all have a responsibility to preserve this engineering marvel for future generations so we can prove that we are pioneers in engineering, merging science and math.

Rather than the government and the ASI bearing responsibility and accountability, everyone must step forward, unite, cooperate, and work together with the government and ASI officials to maintain, protect, and preserve such a historical monument for future generations.

Amazing scientific and mathematical discoveries have been buried for millennia in places like Keezadi, Athichanallur, and other parts of Tamil Nadu and are being explored. The facts of cutting-edge engineering, merging these two fields, from ancient Tamil engineers have remained visible in front of us for the past so many centuries, which sits calmly and majestically at the summit of Tanjore Big Temple Vimana.

The Archimedes principle, the universal theory of gravitation, Newton's Law of Motion, Pascal's principle of fluid pressure, Stevin's hydrostatic paradox and lubrication theory, all had a role in designing the Tanjore Big Temple Vimana.

This volume contains supporting images, diagrams, theories, concepts, formulas, and related computations handled by Tamil engineers in the Chola regime a thousand years ago, the results of which can be seen physically in the construction of the Tanjore Big Temple.

It is in the shape of a pyramid, and the walls were designed and built in the style of a gravity dam to safeguard its stability from its weight. There is no need for a separate deeper foundation beneath the courtyard's base; the stability analysis confirms this. Its base had to be rested on the top of a solid limestone rock mass; therefore, a nominal depth of 1.5 m was just needed as a levelling course.

The massive granite pieces, including the statue of Lord Shivalinga and the Sikhara, were lifted and installed safely and economically using physics principles rather than laying a long sand and stone ramp, involving a large labour force, and troubling a large number of bulls and elephants.

It functioned like a physics laboratory made of granite and can be labelled as "The Granite lab."

Cholan was a very advanced scientist who weighed the earth's mass many centuries ago and tested it in this lab!

The Chola regime's Tamil engineers were able to precisely discover the laws of physics and incorporate them into the design of this lab 700 years before Newton's and Pascal's theories on gravity, fluid pressure, forces, lubrication and so on were revealed.

In this case, can "Newton's Law of Motion" be referred to as "Cholan's Law of Motion," and Newtonian Classical Mechanics be referred to as "Cholan's Mechanics?"

Can Pascal's Principle also be called "Cholan's Principle?"

To build such a large temple, the emperor, Raja Raja Cholan was thirsty.

Persistence and brains can solve any challenge, says the thirsty crow.

In the Panchatantra, stones raised the water, but Cholan reversed that!

The Sikhara completed its mission using buoyancy power.

The buoyancy has worked in tandem with gravity conclusively.

But the buoyancy depends on the weight of the fluid displaced, which is a function of gravitational acceleration.

In the absence of gravity, buoyancy is zero!

Ultimately, gravity is the reason!

Cholas Predated Major discoveries by
600 to 800 Years !!

Simon Stevin
1548 - 1620

Blaise Pascal
1623 - 1662

Raja Raja Cholan
947 - 1015

Henry Cavendish
1731 - 1810

Galileo Galilei
1564 - 1642

Sir Isaac Newton
1642 - 1726

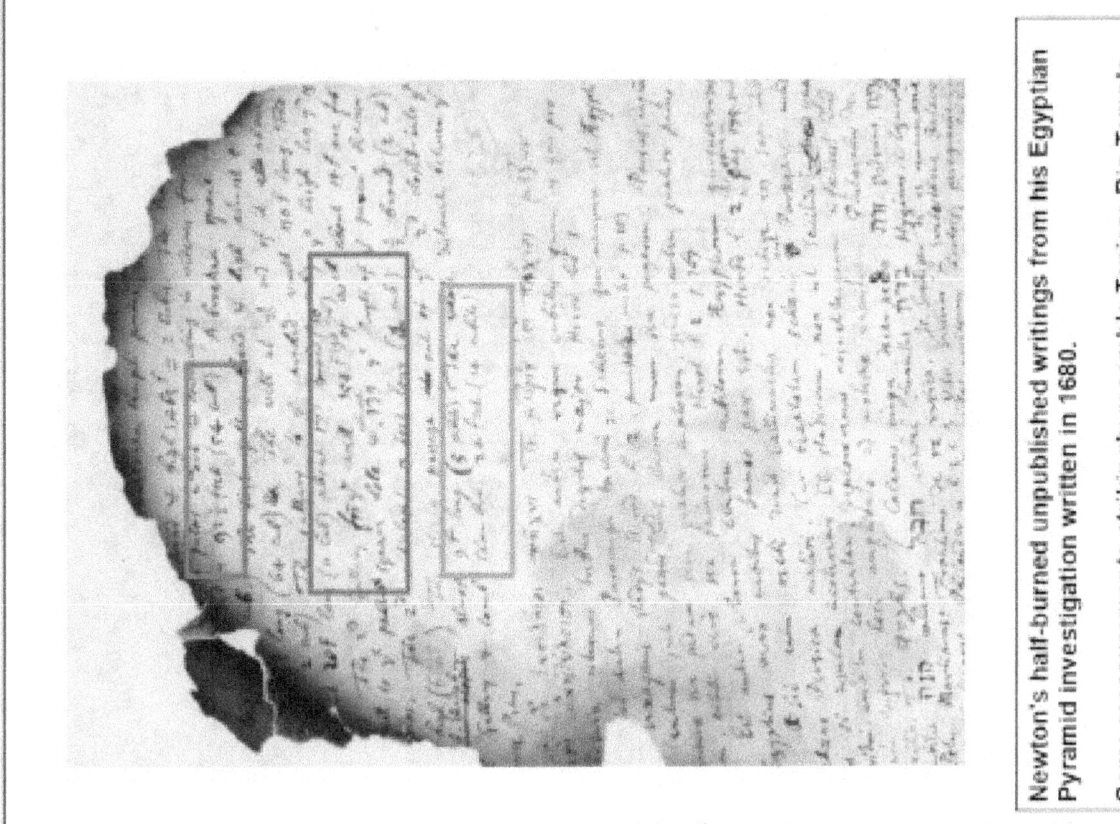

Newton's half-burned unpublished writings from his Egyptian Pyramid investigation written in 1680.

Some measurements strikingly resemble Tanjore Big Temple Tower's.

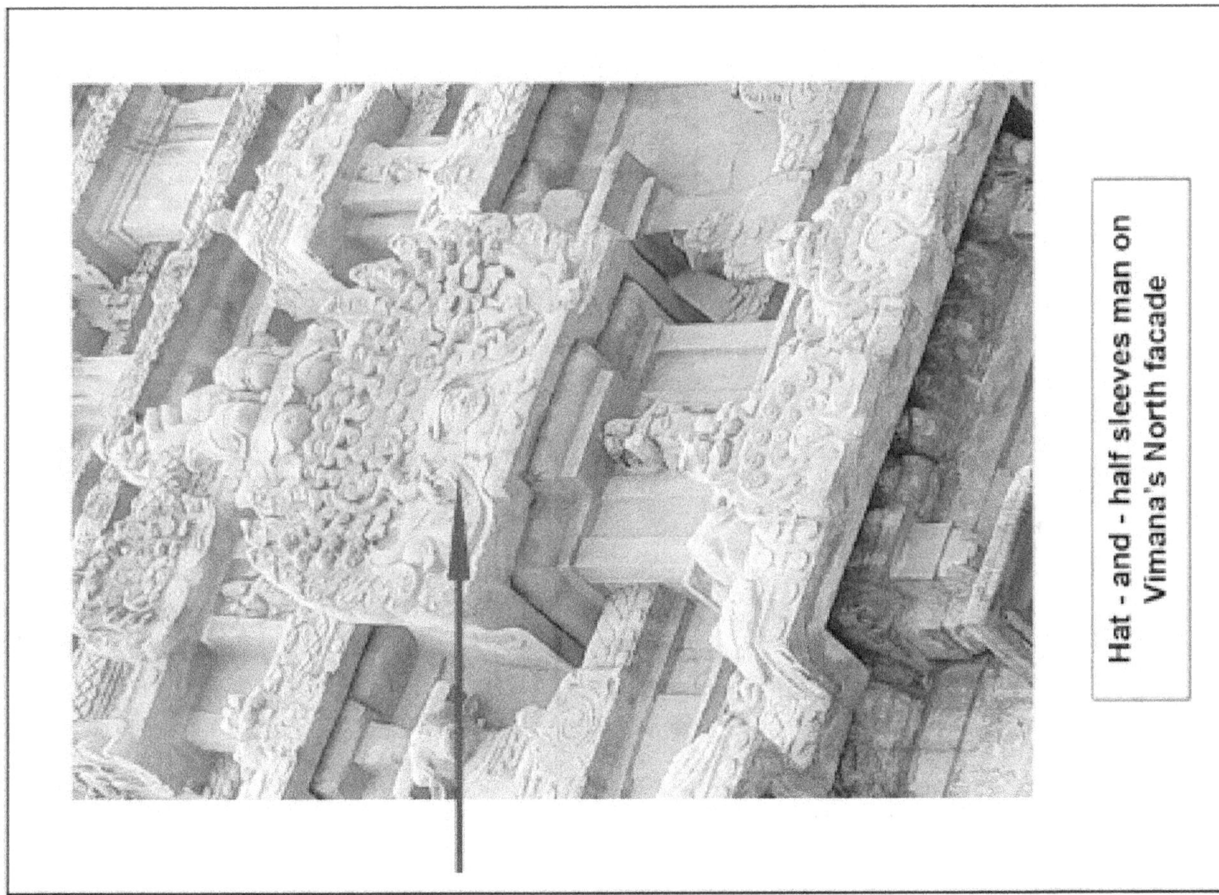

Hat - and - half sleeves man on Vimana's North facade

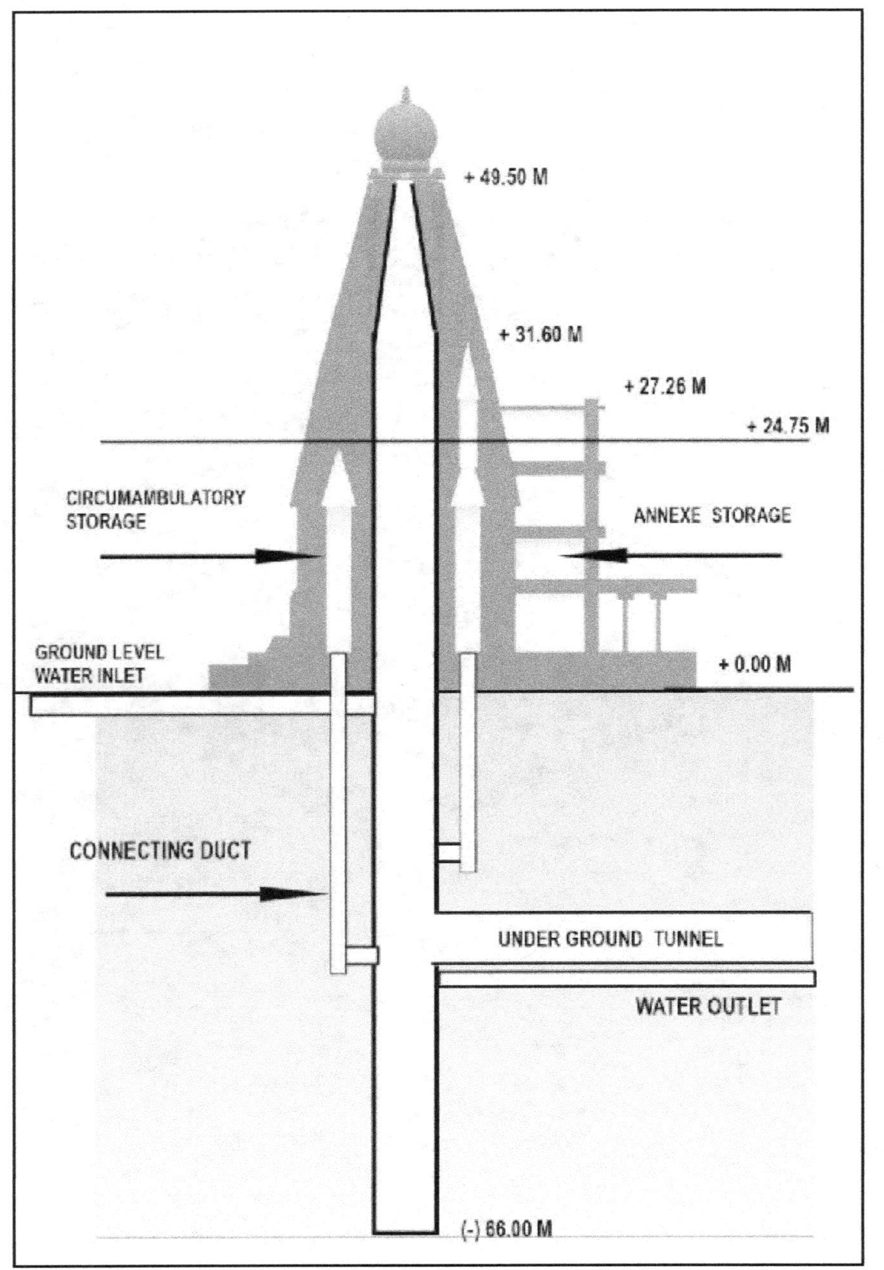
+ 49.50 M
+ 31.60 M
+ 27.26 M
+ 24.75 M
CIRCUMAMBULATORY STORAGE
ANNEXE STORAGE
GROUND LEVEL WATER INLET
+ 0.00 M
CONNECTING DUCT
UNDER GROUND TUNNEL
WATER OUTLET
(-) 66.00 M

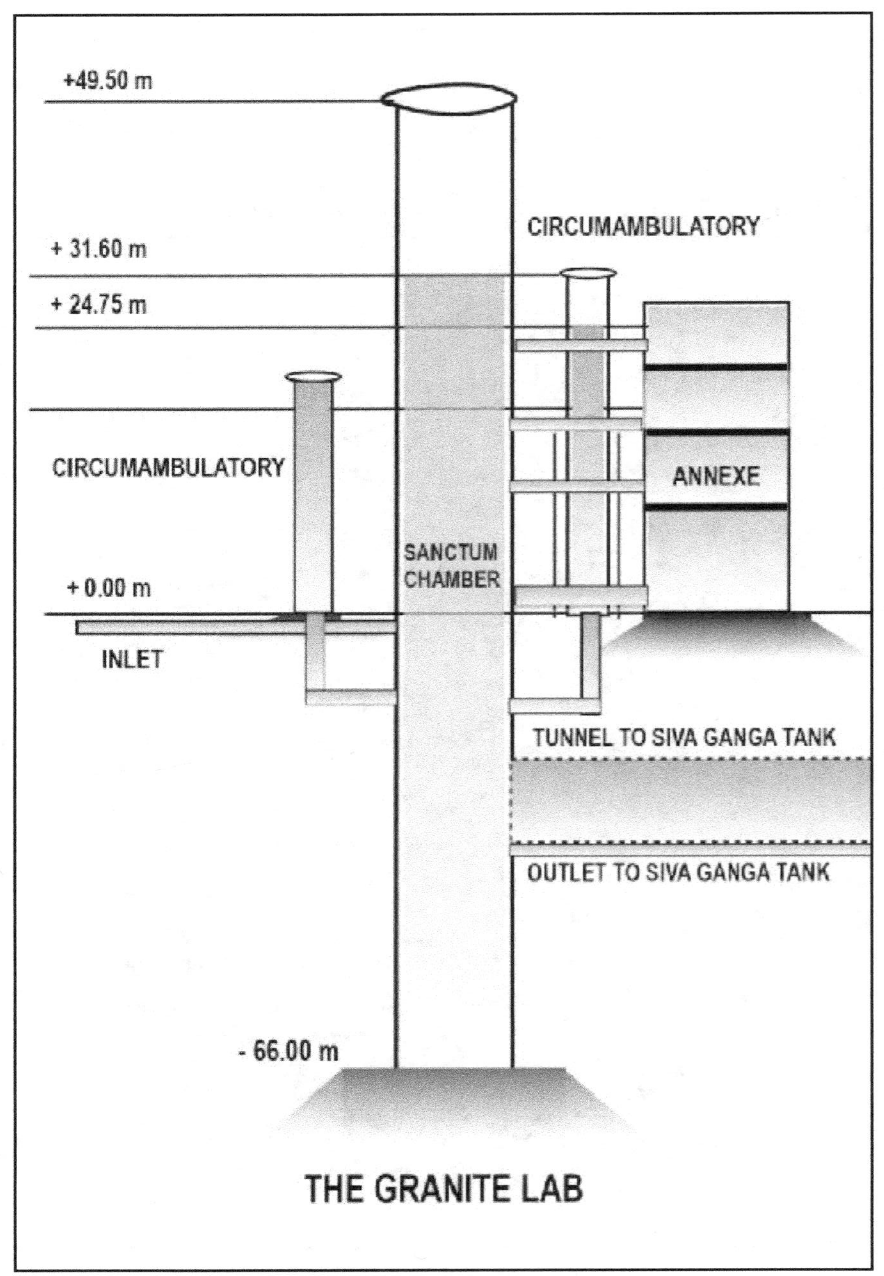
+49.50 m
+ 31.60 m
+ 24.75 m
CIRCUMAMBULATORY
CIRCUMAMBULATORY
ANNEXE
SANCTUM CHAMBER
+ 0.00 m
INLET
TUNNEL TO SIVA GANGA TANK
OUTLET TO SIVA GANGA TANK
- 66.00 m
THE GRANITE LAB

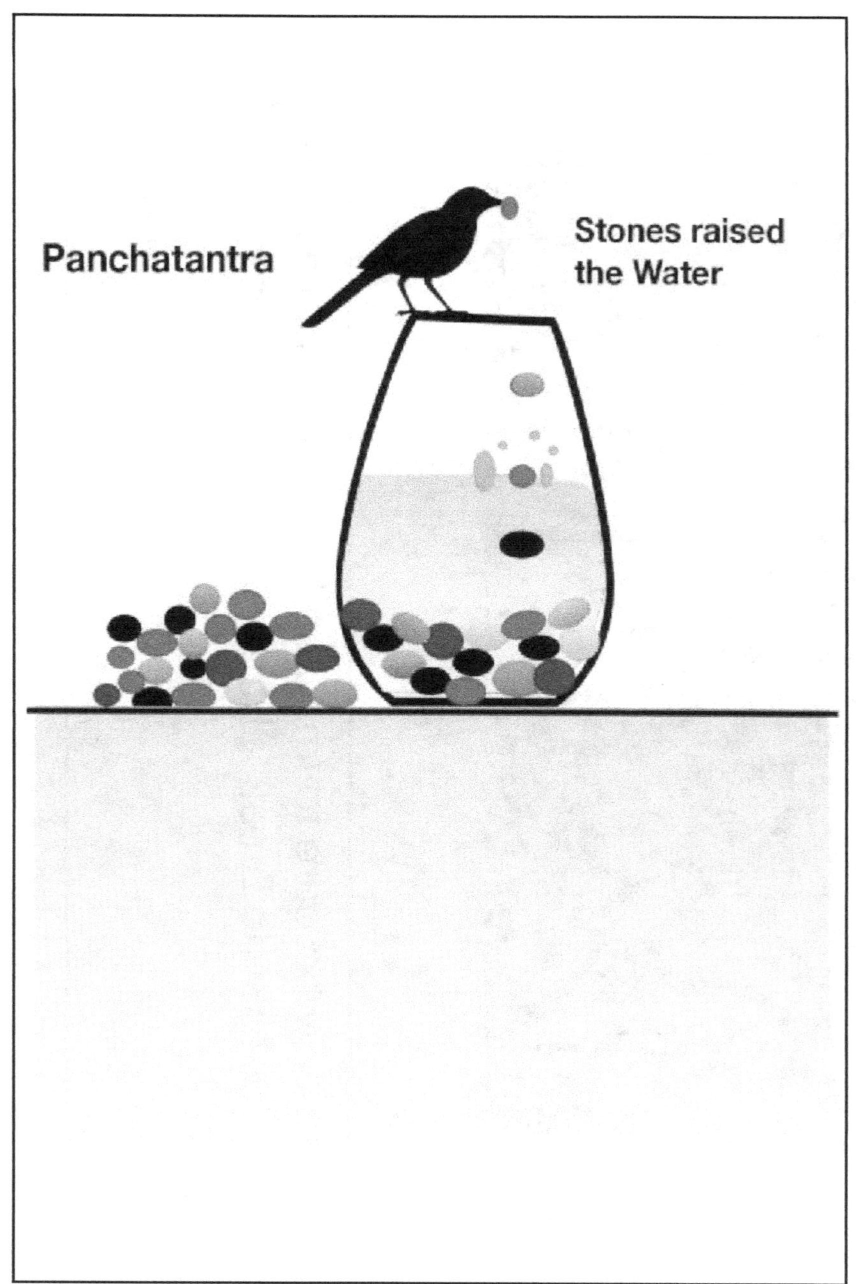

Panchatantra
Stones raised the Water

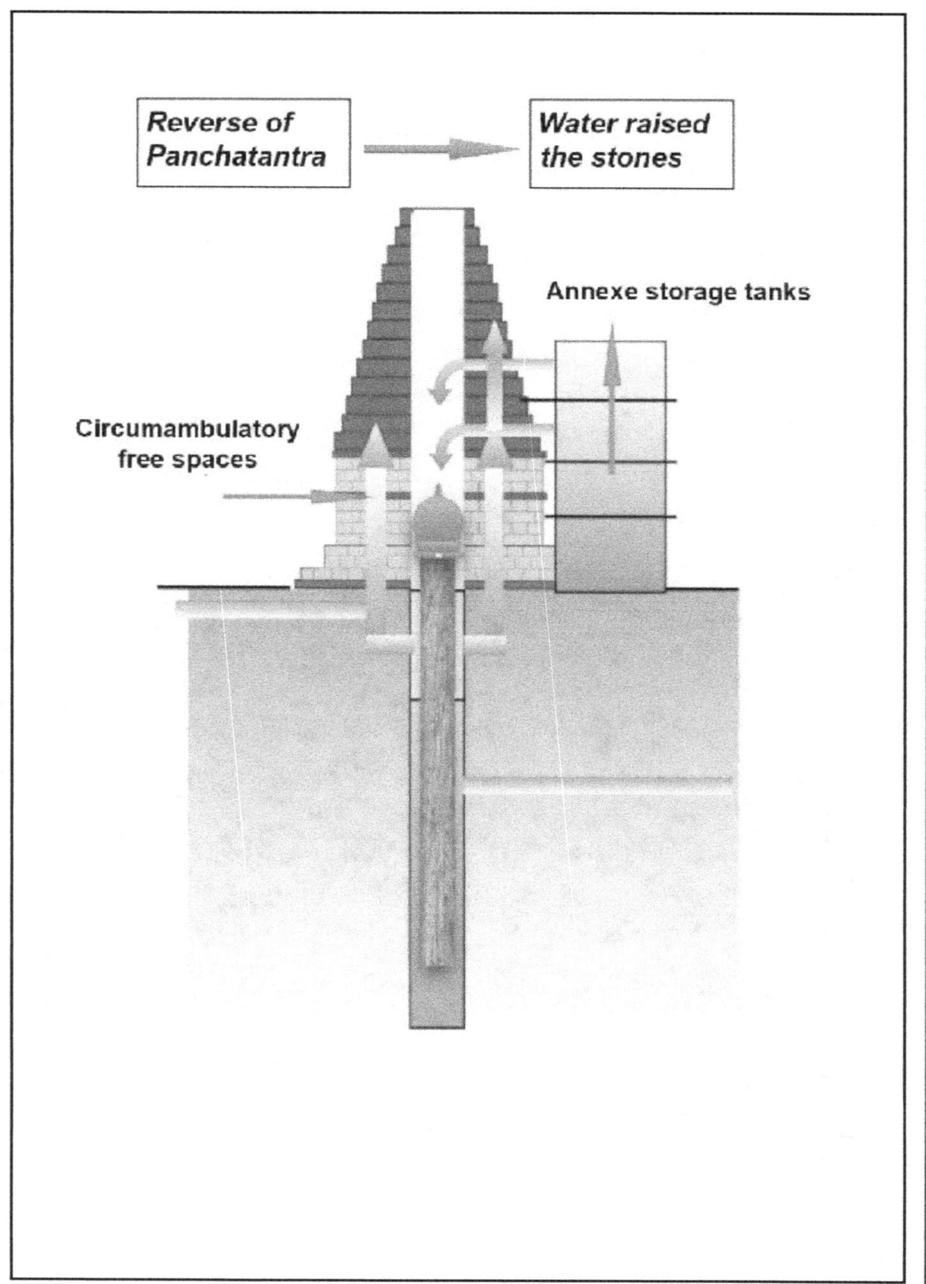

Reverse of Panchatantra
Water raised the stones
Annexe storage tanks
Circumambulatory free spaces

Those who dare to imagine the impossible are the ones who break all the Human limitations !!!

Dr A PJ Abdulkalam

References

Thanjavur -Shree Rajarajeeswaram by Prof C.G. Deivanayagam
Rajarajecharam by Dr Kudavayil Balasubramanian
Images courtesy
Mr E. Ragupathi - Pondicherry
Mr Paranthagam Tamilselvam - History Trails - Pondicherry
Mr P. Thanikainathan - Green Hunt Studio - YouTube